SHAKESPEARE'S SONNETS AND THE BIBLE

Cover Reference:
After the “Chandos” portrait of William Shakespeare.

SHAKESPEARE'S SONNETS AND THE BIBLE

A Spiritual Interpretation with Christian Sources

Ira B. Zinman

Foreword by
HRH The Prince of Wales

World Wisdom

Shakespeare's Sonnets and the Bible:
A Spiritual Interpretation with Christian Sources

Library of Congress Cataloging-in-Publication Data

Zinman, Ira B.
Shakespeare's sonnets and the Bible : a spiritual interpretation with Christian sources / Ira B. Zinman ; foreword by HRH The Prince of Wales.
p. cm.
Includes index.
ISBN 978-1-933316-74-1 (pbk. : alk. paper) -- ISBN 978-1-933316-75-8 (alk. paper) 1. Shakespeare, William, 1564-1616. Sonnets. 2. Shakespeare, William, 1564-1616--Religion. 3. Bible--In literature. 4. Sonnets, English--History and criticism. I. Title.
PR2848.Z56 2009
821'.3--dc22

2009024884

Printed on acid-free paper in The United States of America.

For information address World Wisdom, Inc.
P.O. Box 2682, Bloomington, Indiana 47402-2682
www.worldwisdom.com

This work is
dedicated to
P.Y.

TABLE OF CONTENTS

Foreword by HRH The Prince of Wales		*xi*
Introduction by Ira B. Zinman		*xiii*
The Method Followed		*xix*
Sonnet 1:	"From fairest creatures we desire increase,"	1
Sonnet 2:	"When forty winters shall besiege thy brow,"	4
Sonnet 3:	"Look in thy glass, and tell the face thou viewest,"	7
Sonnet 4:	"Unthrifty loveliness, why dost thou spend"	10
Sonnet 5:	"Those hours, that with gentle work did frame"	13
Sonnet 6:	"Then let not winter's ragged hand deface"	16
Sonnet 7:	"Lo, in the orient when the gracious light"	19
Sonnet 8:	"Music to hear, why hear'st thou music sadly?"	22
Sonnet 9:	"Is it for fear to wet a widow's eye"	25
Sonnet 10:	"For shame deny that thou bear'st love to any,"	28
Sonnet 11:	"As fast as thou shalt wane, so fast thou grow'st,"	31
Sonnet 12:	"When I do count the clock that tells the time,"	34
Sonnet 13:	"O that you were yourself, but, love, you are"	37
Sonnet 14:	"Not from the stars do I my judgment pluck,"	41
Sonnet 15:	"When I consider everything that grows"	44
Sonnet 16:	"But wherefore do not you a mightier way"	47
Sonnet 17:	"Who will believe my verse in time to come,"	50
Sonnet 18:	"Shall I compare thee to a summer's day?"	53
Sonnet 19:	"Devouring Time, blunt thou the lion's paws,"	56
Sonnet 20:	"A woman's face with Nature's own hand painted"	59
Sonnet 21:	"So is it not with me as with that Muse,"	64
Sonnet 22:	"My glass shall not persuade me I am old,"	67
Sonnet 23:	"As an unperfect actor on the stage,"	69
Sonnet 24:	"Mine eye hath play'd the painter and hath stell'd"	72
Sonnet 25:	"Let those who are in favor with their stars"	75
Sonnet 26:	"Lord of my love, to whom in vassalage"	78
Sonnet 27:	"Weary with toil, I haste me to my bed,"	81
Sonnet 28:	"How can I then return in happy plight,"	84
Sonnet 29:	"When, in disgrace with fortune and men's eyes,"	87
Sonnet 30:	"When to the sessions of sweet silent thought"	90
Sonnet 31:	"Thy bosom is endeared with all hearts,"	93
Sonnet 32:	"If thou survive my well-contented day,"	96
Sonnet 33:	"Full many a glorious morning have I seen"	98
Sonnet 34:	"Why didst thou promise such a beauteous day,"	101
Sonnet 35:	"No more be griev'd at that which thou hast done:"	105

Sonnet 36:	"Let me confess that we two must be twain,"	108
Sonnet 37:	"As a decrepit father takes delight"	111
Sonnet 38:	"How can my Muse want subject to invent,"	114
Sonnet 39:	"O how thy worth with manners may I sing,"	117
Sonnet 40:	"Take all my loves, my love, yea take them all,"	120
Sonnet 41:	"Those pretty wrongs that liberty commits,"	123
Sonnet 42:	"That thou hast her, it is not all my grief,"	126
Sonnet 43:	"When most I wink, then do mine eyes best see,"	129
Sonnet 44:	"If the dull substance of my flesh were thought,"	132
Sonnet 45:	"The other two, slight air and purging fire,"	135
Sonnet 46:	"Mine eye and heart are at a mortal war,"	138
Sonnet 47:	"Betwixt mine eye and heart a league is took,"	141
Sonnet 48:	"How careful was I when I took my way,"	144
Sonnet 49:	"Against that time, if ever that time come,"	147
Sonnet 50:	"How heavy do I journey on the way,"	151
Sonnet 51:	"Thus can my love excuse the slow offence"	154
Sonnet 52:	"So am I as the rich, whose blessed key"	157
Sonnet 53:	"What is your substance, whereof are you made,"	161
Sonnet 54:	"O how much more doth beauty beauteous seem,"	164
Sonnet 55:	"Not marble, nor the gilded monuments"	168
Sonnet 56:	"Sweet love, renew thy force; be it not said"	170
Sonnet 57:	"Being your slave, what should I do but tend"	173
Sonnet 58:	"That God forbid that made me first your slave,"	176
Sonnet 59:	"If there be nothing new, but that which is"	178
Sonnet 60:	"Like as the waves make towards the pebbled shore,"	181
Sonnet 61:	"Is it thy will thy image should keep open"	184
Sonnet 62:	"Sin of self-love possesseth all mine eye,"	187
Sonnet 63:	"Against my love shall be, as I am now,"	190
Sonnet 64:	"When I have seen by Time's fell hand defaced"	193
Sonnet 65:	"Since brass, nor stone, nor earth, nor boundless sea,"	196
Sonnet 66:	"Tired with all these, for restful death I cry,"	199
Sonnet 67:	"Ah wherefore with infection should he live,"	202
Sonnet 68:	"Thus in his cheek the map of days outworn,"	205
Sonnet 69:	"Those parts of thee that the world's eye doth view,"	208
Sonnet 70:	"That thou art blamed shall not be thy defect,"	211
Sonnet 71:	"No longer mourn for me when I am dead"	214
Sonnet 72:	"O lest the world should task you to recite,"	216
Sonnet 73:	"That time of year thou mayst in me behold,"	218
Sonnet 74:	"But be contented when that fell arrest,"	221
Sonnet 75:	"So are you to my thoughts as food to life,"	223
Sonnet 76:	"Why is my verse so barren of new pride,"	226
Sonnet 77:	"Thy glass will show thee how thy beauties wear,"	229

Sonnet 78:	"So oft have I invok'd thee for my Muse,"	232
Sonnet 79:	"Whilst I alone did call upon thy aid,"	235
Sonnet 80:	"O how I faint when I of you do write,"	237
Sonnet 81:	"Or I shall live your epitaph to make,"	240
Sonnet 82:	"I grant thou wert not married to my Muse,"	244
Sonnet 83:	"I never saw that you did painting need,"	246
Sonnet 84:	"Who is it that says most, which can say more"	249
Sonnet 85:	"My tongue-tied Muse in manners holds her still,"	252
Sonnet 86:	"Was it the proud full sail of his great verse,"	255
Sonnet 87:	"Farewell, thou art too dear for my possessing,"	258
Sonnet 88:	"When thou shalt be disposed to set me light,"	261
Sonnet 89:	"Say that thou didst forsake me for some fault,"	264
Sonnet 90:	"Then hate me when thou wilt, if ever, now;"	267
Sonnet 91:	"Some glory in their birth, some in their skill,"	270
Sonnet 92:	"But do thy worst to steal thyself away,"	272
Sonnet 93:	"So shall I live, supposing thou art true,"	275
Sonnet 94:	"They that have power to hurt, and will do none,"	278
Sonnet 95:	"How sweet and lovely dost thou make the shame"	282
Sonnet 96:	"Some say thy fault is youth, some wantonness,"	285
Sonnet 97:	"How like a winter hath my absence been"	288
Sonnet 98:	"From you have I been absent in the spring,"	291
Sonnet 99:	"The forward violet thus did I chide:"	293
Sonnet 100:	"Where art thou, Muse, that thou forget'st so long"	295
Sonnet 101:	"O truant Muse, what shall be thy amends"	298
Sonnet 102:	"My love is strengthen'd, though more weak in seeming;"	301
Sonnet 103:	"Alack what poverty my Muse brings forth,"	304
Sonnet 104:	"To me, fair friend, you never can be old,"	307
Sonnet 105:	"Let not my love be call'd idolatry,"	310
Sonnet 106:	"When in the chronicle of wasted time"	313
Sonnet 107:	"Not mine own fears, nor the prophetic soul"	316
Sonnet 108:	"What's in the brain, that ink may character,"	319
Sonnet 109:	"O never say that I was false of heart,"	322
Sonnet 110:	"Alas 'tis true I have gone here and there,"	325
Sonnet 111:	"O for my sake do you with Fortune chide,"	328
Sonnet 112:	"Your love and pity doth the impression fill"	331
Sonnet 113:	"Since I left you, mine eye is in my mind,"	334
Sonnet 114:	"Or whether doth my mind being crown'd with you,"	337
Sonnet 115:	"Those lines that I before have writ do lie,"	340
Sonnet 116:	"Let me not to the marriage of true minds"	343
Sonnet 117:	"Accuse me thus: that I have scanted all"	346
Sonnet 118:	"Like as, to make our appetites more keen,"	349
Sonnet 119:	"What potions have I drunk of Siren tears,"	352

Sonnet 120: "That you were once unkind befriends me now," 356
Sonnet 121: "'Tis better to be vile than vile esteemed," 360
Sonnet 122: "Thy gift, thy tables, are within my brain" 363
Sonnet 123: "No, Time, thou shalt not boast that I do change:" 366
Sonnet 124: "If my dear love were but the child of state," 369
Sonnet 125: "Were't aught to me I bore the canopy," 372
Sonnet 126: "O thou, my lovely boy, who in thy power" 375
Sonnet 127: "In the old age black was not counted fair," 379
Sonnet 128: "How oft, when thou, my music, music play'st," 384
Sonnet 129: "Th' expense of spirit in a waste of shame" 390
Sonnet 130: "My mistress' eyes are nothing like the sun;" 393
Sonnet 131: "Thou art as tyrannous, so as thou art," 397
Sonnet 132: "Thine eyes I love, and they, as pitying me," 401
Sonnet 133: "Beshrew that heart that makes my heart to groan" 404
Sonnet 134: "So, now I have confessed that he is thine," 408
Sonnet 135: "Whoever hath her wish, thou hast thy Will," 412
Sonnet 136: "If thy soul check thee that I come so near," 415
Sonnet 137: "Thou blind fool, love, what dost thou to mine eyes," 419
Sonnet 138: "When my love swears that she is made of truth," 423
Sonnet 139: "O call not me to justify the wrong" 427
Sonnet 140: "Be wise as thou art cruel, do not press" 431
Sonnet 141: "In faith, I do not love thee with mine eyes," 435
Sonnet 142: "Love is my sin, and thy dear virtue hate," 439
Sonnet 143: "Lo, as a careful housewife runs to catch" 443
Sonnet 144: "Two loves I have of comfort and despair," 447
Sonnet 145: "Those lips that Love's own hand did make," 451
Sonnet 146: "Poor soul, the centre of my sinful earth," 455
Sonnet 147: "My love is as a fever, longing still" 458
Sonnet 148: "O me! what eyes hath Love put in my head," 462
Sonnet 149: "Canst thou, O cruel, say I love thee not," 466
Sonnet 150: "O from what power hast thou this pow'rful might," 469
Sonnet 151: "Love is too young to know what conscience is;" 472
Sonnet 152: "In loving thee thou know'st I am forsworn," 475
Sonnet 153: "Cupid laid by his brand and fell asleep." 481
Sonnet 154: "The little Love-god lying once asleep," 483

Acknowledgments 487
Index of First Lines 489
Biographical Note 495

FOREWORD BY HRH THE PRINCE OF WALES

CLARENCE HOUSE

Shakespeare's poetry is surely miraculous. Each of his lines instantly reveals multiple layers of meaning. In his own day they would not just have served those in his audience who were there simply for the action and the apparent drama of his plays but also those, like him, who were steeped in the esoteric learning of the Platonic tradition. These people would have discerned the far deeper meaning of his words, recognising, no doubt, what it was in Shakespeare's art "giving invention light". As Ira Zinman so clearly demonstrates in this admirable work of scholarship, when Shakespeare was away from the theatre he was able in his more private sonnets to speak directly to this particular audience by stripping away apparent narrative and getting to the very heart of things.

By enchanting us with his poetry, Shakespeare opens our minds to the Divine. He, more than any other poet I can think of, understood the importance of symbolism. The constant allusions in his sonnets to the beloved are all references to the Divine spirit for which the human soul longs and this, for me, makes him a figure of universal importance, for he shows us in language so easy to understand that, whichever tradition we may be born into, it is only by attending to the spiritual dimension of our being that we may properly know what it is to be alive.

Our present age, alas, has lost the ability to read this symbolism which is not an arbitrary system of labelling. It is specific to the very nature of things and has the capacity to heighten our awareness of the unity to be found in all of creation. That is to say the Divine: "In all external grace you have some part," as Shakespeare puts it in Sonnet 53. Such a symbol is like a shadow. It reveals to us a fleeting image of the object that casts it. But it is only in the hands of a great and universal artist like Shakespeare, whose vision of the inner, spiritual realm is so direct and whose practical skill with words so acute, that such symbols enchant us so completely. The shadows, as it were, become sharp and outstanding so that we become more profoundly aware of the inner knowledge of the heart.

This is a book that makes leafing compulsive. It demonstrates on every page Shakespeare's deeper meaning. As Ira Zinman puts it in his commentary on perhaps the best known of Shakespeare's sonnets, 18, "the secret is for Man to live in tune with timeless spiritual values". I hope that his meticulous endeavours here will help convey that secret to a world which is desperately in need of a much more sensitive response to the inner reality of things for, as Shakespeare and his truly enlightened contemporaries clearly understood, all of our external endeavours depend upon it absolutely.

INTRODUCTION

Scholars have found in Shakespeare's Sonnets wonderful poetry written about a mysterious youth, a dark lady, and a rival poet, and have presented a myriad of possible interpretations to these and other aspects of the poems. Some believe that the Sonnets are biographical, and it may well be that Shakespeare had one or many individuals in mind as he wrote. Current criticism makes it clear, however, that interpretations which have assumed biographical facts about the author have not succeeded in making out a conclusive case. And as to whether a young man or woman is a central part of the Sonnets, the gender of the addressee in most of the Sonnets is in fact unspecified. Indeed, "Shakespeare is exceptional among the English sonneteers (Sidney, Spenser, and Daniel, for example) in leaving the beloved's gender unspecified in so many of the sonnets: about five-sixths of them in the first 126 and just less than that in the collection entire."[1]

Even without decisive facts about the Sonnets and their origin, "serious scholarly as well as popular interest in the Sonnets seems never to have been greater." This includes publications in the last few decades of several new editions of the Sonnets as well as "significant criticism." "Much of the liveliness of today's criticism of the Sonnets, of course, is fueled by scholarly disagreement; the only complete agreement seems to be on the value of affording careful study of these poems and the cultural conditions from which they emerged."[2]

As for Shakespeare himself, he has been paid almost every kind of tribute, and his works are at the pinnacle of all respected world literature. Emerson, in commenting on Shakespeare, stated: "What point of morals, of manners, of economy, of philosophy, of religion, of taste, of the conduct of life has he not settled?"[3] There is no shortage of commentary on these varied themes. In addition, there have been

[1] Margreta de Grazia, "The Scandal of Shakespeare's Sonnets," quoted in *Shakespeare's Sonnets*, ed. James Schiffer (New York: Garland Publishing, 2000), p. 97.

[2] Ibid., pp. 41-42.

[3] "Shakespeare or, the Poet," in Ralph Waldo Emerson, *Select Essays and Addresses* (New York: Macmillan, 1928), p. 190.

writers, such as Noble and Shaheen, who have identified throughout the plays many passages that are similar to, or echo, an expansive list of Biblical passages.[4]

While there is a growing interest in the Sonnets, it is also true, as Helen Vendler has stated that "rather few sonnets have been examined in detail, since critics tend to dwell on the most famous ten or fifteen out of the total 154; in fact, the *Sonnets* represent the largest tract of unexamined Shakespearean lines left open to scrutiny."[5] This reading of all 154 Sonnets, with close attention to Biblical themes, is an area of inquiry never before undertaken.

The Bible has been identified by several writers as a source of major importance to Shakespeare. As for the Sonnets, there has not generally been an exploration of their religious or spiritual meanings, except to identify verses that are suggestive of Biblical passages. It should be recalled that for writers in Shakespeare's time, it was contrary to English law to make direct reference to religion in their works; it was therefore necessary for such themes to be occluded within the text and beneath a literal reading. Elizabethan audiences were not unaware of the fact that multiple levels of interpretation were to be found in poetry and drama. Edmund Spenser described such to be true, and it is often accepted that great literature can be understood, as Dante has suggested in his *Il Convivio*,[6] on four distinct levels: first, the plain or literal meaning; second, the allegorical meaning; third, the moral meaning; and last, the anagogical or esoteric meaning. Religious or spiritual aspects would thus be found in the three last-mentioned levels of meaning.

While Shakespeare's plays have garnered the major attention with regard to identifying Biblical themes and passages, this area is left without complete exploration in the Sonnets. It is the intent of this work to complete for the Sonnets what has been done for

[4] See, for example, Richmond Noble, *Shakespeare's Biblical Knowledge* (New York: Octagon Books, 1935) and Naseeb Shaheen, *Biblical References in Shakespeare's Plays* (Newark: University of Delaware Press, 1999).

[5] Helen Vendler, *The Art of Shakespeare's Sonnets* (Cambridge: Belknap Press, 1997), p. 13.

[6] See especially Book 2, Chapter 1, available online at: http://dante.ilt.columbia.edu/books/convivi (English translation by Richard Lansing).

Shakespeare's plays. The goal is not to supplant the criticism already in place with a claim for an exclusive interpretation along religious lines. Stephen Booth tells us that "Nothing one says or thinks about a poem can change it. What one says about a poem can sometimes change the angle of a reader's perception of it, but one cannot stop the poem from doing all that it does or argue it into doing what it does not do. No interpretive description of a poem can nullify any of the actions the poem performs upon a reader's understanding."[7] An attempt to argue that one interpretation of the Sonnets is better than another only creates divisiveness. Because one critical commentary throws a shaft of light upon some elements in a poem does not necessarily throw a shadow across the position taken by another, or make it less valid. In his plays and Sonnets, Shakespeare was able to write simultaneously on the levels of literal meaning as well as the allegorical, moral, and anagogical meanings. The Sonnets flow from the same pen as the plays and are filled with equally limitless dimensions.

To assist the reader in understanding the approach to the Sonnets taken in this book, and as an example of the multiple, interpretive readings, Sonnet 7 is here examined in part. The complete treatment of Sonnet 7, with its Theme, Glossary, Commentary, and Suggested Biblical Passages, is found in this book.

SONNET 7

Lo, in the orient when the gracious light
Lifts up his burning head, each under eye
Doth homage to his new-appearing sight,
Serving with looks his sacred majesty;
And having climb'd the steep-up heavenly hill,
Resembling strong youth in his middle age,
Yet mortal looks adore his beauty still,
Attending on his golden pilgrimage.
But when from highmost pitch, with weary car,
Like feeble age, he reeleth from the day,

[7] *Shakespeare's Sonnets*, ed. Stephen Booth (New Haven: Yale Nota Bene, 2000), pp. 514-515.

The eyes, 'fore duteous, now converted are
From his low tract, and look another way:
So thou, thyself outgoing in thy noon,
Unlook'd on diest, unless thou get a son.

The *literal meaning* usually assigned to this sonnet is as follows: The poet is making a comparison of the youth, to whom he is speaking, with the sun, which in its morning beauty in the East is gazed upon with adoration ("*Doth homage*"). This youth is then in the prime of his life. As time progresses to "*his middle age*," his beauty is yet admired ("*adore his beauty still*"). But just as the sun travels across the heavens, so the youth eventually reaches "*feeble age*." As the sun fades, so also, will the youth be neglected when he becomes old ("*outgoing in thy noon*") and die and be forgotten, unless he is able to "*get a son*." The idea is that procreation is needed to carry on one's lineage; otherwise, one is forgotten like the sun set below the horizon.

On a *deeper level*, the *Biblical theme* suggested by this Sonnet reads: Life is a journey of the soul. If it is directed outwardly toward a shallow material life, the inner radiance will not shine forth, but die. When the eye is reverently directed heavenward, the soul may receive "*the gracious light*" of the Spirit and experience the rebirth or resurrection promised by the Son of God. The words in line 1 of the Sonnet, "*orient when the gracious light*," is read as the light of the Spirit described as coming from the East. The "*son*" in the final line of the Sonnet is found in the suggested Bible passage whose text reads: "For as the lightning cometh out of the east, and shineth even unto the west; so shall also the coming of the Son of man be." **(Matt. 24:27)**

This treatment of the Sonnets demonstrates that it is possible to reach various conclusions about the meaning or interpretation of a Sonnet, though it does not seek to make any claims for exclusivity. It is proposed that for a more complete understanding of the Sonnets, one should take a balanced approach, looking at meanings, which as Dante suggests, may be found in the plain or literal interpretation; the allegorical; the level of morality; or the anagogical or esoteric. As with the examination of Shakespeare's plays, it is possible to find all of these meanings, or a combination of them, in the Sonnets.

As mentioned, Shakespeare's Sonnets may be interpreted literally as applying to a youth, lover, other poets, "the dark lady," and the like.

We also find within them an exploration of human love, the beauty of the inner man, the soul, mortality, temptation, time, and death. Nor can one overlook the Biblical themes of lust, greed, gluttony and the other of the "deadly sins," as well as references to man's "nobler part" or "better angel," which writers on the Sonnets have acknowledged as referring to the soul of man.

Shakespeare's Sonnets and the Bible is written to more completely explore the Sonnets; in doing so it seeks to identify themes at the religious and scriptural level of interpretation. This work is offered to the reader for thought and contemplation. It is only a beginning glimpse into the depth of Shakespeare's spiritual heart. Of course, each one will reach his or her own interpretations and conclusions. Indeed, is it not part of what we admire in Shakespeare that he has given ample scope for appreciation to all audiences on all levels of understanding? Like Truth, Shakespeare's nature is multi-dimensional and limitless. *Shakespeare's Sonnets and the Bible* is another facet of the diamond that is Shakespeare himself.

Ira B. Zinman

THE METHOD FOLLOWED

When interpreting a Sonnet, a **Theme** that summarizes the overall scriptural theme of the Sonnet is presented, which is then followed by a **Glossary**. In the **Glossary**, each one of the quatrains of the Sonnet, and then the final couplet, are presented individually with a view toward the scriptural elements contained therein. A **Commentary** follows, which discusses the Sonnet and how it presents scriptural themes. Finally, a few **Biblical Passages** are given whose themes are suggested by the Sonnet.

The King James Version (KJV) of the Bible (published in 1611) is used throughout this work, except as noted in the Commentary. While it is widely accepted that Shakespeare most likely used the earlier Geneva Bible (published in 1560), the meanings of the various passages referenced herein do not significantly change from the Geneva to the KJV version. Therefore, for the reader's ease of reference, the widely-used and available KJV is used in this work.

SONNET 1

From fairest creatures we desire increase,
That thereby beauty's rose might never die,
But as the riper should by time decease,
His tender heir might bear his memory:
But thou, contracted to thine own bright eyes,
Feed'st thy light's flame with self-substantial fuel,
Making a famine where abundance lies,
Thyself thy foe, to thy sweet self too cruel.
Thou that art now the world's fresh ornament
And only herald to the gaudy spring,
Within thine own bud buriest thy content
And, tender churl, mak'st waste in niggarding.
Pity the world, or else this glutton be,
To eat the world's due, by the grave and thee.

THEME

Ever-increasing desires for worldly allurements are the result of delusive attachment. A life ill-spent in acquiring, to the point of greed and gluttony, leads surely to a life of discontentment and spiritual denigration.

GLOSSARY

From fairest creatures we desire increase, That thereby beauty's rose might never die, But as the riper should by time decease, His tender heir might bear his memory:

> For what is perceived as creation's fairest aspects, we possess an insatiable appetite, believing that in having more we are perpetuating happiness. With age and wisdom, one's desire for worldly things should decrease, thereby protecting the tender soul from harmful material attachments that become subconsciously imprinted.

But thou, contracted to thine own bright eyes, Feed'st thy light's flame with self-substantial fuel, Making a famine where abundance lies, Thyself thy foe, to thy sweet self too cruel.

> But you, irrevocably habituated to going after what you see and desire, feed your soul with ego-satisfying desires, depleting your inner resources. You, your own worst enemy, are the slayer of your soul.

Thou that art now the world's fresh ornament And only herald to the gaudy spring, Within thine own bud buriest thy content And, tender churl, mak'st waste in niggarding.

> Today you are everyone's hero, your existence portending a shallow life, your happiness buried before it can flower, and you, for lack of true spiritual effort, never flourish.

Pity the world, or else this glutton be, To eat the world's due, by the grave and thee.

> Turn from the ways of the world. Awake to this folly or fall victim to worldly excesses and be buried with them.

COMMENTARY

Shakespeare cautions against increasing desires for material things under the delusion that these are "*fairest creatures*" that will satisfy man's deepest needs. He says that people are deluded into believing that having more worldly things must be better. "*That thereby beauty's rose might never die.*" Common sense, however, teaches that if a little bit of dessert is good, then eating several helpings of the same will result in feeling sick. As one grows older and supposedly wiser, tempting worldly desires should fall away. "*But as the riper should by time decrease.*" Habitually going after desires of the heart ("*contracted to thine own bright eyes*") destroys the spiritual glow by feeding it with the ego's "*self-substantial fuel.*" The result is "*famine*" where the wealth of Spirit should be: "*Making a famine where abundance lies.*" Happiness lies in starving worldly desires and feeding the soul with actions of a spiritual nature. This theme is also reflected in Sonnet 146.9, 12: "*Then, soul, live thou upon thy servant's loss. . . . Within be fed, without be rich no more.*"

Indulging in worldly excesses, according to Shakespeare, makes a person his own worst enemy: "*Thyself thy foe.*" This is cruel to one's precious soul: "*to thy sweet self too cruel.*" The sweet bud of spiritual happiness never flowers but remains buried: "*within thine own bud buriest thy content.*"

The answer is to shun worldly ways "*or else this glutton be, to eat the world's due,*" the result of which is to be buried spiritually ("*by the grave and thee*") having fallen victim to material excesses.

BIBLICAL PASSAGES SUGGESTED BY SONNET 1

"These are wells without water, clouds that are carried with a tempest; to whom the mist of darkness is reserved for ever. For when they speak great swelling words of vanity, they allure through the lusts of the flesh, through much wantonness, those that were clean escaped from them who live in error. While they promise them liberty, they themselves are the servants of corruption: for of whom a man is overcome, of the same is he brought in bondage. For if after they have escaped the pollutions of the world through the knowledge of the Lord and Savior Jesus Christ, they are again entangled therein, and overcome, the latter end is worse with them than the beginning. For it would have been better for them not to have known the way of righteousness, than, after they have known it, to turn from the holy commandment delivered unto them." **2 Pet. 2:17-21**

"Whose end is destruction, whose God is their belly, and whose glory is in their shame, who mind earthly things." **Phil. 3:19**

"Be not desirous of his dainties; for they are deceitful meat." **Prov. 23:3**

"For the drunkard and the glutton shall come to poverty: and drowsiness shall clothe a man with rags." **Prov. 23:21**

SONNET 2

When forty winters shall besiege thy brow,
And dig deep trenches in thy beauty's field,
Thy youth's proud livery, so gaz'd on now,
Will be a tatter'd weed, of small worth held:
Then being ask'd where all thy beauty lies,
Where all the treasure of thy lusty days,
To say, within thine own deep-sunken eyes,
Were an all-eating shame and thriftless praise.
How much more praise deserv'd thy beauty's use,
If thou couldst answer, "This fair child of mine
Shall sum my count, and make my old excuse,"
Proving his beauty by succession thine.
This were to be new made when thou art old,
And see thy blood warm when thou feel'st it cold.

THEME

"For where your treasure is, there will your heart be also." **(Matt. 6:21)** If life is misspent in worldly, "*lusty days*," one will have regret and shame in old age. If a person lives a God-centered life, he glorifies his soul by giving to his earthly fellows, and reaps a heavenly reward after death.

GLOSSARY

When forty winters shall besiege thy brow, And dig deep trenches in thy beauty's field, Thy youth's proud livery, so gaz'd on now, Will be a tatter'd weed, of small worth held:

> When you are old and gray and your withered youth is spent, the youthful abundance you now possess will be depleted to near nothingness.

Then being ask'd where all thy beauty lies, Where all the treasure of thy lusty days, To say, within thine own deep-sunken eyes, Were an all-eating shame and thriftless praise.

> Then being asked where is your beauty, where is the

profit of a misspent youth, the answer is reflected in your downcast eyes and guilty conscience.

How much more praise deserv'd thy beauty's use, If thou couldst answer, "This fair child of mine Shall sum my count, and make my old excuse," Proving his beauty by succession thine.

How much more precious a life if you could say, "the Spirit that I carry within and my deeds alone speak for me," proving that they are alone your worth and valued legacy.

This were to be new made when thou art old, And see thy blood warm when thou feel'st it cold.

When old age finds the body wanting and waning, we are meant to be uplifted in Spirit by a perpetual flow of inner joy and wisdom.

COMMENTARY

In Sonnet 1, Shakespeare states that with maturity and age should come the wisdom to avoid worldly excesses. In Sonnet 2, Shakespeare describes the old age of one who has been living a life of material excesses. In this Sonnet, he warns that such pursuits lead to an old age of "*tatter'd weed, of small worth.*" The materially-minded will regret the "*lusty days*" and such is reflected in "*deep-sunken eyes*" and is felt as "*an all-eating shame.*" How comforting it would be if a person advanced in years might declare that "my life wisely-lived shall answer in judgment". These are the precious bequests ("*fair child*") of my soul's worth "*proving his beauty by succession thine.*"

It is in living a spiritual life that one is renewed in old age: "*This were to be made new when thou art old.*" Such a goodly life reaps rewards beyond death in the hereafter: "*see thy blood warm when thou feel'st it cold.*"

BIBLICAL PASSAGES SUGGESTED BY SONNET 2

"For where your treasure is, there will your heart be also." **Matt. 6:21**

"Rejoice, O young man, in thy youth; and let thy heart cheer thee in the days of thy youth, and walk in the ways of thine heart, and in the sight of thine eyes: but know thou, that for all these things God will bring thee into judgment. Therefore remove sorrow from thy heart, and put away evil from thy flesh: for childhood and youth are vanity." **Eccl. 11:9-10**

"Therefore if any man be in Christ, he is a new creature: old things are passed away; behold, all things are become new." **2 Cor. 5:17**

SONNET 3

Look in thy glass, and tell the face thou viewest,
Now is the time that face should form another;
Whose fresh repair if now thou not renewest,
Thou dost beguile the world, unbless some mother,
For where is she so fair whose unear'd womb
Disdains the tillage of thy husbandry?
Or who is he so fond will be the tomb
Of his self-love, to stop posterity?
Thou art thy mother's glass, and she in thee
Calls back the lovely April of her prime;
So thou through windows of thine age shalt see,
Despite of wrinkles, this thy golden time.
But if thou live, remember'd not to be,
Die single, and thine image dies with thee.

THEME

One must reflect honestly on choices and change oneself in a positive way. If not, Mother Earth herself will weep for her spiritually lost children living ego-centered lives. Renewal to one's "*golden time*" is possible if one's life becomes spiritually centered.

GLOSSARY

Look in thy glass, and tell the face thou viewest, Now is the time that face should form another; Whose fresh repair if now thou not renewest, Thou dost beguile the world, unbless some mother,

> Look at yourself and your life with honest introspection and realize that it is now time to correct the erroneous ways you have pursued. If you do nothing, you fool the world, but shame the earthly mother who bore you, and the Heavenly Mother who endowed your soul.

For where is she so fair whose unear'd womb Disdains the tillage of thy husbandry? Or who is he so fond will be the tomb Of his self-love, to stop posterity?

> And where is the Mother of Creation so pure, who weeps for her barren offspring whose life is misspent? Who is one so self-consumed that his life is death while he lives?

Thou art thy mother's glass, and she in thee Calls back the lovely April of her prime; So thou through windows of thine age shalt see, Despite of wrinkles this thy golden time.

> The pure essence of your soul is the reflection of Mother Nature herself and the power of that ever-youthful Spirit within, which is all renewing; so you, although past the years of your prime, shall be uplifted and see with wisdom born of awakened soul intuition.

But if thou live, remember'd not to be, Die single, and thine image dies with thee.

> But if you live ignorant of the Spirit within, you are indeed alone, here and hereafter.

COMMENTARY

One should not wait until "*forty winters shall besiege thy brow*" (Sonnet 2.1) to make a change. In Sonnet 3, the Poet insists that now is the time to reflect on one's errors and make a change: "*Look in thy glass, and tell the face thou viewest, Now is the time that face should form another.*"

Shakespeare decries a life in which the soul's true nature is never developed or expressed. This is the "*unear'd womb,*" likened to agricultural planting ("*tillage*"), which yields no harvest. The Spirit within is in the "*tomb*" of the ego's "*self-love.*" One's soul is the reflection of Spirit or the Creative Mother Nature of the Universe ("*thou art thy mother's glass*") who ever restores the fullness of youth: "*Calls back the lovely April of her prime.*" Whoever looks with wisdom within ("*through windows of thine age*") at the soul, no matter the age of the physical body ("*despite of wrinkles*") can be renewed in ever-youthful Spirit: "*this thy golden time.*" One who lives, however, in the tomb of egoistic self-love is not remembered and will "*die single.*" Such a person lives ignorant of the Soul within ("*remember'd not to be*") and suffers a spiritual, as well as a physical death: "*thine image dies with thee.*"

BIBLICAL PASSAGES SUGGESTED BY SONNET 3

"For now we see through a glass, darkly; but then face to face: now I know in part; but then shall I know even as also I am known." **1 Cor. 13:12**

"Let us search and try our ways, and turn again to the Lord." **Lam. 3:40**

"For if a man think himself to be something, when he is nothing, he deceiveth himself. . . . Be not deceived; God is not mocked: for whatsoever a man soweth, that shall he also reap. For he that soweth to his flesh shall of the flesh reap corruption; but he that soweth to the Spirit shall of the Spirit reap life everlasting." **Gal. 6:3, 7-8**

SONNET 4

Unthrifty loveliness, why dost thou spend
Upon thyself thy beauty's legacy?
Nature's bequest gives nothing, but doth lend,
And being frank, she lends to those are free:
Then, beauteous niggard, why dost thou abuse
The bounteous largess given thee to give?
Profitless usurer why dost thou use
So great a sum of sums, yet canst not live?
For having traffic with thyself alone,
Thou of thyself thy sweet self dost deceive:
Then how, when Nature calls thee to be gone,
What acceptable audit canst thou leave?
Thy unus'd beauty must be tomb'd with thee,
Which used, lives th' executor to be.

THEME

Humans are endowed with the unlimited power of the soul, a reflection of Spirit. People may choose to live a limited and limiting ego-centered life or one expressive of the Spirit, which benefits humankind and the soul.

GLOSSARY

Unthrifty loveliness, why dost thou spend Upon thyself thy beauty's legacy? Nature's bequest gives nothing, but doth lend, And being frank, she lends to those are free:

> Oh created spiritual man, why do you waste your soul's wealth on egoistical pursuits? The Creator for this short term of life instills potential, and much is given to those who freely and unselfishly give of their innate spiritual bounty.

Then, beauteous niggard, why dost thou abuse The bounteous largess given thee to give? Profitless usurer why dost thou use So great a sum of sums, yet canst not live?

So why do you, a precious child of God, act small when your wealth is so great? How is it that you waste your life in profitless, worldly pursuits, and still cannot find happiness?

For having traffic with thyself alone, Thou of thyself thy sweet self dost deceive: Then how, when Nature calls thee to be gone, What acceptable audit canst thou leave?

Because your pursuits are self-centered, you live in ignorance of the happiness of your Spirit: When it is your time to die, what of value will you leave behind?

Thy unus'd beauty must be tomb'd with thee, Which used, lives th' executor to be.

All the unspent treasure of your soul must be buried with you, which had it been expressed, would live on after you.

COMMENTARY

Shakespeare continues, in this Sonnet, to chide those who live a self-centered existence while depleting the soul's true beauty: "*thy beauty's legacy.*" In Sonnet 3, Shakespeare refers to the "*tomb of . . . self-love*" (3.8) which causes one to "*die single, and thine image dies with thee.*" (3.14) In this Sonnet, Shakespeare again repeats that the God-given soul is full of bounty to those who are not ignorant of it: "*she lends to those are free.*" If one acts to "*abuse the bounteous largess,*" the soul's unlimited bounty is lost: "*thy unus'd beauty must be tomb'd with thee.*"

Unlike those who cannot leave an "*acceptable audit,*" those who live a life full of spiritual beauty, endow their souls with the grace that confers a benefit in life and assures their place in heaven: "*which used, lives th' executor to be.*" In Sonnet 4, Shakespeare uses the analogy of the executor of a will, who lives on after the deceased to administer the affairs of the estate. The obvious implication is that when the beauty of the soul is spiritually expressed in life, or "*used,*" there is indeed an "*acceptable audit*"; and thus there is a viable estate or legacy bequeathed after the deceased has departed this earthly life.

Plainly stated, Shakespeare says that the more one expresses the soul's "*bounteous largess*" of love, kindness, compassion, and other beautiful qualities, the greater will be the spiritual treasure in this life and always.

BIBLICAL PASSAGES SUGGESTED BY SONNET 4

"Vanity of vanities, saith the Preacher, vanity of vanities; all is vanity. What profit hath a man of all his labor which he taketh under the sun?" **Eccl. 1:2-3**

"Behold, all souls are mine; as the soul of the father, so also the soul of the son is mine: the soul that sinneth, it shall die. But if a man be just, and do that which is lawful and right . . . he shall surely live, saith the Lord God." **Ezek. 18:4-5, 9**

"Know ye not that the unrighteous shall not inherit the kingdom of God? Be not deceived: neither fornicators, nor idolaters, nor adulterers, nor effeminate, nor abusers of themselves with mankind, nor thieves, nor covetous, nor drunkards, nor revilers, nor extortioners, shall inherit the kingdom of God." **1 Cor. 6:9-10**

"For I have no pleasure in the death of him who dieth, saith the Lord God: wherefore turn yourselves, and live ye." **Ezek. 18:32**

SONNET 5

Those hours, that with gentle work did frame
The lovely gaze where every eye doth dwell
Will play the tyrants to the very same
And that unfair which fairly doth excel:
For never-resting time leads summer on
To hideous winter, and confounds him there,
Sap check'd with frost and lusty leaves quite gone,
Beauty o'ersnow'd and bareness everywhere.
Then were not summer's distillation left
A liquid prisoner pent in walls of glass,
Beauty's effect with beauty were bereft,
Nor it nor no remembrance what it was.
But flowers distill'd, though they with winter meet,
Leese but their show, their substance still lives sweet.

THEME

Those who take time in life to discover and express their spiritual nature are renewed and ever exude a sweet nature.

GLOSSARY

Those hours, that with gentle work did frame The lovely gaze where every eye doth dwell Will play the tyrants to the very same And that unfair which fairly doth excel:

> Time spent in quiet meditation awakens the soul with the light of spiritual vision which diminishes the desire for wasteful, materialistic pursuits, and thereby, the allure of inner joy overtakes the mundane.

For never-resting time leads summer on To hideous winter, and confounds him there, Sap check'd with frost and lusty leaves quite gone, Beauty o'ersnow'd and bareness everywhere.

> A life spent restlessly in worldly pursuits ends in ill-health, shallow understanding, and spent energy, a life devoid of beauty that is lifeless in the end.

Then, were not summer's distillation left A liquid prisoner pent in walls of glass, Beauty's effect with beauty were bereft, Nor it nor no remembrance what it was.

> Then the sweet perfume of the soul, kept like a prisoner within, is never released, depriving beauty of its own expression, never known nor remembered for what it truly was.

But flowers distill'd, though they with winter meet, Leese but their show, their substance still lives sweet.

> But having discovered and expressed the spiritual essence within, though the temporary encasement of the physical body is diminished with age, the sweet perfume of the soul ever exudes its sweet fragrance.

COMMENTARY

Shakespeare gives expression to the idea that man is essentially a spiritual being who needs prayer and time spent in peaceful meditation: "*Those hours that with gentle work did frame . . . will play the tyrants to the very same.*" Such activity is revivifying and allows the opportunity for greater peace and understanding: "*and that unfair which fairly doth excel.*" The soul is thus not kept as "*a liquid prisoner in walls of glass. Beauty's effect with beauty were bereft.*" To be born, work, raise a family, and die without the thought of God starves the soul: "*For never-resting time leads summer on to hideous winter, and confounds him there . . . bareness everywhere.*" The soul's garden must be watered with renewed yearning for God and purposeful acts of love, peace, and kindness. The result is a wonderful fulfillment in life, and the guarantee that this awakened consciousness remains with the soul after death. "*But flowers distill'd, though they with winter meet, Leese but their show, their substance still lives sweet.*"

BIBLICAL PASSAGES SUGGESTED BY SONNET 5

"To open the blind eyes, to bring out prisoners from the prison, and them that sit in darkness out of the prison house." **Isa. 42:7**

"When I remember thee upon my bed, and meditate on thee in the night watches. Because thou hast been my help, therefore in the shadow of thy wings will I rejoice." **Ps. 63:6-7**

"For which cause we faint not; but though our outward man perish, yet the inward man is renewed day by day." **2 Cor. 4:16**

"The light of the body is the eye: if therefore thine eye be single, thy whole body shall be full of light." **Matt. 6:22**

SONNET 6

Then let not winter's ragged hand deface
In thee thy summer, ere thou be distill'd:
Make sweet some vial; treasure thou some place
With beauty's treasure ere it be self-kill'd.
That use is not forbidden usury,
Which happies those that pay the willing loan;
That's for thyself to breed another thee,
Or ten times happier, be it ten for one.
Ten times thyself were happier than thou art,
If ten of thine ten times refigur'd thee,
Then what could death do, if thou shouldst depart,
Leaving thee living in posterity?
Be not self-will'd, for thou art much too fair,
To be death's conquest and make worms thine heir.

THEME

Life is wasted if one has not spent time in spiritual pursuits. Selfishness or self-will negates the bright summer light of the Spirit. One's inner light is exponentially expanded by turning inward and eschewing mundane matters. Eventually even death will have no sway over one whose soul appreciates its immortality.

GLOSSARY

Then let not winter's ragged hand deface in thee thy summer, ere thou be distill'd: Make sweet some vial; treasure thou some place With beauty's treasure ere it be self-kill'd.

> Don't be barren and depleted in youth when you should be flourishing and allowing your inner light to shine. Sweeten your life by treasuring inner beauty and quietude before endless worldly pursuits overtake and destroy your happiness.

That use is not forbidden usury, Which happies those that pay the willing loan; That's for thyself to breed another thee, Or ten times happier, be it ten for one.

It is not foolish to steal time away from mundane matters and to invest your time in quiet meditation; this will renew and awaken your soul, and for every hour you borrow from a worldly life for a sacred life, you will reap a tenfold treasure of lasting joy.

Ten times thyself were happier than thou art, If ten of thine ten times refigur'd thee, Then what could death do if thou shouldst depart, Leaving thee living in posterity?

It takes persistent time and effort to spiritualize your nature, but if in Spirit you are multiplied and renewed a hundred fold, then what power could even death have over you who leave as legacy, such wealth of the Spirit?

Be not self-will'd, for thou art much too fair, To be death's conquest and make worms thine heir.

Don't cast your life away being ruled by the ego's worldly desires; you and your sweet soul are much too beautiful to be swallowed up and forgotten in death.

COMMENTARY

Shakespeare is urging us not to waste the prime of life ("*thy summer*") but to free "*the liquid prisoner*" referred to in Sonnet 5.10. The distillation process requires the time to "*make sweet some vial*" by making it a priority ("*treasure*") to spend meaningful moments with "*beauty's treasure*" within the soul before it is "*self-kill'd*" by having egotistical "*traffic with thyself alone.*" (Sonnet 4.9) In the first five Sonnets, Shakespeare decries material excesses that lead to a wasteful, discontented existence. In Sonnet 6, he asserts that those people are happy "*that pay the willing loan*" by borrowing time from egotistic pursuits. The more they develop their inner treasure by reflection and meditation, the greater is their reward: "*ten times refigur'd thee.*" "*Be not self-will'd*" lest the end is "*To be death's conquest.*"

Simply stated, Shakespeare says that even a little time spent in prayer or peaceful activity will be uplifting. It is necessary to make spiritual activity a priority, a necessary necessity. Feeding the Spirit within is more important than feeding endless material desires. Life then would be more fulfilling. "*Within be fed, without be fed no more.*" (Sonnet 146.12)

BIBLICAL PASSAGES SUGGESTED BY SONNET 6

"And he said unto them that stood by, Take from him the pound, and give it to him who hath ten pounds. (And they said unto him, Lord, he hath ten pounds.) For I say unto you, That unto every one which hath shall be given; and from him that hath not, even that he hath shall be taken away from him." **Luke 19:24-26**

"I have been young, and now am old; yet have I not seen the righteous forsaken, nor his seed begging bread." **Ps. 37:25**

"For he hath strengthened the bars of thy gates; he hath blessed thy children within thee." **Ps. 147:13**

SONNET 7

Lo, in the orient when the gracious light
Lifts up his burning head, each under eye
Doth homage to his new-appearing sight,
Serving with looks his sacred majesty;
And having climb'd the steep-up heavenly hill,
Resembling strong youth in his middle age,
Yet mortal looks adore his beauty still,
Attending on his golden pilgrimage.
But when from highmost pitch, with weary car,
Like feeble age, he reeleth from the day,
The eyes ('fore duteous) now converted are
From his low tract, and look another way:
So thou, thyself outgoing in thy noon,
Unlook'd on diest, unless thou get a son.

THEME

Life is a journey of the soul. If it is directed outwardly toward a shallow material life, then the inner radiance does not shine forth, but dies. When the eye is reverently directed heavenward, one may receive "*the gracious light*" of Spirit and experience the rebirth or resurrection promised by the Son of God.

GLOSSARY

Lo, in the orient when the gracious light Lifts up his burning head, each under eye Doth homage to his new-appearing sight, Serving with looks his sacred majesty;

> Look in the east, place of the spiritual eye, when its light raises his consciousness, and he bows reverently to the awakening light of Spirit, concentrating longingly upon his God-given soul within.

And having climb'd the steep-up heavenly hill, Resembling strong youth in his middle age, Yet mortal looks adore his beauty still, Attending on his golden pilgrimage.

And having raised his consciousness toward Spirit, he is filled with strength and vigor in middle age, and even his egoistic nature is cognizant of the nature of the soul within, impelling him along on his spiritual journey.

But when from highmost pitch, with weary car, Like feeble age, he reeleth from the day, The eyes, ('fore duteous) now converted are From his low tract, and look another way:

But when his consciousness is highly evolved, he wearies of body attachment, and like one in old age, who withdraws from outer life, his super-conscious, soul nature is irrevocably turned heavenward, away from the mundane.

So thou, thyself outgoing in thy noon, Unlook'd on diest, unless thou get a son.

So you, in the prime of your days are centered on worldly pursuits, while ignoring your innate spiritual legacy, dying a slow death unless your soul is reborn in the Spirit.

COMMENTARY

Sonnet 3 urges introspection: "*Now is the time that face should form another.*" (Sonnet 3.2) This returns one to a "*golden time.*" (Sonnet 3.12) "*The lovely gaze where every eye doth dwell*" (Sonnet 5.2) becomes the "*new-appearing sight*" in Sonnet 7.

Sonnet 7 describes one who is deeply committed to the spiritual journey, who "*Doth homage to his new-appearing sight.*" On the level of allegory, Sonnet 7 is like the story of the three wise men as they see the star in the east. "*Lo, in the orient when the gracious light Lifts up his burning head.*" "And, behold, the glory of the God of Israel came from the way of the east: and his voice was like a noise of many waters: and the earth shined with his glory." **(Ezek. 43:2)** "And the Glory of the Lord came into the house by way of the gate whose prospect is toward the east." **(Ezek. 43:4)** "Saying, Where is he that is born King of the Jews? for we have seen his star in the east, and are come to worship him." **(Matt. 2:2)**

Shakespeare describes the results of raising one's consciousness by looking into the Light of Spirit. He describes how every spiritual traveler looks to the East, the spiritual eye, and is guided "*each under eye.*" One who is in devotional prayer "*doth homage to his new-appearing sight,*" which symbolically is "the gate whose prospect is toward the east." (**Ezek. 43.4**) For the three wise men, this is Bethlehem. They look upon "*his sacred majesty.*" For the individual this is the soul or "*beauty's treasure.*" (Sonnet 6.4) This journey of the wise men, or the spiritual journey of the soul, is the "*golden pilgrimage.*"

In this journey of the soul, allegorically represented in the story of the wise men, we see that the road of an ego-centered life is long and often wearisome. There is a point of turning away from that sensually-based existence, to which the individual was "*'fore duteous,*" and now he is looking another way, toward the sacred newborn child: "*now converted are from his low tract, and look another way.*" Happy are those who "*pay the willing loan.*" (Sonnet 6.6) Shakespeare urges a person in the prime of his life to be looking in the right direction ("*thyself outgoing in thy noon*") and to pursue a sacred pilgrimage. This means to abandon "*traffic with thyself alone*" (Sonnet 4.9), unless he, unknown to himself and others, is really dying, spiritually speaking: "*unlook'd on diest.*" Salvation lies in getting a "*son*" ("*unless thou get a son*"), meaning rebirth or resurrection of soul-consciousness in God. Rebirth is within the grasp of one who is willing to go on that sacred "*golden pilgrimage.*"

BIBLICAL PASSAGES SUGGESTED BY SONNET 7

"But they that wait upon the Lord shall renew their strength; they shall mount up with wings as eagles; they shall run, and not be weary; and they shall walk, and not faint." **Isa. 40:31**

"The light of the body is the eye: if therefore thine eye be single, thy whole body shall be full of light." **Matt. 6:22**

"For as the lightning cometh out of the east, and shineth even unto the west; so shall also the coming of the Son of man be." **Matt. 24:27**

SONNET 8

Music to hear, why hear'st thou music sadly?
Sweets with sweets war not, joy delights in joy:
Why lov'st thou that which thou receiv'st not gladly,
Or else receiv'st with pleasure thine annoy?
If the true concord of well-tuned sounds,
By unions married, do offend thine ear,
They do but sweetly chide thee, who confounds
In singleness the parts that thou shouldst bear.
Mark how one string, sweet husband to another,
Strikes each in each by mutual ordering;
Resembling sire and child and happy mother,
Who, all in one, one pleasing note do sing:
Whose speechless song, being many, seeming one,
Sings this to thee: "Thou single wilt prove none."

THEME

We are meant to act in sweet, unselfish harmony, playing the music of the divine composer. He who acts alone, for himself alone, lives and dies alone.

GLOSSARY

Music to hear, why hear'st thou music sadly? Sweets with sweets war not, joy delights in joy: Why lov'st thou that which thou receiv'st not gladly, Or else receiv'st with pleasure thine annoy?

> Sweet celestial sounds are for the hearing, so why listen to the discordant notes of ordinary life? When the sweetness of the soul harmonizes with heavenly music there is a symphony of joy: Why do you pursue that which brings discontentment, or that which delights in your undoing?

If the true concord of well-tuned sounds, By unions married, do offend thine ear, They do but sweetly chide thee, who confounds In singleness the parts that thou shouldst bear.

> If those things which bring true harmony in life are some-

thing you cannot abide hearing about, know that their purpose is to gently urge you in the right direction, away from the self-created maze of selfish existence, toward the greater spiritual roles you are meant to play.

Mark how one string, sweet husband to another, Strikes each in each by mutual ordering; Resembling sire and child and happy mother, Who, all in one, one pleasing note do sing:

See how one unselfish action, responded to likewise by another, touches the heart of both as it is intended to be. It is the Creator, His divine children, and all Nature who in unison are playing the sweet music of the One.

Whose speechless song, being many, seeming one, Sings this to thee: "Thou single wilt prove none."

His divine melody, played in many souls, but heard as one symphony, sings to you: "One solitary note for itself played, is nothing."

COMMENTARY

Shakespeare likens God's universal plan to a divine symphony in which all may be aware of "*music to hear.*" Sweet harmonious actions make for concordant joy: "*Sweets with sweets war not, joy delights in joy.*" There is free will to choose right harmonious actions, or to go in the opposite direction, to love "*that which thou receiv'st not gladly, Or else receiv'st with pleasure thine annoy?*" For one "*having traffic with thyself alone*" (Sonnet 4.9), "*the true concord of well-tuned sounds, By unions married, do offend thine ear.*" The purpose of the harmonious music is not to "*annoy*" but to "*sweetly chide*" one to join in harmony with others: "*Strikes in each by mutual ordering; Resembling sire and child and happy mother.*"

There is the symbolism of an ideal family in "*sire and child and happy mother*" who together represent a perfect harmony. To remain alone is to "*die single*" (Sonnet 3.14) and "*to be death's conquest*" (Sonnet 6.14). One who is "*having traffic with* [himself] *alone*" (Sonnet 4.9) condemns his soul. *"unlook'd on diest*" (Sonnet 7.14). One is invited to join and be One with the harmonious, *speechless song*. "*Who, all in one, one pleasing note do sing.*"

BIBLICAL PASSAGES SUGGESTED BY SONNET 8

"Thy watchmen shall lift up the voice; with the voice together shall they sing: for they shall see eye to eye, when the Lord shall bring again Zion." **Isa. 52:8**

"Sing unto God, sing praises to his name: extol him that rideth upon the heavens by his name JAH [Jehovah], and rejoice before him." **Ps. 68:4**

"Blessed is the people that know the joyful sound: they shall walk, O Lord, in the light of thy countenance." **Ps. 89:15**

SONNET 9

Is it for fear to wet a widow's eye
That thou consum'st thyself in single life?
Ah! If thou issueless shalt hap to die,
The world will wail thee, like a makeless wife;
The world will be thy widow, and still weep,
That thou no form of thee hast left behind,
When every private widow well may keep,
By children's eyes her husband's shape in mind.
Look, what an unthrift in the world doth spend
Shifts but his place, for still the world enjoys it;
But beauty's waste hath in the world an end,
And kept unus'd the user so destroys it.
No love toward others in that bosom sits
That on himself such murderous shame commits.

THEME

To live for oneself alone without giving of one's loving nature, is like a family man who leaves a widow and orphaned children, never having imparted to them happiness or anything of lasting value. Both man and mankind suffer when a soul lives without giving expression to the love innate to his being.

GLOSSARY

Is it for fear to wet a widow's eye That thou consum'st thyself in single life? Ah! If thou issueless shalt hap to die, The world will wail thee, like a makeless wife;

> Is it to spare another the grief of your departure that you so selfishly never commit to anyone except yourself? Well, if you, having left no worthwhile legacy, shall die, all mankind will suffer the loss as the mateless wife .

The world will be thy widow, and still weep, That thou no form of thee hast left behind, When every private widow well may keep, By children's eyes her husband's shape in mind.

> The world will be a lesser place, and regret you left noth-

> ing of value behind, although your grief-stricken widow might keep some remembrance of you alive for the children's sake.

Look, what an unthrift in the world doth spend Shifts but his place, for still the world enjoys it; But beauty's waste hath in the world an end, And kept unus'd the user so destroys it.

> See how the profitless spender gads about moving in his little circle, and only the worldly world enjoys it; but the price of never uncovering one's inner beauty is to destroy one's soul-nature within.

No love toward others in that bosom sits That on himself such murderous shame commits.

> Locked deep within, one whose love is never expressed condemns himself to a piteous life, and an empty death.

COMMENTARY

In Sonnet 8, Shakespeare refers to the concordant symphony of life "*resembling sire and child and happy mother, Who, all in one, one pleasing note do sing.*" From the sweet harmony of life and family in Sonnet 8, Shakespeare moves to the theme of the loss of love in "*the world.*" When a single soul expresses "*no love toward others,*" it is like a "*widow*" bereft of a husband's love. Both she and the children suffer the loss. In stating "*That thou consum'st thyself in single life,*" Shakespeare is referring to one who "*Feed'st thy light's flame with self-substantial fuel*" (Sonnet 1.6) of thy "*lusty days.*" (Sonnet 2.6) He is a "*profitless usurer*" (Sonnet 4.7) who will "*traffic with* [himself] *alone.*" (Sonnet 4.9) In Sonnet 9, Shakespeare makes the point that such a person who "*comsum'st* [himself] *in single life*" will be missed in a world of "*well-tuned sounds, By unions married.*" (Sonnet 8.5-6) But the pronouncement, "*Thou single wilt prove none*" (Sonnet 8.14) is a condemnation in Sonnet 9: "*No love toward others in that bosom sits that on himself such murderous shame commits.*" Sonnet 10, which follows, continues the theme of love in man and love in relation to his Creator.

BIBLICAL PASSAGES SUGGESTED BY SONNET 9

"Beloved, let us love one another: for love is of God; and every one that loveth is born of God, and knoweth God. He that loveth not knoweth not God; for God is love." **1 John 4:7-8**

"We know that we have passed from death unto life, because we love the brethren. He that loveth not his brother abideth in death. Whosoever hateth his brother is a murderer: and ye know that no murderer hath eternal life abiding in him." **1 John 3:14-15**

SONNET 10

For shame deny that thou bear'st love to any,
Who for thyself art so unprovident.
Grant, if thou wilt, thou art belov'd of many,
But that thou none lov'st is most evident;
For thou art so possess'd with murderous hate
That 'gainst thyself thou stick'st not to conspire,
Seeking that beauteous roof to ruinate
Which to repair should be thy chief desire.
O, change thy thought, that I may change my mind.
Shall hate be fairer lodg'd than gentle love?
Be, as thy presence is, gracious and kind,
Or to thyself at least kind-hearted prove.
Make thee another self, for love of me,
That beauty still may live in thine or thee.

THEME

Hatred towards others is one of man's most deplorable traits. It is necessary to break the habit of expressing such self-destructive emotions. Altering one's thoughts in a more positive, loving way allows for a blossoming of one's soul. This spiritual change brings greater happiness to the lover and to those around him.

GLOSSARY

For shame deny that thou bear'st love to any, Who for thyself art so unprovident. Grant, if thou wilt, thou art belov'd of many, But that thou none lov'st is most evident;

> You should be ashamed to deny that you harbor love for anyone, as you are only hurting yourself. At least admit that you are loved by many, but clearly, you do not reciprocate.

For thou art so possess'd with murderous hate That 'gainst thyself thou stick'st not to conspire, Seeking that beauteous roof to ruinate Which to repair should be thy chief desire.

You are so filled with an all-consuming hate that you do nothing to deter this self-destructive trait, pursuing instead a course ruinous to your heavenly nature, which should be your deepest desire to repair.

O, change thy thought, that I may change my mind. Shall hate be fairer lodg'd than gentle love? Be, as thy presence is, gracious and kind, Or to thyself at least kind-hearted prove.

Change the way you are thinking and acting so that I too can change my judgment. Is it really better to allow hate to dominate over love? Be gracious and kind toward others as this is your true nature, or at least for the good of your own soul show more kindness.

Make thee another self, for love of me, That beauty still may live in thine or thee.

Be born again spiritually for me, that your soul may be sustained to benefit you and your brethren.

COMMENTARY

Shakespeare comments upon the strongest emotions in man: love and hate. In Sonnet 9 the Poet says, "*No love towards others in that bosom sits That on himself such murderous shame commits.*" (Sonnet 9.13-14) Deep-seated, negative emotional states shut out the light of the Spirit: not even God can reach one who chooses not to be reached. "*O, change thy thought, that I may change thy mind.*" Just to admit that love exists, is better than choosing to hate and is a start in the right direction. "*Grant, if thou wilt, thou art belov'd of many.*" To save one's self truly, it is necessary to change the attitude first and then to act in a different manner. Man is essentially the soul innately endowed with the love of God. "So God created man in his own image, in the image of God created he him; male and female created he them." **(Gen. 1:27)** "*Be, as thy presence is, gracious and kind, Or to thyself at least kind-hearted prove.*" To be "*gracious and kind*" allows the innate beauty of the soul to shine forth from within and cast its light upon others. "*Make thee another self, for love of me, That beauty still may live in thine and thee.*"

It is a Biblical commandment to love God and to love others. It is a "*shame to deny*" that a person can love, for it is his nature, given that man is made in the image of God. "*Change thy thought, that I may change my mind*" again means that the Divine is ever trying to awaken man's awareness of his soul nature. The Lord cannot act, however, unless an individual through the exercise of his free will, chooses spiritual actions.

BIBLICAL PASSAGES SUGGESTED BY SONNET 10

"For as he thinketh in his heart, so is he: Eat and drink, saith he to thee; but his heart is not with thee." **Prov. 23:7**

"Ye that love the Lord, hate evil: he preserveth the souls of his saints; he delivereth them out of the hand of the wicked." **Ps. 97:10**

"Owe no man any thing, but to love one another: for he that loveth another hath fulfilled the law." **Rom. 13:8**

"Beloved, let us love one another: for love is of God; and every one that loveth is born of God, and knoweth God. He that loveth not knoweth not God; for God is love. In this was manifested the love of God toward us, because that God sent his only begotten Son into the world, that we might live through him. Herein is love, not that we loved God, but that he loved us, and sent his Son to be the propitiation for our sins. Beloved, if God so loved us, we ought also to love one another. No man hath seen God at any time. If we love one another, God dwelleth in us, and his love is perfected in us. Hereby know we that we dwell in him, and he in us, because he hath given us of his Spirit." **1 John 4:7-13**

"In this the children of God are manifest, and the children of the devil: whosoever doeth not righteousness is not of God, neither he that loveth not his brother. For this is the message that ye heard from the beginning, that we should love one another." **1 John 3:10-11**

"We know that whosoever is born of God sinneth not; but he that is begotten of God keepeth himself, and that wicked one toucheth him not. And we know that we are of God, and the whole world lieth in wickedness." **1 John 5:18-19**

SONNET 11

As fast as thou shalt wane, so fast thou grow'st,
In one of thine, from that which thou departest,
And that fresh blood which youngly thou bestow'st
Thou mayst call thine when thou from youth convertest.
Herein lies wisdom, beauty, and increase;
Without this, folly, age, and cold decay.
If all were minded so, the times should cease,
And threescore year would make the world away.
Let those whom Nature hath not made for store,
Harsh, featureless, and rude, barrenly perish.
Look, whom she best endow'd, she gave the more;
Which bounteous gift thou shouldst in bounty cherish:
She carv'd thee for her seal, and meant thereby
Thou shouldst print more, not let that copy die.

THEME

The more one abandons worldly, egotistical desires, the more quickly the spiritual nature, with its attendant wisdom and beauty, grows. To do otherwise makes life meaningless and empty. Man is made in the joyous image of God and is meant to express this in his life.

GLOSSARY

As fast as thou shalt wane, so fast thou grow'st, In one of thine, from that which thou departest, And that fresh blood which youngly thou bestow'st Thou mayst call thine when thou from youth convertest.

> As your ego's wayward traits fall away, your spiritual nature will grow, adding new qualities, for those of the ego that are abandoned. Then, that newly-reborn inner life you hold dear becomes firmly established as you completely turn from your old habits.

Herein lies wisdom, beauty, and increase; Without this, folly, age, and cold decay. If all were minded so, the times should cease, And threescore year would make the world away.

> In this way, one finds wisdom, beauty, and spiritual bounty; and without it, life is lifeless and wasted. If everyone would understand this, our lives would change and in one generation the world would be established in a completely new direction.

Let those whom Nature hath not made for store, Harsh, featureless, and rude, barrenly perish. Look, whom she best endow'd, she gave the more; Which bounteous gift thou shouldst in bounty cherish:

> Let those who pursue a wanton life, and who persist in such, reap the emptiness they sow: Look how the Lord has endowed man with an immortal soul, free to express its bounty, and which above all else, should be cherished.

She carv'd thee for her seal, and meant thereby Thou shouldst print more, not let that copy die.

> You are created in the image of God, and you are meant to express the spiritual qualities that are imprinted in your soul, not let them die.

COMMENTARY

Shakespeare again reflects upon the essence of man as the soul. In youth, one is often enticed by harmful temptations. By spurning immature ego-centered pursuits ("*when thou from youth convertest*") one reaps not only personal bounty ("*Herein lies wisdom, beauty, and increase*"), but is an example for change to the world as well. "*If all were minded so, the times should cease And threescore year would make the world away.*" One is to "*cherish*" the Spirit within, and as the Bible states, be fruitful and multiply. "*Look, whom she best endow'd, she gave the more. . . . Thou shouldst print more, not let that copy die.*"

BIBLICAL PASSAGES SUGGESTED BY SONNET 11

"And God said, Let us make man in our image, after our likeness; and let them have dominion over fish of the sea, and over the fowl of the air, and over the cattle, and over all the earth, and over every creeping thing that creepeth on the earth. . . . And God blessed them, and God said unto them, Be fruitful, and multiply, and replenish the earth, and subdue it: and have dominion over the fish of the sea, and over the fowl of the air, and over every living thing that moveth upon the earth." **Gen. 1:26, 28**

"Sow to yourselves in righteousness, reap in mercy; break up your fallow ground: for it is time to seek the Lord, till he come and rain righteousness upon you." **Hos. 10:12**

"Know ye not that ye are the temple of God, and that the Spirit of God dwelleth in you?" **1 Cor. 3:16**

"For if a man think himself to be something, when he is nothing, he deceiveth himself. . . . Be not deceived; God is not mocked: for whatsoever a man soweth, that shall he also reap. For he that soweth to his flesh shall of the flesh reap corruption; but he that soweth to the Spirit shall of the Spirit reap life everlasting." **Gal. 6:3, 7-8**

SONNET 12

When I do count the clock that tells the time,
And see the brave day sunk in hideous night,
When I behold the violet past prime,
And sable curls, all silvered o'er with white;
When lofty trees I see barren of leaves,
Which erst from heat did canopy the herd,
And summer's green all girded up in sheaves,
Borne on the bier with white and bristly beard,
Then of thy beauty do I question make,
That thou among the wastes of time must go,
Since sweets and beauties do themselves forsake,
And die as fast as they see others grow,
And nothing 'gainst Time's scythe can make defence
Save breed, to brave him when he takes thee hence.

THEME

Birth, growth, and death are inevitable and inescapable for mankind, but each one of us possesses a soul that is transcendent. One may choose an ordinary life of material pursuits, or a life that nourishes the awakening of the soul's immortal consciousness, which alone can stand against death.

GLOSSARY

When I do count the clock that tells the time, And see the brave day sunk in hideous night, When I behold the violet past prime, And sable curls, all silvered o'er with white;

> When I make a reckoning of the nature of time, and how sparkling, vibrant life passes into death; when I see the sun's sweet flowers withering, and dark curls aged into silvery gray.

When lofty trees I see barren of leaves, Which erst from heat did canopy the herd, And summer's green all girded up in sheaves, Borne on the bier with white and bristly beard,

When lofty trees are denuded of the foliage that to all creatures once offered solacing shade from the heat, and summer's foliage stands gathered and sheaved in the stillness, a stark ornament of winter's killing frost.

Then of thy beauty do I question make, That thou among the wastes of time must go, Since sweets and beauties do themselves forsake, And die as fast as they see others grow,

It is then I question why your inner light of Spirit must be wasted, having forsaken its sweet beauty, dying in a life of superficiality, while others continue to grow.

And nothing 'gainst Time's scythe can make defence Save breed, to brave him when he takes thee hence.

There is no remedy for death except perpetual renewal of the ever-living Spirit within, which alone defeats bodily death.

COMMENTARY

In Sonnet 12, just as in Sonnets 10 and 11, Shakespeare comments upon the essential nature of man as a soul endowed with immortal spiritual qualities. As for the physical body, Time is man's enemy: "*And nothing 'gainst Time's scythe can make defence.*" We are immortal beings beneath the fleshy cover. Sonnet 10 counsels the elimination of "*murderous hate*" by changing "*thy thought*" and "*to thyself at least kind-hearted prove.*" (Sonnet 10.5, 9, 12) This is how "*beauty still may live in thine and thee.*" It is the renewal of the soul within, which "*'gainst Time's scythe can make defence.*" While Time has its sway over the physical nature, leading inevitably to death, the soul is immortal. Man is free to choose a life leading toward salvation. "*Save breed, to brave him* [death] *when he takes thee hence.*" With the awakening dawn, the dark night loses its hold.

BIBLICAL PASSAGES SUGGESTED BY SONNET 12

"What fruit had ye then in those things whereof ye are now ashamed? for the end of those things is death. But now being made free from sin, and become servants to God, ye have your fruit unto holiness, and the end everlasting life. For the wages of sin is death, but the gift of God is eternal life through Jesus Christ our Lord." **Rom. 6:21-23**

"So when this corruptible shall have put on incorruption, and this mortal shall have put on immortality, then shall be brought to pass the saying that is written, Death is swallowed up in victory. O death, where is thy sting? O grave, where is thy victory? The sting of death is sin; and the strength of sin is the law." **1 Cor. 15:54-56**

"To an inheritance incorruptible, and undefiled, and that fadeth not away, reserved in heaven for you." **1 Pet. 1:4**

SONNET 13

O that you were yourself, but, love, you are
No longer yours than you yourself here live.
Against this coming end you should prepare,
And your sweet semblance to some other give.
So should that beauty which you hold in lease
Find no determination; then you were
Yourself again, after yourself's decease,
When your sweet issue your sweet form should bear.
Who lets so fair a house fall to decay,
Which husbandry in honour might uphold
Against the stormy gusts of winter's day
And barren rage of death's eternal cold?
O none but unthrifts, dear my love you know
You had a father, let your son say so.

THEME

Each is the spiritual child of God. Give less to superficial allures so that the inner beauty might be awakened to its heavenly stature, and the sweetness of that life which the heavenly Father intended.

GLOSSARY

O that you were yourself, but, love, you are No longer yours than you yourself here live. Against this coming end you should prepare, And your sweet semblance to some other give.

> If you could be that spiritual being you were created to be! But, dear one, you are only that to the extent that you develop your spiritual nature. Prepare for life's end and leave a legacy of spiritual sweetness.

So should that beauty which you hold in lease Find no determination; then you were Yourself again, after yourself's decease, When your sweet issue your sweet form should bear.

> The physical body, which the soul temporarily inhabits, should not be the object of your attention. By decreasing

> the ego's sensuous desires, you will grow spiritually. The body will then house a renewed, sweetened soul.

Who lets so fair a house fall to decay, Which husbandry in honour might uphold Against the stormy gusts of winter's day And barren rage of death's eternal cold?

> Who allows their life to be wasted when a few right choices and proper direction would have been a bulwark against life's vicissitudes, and the futile cry for release from the empty sentence of death?

O, none but unthrifts, dear my love you know You had a father, let your son say so.

> None but the wasteful. Dear is the love I have for you, that you might know you have a caring heavenly Father: let your awakened and reborn soul affirm it.

COMMENTARY

In the first group of Sonnets preceding Sonnet 13, Shakespeare repeatedly admonishes against wasting the beauty and sweetness of the soul. In Sonnet 1, he says "*thou, contracted to thine own bright eyes*" and "*Making a famine where abundance lies.*" (Sonnet 1.5, 7) In Sonnet 2, the misspent youth gathering "*all the treasure of thy lusty days . . . Will be a tatter'd weed, of small worth . . . When forty winters shall besiege thy brow.*" (Sonnet 2.6, 4, 1) In Sonnet 3, the Poet addresses one who needs a "*fresh repair*"; otherwise, he will be entombed by "*self-love*" and "*live, remember'd not to be,* [and] *Die single.*" (Sonnet 3.3, 8, 13-14) Sonnet 4 clearly asks: "*Unthrifty loveliness, why dost thou spend Upon thyself thy beauty's legacy?*" (Sonnet 4.1-2) This wasteful expenditure on external pleasures spells the demise of the spiritual nature. "*Thy unus'd beauty must be tomb'd with thee.*" (Sonnet 4.13) The soul is compared, in Sonnet 5, to the lovely fragrance of summer flowers kept as "*A liquid prisoner pent in walls of glass*" (Sonnet 5.10), suggesting a sealed perfume bottle which is never opened. But if released, these "*flowers distill'd, though they with winter meet . . . their substance still lives sweet.*" (Sonnet 5.13-14)

Sonnet 6 strongly encourages the one addressed to "*Make sweet some vial; treasure thou some place With beauty's treasure ere it be self-kill'd.*" (Sonnet

6.3-4) "*Be not self-will'd, for thou are much too fair, To be death's conquest and make worms thine heir.*" (Sonnet 6.13-14) Here again, Shakespeare admonishes one not to be "*self-will'd,*" but to express "*beauty's treasure,*" the inner spiritual qualities and thus avoid being "*death's conquest.*"

Addressing the listener in Sonnet 7, Shakespeare states that in the prime of life, "*thy noon,*" one should be "*attending on his golden pilgrimage,*" which means to be climbing the "*heavenly hill*" of a spiritual journey. (Sonnet 7.13, 8, 5)

One living for himself alone in Sonnet 8, misses out on the "*music to hear,*" and does not join in the "*true concord of well-tuned sounds.*" (Sonnet 8.1, 5) The result is that "*Thou single wilt prove none.*" (Sonnet 8.14)

Sonnet 9 addresses one who expresses "*No love toward others.*" The result is "*That on himself such murderous shame commits.*" (Sonnet 9.13, 14)

Sonnet 11 encourages one to allow some bad habit to "*wane*" and "*as fast as*" this is done, "*so fast thou grow'st.*" (Sonnet 11.1) To do this shows that one expresses "*wisdom, beauty, and increase,*" but "*without this, folly, age, and cold decay.*" (Sonnet 11.5-6)

Sonnet 12 questions why one would allow the spiritual self to be lost and forsaken. "*Then of thy beauty do I question make, That thou among the wastes of time must go, Since sweets and beauties do themselves forsake.*" (Sonnet 12.9-11) To live in this way is a certain sentence of death since "*Nothing 'gainst Time's scythe can make defence.*" (Sonnet 12.13) The only way out again is to live life in spiritual renewal. This spiritual renewal, like "*flowers distill'd*" in Sonnet 5.13, and the "*seal*" that "*Thou shouldst print more*" in Sonnet 11.13, 14, is the same as the admonition to "*breed*" in Sonnet 12.14. Once this spiritually-oriented life begins, one can "*brave*" death. (Sonnet 12.14)

In Sonnet 13, Shakespeare admonishes one to live as one's true self, a child of God. "*O that you were yourself.*" He says that one is not true to oneself, and is not preparing for the end of life, unless one's spiritual nature is expressed and shared with another person. "*No longer yours than you yourself here live. Against this coming end you should prepare, And your sweet semblance to some other give.*" (Sonnet 13.2-4)

Not allowing the inner spiritual beauty to express itself, is to diminish one's inner being. "*So should that beauty which you hold in lease Find no determination; then you were Yourself again, after yourself's decease.*"

The Poet asks who would waste his spiritual inheritance and lose salvation when a little self-control that honors the soul would be enough. "*Who lets so fair a house fall to decay, Which husbandry in honour might uphold Against the stormy gusts of winter's day And barren rage of death's eternal cold?*" Only foolish wasteful "*unthrifts*." This also harkens back to the earlier Sonnets where waste makes "*a famine*" (Sonnet 1.7), or "*a tatter'd weed*." (Sonnet 2.4) It is the "*Unthrifty loveliness*" of Sonnet 4.1, "*an unthrift in the world*" (Sonnet 9.9), and the "*wastes of time*" in Sonnet 12.10 who squander their spiritual inheritance. A resurrected, renewed soul would proclaim the glory and grace of the heavenly Father: "*dear my love you know You had a father, let your son say so*."

BIBLICAL PASSAGES SUGGESTED BY SONNET 13

"But the fruit of the Spirit is love, joy, peace, longsuffering, gentleness, goodness, faith." **Gal. 5:22**

"Behold, what manner of love the Father hath bestowed upon us, that we should be called the sons of God: therefore the world knoweth us not, because it knew him not." **1 John 3:1**

"Bless the Lord, O my soul: and all that is within me, bless his holy name." **Ps. 103:1**

"The Lord preserveth the simple: I was brought low, and he helped me. Return unto thy rest, O my soul; for the Lord hath dealt bountifully with thee." **Ps. 116:6-7**

"Wherefore do ye spend money for that which is not bread? and your labor for that which satisfieth not? hearken diligently unto me, and eat ye that which is good, and let your soul delight itself in fatness." **Isa. 55:2**

"For what is a man profited, if he shall gain the whole world, and lose his own soul? Or what shall a man give in exchange for his soul?" **Matt. 16:26**

SONNET 14

Not from the stars do I my judgment pluck,
And yet methinks I have astronomy;
But not to tell of good or evil luck,
Of plagues, of dearths, or seasons' quality;
Nor can I fortune to brief minutes tell,
Pointing to each his thunder, rain, and wind,
Or say with princes if it shall go well,
By oft predict that I in heaven find,
But from thine eyes my knowledge I derive,
And constant stars in them I read such art
As truth and beauty shall together thrive,
If from thyself to store thou wouldst convert;
Or else of thee this I prognosticate:
Thy end is truth's and beauty's doom and date.

THEME

Man is endowed with the gift of intuition, a spiritual quality. It should be used to see Truth and Beauty and to help others see these qualities in themselves. To those who spurn Truth and Beauty and live for themselves alone, their predictable end is spiritual demise.

GLOSSARY

Not from the stars do I my judgment pluck, And yet methinks I have astronomy; But not to tell of good or evil luck, Of plagues, of dearths, or seasons' quality;

> I do not base my opinions on the movement of the stars; but I do think I have some knowledge along these lines, but not to prognosticate about good or bad luck, or plagues, droughts, or opportune conditions.

Nor can I fortune to brief minutes tell, Pointing to each his thunder, rain, and wind, Or say with princes if it shall go well, By oft predict that I in heaven find,

> Nor am I able to provide minute details of each person's time of good, bad, or other omens, or reveal to princes

> whether things will go well, but I do somewhat often receive insight through soulful intuition.

But from thine eyes my knowledge I derive, And constant stars in them I read such art As truth and beauty shall together thrive, If from thyself to store thou wouldst convert;

> But from your eyes, I discern many things, as they are windows to the soul that reveal to me things like Truth and Beauty, which would flourish in you if you would turn aside from self-centered pursuits.

Or else of thee this I prognosticate: Thy end is truth's and beauty's doom and date.

> Otherwise I can truly predict for you: Your life's script is the condemnation of the Truth and Beauty that might have been.

COMMENTARY

Shakespeare says that one does not need to be an astrologer or fortune teller to be able to look at another's life and see what favorable or unfortunate path he is set upon. "*Not from the stars do I my judgment pluck.*" To live for oneself ("*Thyself to store*") means to live in self-condemnation and limitation. It has been said that the "eyes are the windows to the soul." Here the Poet declares that "*from thine eyes my knowledge I derive.*" He is also addressing himself to the gift of intuition developed in those whose calm vision reflects inner tranquility, and which is likened to "*constant stars.*" This is the "*lovely gaze*" in Sonnet 5.2 and the "*new appearing sight*" in Sonnet 7.3. Unless one turns away from self-serving, egotistical pursuits ("*If from thyself to store thou wouldst convert*"), it requires no gift of a seer to prognosticate a sad ending. "*Thy end is Truth's and Beauty's doom and date.*" This is similar to previous Sonnets, such as Sonnet 3, wherein the one addressed will "*die single, and thine image dies with thee.*" (Sonnet 3.14) This "*image*" and "*Truth and Beauty*" refer again to qualities of the soul, the image of God in man.

BIBLICAL PASSAGES SUGGESTED BY SONNET 14

"When thou with rebukes dost correct man for iniquity, thou makest his beauty to consume away like a moth: surely every man is vanity." **Ps. 39:11**

"Like sheep they are laid in the grave; death shall feed on them; and the upright shall have dominion over them in the morning; and their beauty shall consume in the grave from their dwelling." **Ps. 49:14**

"Those that be planted in the house of the Lord shall flourish in the courts of our God." **Ps. 92:13**

"Whatsoever thy hand findeth to do, do it with thy might; for there is no work, nor device, nor knowledge, nor wisdom, in the grave, whither thou goest." **Eccl. 9:10**

"So God created man in his own image, in the image of God created he him; male and female created he them." **Gen. 1:27**

SONNET 15

When I consider everything that grows
Holds in perfection but a little moment,
That this huge stage presenteth nought but shows
Whereon the stars in secret influence comment;
When I perceive that men as plants increase,
Cheered and check'd e'en by the self-same sky,
Vaunt in their youthful sap, at height decrease,
And wear their brave state out of memory;
Then the conceit of this inconstant stay
Sets you most rich in youth before my sight,
Where wasteful time debateth with decay,
To change your day of youth to sullied night;
And, all in war with time for love of you,
As he takes from you, I engraft you new.

THEME

One life is a short span compared to all eternity, and it is a stage upon which the cosmic Director plays the drama of life and death. Mankind would be lost but for the Love of God which ever showers His children with grace, and keeps them ever hopeful and renewed.

GLOSSARY

When I consider everything that grows Holds in perfection but a little moment, That this huge stage presenteth nought but shows Whereon the stars in secret influence comment;

> When I think of all living things, and how all creation is perfect in its time, and that the world is a theater in which shows are being played, and upon which the heavenly spheres cast their unseen influence;

When I perceive that men as plants increase, Cheered and check'd e'en by the self-same sky, Vaunt in their youthful sap, at height decrease, And wear their brave state out of memory;

> When I see that men, like the plants, also wax and wane

by the same positive or negative universal laws that operate from above; they thrive in their energetic youth, then pass their prime, forgetting the vigor that once was.

Then the conceit of this inconstant stay Sets you most rich in youth before my sight, Where wasteful time debateth with decay, To change your day of youth to sullied night;

Then comes the pointed reminder that this world is ephemeral; and I see You the ever-eternal Source, but time and decay intertwine in their way to debase your fount of renewing life into withered old age.

And, all in war with time for love of you, As he takes from you, I engraft you new.

And in the battle against time's march, I offer love to you; as life ebbs in the physical body, I uphold you with soulful renewal.

COMMENTARY

Shakespeare has likened the world to a stage upon which man enacts a small part and then is gone. "*When I consider everything that grows Holds in perfection but a little moment, That this huge stage presenteth naught but shows.*" The world is the creation of God, as spoken of in **Genesis 1:1**: "In the beginning God created the heaven and the earth." In the play *As You Like It*, Shakespeare expresses the same sentiment: "all the world's a stage, the men and women merely players." (II.vii.139-140) There is birth, fortune and loss, old age and death where "*time debateth with decay.*" In youth "*men as plants increase,*" but soon youth is "*check'd,*" and the "*youthful sap, at height decrease*[s]." "[*T*]*ime*" and "*decay . . .change your day of youth to sullied night.*" There is a "*war*" for the youth's soul. "[*T*]*ime*" is marching toward "*decay*" and death, and the Poet speaks as if he is paraphrasing the words of the Lord, saying "*I engraft you new,*" meaning "I renew your spirit." As an observer and expounder of truth, the Poet does in fact bring a message of hope and redemption to help men on the stage of life play their parts in a more divine way.

BIBLICAL VERSES SUGGESTED BY SONNET 15

"Hast thou not known? hast thou not heard, that the everlasting God, the Lord, the Creator of the ends of the earth, fainteth not, neither is weary? there is no searching of his understanding. He giveth power to the faint; and to them that have no might he increaseth strength. Even the youths shall faint and be weary, and the young men shall utterly fall. But they that wait upon the Lord shall renew their strength; they shall mount up with wings as eagles; they shall run, and not be weary; and they shall walk, and not faint." **Isa. 40:28-31**

"Thou, even thou, art Lord alone; thou hast made heaven, the heaven of heavens, with all their host, the earth, and all things that are therein, the seas, and all that is therein, and thou preservest them all; and the host of heaven worshippeth thee." **Neh. 9:6**

"Who redeemeth thy life from destruction; who crowneth thee with lovingkindess and tender mercies; Who satisfieth thy mouth with good things; so that thy youth is renewed like the eagle's." **Ps. 103:4-5**

"And have put on the new man, which is renewed in knowledge after the image of him that created him." **Col. 3:10**

"And be not conformed to this world; but be ye transformed by the renewing of your mind, that ye may prove what is that good, and acceptable, and perfect, will of God." **Rom. 12:2**

SONNET 16

But wherefore do not you a mightier way
Make war upon this bloody tyrant, Time?
And fortify yourself in your decay
With means more blessed than my barren rhyme?
Now stand you on the top of happy hours,
And many maiden gardens, yet unset,
With virtuous wish would bear you living flowers,
Much liker than your painted counterfeit:
So should the lines of life that life repair
Which this Time's pencil, or my pupil pen,
Neither in inward worth nor outward fair
Can make you live yourself in eyes of men.
To give away yourself, keeps yourself still;
And you must live, drawn by your own sweet skill.

THEME

To win the battle of life, one must start in youth to plant "*living flowers*" that yield positive results. Each one needs to learn from mistakes and rewrite the story of his or her life. No one can do this for us. The stage play of one's life will be as every person in the role of player and playwright determines it to be.

GLOSSARY

But wherefore do not you a mightier way Make war upon this bloody tyrant, Time? And fortify yourself in your decay With means more blessed than my barren rhyme?

> In what ways do you strengthen your life and make war upon that bloody tyrant, Time? And fortify your spiritual self against decay by blessed means more powerful than my words, which can encourage but are barren if not heeded.

Now stand you on the top of happy hours, And many maiden gardens, yet unset, With virtuous wish would bear you living flowers, Much liker than your painted counterfeit:

> Now you stand high on the peak of your happiest time of life. There are many possibilities for you, yet untried. Virtuous desires would yield for you a flowering of life, much more like your true inner being, than the superficial, false existence you have created.

So should the lines of life that life repair, Which this Time's pencil, or my pupil pen, Neither in inward worth nor outward fair Can make you live yourself in eyes of men.

> So should the stage script that is written for each person change in a positive way as one learns life's lessons, which neither ordained manuscript, nor my novice verse, can make your inner worth, nor outward behavior change, as this is solely within your own choosing as to how you will live your life in the eyes of the world.

To give away yourself, keeps yourself still; And you must live, drawn by your own sweet skill.

> To waste away your inner spiritual worth means that your soul-nature remains dormant, and your life will be, as you have by your actions, ordained it to be.

COMMENTARY

In Sonnet 16 Shakespeare continues the theme previously expressed in Sonnet 15. Life is like a stage play. Individuals are not marionettes because each one has the free choice "*to make war upon this bloody tyrant, Time.*" In Sonnet 15, we see that the divine Playwright has not left us adrift to the vagaries of time and fate, but watches over His children with love and grace. In this Sonnet, we see that in the prime of youth, one must take on the responsibility ("*stand you on the top of happy hours . . . with virtuous wish*") for the battle of life in "*a mightier way.*" One can read encouraging words, but these are useless "*barren rhyme,*" unless more spiritual means are used ("*means more blessed*") to fight the war "*and fortify yourself in your decay.*" Each person has "*maiden*" ground to till, and what flowers blossom depends upon the virtuous nature of one's deepest wishes and actions. "*With virtuous wish would bear you living flowers.*" As one learns life's lessons, one must alter the script of one's life, which is being written by the personal choices one makes. "*So should the lines of life repair.*" Neither the script of one's life, nor the Poet's pen alone can make a person change how he appears before others, unless he himself chooses to live and act differently. "*Neither in inward worth nor outward fair, can make you live yourself in eyes of men.*" Shakespeare declares that if a person continues to live a wonton life, ("*to give away yourself*") his inner spirit remains "*still,*" and he must then act out the part that he has so skillfully (or unskillfully) written for himself. "*And you must live, drawn by your own sweet skill.*"

BIBLICAL PASSAGES SUGGESTED BY SONNET 16

"Rejoice, O young man, in thy youth; and let thy heart cheer thee in the days of thy youth, and walk in the ways of thine heart, and in the sight of thine eyes: but know thou, that for all these things God will bring thee into judgment." **Eccl. 11:9**

"Be not deceived; God is not mocked: for whatsoever a man soweth, that shall he also reap. For he that soweth to his flesh shall of the flesh reap corruption; but he that soweth to the Spirit shall of the Spirit reap life everlasting." **Gal. 6:7-8**

"The lines are fallen unto me in pleasant places; yea, I have a goodly heritage." **Ps. 16:6**

"For precept must be upon precept, precept upon precept; line upon line, line upon line; here a little, and there a little." **Isa. 28:10**

SONNET 17

Who will believe my verse in time to come,
If it were fill'd with your most high deserts?
Though yet heaven knows it is but as a tomb
Which hides your life and shows not half your parts.
If I could write the beauty of your eyes,
And in fresh numbers number all your graces,
The age to come would say, "This poet lies.
Such heavenly touches ne'er touch'd earthly faces."
So should my papers, yellowed with their age,
Be scorn'd, like old men of less truth than tongue,
And your true rights be term'd a poet's rage
And stretched metre of an antique song.
But were some child of yours alive that time,
You should live twice, in it and in my rhyme.

THEME

Spiritual truths are often not readily apparent in scriptures or verse. Uncovering the deeper meaning requires a heightened awareness, which is in itself a sign of spiritual growth.

GLOSSARY

Who will believe my verse in time to come, If it were fill'd with your most high deserts? Though yet heaven knows it is but as a tomb Which hides your life and shows not half your parts.

> Who will believe my verse in time to come if it were filled with words of Your praise and merit? Yet heaven knows that such verse is but a dim shadow which fails to reveal Your true light and shows only a portion of Your true nature.

If I could write the beauty of your eyes, And in fresh numbers number all your graces, The age to come would say, "This poet lies. Such heavenly touches ne'er touch'd earthly faces."

> If I could truly express in words the beauty in Your eyes, and in limitless new verses could recount your virtues,

> those who come after would say, "This poet lies. Such wondrous qualities were not found in mortal beings."

So should my papers, yellowed with their age, Be scorn'd, like old men of less truth than tongue, And your true rights be term'd a poet's rage And stretched metre of an antique song.

> So shall my poems, yellowed with age, be scorned like old men who tell tall tales, and Your true virtues be called a poet's romantic ravings, and exaggerated verse of some long-forgotten sonnet.

But were some child of yours alive that time, You should live twice, in it and in my rhyme.

> But should a spiritually-awakened child of Yours be alive in the future who understands the truth hidden in my poems, You shall live twice, once in the evolved consciousness of that soul, and also in my living verse.

COMMENTARY

Shakespeare wonders in Sonnet 17 who will understand his verse "*in time to come*," if it were filled with truest, most deserving praise ("*most high deserts*"). "[*H*]*eaven knows*" the Sonnets have a hidden meaning ("*hides your life*") that cannot fully express the true nature of Spirit "*and shows not half your parts.*" Shakespeare has, in spiritual vision, experienced "*the beauty of your eyes.*" If in innumerable lines, he would attempt to express Divine Grace, misunderstanding readers of his verse would call Shakespeare a liar, not comprehending that his poems refer not to "*earthly faces*," but to Spirit. When spiritually-attuned souls should in the future—"*some child of yours alive that time*"—read "*my rhyme*," the Lord will be awakened in their hearts, and in the Sonnets; thus it will "*live twice.*"

Shakespeare in Sonnet 17 declares a truth of scriptural interpretation, i.e., that there are hidden and esoteric meanings that are revealed to those with deeper understanding and perspicacity.

BIBLICAL PASSAGES SUGGESTED BY SONNET 17

"I have not hid thy righteousness within my heart; I have declared thy faithfulness and thy salvation: I have not concealed thy lovingkindness and thy truth from the great congregation." **Ps. 40:10**

"But we speak the wisdom of God in a mystery, even the hidden wisdom, which God ordained before the world unto our glory: Which none of the princes of this world knew: for had they known it, they would not have crucified the Lord of glory." **1 Cor. 2:7-8**

"At that time Jesus answered and said, I thank thee, O Father, Lord of heaven and earth, because thou hast hid these things from the wise and prudent, and hast revealed them unto babes." **Matt. 11:25**

"How that by revelation he made known unto me the mystery; (as I wrote afore in few words, Whereby, when ye read, ye may understand my knowledge in the mystery of Christ) Which in other ages was not made known unto the sons of men, as it is now revealed unto his holy apostles and prophets by the Spirit." **Eph. 3:3-5**

SONNET 18

Shall I compare thee to a summer's day?
Thou art more lovely and more temperate:
Rough winds do shake the darling buds of May,
And summer's lease hath all too short a date:
Sometime too hot the eye of heaven shines,
And often is his gold complexion dimm'd;
And every fair from fair sometime declines,
By chance, or nature's changing course untrimm'd;
But thy eternal summer shall not fade,
Nor lose possession of that fair thou ow'st,
Nor shall death brag thou wander'st in his shade,
When in eternal lines to time thou grow'st.
So long as man can breathe, or eyes can see,
So long lives this, and this gives life to thee.

THEME

Eternal summer and eternal Life are attributes of the Spirit. For those who live according to the highest spiritual precepts, the beauty of the Spirit, found in the soul of man, is everlasting and outshines the seasons of life.

GLOSSARY

Shall I compare thee to a summer's day? Thou art more lovely and more temperate: Rough winds do shake the darling buds of May, And summer's lease hath all too short a date:

> Shall I compare thee to a summer's day? Thou art more beautiful and more balanced in Thy Nature. The rough times are difficult in the springtime of life, and the flourishing times are all too short:

Sometime too hot the eye of heaven shines, And often is his gold complexion dimm'd; And every fair from fair sometime declines, By chance, or nature's changing course untrimm'd;

> Often in our lives, we feel the eyes of heaven hotly upon

> us, and at other times the golden face of Spirit is only dimly perceived; and every beautiful and flowering thing begins to decline, either by misfortune or due to the course of nature.

But thy eternal summer shall not fade, Nor lose possession of that fair thou ow'st, Nor shall death brag thou wander'st in his shade, When in eternal lines to time thou grow'st.

> But thy soulful flourishing shall never fade, nor lose its vibrancy and beauty, nor shall death be able to touch you. When you live your life in spiritual renewal, time cannot touch you, and your flowering never ceases.

So long as man can breathe, or eyes can see, So long lives this, and this gives life to thee.

> So long as man can breathe, or eyes can see, so long lives this eternal way of life, and this gives everlasting life to Thee.

COMMENTARY

Shakespeare frequently borrowed from scriptural sources, as has been well-documented in Noble, Shaheen, and others. Sonnet 18 suggests the following from Isaiah, "To whom then will ye liken God? or what likeness will ye compare unto him?" **(Isa. 40:18)**

In Sonnet 18 Shakespeare continues the theme of man's spiritual renewal explored in Sonnets 15, 16, and 17. Time is the "*bloody tyrant*" (Sonnet 16.2) and, as in Sonnet 15, time seems to conspire with "*decay . . . To change your day of youth to sullied night.*" (Sonnet 15.11-12) Man must exercise his free will to choose "*means more blessed than my barren rhyme*" so "*virtuous wish would bear you living flowers.*" (Sonnet 16.4, 7)

Sonnet 17 provides a transition from Sonnets 15 and 16 to Sonnet 18. In Sonnet 17, Shakespeare laments that even if he could express the praises of the Divine, few would understand. "*If I could write the beauty of your eyes, and in fresh numbers number all your graces, the age to come would say, 'This poet lies.'*" (Sonnet 17.5-7)

In Sonnet 17, Shakespeare avers that when spiritually-attuned souls should in the future ("*some child of yours alive that time*") read "*my rhyme*" they may be spiritually inspired and gain from a deeper understanding of the Sonnets; thus they will "*live twice.*" (Sonnet 17.13-14)

Again in Sonnet 17.5-6, our Poet says: "*If I could write the beauty of your eyes, and in fresh numbers number all your graces,*" few would understand that this refers to the soul of man, which is a reflection of the beauty contained in Spirit. "I have said, Ye are gods; and all of you are children of the most High." (**Ps. 82.6**)

In Sonnet 18, Shakespeare considers the possibility of comparing the Spirit, in its aspect of Beauty in creation, to a "*summer's day.*" As the soul of man is made in the image of the Creator, it also contains all the perfection of an idyllic "*summer's day.*" While the Spirit, however, is changeless and perfect, man must live upon this "*huge stage* [which] *presenteth nought but shows.*" (Sonnet 15.3) Life is full of changing fortunes ("*rough winds*") and our days are few as "*summer's lease hath all too short a date.*" Even when all seems to be flourishing, misfortune and the vagaries of life pursue man's footsteps. "*And every fair from fair sometime declines, By chance, or nature's changing course untrimm'd.*"

A "*summer's day*" fades, but the Spirit, an innate reflection in man's soul, manifests Beauty which does not diminish—"*But thy eternal summer shall not fade.*" The secret is for man to live in "*lines of life that life repair*" (Sonnet 16.9) or "*in eternal lines to time.*" The choice to live "*in eternal lines to time*" means to consciously pursue a life in tune with timeless spiritual values. In this way, one is renewed in Spirit ("*I engraft you new*") (Sonnet 15.14) and such a course of pursuit "*gives life to thee.*"

BIBLICAL PASSAGES SUGGESTED BY SONNET 18

"When I consider thy heavens, the work of thy fingers, the moon and the stars, which thou hast ordained; What is man, that thou art mindful of him? and the son of man, that thou visitest him? For thou hast made him a little lower than the angels, and hast crowned him with glory and honor." Ps. **8:3-5**

"Howbeit that was not first which is spiritual, but that which is natural; and afterward that which is spiritual. The first man is of the earth, earthy: the second man is the Lord from heaven. As is the earthy, such are they also that are earthy: and as is the heavenly, such are they also that are heavenly. And as we have borne the image of the earthy, we shall also bear the image of the heavenly." **1 Cor. 15:46-49**

"The last enemy that shall be destroyed is death." **1 Cor. 15:26**

SONNET 19

Devouring Time, blunt thou the lion's paws,
And make the earth devour her own sweet brood;
Pluck the keen teeth from the fierce tiger's jaws,
And burn the long-liv'd phoenix in her blood;
Make glad and sorry seasons as thou fleet'st,
And do whate'er thou wilt, swift-footed Time,
To the wide world and all her fading sweets;
But I forbid thee one most heinous crime:
O, carve not with thy hours my love's fair brow,
Nor draw no lines there with thine antique pen.
Him in thy course untainted do allow,
For beauty's pattern to succeeding men.
Yet do thy worst, old Time, despite thy wrong,
My love shall in my verse ever live young.

THEME

All created things come to an end, except for Love and Beauty as these are attributes of eternal Spirit.

GLOSSARY

Devouring Time, blunt thou the lion's paws, And make the earth devour her own sweet brood; Pluck the keen teeth from the fierce tiger's jaws, And burn the long-liv'd phoenix in her blood;

> Time eventually swallows all creatures and absorbs creation back into itself, plucks the ferocity from the tiger's jaws, and consumes the eternal phoenix while she lives;

Make glad and sorry seasons as thou fleet'st, And do whate'er thou wilt, swift-footed Time, To the wide world and all her fading sweets; But I forbid thee one most heinous crime:

> Swift-footed Time, make happy and sad seasons of life, and do whatever you will to the world, and to all the short-lived beauties of nature; but I forbid you one most heinous crime:

O, carve not with thy hours my love's fair brow, Nor draw no lines there with thine antique pen. Him in thy course untainted do allow, For beauty's pattern to succeeding men.

> Leave untouched by your pendulum scythe my love's fair countenance, nor dare to attempt to place a wrinkle thereon; him you shall allow to go unblemished in your course, as a model of spiritual purity to succeeding generations.

Yet do thy worst, old Time, despite thy wrong, My love shall in my verse ever live young.

> Nevertheless, do your worst, old Time, despite your inflictions, my love expressed in my verse shall ever live on fresh and new.

COMMENTARY

Shakespeare again returns to the theme of "*Devouring Time.*" In Sonnet 15.11, it is "*wasteful time*"; in Sonnet 16.2, the "*bloody tyrant time*". In Sonnet 19, the Poet describes how time causes all things to pass: "*blunt thou the lion's paws, And make the earth devour her own sweet brood; Pluck the keen teeth from the fierce tiger's jaws, And burn the long-liv'd phoenix in her blood.*"

Shakespeare points out that the earth and all things have their time and seasons. "*Make glad and sorry seasons.*" Time plays no favorites, it simply marches on, and the text of history records the many dramas of this world. "*And do whate'er thou wilt, swift-footed Time, To the world and all her fading sweets.*" But even Time is a creation of Spirit, and therefore it has no power over Eternal attributes ("*beauty's pattern*") such as Truth, Love, and Beauty. "*Him in thy course untainted do allow . . . Yet do thy worst, old Time despite thy wrong, My love shall in my verse ever live young.*" So every person should try to live in "*beauty's pattern,*" and be a good example for "*succeeding men*" to follow. It is by the example of one's life that others are changed. Truths such as these shall never fade with time but will "*ever be young.*"

BIBLICAL PASSAGES SUGGESTED BY SONNET 19

"The grass withereth, the flower fadeth: but the word of our God shall stand forever." **Isa. 40:8**

"The lines are fallen unto me in pleasant places; yea, I have a goodly heritage." **Ps. 16:6**

"I returned, and saw under the sun, that the race is not to the swift, nor the battle to the strong, neither yet bread to the wise, nor yet riches to men of understanding, nor yet favor to men of skill; but time and chance happeneth to them all." **Eccl. 9:11**

"Now when I passed by thee, and looked upon thee, behold, thy time was the time of love; and I spread my skirt over thee, and covered thy nakedness: yea, I sware unto thee, and entered into a covenant with thee, saith the Lord God, and thou becamest mine." **Ezek. 16:8**

"Heaven and earth shall pass away: but my words shall not pass away." **Mark 13:31**

SONNET 20

A woman's face with Nature's own hand painted
Hast thou, the master mistress of my passion,
A woman's gentle heart, but not acquainted
With shifting change, as is false women's fashion;
An eye more bright than theirs, less false in rolling,
Gilding the object whereupon it gazeth,
A man in hue all hues in his controlling,
Which steals men's eyes and women's souls amazeth.
And for a woman wert thou first created;
Till Nature, as she wrought thee, fell a-doting,
And by addition me of thee defeated,
By adding one thing to my purpose nothing.
But since she prick'd thee out for women's pleasure,
Mine be thy love, and thy love's use their treasure.

THEME

The Lord of the Universe, whether it be the Western concept of Father, or the Eastern concept of divine Mother or Nature, is still the same. Man, made in the image of God, has a divine soul, but according to Genesis, has fallen from grace. In earthly existence, man's soul and his sensually-enticed ego—symbolically his male and female aspects of divine mind and worldly nature respectively—are in a battle for supremacy.

GLOSSARY

A woman's face with Nature's own hand painted Hast thou, the master mistress of my passion. A woman's gentle heart, but not acquainted With shifting change, as is false women's fashion;

> The divine Artist who created all things is without form, but for me, I personify God as the divine Mother, which is the heavenly Father-divine Mother Nature of my soul's ardor [The Divine is pluralized in Gen. 1:26: "And God said, Let us make man in our image, after our likeness: and let them have dominion over the fish of the sea, and

over the fowl of the air, and over the cattle, and over all the earth, and over every creeping thing that creepeth upon the earth."]; Her Nature is changeless, unconditional Love, not the shifting and changing nature of a sensuous, earthly woman who is imperfect;

An eye more bright than theirs, less false in rolling, Gilding the object whereupon it gazeth, A man in hue all hues in his controlling, Which steals men's eyes and woman's souls amazeth.

An all-seeing eye of spiritual vision finds less falsehood in its survey of creation, and beholds goodness in that upon which it doth gaze. "And God saw every thing that he had made, and behold, it was very good." (Gen. 1:31) A man of such spiritual vision is surrounded by a divine Presence and is in control of his senses, reason, and emotions. Men look with wonder and envy at such a one, and women's souls are touched and confounded in the presence of such a person of spiritual esteem.

And for a woman wert thou first created; Till Nature, as she wrought thee, fell a-doting, And by addition me of thee defeated, By adding one thing to my purpose nothing.

As a soul, made in the image of God, was man first created. The creative Spirit of God is Mother Nature who fashioned this image: "in the image of God created he him; male and female created he them." (Gen. 1:27) Man, as a soul, became entrapped in a body where it might be "*defeated*" or brought down by sensual pleasures. Adding the bodily encasement with its sensual aspects added nothing.

But since she prick'd thee out for women's pleasure, Mine be thy love, and thy love's use their treasure.

But since man has been marked for bodily pleasure by woman, let my love alone be of Thee, Beloved Spirit, and let human love, however men and women use it, be their treasure.

COMMENTARY

From Genesis we understand that God is beyond creation and is without form. In worship, Western man prays generally to the heavenly Father, while in some traditions, the concept of divine Mother Nature or Compassionate Mother of God ("*A woman's face with Nature's own hand painted*") is often the object of a devotee's adoration. The heavenly Father and divine Mother are "*the master mistress*" of the Poet's passion. Divine Mother of Nature is changeless, characterized by unconditional Love and Compassion, as opposed to the changeable, inconsistent love of humans. "*With shifting change, as is false women's fashion.*" The author refers to "*An eye more bright,*" which is the singular form, not the plural. This metaphor for the divine, all-seeing spiritual eye and spiritual vision is often used by Shakespeare. This all-seeing eye perceives Truth and falsehood or shadows, and therefore that which it beholds is goodness. "And God saw every thing that he had made, and behold, it was very good." **(Gen. 1:31)** "*An eye more bright,*" being not vainly oriented, is "*less false in rolling,*" meaning that it is not a roving eye attracted to worldly allures. Spiritual vision sees the Divine gold in creation. It is "*Gilding the object whereupon it gazeth.*" "*A man in hue*" is one who reflects divine Virtue. He has "*all hues in his controlling*" meaning that he is in command of his senses, reason, and emotions and is not diverted by being "*false in rolling.*" Such a person is the envy of men, and confounds the souls of women in amazement. "*Which steals men's eyes and women's soul amazeth.*"

In **Genesis 1:26** we read: "And God said, Let us make man in our image, after our likeness." Note that the Lord says, "Let us." This is in the plural. One may understand this as God the Father, Absolute beyond creation, and Nature, the creative aspect of God, sometimes called Mother Nature. In the next verse we read: "So God created man in his own image, in the image of God created he him; male and female created he them." **(Gen. 1:27)** In further understanding Sonnet 20, First Corinthians is cited: "For a man indeed ought not to cover his head, forasmuch as he is the image and glory of God: but the woman is the glory of the man. For the man is not of the woman; but the woman of the man. . . . Nevertheless neither is the man without the woman, neither the woman without the man, in the Lord. For as the woman is of the man, even so is the man also by the woman; but all things of

God." **(1 Cor. 11:7-9, 11-12)**

In the Middle Ages, and into Shakespeare's sixteenth century, the concept of the fall of man from grace by the sin committed in the Garden of Eden hung heavily in the consciousness of many. The idea that man was born into sin and was barely able to climb the ladder of redemption without a life free of sin and the grace of God, seems to have been contemplated by Shakespeare in writing Sonnet 20.

In this Sonnet, man is depicted as the ideal spiritual man ("*A man in hue all hues in his controlling*") and also as the fallen man and woman ("*With shifting change, as is false women's fashion*") who are "*false in rolling*."

Shakespeare states that the "*master mistress*" of his passion has "*A woman's gentle heart.*" He opines that "*for a woman wert thou first created.*" This means that man's spiritual soul had the "*gentle heart*" of pure Love as first conceived, and before the fall when "God sent him forth from the garden of Eden." **(Gen. 3:23)**

What the Poet suggests is that the Lord created "*this huge stage*" (Sonnet 15.3) of creation with the idea of creating man and woman not just as elevated beings in Eden, but as physical beings outside of the garden's heavenly gates. **(Gen. 3:24)** In their physical state, Adam and Eve felt "naked" **(Gen. 3:11)** and had lost their pure divine nature. The thought of man and woman as physical beings came about as the conception of man, as a spiritual man or woman, was idealized. "*Till Nature, as she wrought thee, fell a-doting.*" Notice Shakespeare says Nature "*fell,*" the same as Adam and Even fell from the heavenly sphere to the earthly.

In this fall, "*by addition*" of man's sensual, physical nature, he was prevented from seeing with spiritual vision: "*by addition me of thee defeated.*" There is also the connotation that by the addition to Adam of Eve, who yielded to the serpent, his lofty spiritual place and vision was "*defeated.*" He goes on in this vein by saying that "*By adding one thing to my purpose nothing.*" This can refer either to the addition of Eve, or the addition of "*one thing,*" meaning the sensually-oriented ego consciousness. In either instance, for man's spiritual "*purpose*" or goal, which is to make his way back to God, this or these added "*nothing.*"

Finally, the Poet says that since "*Nature*" created both spiritual man as a soul, and the physical man with his sense-bound ego, man has a choice through free will. Men and woman can choose either to have a life being "*prick'd . . . out for women's pleasure*" or choose love of the Divine as their goal. "*Mine be thy love.*" In either case, Shakespeare, the Poet, only wishes to experience pure divine love, and let others "*use*" love, presumably in the less-than-divine sense, and make it "*their treasure.*" "For where your treasure is, there will your heart be also." **(Matt. 6:21)**

BIBLICAL PASSAGES SUGGESTED BY SONNET 20

"The light of the body is the eye: therefore when thine eye is single, thy whole body also is full of light; but when thine eye is evil, thy body also is full of darkness." **Luke 11:34**

"So God created man in his own image, in the image of God created he him; male and female created he them." **Gen. 1:27**

"And the Spirit and the bride say, Come. And let him that heareth say, Come. And let him that is athirst come. And whosoever will, let him take the water of life freely." **Rev. 22:17**

"Whither is thy beloved gone, O thou fairest among women? whither is thy beloved turned aside? that we may seek him with thee." **Song of Sol. 6:1**

SONNET 21

So is it not with me as with that Muse,
Stirr'd by a painted beauty to his verse,
Who heaven itself for ornament doth use
And every fair with his fair doth rehearse,
Making a couplement of proud compare,
With sun and moon, with earth and sea's rich gems,
With April's first-born flowers, and all things rare
That heaven's air in this huge rondure hems.
O let me, true in love, but truly write,
And then believe me, my love is as fair
As any mother's child, though not so bright
As those gold candles fixed in heaven's air:
Let them say more that like of hearsay well;
I will not praise that purpose not to sell.

THEME

Many are those who express themselves using flowery language but are without a deep sense of realization or understanding of the true, deeper meaning of words used in verse. The noble and truly wise person speaks with a heart of understanding, but not to impress anyone or to acquire riches thereby.

GLOSSARY

So is it not with me as with that Muse, Stirr'd by a painted beauty to his verse, Who heaven itself for ornament doth use And every fair with his fair doth rehearse,

> It is not like me to write as the amusing poets who incorporate artificial beauty in their verse, who use heaven itself as an ornament, comparing shallow beauty with everything else beautiful.

Making a couplement of proud compare, With sun and moon, with earth and sea's rich gems, With April's first-born flowers, and all things rare That heaven's air in this huge rondure hems.

Creating couplets of proud comparisons with sun and moon, earth, and the sea's rich gems, with the beauty of early April flowers and everything else of rare beauty under the sky's airy canopy.

O let me, true in love, but truly write, And then believe me, my love is as fair As any mother's child, though not so bright As those gold candles fixed in heaven's air:

Oh let me, who is true in love, write from true inspiration, and then believe me, my love is as true as any mother's child, though not so illuminated as those of greater realization whose consciousness is fixed in heavenly spheres.

Let them say more that like of hearsay well; I will not praise that purpose not to sell.

Let others write mere words from borrowed understanding, I will not appraise myself likewise just to sell my verse.

COMMENTARY

The author bemoans the state of things when shallow poets fill the air with "*painted beauty*," but who in themselves have no depth of true understanding. Shakespeare, as Poet, says his love is real and true "*As any mother's child*," but that there are others whose depth of understanding is like illuminated lights ("*gold candles fix'd in heaven's air*") that reach the sky. The "*gold candles*" signify the light of spiritual understanding.

BIBLICAL PASSAGES SUGGESTED BY SONNET 21

"And said unto me, What seest thou? And I said, I have looked, and behold a candlestick all of gold, with a bowl upon the top of it, and his seven lamps thereon, and seven pipes to the seven lamps, which are upon the top thereof: . . . And I answered again, and said unto him, What be these two olive branches which through the two golden pipes empty the golden oil out of themselves? And he answered me and said, Knowest thou not what these be? And I said, No, my lord. Then said he, These are the two anointed ones, that stand by the Lord of the whole earth." **Zech. 4:2, 12-14**

"For thou wilt light my candle: the Lord my God will enlighten my darkness." Ps. **18:28**

SONNET 22

My glass shall not persuade me I am old,
So long as youth and thou are of one date;
But when in thee time's furrows I behold,
Then look I death my days should expiate.
For all that beauty that doth cover thee
Is but the seemly raiment of my heart,
Which in thy breast doth live, as thine in me.
How can I then be elder than thou art?
O therefore, love, be of thyself so wary
As I, not for myself, but for thee will,
Bearing thy heart, which I will keep so chary
As tender nurse her babe from faring ill.
Presume not on thy heart when mine is slain;
Thou gav'st me thine, not to give back again.

THEME

Love is ageless and timeless. Once it is given, it should be cherished and guarded. It is unconditionally and irrevocably bestowed.

GLOSSARY

My glass shall not persuade me I am old, So long as youth and thou are of one date; But when in thee time's furrows I behold, Then look I death my days should expiate.

> The mirror shall not persuade me that I am old so long as you have your youth; but when I see aging in you, then I look to death for final release.

For all that beauty that doth cover thee Is but the seemly raiment of my heart, Which in thy breast doth live, as thine in me. How can I then be elder than thou art?

> All the beauty I behold in Thee, is but the fair garment of my heart, which in your breast lives, as yours in me. How can I then be older than you?

O therefore, love, be of thyself so wary As I, not for myself, but for thee will. Bearing thy heart, which I will keep so chary As tender nurse her babe from faring ill.

> O therefore, love, be watchful of yourself, as I, not for myself, but for you will; carrying your heart, which I will so carefully keep as a tender nurse guards her babe from harm.

Presume not on thy heart when mine is slain; Thou gav'st me thine, not to give back again.

> Do not look for your heart when mine is slain; you gave me yours, never to give back again.

COMMENTARY

In spite of physical aging, love is invigorating and keeps one feeling alive and youthful. "*My glass shall not persuade me I am old, So long as youth and thou are of one date.*" One sees beauty in the beloved, and in true love there is unity of soul, in this life and beyond. Unconditional love and friendship are precious for all time.

BIBLICAL PASSAGES SUGGESTED BY SONNET 22

"And we have known and believed the love that God hath to us. God is love; and he that dwelleth in love dwelleth in God, and God in him. Herein is our love made perfect, that we may have boldness in the day of judgment: because as he is, so are we in this world." **1 John 4:16-17**

"A friend loveth at all times, and a brother is born for adversity." **Prov. 17:17**

"A man that hath friends must shew himself friendly: and there is a friend that sticketh closer than a brother." **Prov. 18:24**

"Greater love hath no man than this, that a man lay down his life for his friends." **John 15:13**

"And Jonathan caused David to swear again, because he loved him: for he loved him as he loved his own soul." **1 Sam. 20:17**

SONNET 23

As an unperfect actor on the stage,
Who with his fear is put besides his part,
Or some fierce thing replete with too much rage,
Whose strength's abundance weakens his own heart;
So I, for fear of trust, forget to say
The perfect ceremony of love's rite,
And in mine own love's strength seem to decay,
O'ercharg'd with burden of mine own love's might.
O, let my books be then the eloquence
And dumb presagers of my speaking breast,
Who plead for love, and look for recompense,
More than that tongue that more hath more express'd.
O learn to read what silent love hath writ.
To hear with eyes belongs to love's fine wit.

THEME

Most men are, with the exception of a few, imperfect actors on the stage of life. Some are fortunate that they can express in non-verbal ways what their shortcomings prevent them from expressing outwardly.

GLOSSARY

As an unperfect actor on the stage, Who with his fear is put besides his part, Or some fierce thing replete with too much rage, Whose strength's abundance weakens his own heart;

> As an unperfected actor on the stage, who because of his fear, cannot correctly play his part, or some bestial thing filled with rage, whose very force and strength weakens his own heart.

So I, for fear of trust, forget to say The perfect ceremony of love's rite, And in mine own love's strength seem to decay, O'ercharg'd with burden of mine own love's might.

> So I, for fear of trusting, forget to say the perfect ceremo-

> ny of life's marriage ritual, and my own love's strength is weakened by fear and forgetfulness. Yet I am bristling with the burning ardor of my love (to express itself).

O, let my books be then the eloquence And dumb presagers of my speaking breast, Who plead for love, and look for recompense, More than that tongue that more hath more express'd.

> O, let my books be then the eloquence and silent presagers of what is in my heart, who make love's plea, and look for recompense, more than that (forgetful) tongue that, if only, it could more fully have expressed with completeness (my love).

O learn to read what silent love hath writ, To hear with eyes belongs to love's fine wit.

> O, learn to read what silent love has written: to have understanding of what one sees is the nature of love's finely tuned expression.

COMMENTARY

The world or life, likened to a stage, is the metaphor. The "*unperfect actor*" could better play his part if "*his fear*" and some "*fierce thing*" did not weaken "*his own heart,*" meaning his better judgment and emotional strength. "*Fear*" and lack of trust are very "*fierce things*" that impede true expression. They keep one from completing "*the perfect ceremony of love's rite,*" an analogy to the marriage ceremony, or in the esoteric sense, the uniting of soul with Spirit.

The power of "*mine own love's might*" and "*love's strength*" weigh against the "*fear of trust*" and are a "*burden*" upon "*fierce things*" that may "*weaken*" the heart of an "*unperfect actor.*" Let "*books,*" speak more eloquently ("*my speaking breast*") of love. This silent song of "*dumb presagers*" will be heard by those with true understanding; while others who are the false poets who "*plead for love,*" speak loudly but say little. "*Who plead for love, and look for recompense, more than that tongue that more hath more express'd.*" Learn to read "*what silent love hath writ*" truly. Those with eyes to see can hear the silent speaking voice of love. "*To hear with eyes belongs to love's fine wit.*"

BIBLICAL PASSAGES SUGGESTED BY SONNET 23

"Say to them that are of a fearful heart, Be strong, fear not: behold, your God will come with vengeance, even God with a recompense; he will come and save you. Then the eyes of the blind shall be opened, and the ears of the deaf shall be unstopped." **Isa. 35:4-5**

"I have heard of thee by the hearing of the ear: but now mine eye seeth thee." **Job 42:5**

SONNET 24

Mine eye hath play'd the painter and hath stell'd
Thy beauty's form in table of my heart.
My body is the frame wherein 'tis held,
And perspective it is best painter's art.
For through the painter must you see his skill,
To find where your true image pictur'd lies,
Which in my bosom's shop is hanging still,
That hath his windows glazed with thine eyes.
Now see what good turns eyes for eyes have done:
Mine eyes have drawn thy shape, and thine for me
Are windows to my breast, where-through the sun
Delights to peep, to gaze therein on thee.
Yet eyes this cunning want to grace their art,
They draw but what they see, know not the heart.

THEME

The inner eye of intuitive perception is the best source for understanding and expression. The uniqueness of each one is found by looking within at "*beauty's form*" in the heart. No matter how deeply we are able to penetrate the windows of our souls, however, we will never be able to fully exhaust or comprehend the true nature of Spirit, hovering in the stillness of the soul.

GLOSSARY

Mine eye hath play'd the painter and hath stell'd Thy beauty's form in table of my heart. My body is the frame wherein 'tis held, And perspective it is best painter's art.

> My eye has fixed the image of Thy beauty's form upon the tablet of my heart; my body is only the frame wherein it is held, and this perfect perception is the essence of the painter's art.

For through the painter must you see his skill, To find where your true image pictur'd lies, Which in my bosom's shop is hanging still, That hath his windows glazed with thine eyes.

For through a deeper understanding of the painter, you must find something unique about your own true self, which in my heart's workings hovers in stillness, and the windows (of my soul) are glazed with the sight of Thee.

Now see what good turns eyes for eyes have done: Mine eyes have drawn thy shape, and thine for me Are windows to my breast, where-through the sun Delights to peep, to gaze therein on thee.

Now see what good spiritual sight has done to open (mortal) eyes: my eyes have perceived Thy nature; and the spiritual light is a window into my heart, through which the light of (my) understanding delights to peep, to look longingly upon Thee.

Yet eyes this cunning want to grace their art, They draw but what they see, know not the heart.

Yet ordinary human eyes, although cunning, lack the ability to give full expression. They portray what they see physically, but they lack the spiritual vision to comprehend the soul's true nature.

COMMENTARY

Shakespeare uses the metaphor of the artist who tries to capture an image with his eye. A painter with the perspective of the spiritual eye is able to perceive "*beauty's form in* [the] *table of*" the heart.

In other words, the common artist paints upon a "*table*" or canvas what he sees outwardly. The spiritual artist is like the Poet in Sonnet 23.13 who can inscribe what "*silent love hath writ.*" This painter sees true "*beauty's form*" as being an essential soul quality of the "*heart,*" and not an outward material manifestation.

The human body is then as a "*frame*" in which the heart is encased. "*My body is the frame wherein 'tis held and perspective it is best painter's art.*"

A true conception of the "*painter's art*" comes by an understanding of the painter's perspective. "*For through the painter must you see his skill.*" The "*true image*" of man **(Gen. 1:26)** is a spiritual concept that is perceived with spiritual vision. In Sonnet 23.14, we read: "*To hear with eyes belongs to love's fine wit.*" To see with opened eyes, requires spiritual understanding. "When the ear heard me, then it blessed me; and when the eye saw me, it gave witness to me." **(Job 29:11)**

It is in the stillness that one receives such vision and spiritual perception. "Be still, and know that I am God: I will be exalted among the heathen, I will be exalted in the earth." **(Ps. 46.10)** In the lines: "*To find where your true image pictur'd lies, Which in my bosom's shop is hanging still,*" Shakespeare refers to the act of perceiving in stillness or meditation; thus metaphorically, as one whose "*shop*" is in the heart or "*bosom.*" The "*true image pictur'd*" is not a physical portrait, but a spiritual image. Having "*windows glazed*" refers to artistic decoration in the material sense, but spiritually speaking, the reference, "*glazed with thine eyes*" refers to the beholder's being captivated by Divine vision.

By the divine Grace, the Light of Spirit is perceived, in the spiritual eye, and the beholder may then fix his gaze upon it. "*Now see what good turns eyes for eyes have done: Mine eyes have drawn they shape, and thine for me Are windows to my breast, where-through the sun Delights to peep, to gaze therein on thee.*" "The light of the body is the eye: if therefore thine eye be single, thy whole body shall be full of light." **(Matt. 6:22)**

Some painters have "*cunning*" eyes wanting in grace, which see only the mundane and "*know not the heart*" of Spirit. "*Yet eyes this cunning want to grace their art, They draw but what they see, know not the heart.*"

BIBLICAL PASSAGES SUGGESTED BY SONNET 24

"When the ear heard me, then it blessed me; and when the eye saw me, it gave witness to me." **Job 29:11**

"The light of the body is the eye: if therefore thine eye be single, thy whole body shall be full of light." **Matt. 6:22**

"What? Know ye not that your body is the temple of the Holy Ghost which is in you, which ye have of God, and ye are not your own?" **1 Cor. 6:19**

"Know ye not that ye are the temple of God, and that the Spirit of God dwelleth in you? If any man defile the temple of God, him shall God destroy; for the temple of God is holy, which temple ye are." **1 Cor. 3:16-17**

"Be still, and know that I am God: I will be exalted among the heathen, I will be exalted in the earth." **Ps. 46:10**

SONNET 25

Let those who are in favor with their stars
Of public honour and proud titles boast,
Whilst I, whom fortune of such triumph bars,
Unlook'd for joy in that I honour most.
Great princes' favourites their fair leaves spread,
But as the marigold at the sun's eye,
And in themselves their pride lies buried,
For at a frown they in their glory die.
The painful warrior famoused for fight,
After a thousand victories once foil'd,
Is from the book of honour razed quite,
And all the rest forgot for which he toil'd:
Then happy I, that love and am belov'd,
Where I may not remove, nor be remov'd.

THEME

Vainglorious pride is short-lived and vanishes with the tide of fortune or misfortune. One true measure of a person is in how much he or she loves and is loved.

GLOSSARY

Let those who are in favour with their stars Of public honour and proud titles boast, Whilst I, whom fortune of such triumph bars, Unlook'd for joy in that I honour most.

> Let those who are in favor with their stars of public honor and proud position boast, while I, whose fortune has bestowed no such triumphs, find I take joy in what I honor most.

Great princes' favourites their fair leaves spread, But as the marigold at the sun's eye, And in themselves their pride lies buried, For at a frown they in their glory die.

> Great princes' favorites strut about in public display just as marigolds that show their flowery faces in the sun-

> shine. Their pride is hidden within themselves, but the moment they are cast from favor, and the limelight dims, their glory dies.

The painful warrior famoused for fight, After a thousand victories once foil'd, Is from the book of honour razed quite, And all the rest forgot for which he toil'd:

> A warrior through painstaking effort becomes famous for his many victories in battle. But if he suffers one defeat after a thousand victories, he is then removed from the role of the honored, and all of his other achievements are quickly forgotten.

Then happy I, that love and am belov'd, Where I may not remove nor be remov'd.

> Then happy am I who loves and is loved from a secure place from which I may not ever depart, nor ever be removed.

COMMENTARY

Man's earthly sojourn is too short to put pride and position ahead of love. "*Let those who are in favour with their stars Of public honour and proud titles boast, Whilst I, whom fortune of such triumph bars, Unlook'd for joy in that I honour most.*" "Remove far from me vanity and lies: give me neither poverty nor riches; feed me with food convenient for me: Lest I be full, and deny thee, and say, Who is the Lord? Or lest I be poor, and steal, and take the name of my God in vain." **(Prov. 30:8-9)** It is better to connect one's life to immutable values like love. The flattery of others and attendant pride leads to one's downfall. "*Great princes' favourites their fair leaves spread But as the marigold at the sun's eye, And in themselves their pride lies buried, for at a frown they in their glory die.*" From unconditional loving there is no departure, and no one can take this precious gift from us. "*Then happy I, that love and am belov'd, Where I may not remove nor be remov'd.*"

BIBLICAL PASSAGES SUGGESTED BY SONNET 25

"Love not the world, neither the things that are in the world. If any man love the world, the love of the Father is not in him." **1 John 2:15**

"Set me as a seal upon thine heart, as a seal upon thine arm: for love is strong as death; jealousy is cruel as the grave: the coals thereof are coals of fire, which hath a most vehement flame." **Song of Sol. 8:6**

"It is better to trust in the Lord than to put confidence in man." **Ps. 118:8**

SONNET 26

Lord of my love, to whom in vassalage
Thy merit hath my duty strongly knit,
To thee I send this written ambassage,
To witness duty, not to show my wit.
Duty so great, which wit so poor as mine
May make seem bare, in wanting words to show it,
But that I hope some good conceit of thine
In thy soul's thought, all naked, will bestow it;
Till whatsoever star that guides my moving
Points on me graciously with fair aspect,
And puts apparel on my tatter'd loving,
To show me worthy of thy sweet respect.
Then may I dare to boast how I do love thee;
Till then, not show my head where thou mayst prove me.

THEME

Man's love for God is his highest duty, but he may often question his merit before the Divine. It is better to silently bow one's head in humility until one is clothed with spiritual direction to speak openly of the spiritual affection in one's heart.

GLOSSARY

Lord of my love, to whom in vassalage Thy merit hath my duty strongly knit, To thee I send this written ambassage, To witness duty, not to show my wit.

> Lord of my love to whom I am in reverent service, Thy merit is the objective woven into my every duty. This writing is my messenger and witness to Thee of my faithfulness, and not a show of intellectual ability.

Duty so great, which wit so poor as mine May make seem bare, in wanting words to show it, But that I hope some good conceit of thine In thy soul's thought, all naked, will bestow it;

> My duty is so great, but it may appear to be wanting because I lack the wit to find words to properly express it.

I hope for some inspiration from Thy infinite source that may come to my mind from the fount of purity within my soul.

Till whatsoever star that guides my moving Points on me graciously with fair aspect, And puts apparel on my tatter'd loving, To show me worthy of thy sweet respect.

Until whatsoever star that guides the direction of my life graciously bestows upon me good fortune, and clothes my imperfect expression of love, to show me worthy of Thy sweet recognition.

Then may I dare to boast how I do love thee; Till then, not show my head where thou mayst prove me.

Then may I dare to express openly how I do love Thee; till then I will keep my head bowed in humility where Thou may yet test me.

COMMENTARY

In Sonnet 26, Shakespeare is saying that yearning for God and seeking earnestly for Him go together. The Poet prays, but is not certain, if God is listening or finds merit in him: "*show me worthy of thy sweet respect.*" "Hear, O Lord, when I cry with my voice: have mercy also upon me, and answer me." **(Ps. 27:7)** When the Lord "*puts apparel,*" it means to clothe with grace. Upon receipt of this grace, the Poet's "*tatter'd loving*" will then be changed, and then he will "*boast how I do love thee.*" "I will greatly rejoice in the Lord, my soul shall be joyful in my God; for he hath clothed me with the garments of salvation, he hath covered me with the robe of righteousness, as a bridegroom decketh himself with ornaments, and as a bride adorneth herself with her jewels." **(Isa. 61:10)**

"*All naked*" in line 8, means in purity, as Adam and Eve who were pure in their nakedness: "And they were both naked, the man and his wife, and were not ashamed." **(Gen. 2:25)** Until one receives the Divine "*apparel,*" one is spiritually bare, and thus uncertain of God's response. When such a time occurs that the Poet receives "*apparel*" and is attuned to God's message, he will want to share it openly. "*Then may*

I dare to boast how I do love thee." "Let the heavens be glad, and let the earth rejoice: and let men say among the nations, The Lord reigneth." (**1 Chron. 16:31**) "Now therefore arise, O Lord God, into thy resting place, thou, and the ark of thy strength: let thy priests, O Lord God, be clothed with salvation, and let thy saints rejoice in goodness." (**2 Chron. 6:41**)

If the Poet were to speak out or boast too quickly, the Lord would be certain to test him, so it is better to walk humbly with God until he is pointed "*graciously with fair aspect.*" "*Till then, not show my head where thou mayst prove me.*"

BIBLICAL PASSAGES SUGGESTED BY SONNET 26

"He hath shewed thee, O man, what is good; and what doth the Lord require of thee, but to do justly, and to love mercy, and to walk humbly with thy God?" **Mic. 6:8**

"And he said, I will make all my goodness pass before thee, and I will proclaim the name of the Lord before thee; and will be gracious to whom I will be gracious, and will shew mercy on whom I will shew mercy." **Exod. 33:19**

"For thus saith the high and lofty One that inhabiteth eternity, whose name is Holy; I dwell in the high and holy place, with him also that is of a contrite and humble spirit, to revive the spirit of the humble, and to revive the heart of the contrite ones." **Isa. 57:15**

"Humble yourselves therefore under the mighty hand of God, that he may exalt you in due time." **1 Pet. 5:6**

SONNET 27

Weary with toil, I haste me to my bed,
The dear repose for limbs with travail tired,
But then begins a journey in my head
To work my mind, when body's work's expired.
For then my thoughts, from far where I abide,
Intend a zealous pilgrimage to thee,
And keep my drooping eyelids open wide,
Looking on darkness which the blind do see:
Save that my soul's imaginary sight
Presents thy shadow to my sightless view,
Which, like a jewel hung in ghastly night,
Makes black night beauteous, and her old face new.
Lo, thus, by day my limbs, by night my mind,
For thee, and for myself, no quiet find.

THEME

After work should come prayer and meditation. With closed eyes there is darkness, but with spiritual vision, there is light.

GLOSSARY

Weary with toil, I haste me to my bed, The dear repose for limbs with travail tired, But then begins a journey in my head To work my mind, when body's work's expired.

> Weary with toil, I hurry to my bed, and the welcome rest for limbs tired from travel; but then begins a journey of the mind, when bodily activities have ceased.

For then my thoughts, from far where I abide, Intend a zealous pilgrimage to thee, And keep my drooping eyelids open wide, Looking on darkness which the blind do see:

> For then my thoughts, far from where I lie, make a zealous pilgrimage to Thee, and keep my drooping eyelids open wide, peering into what the blind see as darkness:

Save that my soul's imaginary sight Presents thy shadow to my sightless view, Which, like a jewel hung in ghastly night, Makes black night beauteous, and her old face new.

> Only my soul's power of vision brings Thy Spirit to my sightless view, which like a jewel suspended in silent darkness, makes the black night beautiful and illuminates her ancient face.

Lo, thus, by day my limbs, by night my mind, For thee, and for myself, no quiet find.

> So it is, by day my limbs, and by night my mind, seeking Thee, and for myself no quiet do I find.

COMMENTARY

When the body is quiet, thoughts can make their mental "*pilgrimage*," a sacred journey, toward God. "*Weary with toil, I haste me to my bed, The dear repose for limbs with travail tired, But then begins a journey in my head.*" The line "*dear repose for limbs with travail tired,*" suggest a journey with use of the word "*travail.*" One may also infer that there is a suggestion of "*travail*" in the journey of the "*limbs,*" "*Weary with toil.*" Life's journey is travail until one begins one's "*golden pilgrimage*" (Sonnet 7.8) in search of a more spiritual life. "For we know that the whole creation groaneth and travaileth in pain together until now." **(Rom. 8:22)** This continues until there is "the redemption of our body." **(Rom. 8:23)**

In Sonnet 27, the Poet says, "*weary with toil, I haste me to my bed.*" He has the "*star*" that guides his moving and points him "*graciously with fair aspect*" (Sonnet 26.9-10) in the right direction. It is toward his rest and "*the dear repose for limbs with travail tired.*" "My soul shall be satisfied. . . . When I remember thee upon my bed, and meditate on thee in the night watches. Because thou hast been my help, therefore in the shadow of thy wings will I rejoice." **(Ps. 63:5-7)**

One who engages in prayerful meditation may eventually perceive a spiritual light in the darkness behind closed eyes, "*like a jewel hung in ghastly night.*" Such vision has been written about by saints, and is mentioned in previously-cited Bible passages referring to the spiritual eye. Many who have described near-death experiences also have recounted a vision of light. The hymn "Amazing Grace" contains the verse "I was blind, but now I see." "The Lord openeth the eyes of the blind." (**Ps. 146:8**) How to see the light is further told in scripture. "Be still, and know that I am God." (**Ps. 46:10**) In other words, says the Poet, "quiet the body and mind, go meditate and pray." Shakespeare was no stranger to meditation, as his Sonnets reveal. In the end, one can lay down the burden, being "*weary with toil*," and enter into grace and repose in the Lord.

BIBLICAL PASSAGES SUGGESTED BY SONNET 27

"Come unto me, all ye that labor and are heavy laden, and I will give you rest." **Matt. 11:28**

"For he that is entered into his rest, he also hath ceased from his own works, as God did from his. Let us labor therefore to enter into that rest, lest any man fall after the same example of unbelief." **Heb. 4:10-11**

SONNET 28

How can I then return in happy plight,
That am debarr'd the benefit of rest?
When day's oppression is not eas'd by night,
But day by night, and night by day oppress'd;
And each, though enemies to either's reign,
Do in consent shake hands to torture me,
The one by toil, the other to complain
How far I toil, still further off from thee.
I tell the day to please him thou art bright,
And dost him grace when clouds do blot the heaven.
So flatter I the swart-complexion'd night,
When sparkling stars twire not thou gild'st the even.
But day doth daily draw my sorrows longer,
And night doth nightly make grief's strength seem stronger.

THEME

Life's toil can seem never ending. It is important to try and stay positive, although some difficult periods of life seem to give no respite. Earthly existence is a dualistic show of ever-revolving periods of bright and dark events and conditions.

GLOSSARY

How can I then return in happy plight, That am debarr'd the benefit of rest? When day's oppression is not eas'd by night, But day by night, and night by day oppress'd;

How can I return home in good health, when I am prevented from getting proper rest? When day's oppression is not eased by night, and night and day the oppression continues.

And each, though enemies to either's reign, Do in consent shake hands to torture me, The one by toil, the other to complain How far I toil, still further off from thee.

And each, though usually enemies in each other's reign,

do now conspire to torture me, the one by travail, and the other to complain about my day's labor, how it keeps me ever farther from Thee.

I tell the day, to please him, thou art bright And dost him grace when clouds do blot the heaven. So flatter I the swart-complexion'd night, When sparkling stars twire not thou gild'st the even.

I tell day, to please him, thou art bright with the grace of light when clouds do blot the heavens. I also flatter the dark-covered night, saying that when stars are not seen twinkling, thou dost still glitter as gold at eventide.

But day doth daily draw my sorrows longer, And night doth nightly make grief's strength seem stronger.

But each day daily makes my sorrow seem longer and the night, nightly makes my lengthening grief seem stronger.

COMMENTARY

The Poet expresses what many feel who are faced with seemingly endless work day and night. "*When day's oppression is not eas'd by night, but day by night, and night by day oppress'd.*" Principal labor by day and "*by night my mind*" (Sonnet 27.13) "[*d*]*o in consent shake hands to torture me.*" To placate day and night who oppress him, the Poet, in flattery of each, commends the "*grace*" of the light of day even if blotted by clouds, and the golden light of night, although the twinkling stars are hidden from view: "*when sparkling stars twire not thou gild'st the even.*"

In spite of this flattery, which the Poet hopes will assuage his grief, "*day doth daily draw my sorrows longer, and night doth nightly make grief's strength seem stronger.*" The source of the Poet's sorrow is that he is "*debarr'd the benefit of rest,*" which is sought through the "*zealous pilgrimage*" of Sonnet 27. This rest is, as explained in Sonnet 27's Commentary, the spiritual repose sought by the Poet in his "*soul's imaginary sight.*" (Sonnet 27.9) His quest is for the "*jewel*" that "*makes black night beauteous,*" (Sonnet 27.11, 12) and it continues "*by day*" and "*by night*" and offers "*no quiet*" or rest. (Sonnet 27.13,14) Thus we see in Sonnet 28 that the Poet is full of "*sorrows*" as his "*journey*" (Sonnet 27.3), has not yielded the object of his searching.

In spite of this, the Poet seeks solace in knowing that even on days when "*clouds do blot the heaven*" that, by "*grace*," the day is "*bright*." Metaphorically, when one's life seems dark, still the grace of Spirit is present, even if not seen. Also in the evenness of spiritual perception, the golden light shines through. "*When sparkling stars twire not thou gild'st the even*."

The Poet seems beset with grief as he tries to recall that the Lord's grace is ever-present in this clouds-of-day and gilded-night metaphor during his "*zealous pilgrimage*." (Sonnet 27.7)

BIBLICAL PASSAGES SUGGESTED BY SONNET 28

"And the Lord went before them by day in a pillar of a cloud, to lead them the way; and by night in a pillar of fire, to give them light; to go by day and night." **Exod. 13:21**

"Then we which are alive and remain shall be caught up together with them in the clouds, to meet the Lord in the air: and so shall we ever be with the Lord." **1 Thess. 4:17**

The Sonnets are richly imbued with spiritual metaphor. In this Sonnet, Shakespeare sounds like the Psalmist: "In the day of my trouble I sought the Lord: my sore ran in the night, and ceased not: my soul refused to be comforted." **Ps. 77:2**

But see what becomes of our Poet in Sonnet 29.

SONNET 29

When, in disgrace with fortune and men's eyes,
I all alone beweep my outcast state,
And trouble deaf heaven with my bootless cries,
And look upon myself, and curse my fate,
Wishing me like to one more rich in hope,
Featur'd like him, like him with friends possess'd,
Desiring this man's art, and that man's scope,
With what I most enjoy contented least;
Yet in these thoughts myself almost despising,
Haply I think on thee, and then my state,
Like to the lark at break of day arising
From sullen earth, sings hymns at heaven's gate,
For thy sweet love remember'd such wealth brings,
That then I scorn to change my state with kings.

THEME

One's place in life is unique. Each one has a part to play in the Divine drama, and when one forgets this, and wishes for another, the thought of God in one's life should bring one to one's senses and fill one with gratitude and thanksgiving. "But seek ye first the kingdom of God, and his righteousness; and all these things shall be added unto you." **(Matt. 6:33)**

GLOSSARY

When, in disgrace with fortune and men's eyes, I all alone beweep my outcast state, And trouble deaf heaven with my bootless cries, And look upon myself, and curse my fate,

> When in disgrace with fortune and in men's eyes, I all alone bemoan my outcast state, and importune the non-responsive heaven with my unavailing cries, and look upon myself,

Wishing me like to one more rich in hope, Featur'd like him, like him with friends possess'd, Desiring this man's art, and that man's scope, With what I most enjoy contented least;

> Wishing I were like someone more rich in hope, with fine appearance and many friends, desiring this man's skill and another's scope, I am contented little with what I have and should enjoy the most.

Yet in these thoughts myself almost despising, Haply I think on thee, and then my state, Like to the lark at break of day arising From sullen earth, sings hymns at heaven's gate,

> Even as I think such thoughts I despise myself for them, but when, by good fortune I think of Thee, then my state of mind is like the song of the lark arising from the gloomy earth at the break of day, serenading with hymns at the gates of heaven.

For thy sweet love remember'd such wealth brings, That then I scorn to change my state with kings

> In the remembrance of Thy Love, I am filled with sweet abundance. Then I scorn the thought of ever changing places with kings.

COMMENTARY

At the start of Sonnet 29, the Poet says: "*I all alone beweep my outcast state, and trouble deaf heaven with my bootless cries, and look upon myself, and curse my fate.*" The Poet has sunk under the weight of sorrows and grief expressed in Sonnet 28. Shakespeare's Sonnet sounds much like King David in Psalm 55: "Give ear to my prayer, O God; and hide not thyself from my supplication. Attend unto me, and hear me: I mourn in my complaint, and make a noise." **(Ps. 55:1-2)** This is the state that periodically befalls most people, and as the grass seems greener elsewhere, one may wish to exchange places with another. "*Wishing me like to one more rich in hope, Featur'd like him, like him with friend's possess'd, Desiring this man's art, and that man's scope.*"

In Sonnet 27.13-14, the Poet's anguish continued day and night. "*Lo, thus, by day my limbs, by night my mind, For thee, and for myself, no quiet find.*"

"In the day of my trouble I sought the Lord: my sore ran in the night, and ceased not: my soul refused to be comforted." **(Ps. 77:2)**

Now see where the Poet has come to: "*From sullen earth, sings hymns at heaven's gate, For thy sweet love remember'd such wealth brings, That then I scorn to change my state with kings.*"

BIBLICAL PASSAGES SUGGESTED BY SONNET 29

"I call to remembrance my song ("*like to the lark . . . sings hymns at heaven's gate*") in the night: I commune with mine own heart: and my spirit made diligent search." **Ps. 77:6**

"The Lord is my strength and song, and is become my salvation." **Ps. 118:14**

"O Lord my God, I cried unto thee, and thou hast healed me. O Lord, thou hast brought up my soul from the grave: thou hast kept me alive, that I should not go down in the pit. Sing unto the Lord, O ye saints of his, and give thanks at the remembrance of his holiness." **Ps. 30:2-4**

"Thou hast turned for me my mourning into dancing: thou hast put off my sackcloth, and girded me with gladness." **Ps. 30:11**

It is no wonder that with his "*sweet love remember'd*," the Poet is filled "*with abundance*" and he then scorns the thought of ever changing places "*with kings.*"

SONNET 30

When to the sessions of sweet silent thought
I summon up remembrance of things past,
I sigh the lack of many a thing I sought,
And with old woes new wail my dear time's waste.
Then can I drown an eye, unus'd to flow,
For precious friends hid in death's dateless night,
And weep afresh love's long since cancell'd woe,
And moan th' expense of many a vanish'd sight.
Then can I grieve at grievances foregone,
And heavily from woe to woe tell o'er
The sad account of fore-bemoaned moan,
Which I new pay as if not paid before.
But if the while I think on thee, dear friend,
All losses are restor'd, and sorrows end.

THEME

It is not good to dwell on past errors or wrongs. These keep one from moving forward on the journey of the soul. Remembrance of God restores one to wholeness and effaces all sorrow.

GLOSSARY

When to the sessions of sweet silent thought I summon up remembrance of things past, I sigh the lack of many a thing I sought, And with old woes new wail my dear time's waste.

> When in time of sweet thought I summon the memory of things past, I regret my failure to accomplish things I sought after, and with sorrowful memories lament again those precious wasted years of my life:

Then can I drown an eye, unus'd to flow, For precious friends hid in death's dateless night, And weep afresh love's long since cancell'd woe, And moan th' expense of many a vanish'd sight.

> Then again I shed tears from dry eyes, for dear friends hidden behind the eternal gates of death, and weep again

for sorrows that love had washed away; and lament the heavy cost of my forgotten sins.

Then can I grieve at grievances foregone, And heavily from woe to woe tell o'er The sad account of fore-bemoaned moan, Which I new pay as if not paid before.

Then I can grieve over past wrongs, which weigh heavily upon me as I recount them and the sorrowful debt incurred due to previously grieved wrongs, which I continue to pay for as if my slate was never cleared.

But if the while I think on thee, dear friend, All losses are restor'd, and sorrows end.

But if all the while I think of Thee, dear Friend, all losses are restored and my sorrows end.

COMMENTARY

In Sonnet 30, the Poet recalls moments when his thoughts again dwell on forgotten woes. He then suffers in their remembrance. "*When to the sessions of sweet silent thought I summon up remembrance of things past, I sigh the lack of many a thing I sought, And with old woes new wail my dear time's waste.*" It is a burdensome weight to recount old sorrows and old hurts. Recalling past memories has brought the Poet down from the lofty state of Sonnet 29.13, where "*sweet love remember'd such wealth brings.*" This state of elevated consciousness cannot be maintained when the weight of past wrongs, sorrows, or grievances still hold sway over the Poet's mind and emotions. "*Old woes*" are wept for again; the dry eye again is "*drown*[ed]" for "*friends hid in death's dateless night.*" There is grief for "*grievances foregone,*" and all of this lies heavily as a "*sad account*" for which the Poet must render "*new pay as if not paid before.*"

But the Poet curbs his grievous thoughts, and again brings to remembrance his "*dear friend,*" the Lord, and then "*All losses are restor'd, and sorrows end.*"

BIBLICAL PASSAGES SUGGESTED BY SONNET 30

"Remember ye not the former things, neither consider the things of old. Behold, I will do a new thing; now it shall spring forth; shall ye not know it? I will even make a way in the wilderness, and rivers in the desert." Isa. **43:18-19**

"Thy sun shall no more go down; neither shall thy moon withdraw itself; for the Lord shall be thine everlasting light, and the days of thy mourning shall be ended." **Isa. 60:20**

"When my soul fainted within me I remembered the Lord: and my prayer came in unto thee, into thine holy temple." **Jon. 2:7**

SONNET 31

Thy bosom is endeared with all hearts,
Which I by lacking have supposed dead,
And there reigns Love, and all Love's loving parts,
And all those friends which I thought buried.
How many a holy and obsequious tear
Hath dear religious love stol'n from mine eye,
As interest of the dead, which now appear,
But things remov'd that hidden in thee lie.
Thou art the grave where buried love doth live,
Hung with the trophies of my lovers gone,
Who all their parts of me to thee did give,
That due of many, now is thine alone.
Their images I lov'd I view in thee,
And thou (all they) hast all the all of me.

THEME

God is the source, fountain, and final repository of all love. When we feel deepest love for the supreme Beloved, we will be reassured in our love for those departed, now in Him.

GLOSSARY

Thy bosom is endeared with all hearts, Which I by lacking have supposed dead, And there reigns Love, and all Love's loving parts, And all those friends which I thought buried.

Thy Heart is the beloved repository of all hearts. I, for lack of understanding, mistakenly believed the departed ones forever lost. In Thy Love reigns the love of all beings, including those of friends I thought buried.

How many a holy and obsequious tear Hath dear religious love stol'n from mine eye, As interest of the dead, which now appear, But things remov'd that hidden in thee lie.

How many sacred, surrendered tears has my spiritual journey of religious love extracted from my eye, in

> mourning for the dead. They seemed to be removed from me; but now appear and lie hidden in Thy bosom.

Thou art the grave where buried love doth live, Hung with the trophies of my lovers gone, Who all their parts of me to thee did give, That due of many, now is thine alone.

> Thou art the resting place where buried love still lives, hung with the trophies of my past loves, who render unto Thee all the love which once was mine alone.

Their images I lov'd I view in thee, And thou (all they) hast all the all of me.

> Their images, I loved, and I now see them in Thee; and Thou, the supreme Beloved, has the all and all of me.

COMMENTARY

The Poet declares that the bosom of God is the haven of love for all hearts. "*Thy bosom is endeared with all hearts.*" So many tears are shed for the loss of loved ones who in reality are being well attended in the Heart of God. "*Which I by lacking have supposed dead, And there reigns Love, and all Love's loving parts, And all those friends which I thought buried.*" "And God shall wipe away all tears from their eyes; and there shall be no more death, neither sorrow, nor crying, neither shall there be any more pain: for the former things are passed away." **(Rev. 21:4)**

In the final analysis, God is Love, and the love received by all, from father, mother, friend, and lover, is God's Love. "*And there reigns Love, and all Love's loving parts.*" He is the One who loves us through all receptive and giving hearts. "For whether we live, we live unto the Lord; and whether we die, we die unto the Lord: whether we live therefore, or die, we are the Lord's." **(Rom. 14:8)** The Poet realizes that "*Thou* [the Lord] *art the grave where buried love doth live. . . . Their images I lov'd I view in thee.*" "Neither can they die any more: for they are equal unto the angels; and are the children of God, being the children of the resurrection. Now that the dead are raised, even Moses shewed at the bush, when he calleth the Lord the God of Abraham, and the God of Isaac, and the God of Jacob. For he is not a God of the dead, but of the living: for all live unto him." **(Luke 20:36-38)**

Shakespeare refers in line 12 to the "*due*" of many, which is a word play on "dew." "Thy dead men shall live, together with my dead body shall they arise. Awake and sing, ye that dwell in dust; for thy dew is as the dew of herbs, and the earth shall cast out the dead." **(Isa. 26:19)** "*Due*" also suggests an accounting on the "*interest of the dead.*"

Shakespeare declares that "*all those friends which I thought buried . . . now appear,*" and "*lovers gone . . . I view in thee.*" Literally he is saying that in spiritual vision he sees departed loved ones. Many have seen images or visions of departed loved ones. The saints are notable examples, but humble folk like the famous horticulturist, Luther Burbank, shyly confided that he saw his mother in visions, after her death. Also, in states of religious ecstasy or deep meditative states, and in near-death experiences, many have seen departed souls.

Shakespeare's Sonnet expresses a deep and abiding spiritual faith and understanding. The last two lines of Sonnet 31 convey the message that Shakespeare was among the ranks of those whose spiritual attainment permitted him in states of ecstasy or deep meditative states to see in visions loved ones who had passed on.

BIBLICAL PASSAGES SUGGESTED BY SONNET 31

"And I saw a great white throne, and him that sat on it, from whose face the earth and the heaven fled away; and there was found no place for them. And I saw the dead, small and great, stand before God; and the books were opened: and another book was opened, which is the book of life: and the dead were judged out of those things which were written in the books, according to their works." **Rev. 20:11-12**

"Have the gates of death been opened unto thee? or hast thou seen the doors of the shadow of death?" **Job 38:17**

SONNET 32

If thou survive my well-contented day,
When that churl Death my bones with dust shall cover,
And shalt by fortune once more re-survey
These poor rude lines of thy deceased lover,
Compare them with the bett'ring of the time,
And though they be outstripp'd by every pen,
Reserve them for my love, not for their rhyme,
Exceeded by the height of happier men.
O then vouchsafe me but this loving thought:
"Had my friend's Muse grown with this growing age,
A dearer birth than this his love had brought,
To march in ranks of better equipage;
But since he died, and poets better prove,
Theirs for their style I'll read, his for his love."

THEME

All writers and works of art come and go, but those imbued with truth, sincerity, and love will continue over time to inspire audiences and be read, and re-read by future generations.

GLOSSARY

If thou survive my well-contented day, When that churl Death my bones with dust shall cover, And shalt by fortune once more re-survey These poor rude lines of thy deceased lover,

> If you survive that final blessed day when rude death shall cover my bones with dust, and shall perchance once more look over these poor offerings of verse of thy deceased friend,

Compare them with the bett'ring of the time, And though they be outstripp'd by every pen, Reserve them for my love, not for their rhyme, Exceeded by the height of happier men.

> Compare them with the better verse of that time, and though they are surpassed by other poets, preserve them

for the love in them, not for their rhyme, which is exceeded by the works of more fortunate writers.

O then vouchsafe me but this loving thought: "Had my friend's Muse grown with this growing age, A dearer birth than this his love had brought, To march in ranks of better equipage;

Oh, then grant me this one loving thought: "Had my friend's poetry grown with time in this improving age (of literary skill), a much dearer love than this would have come forth to march in the ranks of those more skillfully endowed:

But since he died, and poets better prove, Theirs for their style I'll read, his for his love."

But since he died, and poets now are better, theirs I will read for their style, and his for the love he shared."

COMMENTARY

To the reader of his work, Shakespeare, in his modesty, submits his "*poor rude lines*" for comparison and re-evaluation against other writers who may have achieved greater fame. "*Compare them with the bett'ring of the time.*" But he asks to be granted one thing: that his reader feel the deep loving thoughts with which his verse is imbued. "*Reserve them for my love, not for their rhyme.*" This love of Spirit, and faith in God is so touchingly reflected in his works, that for all time he should be read and appreciated for these qualities alone, if nothing else. "*'Had my friend's Muse grown with this growing age, A dearer birth than this his love had brought, To march in ranks of better equipage; But since he died, and poets better prove, Theirs for their style I'll read, his for his love.'*"

SONNET 33

Full many a glorious morning have I seen
Flatter the mountain-tops with sovereign eye,
Kissing with golden face the meadows green,
Gilding pale streams with heavenly alchemy,
Anon permit the basest clouds to ride
With ugly rack on his celestial face,
And from the forlorn world his visage hide,
Stealing unseen to west with this disgrace:
Even so my sun one early morn did shine,
With all-triumphant splendor on my brow;
But out alack, he was but one hour mine,
The region cloud hath mask'd him from me now,
Yet him for this my love no whit disdaineth;
Suns of the world may stain when heaven's sun staineth.

THEME

The Light of the spiritual eye is so very beautiful that one feels forlorn when it cannot be seen. It is more radiant than the light of the earthly sun.

GLOSSARY

Full many a glorious morning have I seen Flatter the mountain-tops with sovereign eye, Kissing with golden face the meadows green, Gilding pale streams with heavenly alchemy,

> Many are the glorious mornings I have seen where the sun beautifies the mountain tops with sovereign eye, kissing green meadows with golden light, and gilding pale streams with heavenly magic light.

Anon permit the basest clouds to ride With ugly rack on his celestial face, And from the forlorn world his visage hide, Stealing unseen to west with this disgrace:

> Later to allow the darkest clouds to ride with ugly torment across His heavenly face, and hide His face from a

forlorn world, stealing unseen to the west with this disgrace:

Even so my sun one early morn did shine, With all-triumphant splendour on my brow; But out alack, he was but one hour mine, The region cloud hath mask'd him from me now,

Even so, my sun one early morning did shine with complete triumphant splendor on my brow. But out in the open, alas, He was but one hour mine. But now, the high clouds cover Him.

Yet him for this my love no whit disdaineth; Suns of the world may stain when heaven's sun staineth.

Yet my love for Him is not the least diminished; earthy suns lose their luster in comparison to the celestial Light that shines. (Within the spiritual eye)

COMMENTARY

Shakespeare repeats his use of the spiritual "*sovereign*" eye through which all is transformed into golden light. It is tormenting, like being on the "*ugly rack*" of torture, when the celestial vision is hidden behind the lowest "*basest*" clouds of consciousness. When "*basest clouds . . . ride with ugly rack*," the world is "*forlorn*" as they steal "*unseen to* [the] *west.*" As discussed in Sonnet 7, the way of the East, "*the orient*," refers to the spiritual while the west refers to the "*basest*" of worldly temptations. "These are wells without water, clouds that are carried with a tempest; to whom the mist of darkness is reserved for ever." **(2 Pet. 2:17)** "And, behold, the glory of the God of Israel came from the way of the east: and his voice was like a noise of many waters: and the earth shined with his glory. . . . And the glory of the Lord came into the house by the way of the gate whose prospect is toward the east." **(Ezek. 43:2, 4)** By way of contrast, the Bible refers to the "pillar of a cloud," which rather than obscure "*his celestial face*," lights the way. "And the Lord went before them by day in a pillar of a cloud, to lead them the way; and by night in a pillar of fire, to give them light; to go by day and night." **(Exod. 13:21)** "And the angel of God, which went before the camp of Israel, removed and went behind them; and the pillar of the cloud went from before their face, and stood behind them" **(Exod. 14:19)** The cloud metaphor is unmistakable. Shakespeare writes not as one who merely reads scripture, but as one who lived illuminating experiences. His love for the Lord is not diminished nor commandeered by the lesser lights ("*west*") of earthbound "*suns of the world*," but is sustained by the pure Light of "*heaven's sun*."

SONNET 34

Why didst thou promise such a beauteous day,
And make me travel forth without my cloak,
To let base clouds o'ertake me in my way,
Hiding thy bravery in their rotten smoke?
'Tis not enough that through the cloud thou break,
To dry the rain on my storm-beaten face,
For no man well of such a salve can speak
That heals the wound, and cures not the disgrace.
Nor can thy shame give physic to my grief;
Though thou repent, yet I have still the loss:
The offender's sorrow lends but weak relief
To him that bears the strong offence's cross.
Ah, but those tears are pearl which thy love sheds,
And they are rich and ransom all ill deeds.

THEME

Weep and shed tears for God, and He will answer, healing all sorrow of the moment. Such tears for the love of God release devotion and are a redeeming treasure that heals all past sorrows.

GLOSSARY

Why didst thou promise such a beauteous day, And make me travel forth without my cloak, To let base clouds o'ertake me in my way, Hiding thy bravery in their rotten smoke?

> Why didst Thou promise such a perfect day of beauty, and cause me to travel without my cloak (covering that shields one from outer disturbances); to let lowest, restless, worldly thoughts ("*base clouds*") overtake me in my way (to Thee), hiding Thy splendor in their rotten smoke?

'Tis not enough that through the cloud thou break, To dry the rain on my storm-beaten face, For no man well of such a salve can speak That heals the wound, and cures not the disgrace.

> It is not enough, that through the base cloud, Thou dost shine through, to dry the anguished tears from my face; for no man can speak well of such a salve that relieves the hurt, but cannot cure my inner disgrace.

Nor can thy shame give physic to my grief; Though thou repent, yet I have still the loss: The offender's sorrow lends but weak relief To him that bears the strong offence's cross.

> Nor can thy feeling of shame give relief to my sorrow. Even if you, my child, are repentant, yet I still have the loss; the offender's sorrow gives little relief to the one who bears the grievous offence's loss.

Ah, but those tears are pearl which thy love sheds, And they are rich and ransom all ill deeds

> Ah, but those repentant tears, shed out of love, are pearls, and they are my treasure and redeem all wrongs done.

COMMENTARY

Shakespeare's use of "*cloud*" metaphors refer generally to worldly thoughts and actions that obscure the spiritual. They are compared to "*rotten smoke*" that hides "*thy bravery.*" Eventually the Lord answers the wails of his pleading child and gives relief, but the disgrace remains for not having cloaked himself from worldly thoughts. The Poet blames the Lord for making him "*travel forth without my* [his] *cloak.*" "If I had not come and spoken unto them, they had not had sin: but now they have no cloak for their sin." **(John 15:22)** "Then Job arose, and rent his mantle, and shaved his head, and fell down upon the ground, and worshiped." **(Job 1:20)** "But thou, when thou prayest, enter into thy closet, and when thou hast shut thy door, pray to thy Father which is in secret; and thy Father which seeth in secret shall reward thee openly." **(Matt. 6:6)**

The Lord comes when He will "*to dry the rain on my storm-beaten face.*" The Poet says that the Lord's compassion is like a "*salve*" that soothes, but does not cure the underlying "*disgrace*" of man's innate worldly tendencies. The Lord does not like his children to suffer, and while man has a God-given conscience, which guides him through guilt and "*shame*" to repent, this does little for "*him who bears the strong offence's cross*" of disgrace. In other words, man is tempted by worldly allurements, and the Lord, "repents," in a manner of speaking, for planting evil in creation by giving man a guiding conscience. Note that for the child who sins, the Lord says, "*Though thou repent, yet I have still the loss.*" But for the sinner, there is but "*weak relief*" as the one who "*bears the strong offence's cross.*" In a double meaning, the Poet shows that the Lord who redeems also bears the cross of many sinners.

Finally, out of "*disgrace,*" the repentant child, out of love for the Lord, sheds the "*tears* [that] *are pearl.*" They are the true treasure that brings the ransom of forgiveness. "*Ah, but those tears are pearl which thy love sheds, And they are rich and ransom all ill deeds.*" "Again, the kingdom of heaven is like unto treasure hid in a field; the which when a man hath found, he hideth, and for joy thereof goeth and selleth all that he hath, and buyeth that field. Again, the kingdom of heaven is like unto a merchant man, seeking goodly pearls:" **(Matt. 13:44-45)** "They that sow in tears shall reap in joy. He that goeth forth and weepeth, bearing precious seed, shall doubtless come again with rejoicing, bringing his sheaves with him." **(Ps. 126:5-6)**

In Sonnets 33 and 34, Shakespeare carries on the themes of reaching up toward God and falling back again. The Lord, "*his visage hide*[s], *stealing unseen to the west.*" (Sonnet 33.7-8) Sonnet 34 describes a roller coaster of changing emotions: at first there is the "*promise of such a beauteous day*" with happy anticipation, then our traveler is "*without* [his] *my cloak*" so that "*base clouds*" of worldly thoughts and restlessness shrivel him to tears on his "*storm-beaten face.*" The sweet tears of devotional longing are "*pearls*" that renew his heart and ransom him from all "*ill deeds.*" He accuses the Lord, in Sonnet 34, of shame from which the Lord repents (for having created evil and temptation), but God's sorrow, for the exacting nature of his Divine Law by which man must use free will to return to Him, is but "*weak relief*" to him that bears "*the strong offence's cross.*" While universal law is unbending, the Lord is approachable through love and devotion, and ultimately responds thereto.

BIBLICAL PASSAGES SUGGESTED BY SONNET 34

"For out of much affliction and anguish of heart I wrote unto you with many tears; not that ye should be grieved, but that ye might know the love which I have more abundantly unto you. . . . Wherefore I beseech you that ye would confirm your love toward him." **2 Cor. 2:4, 8**

"Who comforteth us in all our tribulation, that we may be able to comfort them which are in any trouble, by the comfort wherewith we ourselves are comforted of God. . . . For we would not, brethren, have you ignorant of our trouble which came to us in Asia, that we were pressed out of measure, above strength, insomuch that we despaired even of life." **2 Cor. 1:4, 8**

"For our light affliction, which is but for a moment, worketh for us a far more exceeding and eternal weight of glory; While we look not at the things which are seen, but at the things which are not seen: for the things which are seen are temporal; but the things which are not seen are eternal." **2 Cor. 4:17-18**

"Behold, happy is the man whom God correcteth: therefore despise not thou the chastening of the Almighty: For he maketh sore, and bindeth up: he woundeth, and his hands make whole." **Job 5:17-18**

SONNET 35

No more be griev'd at that which thou hast done:
Roses have thorns, and silver fountains mud;
Clouds and eclipses stain both moon and sun,
And loathsome canker lives in sweetest bud.
All men make faults, and even I in this,
Authorising thy trespass with compare,
Myself corrupting, salving thy amiss,
Excusing thy sins more than thy sins are;
For to thy sensual fault I bring in sense,
Thy adverse party is thy advocate,
And 'gainst myself a lawful plea commence:
Such civil war is in my love and hate,
That I an accessary needs must be
To that sweet thief which sourly robs from me.

THEME

The Lord does not want man to be overly grieved of conscience for sin. The Lord is the creator of worldly temptations. He is an "*accessary*" to man's actions and suffers when His children are overcome by sin and grief.

GLOSSARY

No more be griev'd at that which thou hast done: Roses have thorns, and silver fountains mud; Clouds and eclipses stain both moon and sun, And loathsome canker lives in sweetest bud.

> No more be grieved by what you have done. Roses have thorns, and silver fountains mud; clouds and eclipses darken both moon and sun, and the ugliest decay is within the sweetest buds.

All men make faults, and even I in this, Authorising thy trespass with compare, Myself corrupting, salving thy amiss, Excusing thy sins more than thy sins are;

> All men commit wrongs, and even I in this, must take responsibility for having made the relative states of good

and evil, My own Creation with its temptations.. But I also forgive, excusing your sins repeatedly, and showing more compassion than the weight of man's great sins.

For to thy sensual fault I bring in sense, Thy adverse party is thy advocate, And 'gainst myself a lawful plea commence: Such civil war is in my love and hate,

To your reasoning mind, I give the power of free will to choose correctly that you might overcome sensual allurements. There is evil in My creation, so I, too, must be your advocate—and against this evil, I institute the Divine laws of Justice and Mercy to do battle in the world of good and evil.

That I an accessary needs must be To that sweet thief which sourly robs from me.

Because I am by necessity a willing accomplice to that sweet thief which sourly robs from Me the love of My children.

COMMENTARY

We have seen how in Sonnets 33 and 34 mankind suffers, and how the Lord suffers with him, until man reaches upward with his thoughts and tears to be made finally whole by "the chastening of the Almighty" who "correcteth" for man's own sake and happiness. Sonnet 35 is the Poet's Divine monologue, as if the Lord speaks directly to his children. "Behold, happy is the man whom God correcteth: therefore despise not thou the chastening of the Almighty: For he maketh sore, and bindeth up: he woundeth, and his hands make whole." **(Job 5:17-18)** In Sonnet 35, Shakespeare speaks for the Lord to man: "*No more be griev'd at that which thou hast done.*" All creation is filled with alternating states of good and evil, beauty and ugliness. "*Roses have thorns, and silver fountains mud; Clouds and eclipses stain both moon and sun, And loathsome canker lives in sweetest bud.*" Man should not be overly wrought: "*No more be griev'd,*" as "*all men make faults.*" Creation is filled with temptations made by the Lord. So He is the one "*authorising,*" or making possible sin or the "*trespass*" of "*all men.*" "I am understanding," **(Prov. 8:14)** says the Lord, "*I bring in sense*" to explain the nature of things, and I am your advocate, and complain "*'gainst myself*," engaging in an eternal battle or "*civil war . . . in my love and hate*." This "*love and hate*" in the created world is the allurement of multitudinous temptations. The alternating, apparent opposites of worldly creation, life and death, pain, pleasure, beauty, ugliness, good and evil, are ever-existent and keep man's attention upon the worldly drama. Such is the play of light and shadow ("*clouds . . . eclipses . . . moon*" and "*sun*") in which "*all men make faults*," and the Creator who is the "*adverse party*" in making the world as it is, must also be man's "*advocate*" who must forgive, "*excusing thy* [man's] *sins*." This sin is hated as it is against the soul's nature. "He hath made every thing beautiful in his time: also he hath set the world in their heart, so that no man can find out the work that God maketh from the beginning to the end." **(Eccl. 3:11)** "Thorns also and thistles shall it bring forth to thee; and thou shalt eat the herb of the field. . . . And the Lord God said, Behold, the man is become as one of us, to know good and evil: and now, lest he put forth his hand, and take also of the tree of life, and eat, and live for ever." **(Gen. 3:18, 22)** "She is a tree of life to them that lay hold upon her: and happy is every one that retaineth her." **(Prov. 3:18)**

In the final couplet, we see that the Lord speaks as "*an accessary*." All that exists, including evil is part of creation. "I form the light, and create darkness: I make peace, and create evil: I the Lord do all these things." **(Isa. 45:7)** The Lord suffers with man in this creation. Evil and worldly allurements are a "*sweet thief*" that carry man away from God. The Lord grieves as the "*sweet thief . . . robs*" man's love from Him. "In their afflictions, he was afflicted, and the angel of his presence saved them: in his love and in his pity he redeemed them; and he bore them, and carried them all the days of old." **(Isa. 63:9)**

SONNET 36

Let me confess that we two must be twain,
Although our undivided loves are one.
So shall those blots that do with me remain,
Without thy help, by me be borne alone.
In our two loves there is but one respect,
Though in our lives a separable spite,
Which though it alter not love's sole effect,
Yet doth it steal sweet hours from love's delight.
I may not evermore acknowledge thee,
Lest my bewailed guilt should do thee shame,
Nor thou with public kindness honour me,
Unless thou take that honour from thy name:
But do not so; I love thee in such sort
As thou being mine, mine is thy good report.

THEME

The love of God and man are one Love because they are from the same eternal source. Man cannot fully communicate what God is, or communicate his deep love for God; but in loving God deeply, man's life begins to change, and the example of that life speaks more eloquently of God than words ever can.

GLOSSARY

Let me confess that we two must be twain, Although our undivided loves are one. So shall those blots that do with me remain, Without thy help, by me be borne alone.

> Let me confess that we two must be separate although our divided loves are truly inseparable: So shall those imperfections that remain with me, continue to be borne alone, without Thy help.

In our two loves there is but one respect, Though in our lives a separable spite, Which, though it alter not love's sole effect, Yet doth it steal sweet hours from love's delight.

In our two loves, there is but one natural aspect which connects us. ["Now there are diversities of gifts, but the same Spirit." **(1 Cor. 12:4)** "For as we have many members in one body, and all members have not the same office." **(Rom. 12:4)**] In life, however, there is a seeming separation which, beneath the surface, does not destroy the power of Love, yet keeps man from feeling his oneness with the Spirit.

I may not evermore acknowledge thee, Lest my bewailed guilt should do thee shame, Nor thou with public kindness honour me, Unless thou take that honour from thy name:

I may not always acknowledge Thee openly, lest my grievous shames cause some to say the Lord has rewarded my sins. Do not cause honor to come upon me with public recognition, unless such public recognition lauds Thy name which is honored thereby.

But do not so; I love thee in such sort As thou being mine, mine is thy good report.

But do not do so. It is enough that Thou art mine, and the nature of the love I have for Thee is what speaks (reports) so well of Thee. It is honor and recognition enough just to have love for Thee and Thy loving response.

COMMENTARY

In Sonnets 21, 25, 26, 29, 30, 32, and 35 Shakespeare writes on the theme of his love for God and his opinion of public honor. In Sonnet 21.9, he says "*O let me, true in love, but truly write.*" In Sonnet 25.14, the Poet does not want public honor, but is happy to be endowed with a permanent love that cannot "*be removed.*" In Sonnet 26.2, he speaks of his duty, which is "*strongly knit,*" and which he cannot adequately express in written form because of a "*wit so poor as mine . . .* [I am] *wanting words to show it.*" (Sonnet 26.5, 6) Only when his imperfect "*tottered loving*" (Sonnet 26.11) is clothed by grace with "*fair aspect*" (Sonnet 26.10) to show him worthy of "*sweet respect*" (Sonnet 26.12) does he dare to openly "*boast*" (Sonnet 26.13) of how he loves God.

Until then he will "*not show* [his] *my head*" openly (Sonnet 26.14). In Sonnets 29 and 30, the Poet is content just to "*Haply think on thee . . . for thy sweet love remember'd such wealth brings*"(Sonnet 29.10, 13), and "*while I think on thee, dear friend, all losses are restor'd and sorrows end.*" (Sonnet 30.13-14) In Sonnet 32, our Poet exhorts his readers to resurvey these "*poor rude lines*" not for their style, but for the love expressed therein (Sonnet 32.4). His poetry flows from the love and thought of God.

Now, in Sonnet 36, he will never more acknowledge or "*confess*" publicly to having knowledge of God lest his oft-lamented shortcomings, "*bewailed guilt,*" and "*blots*" do shame to the Lord: "*Lest my bewailed guilt should do thee shame.*" The Poet's "*poor rude lines*" (Sonnet 32.4) cannot do justice, thus he would "*do thee* [God] *shame.*" (Note his play on the words "*confess*" and "*guilt.*") Nor does the author want public recognition by the Lord's sweet "*kindness*"—which fortune may cause to come upon him publicly—unless the honor is understood as being the Lord's ("*from thy name*"). In other words, if the love of God is recognized in his poetry, the honor is from God's name being recognized as the source of Love expressed in his writing, not the Poet's fame, or the temporary honors given to "*great princes' favorites*" (Sonnet 25.5). "Better it is to be of an humble spirit with the lowly, than to divide the spoil with the proud." **(Prov. 16:19)** Of "*such sort*" is the Poet's love for God: he prefers to keep his head bowed ("*not show my head*" [Sonnet 26.14]). How endearing is man's loved-imbued outpouring of the soul. "For thus saith the high and lofty One that inhabiteth eternity, whose name is Holy; I dwell in the high and holy place, with him also that is of a contrite and humble spirit, to revive the spirit of the humble, and to revive the heart of the contrite ones." **(Isa. 57:15)** "For I say, through the grace given unto me, to every man that is among you, not to think of himself more highly than he ought to think; but to think soberly, according as God hath dealt to every man the measure of faith." **(Rom. 12:3)**

SONNET 37

As a decrepit father takes delight
To see his active child do deeds of youth,
So I, made lame by Fortune's dearest spite,
Take all my comfort of thy worth and truth.
For whether beauty, birth, or wealth, or wit,
Or any of these all, or all, or more,
Entitled in thy parts do crowned sit,
I make my love engrafted to this store.
So then I am not lame, poor, nor despis'd,
Whilst that this shadow doth such substance give,
That I in thy abundance am suffic'd,
And by a part of all thy glory live.
Look what is best, that best I wish in thee,
This wish I have; then ten times happy me!

THEME

The nature of life is such that each one must look back upon his fortunes or misfortunes and accept with grace his place in the world. Our true comfort and sustenance is not derived from physical but from spiritual abundance. In the last analysis, one should seek the best from God, and the best is what will be provided.

GLOSSARY

As a decrepit father takes delight To see his active child do deeds of youth, So I, made lame by Fortune's dearest spite, Take all my comfort of thy worth and truth.

> As a decrepit father takes delight to see his active child engaged in youthful activities, so I, made lame by the consequence of dear misfortune, take all my comfort from Thy Truth and Beauty.

For whether beauty, birth, or wealth, or wit, Or any of these all, or all, or more, Entitled in thy parts do crowned sit, I make my love engrafted to this store.

> For whether Beauty, Eternity, or Bounty, or Wisdom or

any of these, or all of them or more than these sit among the crowning attributes of Thy nature, I derive my love's nourishment from all of these.

So then I am not lame, poor, nor despis'd, Whilst that this shadow doth such substance give, That I in thy abundance am suffic'd, And by a part of all thy glory live.

So then, I am not lame, poor, nor despised, as these are a false shadow; I am fulfilled by Thy abundance and live gratefully receiving only a part of Thy glory.

Look what is best, that best I wish in thee, This wish I have; then ten times happy me!

Whatever is best, I wish to find in Thee. This wish I have is the source of greatest happiness in me!

COMMENTARY

Often Shakespeare revisits themes of the temporal body, the short-sightedness of attending to it, and the ego's desires at the expense of the immortal soul. In Sonnets 2, 3, 11, and 12 for example, the Poet explores the theme of spiritual renewal. In Sonnet 37, the presumably older and wiser Poet, is now lame. Fate and fortune do not play favorites: it is man who has free will, and by spiritual law, must reap what he sows. This is not for man's harm, but only that the Lord might correct through "*dearest spite.*" Physical age does not matter if soulful comfort is found in the Lord's bounty. "*So I, made lame by fortune's dearest spite, Take all my comfort of thy worth and truth.*" "*Engrafting*" one's love to the crowning, "[*e*]*ntitled*" aspects of Spirit's abundance, supersedes physical lameness or shortcomings, and one is completely sustained and lives "*by a part*" of God's "*glory*" and grace. In surrendering one's life to God with faith, one feels that all good things ("*what is best*") are to be sought from God. The very act of surrender itself is so freeing, that the Poet finds abundant joy in it: "*Ten times happy me.*"

BIBLICAL PASSAGES SUGGESTED BY SONNET 37

"For whom the Lord loveth he correcteth; even as a father the son in whom he delighteth." **Prov. 3:12**

"Behold, happy is the man whom God correcteth: therefore despise not thou the chastening of the Almighty." **Job 5:17**

"For whom the Lord loveth he chasteneth, and scourgeth every son whom he receiveth. If ye endure chastening, God dealeth with you as with sons; for what son is he whom the father chasteneth not? . . . For they verily for a few days chastened us after their own pleasure; but he for our profit, that we might be partakers of his holiness. Now no chastening for the present seemeth to be joyous, but grievous: nevertheless afterward it yieldeth the peaceable fruit of righteousness unto them which are exercised thereby. Wherefore lift up the hands which hang down, and the feeble knees; And make straight paths for your feet, lest that which is lame be turned out of the way; but let it rather be healed." **Heb. 12:6-7, 10-13**

SONNET 38

How can my Muse want subject to invent,
While thou dost breathe, that pour'st into my verse
Thine own sweet argument, too excellent
For every vulgar paper to rehearse?
O give thyself the thanks, if aught in me
Worthy perusal stand against thy sight;
For who's so dumb that cannot write to thee,
When thou thyself dost give invention light?
Be thou the tenth Muse, ten times more in worth
Than those old nine which rhymers invocate;
And he that calls on thee, let him bring forth
Eternal numbers to outlive long date.
If my slight Muse do please these curious days,
The pain be mine, but thine shall be the praise.

THEME

All creative inspiration which stands the test of time comes from God, the ultimate Creator whose fount of originality is exhaustless. That which is founded upon the commonplace, ever remains common work.

GLOSSARY

How can my Muse want subject to invent, While thou dost breathe, that pour'st into my verse Thine own sweet argument, too excellent For every vulgar paper to rehearse?

> How can my poetry ever lack in themes to write about while Thou dost breathe life into my soul, and when Thou dost pour into my verse Thine own sweet inspirations, too excellent for commonplace writings to set out?

O give thyself the thanks, if aught in me Worthy perusal stand against thy sight; For who's so dumb that cannot write to thee, When thou thyself dost give invention light?

All the credit belongs to Thee, if there is anything in me worthy of perusal that stands up in Thy sight; for who is so lacking, that he cannot write words to Thee when it is Thou who dost provide creative inspiration?

Be thou the tenth Muse, ten times more in worth Than those old nine which rhymers invocate; And he that calls on thee, let him bring forth Eternal numbers to outlive long date.

Thou art the ultimate Poet, infinitely more in worth than those lesser muses who are called on for inspiration. And he that calls upon Thee, let him bring forth verse that is eternally appreciated for its majestic worth and inspiration.

If my slight Muse do please these curious days, The pain be mine, but thine shall be the praise.

If my humble poetry is pleasing in these literary times, the effort is mine, but to Thee belongs all the praise.

COMMENTARY

Whenever lacking in inspiration or inventiveness, one should turn within toward the innate fountain of creativity, the spark of Spirit inherent in the soul. "*How can my Muse want subject to invent, While thou does breathe, that pour'st into my verse.*" Then there is no one so "*dumb*" or dull who cannot benefit from "*invention light.*" This inspiration may take time to develop or "*bring forth.*" The Sonnet labels the muses of artistic inspiration the "*old nine*" who "*rhymers invocate,*" or call upon. These cannot compare with the "*tenth Muse,*" whose "*sweet argument*" is "*too excellent*" and beyond the reach of the "*vulgar*" or commonplace. In humility, one gives credit to the true source of inspiration: "*thine shall be the praise,*" the One who is the ultimate Poet, "*the tenth Muse,*" the divine Fountain of beauty, truth, and eloquence.

BIBLICAL PASSAGES SUGGESTED BY SONNET 38

"The entrance of thy words giveth light; it giveth understanding unto the simple." **Ps. 119:130**

"The grass withereth, the flower fadeth: but the word of our God shall stand for ever." **Isa. 40:8**

"The Lord God hath given me the tongue of the learned, that I should know how to speak a word in season to him that is weary: he wakeneth morning by morning, he wakeneth mine ear to hear as the learned." **Isa. 50:4**

"Now therefore go, and I will be with thy mouth, and teach thee what thou shalt say." **Exod. 4:12**

"Which things also we speak, not in words which man's wisdom teacheth, but which the Holy Ghost teacheth; comparing spiritual things with spiritual." **1 Cor. 2:13**

SONNET 39

O how thy worth with manners may I sing,
When thou art all the better part of me?
What can mine own praise to mine own self bring?
And what is't but mine own when I praise thee?
Even for this let us divided live,
And our dear love lose name of single one,
That by this separation I may give
That due to thee, which thou deserv'st alone.
O absence! what a torment wouldst thou prove,
Were it not thy sour leisure gave sweet leave
To entertain the time with thoughts of love,
Which time and thoughts so sweetly doth deceive,
And that thou teachest how to make one twain,
By praising him here who doth hence remain.

THEME

The soul is a sacred part of Spirit, and no words alone can adequately praise or appraise it. Man must give "*due*" "*praise*" to the Spirit, which is the "*better part*" in man. If one mostly devotes time and thought to worldly things, one is deceived. Then the separation between soul and Spirit is "*twain,*" and the ego-imbued self must "*remain*" earthbound.

GLOSSARY

O how thy worth with manners may I sing, When thou art all the better part of me? What can mine own praise to mine own self bring? And what is't but mine own when I praise thee?

> O how may I praise Thee in a mannerly way, when Thou art everything that is the better part of me? What can my own (meager) praise add to the divine soul that is already mine? And what is it but my own (soul) when I praise thee?

Even for this let us divided live, And our dear love lose name of single one, That by this separation I may give That due to thee, which thou deserv'st alone.

> Even for this, let us in divided consciousness appear to exist separately (as soul and Spirit); and let our precious Love, although in realty one, not be called such; that by this separation I may give to Thee that which Thou alone deserves.

O absence! What a torment wouldst thou prove, Were it not thy sour leisure gave sweet leave To entertain the time with thought of love, Which time and thoughts so sweetly doth deceive,

> O absence! What torment it would prove to be, were it not that bitter leisure time provides sweet moments to entertain thoughts of love. On the contrary, passing time in useless actions may seem a delight, but in reality is a deceptive distraction.

And that thou teachest how to make one twain, By praising him here who doth hence remain.

> Thou teachest how to make the oneness of Spirit and soul appear to be separate. By man's praising and lauding worldly entertainments, he only enhances his selfish, ego nature, which then must remain earthbound in a worldly grave.

COMMENTARY

Shakespeare again visits the theme of Spirit as one, instead of separate "[e]*ntitled*," crowning parts, or natures like "*worth and truth*" (Sonnet 37.7, 4). The Poet addresses again the over-arching Spirit and the incarnate soul in man. The soul is the spark of Spirit, which the Poet calls "*the better part of me*." When any man praises the ego-oriented self, the Poet asks, "*What can mine own praise to mine own self bring?*" If the soul in man is praised, he is praising the spiritual aspect. "*And what is't but mine own when I praise thee?*" Praising the egotistical self means man must live ignorant of his spiritual nature. "*Even for this let us divided live.*" The ego, which is identified with self-"*praise*," or attachment to material existence, feels itself as separated and lives a "*divided*" life. A saving grace is to fill time of "*absence*" with "*thoughts of love*." In loving God, one is freed from the "*torment*" of this apparent separation ("*absence*") until the soul finds salvation by finally realizing itself as the "*better part*" of this human form which it temporarily inhabits. To live for the selfish egotistical nature means that one remains earthbound, and is left behind in a manner of speaking. "*By praising him here who doth hence remain.*" Then it shall be the "*worms*" who inherit the remains of a life lived in ego-oriented excess (see Sonnet 146.7).

SONNET 40

Take all my loves, my love, yea take them all,
What hast thou then more than thou hadst before?
No love, my love, that thou mayst true love call;
All mine was thine before thou hadst this more.
Then if for my love thou my love receivest,
I cannot blame thee for my love thou usest;
But yet be blam'd, if thou thyself deceivest
By wilful taste of what thyself refusest.
I do forgive thy robbery, gentle thief,
Although thou steal thee all my poverty;
And yet, love knows it is a greater grief
To bear love's wrong than hate's known injury.
Lascivious grace, in whom all ill well shows,
Kill me with spites; yet we must not be foes.

THEME

The Lord is a jealous God, and man must have no other "loves" except Him; otherwise he is only hurting himself.

GLOSSARY

Take all my loves, my love, yea take them all, What hast thou then more than thou hadst before? No love, my love, that thou mayst true love call; All mine was thine before thou hadst this more.

> Take all things that I love, my Beloved, yes, take them all. What hast Thou then more than Thou hadst before? No love at all, my Beloved, that Thou mayest call true love. All that was mine was Thine before Thou didst add this to it.

Then, if for my love thou my love receivest, I cannot blame thee for my love thou usest; But yet be blam'd, if thou thyself deceivest By willful taste of what thyself refusest.

> Then, if for love of me, Thou receivest my love, I cannot blame Thee for using my love as Thou wilt; but still

Thou art to blame, if Thou deceivest my true self. But still, Thou art to blame for willfully creating sensual enjoyments which are repugnant to enjoyment of that which is spiritual.

I do forgive thy robbery, gentle thief, Although though steal thee all my poverty; And yet, love knows it is a greater grief To bear love's wrong than hate's known injury.

I do forgive Thy robbery, gentle Thief, although Thou dost steal for Thyself all the little I do possess. Even so, true love knows it is a greater grief to bear wrong committed against love, than injury from hatred.

Lascivious grace, in whom all ill well shows, Kill me with spites; yet we must not be foes.

Egoistic attachments created by lascivious grace quickly show their colors, which kill the soul with injuries. Even so, we must not be enemies.

COMMENTARY

"All which I took from thee I did but take, Not for thy harms, But just that thou might'st seek it in My arms. All which thy child's mistake Fancies as lost, I have stored for thee at home; Rise, clasp My hand, and come!" (Francis Thompson, "The Hound of Heaven"). The Lord wants all of the love of His children. Man's desires are the "*love*" of his worldly heart. The Lord will take from man the objects of his lesser desires. Even so, this does not give God anything additional ("*more than thou hadst before*") as everything already belonged to Him. The loss of worldly things teaches that true happiness, which fills the void in the soul, is not in earthly possessions or people, but in God alone. "*No love, my love, that thou mayst true love call; All mine was thine before thou hadst this more.*"

It is true that God created earthly pleasures and may be blamed for deceiving His children with them. "*But yet be blamed, if thou this self deceivest.*" Worldly attachments ("*willful taste*") keep man from fully surrendering to God, and are "*of what thyself refusest.*" One cannot hold on to worldly allurements and still expect to have higher soul awareness of the Spirit. The Lord is a "*gentle thief*" who dispossesses, or robs man of lesser ego desires ("*all my poverty*"). It would be "*a greater grief*" to commit a wrong against the Love of Spirit by having a "*love*," or desire for worldly temptations, than to lament the absence of earthly pleasures in lieu of spiritual communion. "*And yet, love knows it is a greater grief to bear love's wrong than hate's known injury.*"

The Lord created this world with tempting grace, but tinged with allurements to entrap man if he wrongfully uses his free will. "*Lascivious grace, in whom all ill well shows.*" Eventually the harmful results are felt ("*all ill well shows*") and the human soul suffers with "*spites*" by reaping what has been sown. Yet one must not "kick against the pricks" (**Acts 9:5**) and "*be foes*," as a result of injuries or "*spites*," as these are only a means to teach us to use the faculties of reason and discrimination more wisely. Man is punished, or corrected, so he might eventually break free from all lesser earthly loves and attachments.

In Sonnet 39.12, Shakespeare says, "*so sweetly*" do our thoughts and time deceive us. God is teaching his children that by self-"*praise*," or ego attachment, this makes "*one twain*," and keeps one identified with the sensual body and its desires, thus perpetuating a separation of soul from Spirit (Sonnet 39.3, 13). In Sonnet 40, the Poet tells us that God will tempt man with earthly deceptions, and these he must learn to overcome by wise discrimination if he is to progress spiritually.

BIBLICAL PASSAGES SUGGESTED BY SONNET 40

"Thou shalt not make unto thee any graven image, or any likeness of any thing that is in heaven above, or that is in the earth beneath, or that is in the water under the earth: Thou shalt not bow down thyself to them, nor serve them: for I the Lord thy God am a jealous god, visiting the iniquity of the fathers upon the children unto the third and fourth generation of them that hate me." **Exod. 20:4-5**

"For thou shalt worship no other god: for the Lord, whose name is Jealous, is a jealous God:" **Exod. 34:14**

SONNET 41

Those pretty wrongs that liberty commits,
When I am sometimes absent from thy heart,
Thy beauty and thy years full well befits,
For still temptation follows where thou art.
Gentle thou art, and therefore to be won,
Beauteous thou art, therefore to be assailed;
And when a woman woos, what woman's son
Will sourly leave her till he have prevailed?
Ay me! but yet thou might'st my seat forbear,
And chide thy beauty and thy straying youth,
Who lead thee in their riot even there
Where thou art forc'd to break a twofold truth:
Hers, by thy beauty tempting her to thee,
Thine, by thy beauty being false to me.

THEME

Even while one pursues God, temptation is ever close at hand. The Lord is worth winning above all else, but temptation is to be conquered before the battle is over.

GLOSSARY

Those pretty wrongs that liberty commits, When I am sometimes absent from thy heart, Thy beauty and thy years full well befits, For still temptation follows where thou art.

> Having free will sometimes leads to my yielding to petty temptations. When I am sometimes (mentally) absent from the thought of Thy love, it is Thy beauty and the years of loving grace that are my anchor still, even when temptations are everywhere present.

Gentle thou art, and therefore to be won, Beauteous thou art, therefore to be assailed; And when a woman woos, what woman's son Will sourly leave her till he have prevailed?

> Gentle Thou art, and therefore well-worth winning.

> Thou art Beauty, and therefore every obstacle is to be assailed to know Thee; and when a woman is in love's pursuit, what earthly man will suffer the bitterness of leaving her until he has prevailed?

Ay me! but yet thou might'st my seat forbear, And chide thy beauty and thy straying youth, Who lead thee in their riot even there Where thou art forc'd to break a twofold truth:

> Alas, even Thou mightest make allowance for the situation I am in, and chide Thy earthly temptations, and the indiscretions of immature youth who come to man before knowing Thee. These wreak havoc in man while he is in the temporal body, and so Thou art forced to break a two-fold truth:

Hers, by the beauty tempting her to thee, Thine, by thy beauty being false to me.

> My soul's (the loved one) by Thy unsurpassable Beauty attracting my soul to Thee, and Thine (the Eternal Beloved) by Thine earthly temptation's being false to me.

COMMENTARY

When the heart is fixed upon God, man is strong in willpower, but when temptations cause him to be "*sometimes absent*," he may use, or misuse, his free will and commit "*pretty wrongs*." No matter how alluring is the beauty of Spirit ("*thy beauty*") or how many years one is on a spiritual course ("*years full well befits*"), still temptation is ever near. In earthly life, the worldly man attends to the woman who woos him, and yet the Lord is Beauty and "*gentle*" sweetness itself, worth winning and assailing all obstacles to obtain. "*Gentle thou art, and therefore to be won, beauteous thou art, therefore to be assailed*." Man is not entirely to blame because the Lord created temptations; and while man's immature wisdom ("*straying youth*") comes before the realization of truth, sensual allurements run riot with the human ego: "*and chide thy beauty and thy straying youth, who lead thee in their riot even there*." The eternal promise of the Beloved of the Universe to His children is that salvation will eventually come; but before that occurs, there seems to be a twofold breaking of the truth. "*Where thou art forc'd to break a twofold truth.*" The first is that of the soul being lured to seek God and being yet unable to fill the heart's void immediately because of worldly desires; and second, that of the Spirit which seeks the return of the soul, but which places the obstacles of temptation before man to test whether he really wants God, the Giver, more than His earthly gifts. "*Hers, by thy beauty tempting her to thee, Thine, by thy beauty being false to me.*"

BIBLICAL PASSAGES SUGGESTED BY SONNET 41

"There hath no temptation taken you but such as is common to man: but God is faithful, who will not suffer you to be tempted above that ye are able; but will with the temptation also make a way to escape, that ye may be able to bear it." **1 Cor. 10:13**

"Hear, O heavens, and give ear, O earth: for the Lord hath spoken, I have nourished and brought up children, and they have rebelled against me. The ox knoweth his owner, and the ass his master's crib: but Israel doth not know, my people doth not consider." **Isa. 1:2-3**

"Because thou has kept the word of my patience, I also will keep thee from the hour of temptation, which shall come upon all the world, to try them that dwell upon the earth." **Rev. 3:10**

SONNET 42

That thou hast her, it is not all my grief,
And yet it may be said I lov'd her dearly;
That she hath thee, is of my wailing chief,
A loss in love that touches me more nearly.
Loving offenders, thus I will excuse ye:
Thou dost love her, because thou know'st I love her,
And for my sake even so doth she abuse me,
Suffering my friend for my sake to approve her.
If I lose thee, my loss is my love's gain,
And losing her, my friend hath found that loss;
Both find each other, and I lose both twain,
And both for my sake lay on me this cross.
But here's the joy, my friend and I are one,
Sweet flattery, then she loves but me alone.

THEME

Our deepest attachments, even human love, may be taken from us as a Divine test. The Lord's love of us is the reason for testing us, and the temptation also offends man's soul nature. In the end, man realizes that love was always one. The Lord never tests beyond man's capacity to overcome. All is sweet delusion, "*flattery*," and man finally realizes that God's love was never absent from his children but was ever constant.

GLOSSARY

That thou hast her, it is not all my grief, And yet it may be said that I lov'd her dearly; That she hath thee, is of my wailing chief, A loss in love that touches me more nearly.

> That my human love is in your hands, is not all for which I grieve, and yet it may be said I loved in a way that was costly to me. Within my soul is a spark of divine Love which is Thine, and my complaint is the loss of this greater Love, which I feel most near to my heart.

Loving offenders, thus I will excuse ye: Thou dost love her, because thou know'st I love her, And for my sake even so doth she abuse me, Suffering my friend for my sake to approve her.

> My lesser human loves cause me grief, but I excuse the offense knowing why Thou has created them. Thou dost love to create human love knowing man would be beguiled by it. For my sake, (to free me from attachment), human love causes me grief. My divine Friend permits loving temptations so that ultimately I might learn to choose the spiritual over the temporal, and to see the Lord as the true source of all Love.

If I lose thee, my loss is my love's gain, And losing her, my friend hath found that loss; Both find each other, and I lose both twain, And both for my sake lay on me this cross.

> If I lose attachment to a single human love, my loss is a victory and is a gain in true love for my soul. The Lord accepts the surrender of limiting human attachments. Both love for the human and Divine merge, and I lose my limiting attachment for earthly love in the love of Spirit. Human love, and love for the Divine, were created that I might learn to overcome the earthly and find redemption at the feet of the Eternal.

But here's the joy, my friend and I are one; Sweet flattery, Then she loves but me alone.

> But here is the joy, the Lord and I are one. This is the sweetest attraction, knowing that all along my life's journey, my dear Beloved always loved me alone.

COMMENTARY

Shakespeare in Sonnet 41 speaks about temptation. Many temptations are obvious, but man does not usually feel that human relationships, "*pretty wrongs*" (Sonnet 41.1), are also attachments. In Sonnet 42, the Poet explores human love, and love Divine.

Human love was created for man's upliftment, but it can also cause grief. "*That thou hast her, it is not all my grief.*" The soul of man is where divine Love is placed, but perfect communion with divine Love is rare. Instead man seeks love in human relationships to fill the void in his heart and soul, and this costs him "*dearly.*" It is "*a loss in love*" that touches him within, on the level of the spiritual, which is closer to his true soulful nature: "*a loss in love that touches me more nearly.*"

Human love was made part of creation to teach man to love as one on the "*cross.*" Life also is often tinged with grief. So these earthly experiences are "*loving offenders*" until soul and Spirit "*find each other.*" In spiritual union, man loses the grief and "*wailing*" experienced in limiting human attachments over the "*loss in love*" while his soul experienced separation from the Spirit. Now the Poet says: "*I lose both twain.*" The Poet understands, however, that his experiences were necessary. "*Both for my sake lay on me this cross.*" He is now bathed in "*the joy*" realizing the truth that "*my friend and I are one.*" In reality, man and God are never apart. Sweet divine Love imparts the message that makes man feel that "*she loves but me alone.*" The "*cross*" of "*wailing*" and "*grief*" becomes the cross of redemption, love, and "*joy.*"

BIBLICAL PASSAGES SUGGESTED BY SONNET 42

"And we have known and believed the love that God hath to us. God is love; and he that dwelleth in love dwelleth in God, and God in him." **1 John 4:16**

"As the Father hath loved me, so have I loved you: continue ye in my love." **John 15:9**

SONNET 43

When most I wink, then do mine eyes best see,
For all the day they view things unrespected,
But when I sleep, in dreams they look on thee,
And darkly bright, are bright in dark directed.
Then thou, whose shadow shadows doth make bright,
How would thy shadow's form form happy show
To the clear day with thy much clearer light,
When to unseeing eyes thy shade shines so?
How would, I say, mine eyes be blessed made,
By looking on thee in the living day,
When in dead night thy fair imperfect shade
Through heavy sleep on sightless eyes doth stay?
All days are nights to see till I see thee,
And nights bright days when dreams do show thee me.

THEME

Meditative eyes are fixed, sometimes half closed ("*wink*") upon the spiritual eye, which becomes illuminated by the light of the Spirit. To those blessed to see the spiritual Light, there are occasional visions, but even without visions, the Light is most pure when compared to the "common" light of day.

GLOSSARY

When most I wink, then do mine eyes best see, For all the day they view things unrespected, But when I sleep, in dreams they look on thee, And darkly bright, are bright in dark directed.

> When I have eyes half closed, then do my eyes see best, for throughout the day they view things of little value; but when my senses are withdrawn, in visions I look on Thee, and the darkness is illuminated, and my eyes become intensely directed rays of light.

Then thou, whose shadow shadows doth make bright, How would thy shadow's form form happy show To the clear day with thy much clearer light, When to unseeing eyes thy shade shines so?

> Then Thou, whose Image brightens the darkness, how would Thine appearance, as this created world, produce such a joyful vision in the clear light of day, when to unseeing eyes, this shadow image of the world seems to be all that shines for them?

How would, I say, mine eyes be blessed made, By looking on thee in the living day, When in dead night thy fair imperfect shade Through heavy sleep on sightless eyes doth stay?

> How would, I say, that my eyes are truly blessed by looking on Thee in the living light of vision, when in futile darkness Thy fair, but imperfect shadow image, is all that is seen by blind eyes fixed in the slumber of material existence?

All days are nights to see till I see thee, And nights bright days when dreams do show thee me.

> All my days are filled with darkness until I see Thee; and the nights become illuminated like living day, when visions do show Thee to me.

COMMENTARY

When eyes are half closed or closed as if in sleep, this is the focus of one in meditation upon the spiritual eye ("*When most I wink, then do mine eyes best see*"), a theme visited in many Sonnets by Shakespeare. In the daylight, one sees the material creation and "*view*[s] *things unrespected.*" The Poet's eyes are "*directed*" and, as in dreams, are able to "*look on thee,*" and then the darkness becomes illuminated. "*In dreams they look on thee, And darkly bright, are bright in dark directed.*" The image of spiritual light illuminates the darkness and provides joy. "*Then thou, whose shadow shadows doth make bright, How would thy shadow's form form happy show.*"

Spirit is that which is real, and the world is only a "*shadow*" of the Creator. To the "*unseeing eyes,*" there is only darkness. Those fortunate to behold the spiritual Light, feel blessed ("*mine eyes be blessed*") "[*T*]*o unseeing eyes thy shade shines so. How would, I say, mine eyes be blessed made by looking on thee in the living day.*" Those who are steeped in material pursuits and delusion are like one's in "*heavy sleep*" who have "*sightless eyes*." Shakespeare again demonstrates that he has reached a higher level of spiritual understanding and consciousness by his profound description of one who sees the light of the Spirit. "*All days are nights to see till I see thee, And nights bright days when dreams do show thee me.*"

BIBLICAL PASSAGES SUGGESTED BY SONNET 43

"The Lord openeth the eyes of the blind: the Lord raiseth them that are bowed down: the Lord loveth the righteous:" **Ps. 146:8**

"To open the blind eyes, to bring out the prisoners from the prison, and them that sit in darkness out of the prison house." **Isa. 42:7**

"We grope for the wall like the blind, and we grope as if we had no eyes: we stumble at noon day as in the night; we are in desolate places as dead men." **Isa. 59:10**

"But if thine eye be evil, thy whole body shall be full of darkness. If therefore the light that is in thee be darkness, how great is that darkness!" **Matt. 6:23**

"I have heard of thee by the hearing of the ear: but now mine eye seeth thee." **Job 42:5**

"And the light shineth in darkness; and the darkness comprehended it not." **John 1:5**

"Therefore night shall be unto you, that ye shall not have a vision; and it shall be dark unto you, that ye shall not divine; and the sun shall go down over the prophets, and the day shall be dark over them." **Mic. 3:6**

"They know not, neither will they understand; they walk on in darkness: all the foundations of the earth are out of course." **Ps. 82:5**

SONNET 44

If the dull substance of my flesh were thought,
Injurious distance should not stop my way;
For then, despite of space, I would be brought,
From limits far remote, where thou dost stay.
No matter then although my foot did stand
Upon the furthest earth remov'd from thee;
For nimble thought can jump both sea and land,
As soon as think the place where he would be.
But, ah, thought kills me that I am not thought
To leap large lengths of miles when thou art gone,
But that, so much of earth and water wrought,
I must attend time's leisure with my moan.
Receiving nought by elements so slow
But heavy tears, badges of either's woe.

THEME

If a man could experience pure Consciousness, he could transcend time and space by thought alone. Identified with the heavy overcoat of the fleshy body, one must travel at the convenience of lumbering time.

GLOSSARY

If the dull substance of my flesh were thought, Injurious distance should not stop my way; For then, despite of space, I would be brought, From limits far remote, where thou dost stay.

> If the gross material substance of my flesh were converted to thought or consciousness, the impediment of physical distance could not bar my passage. For then, in spite of any distance, I would be brought from the farthest corners of the universe, to where Thou art.

No matter then although my foot did stand Upon the furthest earth remov'd from thee; For nimble thought can jump both sea and land, As soon as think the place where he would be.

> It would be of no consequence then, although my foot did stand upon the farthest corner of the earth removed from thee. For nimble thought can jump both sea and land, as soon as I think the place where He would be.

But, ah, thought kills me that I am not thought To leap large lengths of miles when thou art gone, But that, so much of earth and water wrought, I must attend time's leisure with my moan.

> But, ah! taking thought of myself (as flesh) kills me in that I am not pure Consciousness, able to leap stupendous distances when Thou art gone. Being made as a earth and water, I must wait with my complaint while time moves at its own pace.

Receiving nought by elements so slow But heavy tears, badges of either's woe.

> Receiving nothing from this gross bodily vesture but heavy tears, and the accompanying woeful badges of this physical form.

COMMENTARY

Shakespeare reflects upon the thoughts of man that are usually centered upon the physical body and this material world. If one could think of the physical "*dull substance of the flesh*" existing as thought or consciousness, physical distance would not be an obstacle—"*injurious distance should not stop my way.*" In thought alone, one can be in another place: "*despite of space. . . . For nimble thought can jump both sea and land.*" The soul, wrongly identifying itself with limited physical form, and not as part of Spirit, is prevented from experiencing the realization of higher consciousness. "*But, ah! thought kills me that I am not thought.*" Until the Poet can reach an elevated state of awareness, his complaint is that he cannot "*leap large lengths of miles when thou art gone.*" Identified with his flesh of "*earth and water,*" man "*must attend time's leisure*" with his "*moan*" and "*heavy tears.*" These are the "*badges*" or signs that one is still attached to the "*dull substance of the flesh.*"

BIBLICAL PASSAGES SUGGESTED BY SONNET 44

"I thank God through Jesus Christ our Lord. So then with the mind I myself serve the law of God; but with the flesh the law of sin." **Rom. 7:25**

"But ye are not in the flesh, but in the Spirit, if so be that the Spirit of God dwell in you. Now if any man have not the Spirit of Christ, he is none of his." **Rom. 8:9**

SONNET 45

The other two, slight air and purging fire,
Are both with thee, wherever I abide;
The first my thought, the other my desire,
These present-absent with swift motion slide.
For when these quicker elements are gone
In tender embassy of love to thee,
My life, being made of four, with two alone
Sinks down to death, oppress'd with melancholy;
Until life's composition be recured
By those sweet messengers return'd from thee,
Who even but now come back again, assur'd
Of thy fair health, recounting it to me:
This told, I joy; but then no longer glad,
I send them back again, and straight grow sad.

THEME

The earthbound soul is in a constant battle to be reunited with Spirit. It is dragged down by the ego's desires and uplifted by spiritual thoughts. Sadness accompanies fleshly attachments while joy attends soulful prayers of love for the Divine, and the Lord's sweet response.

GLOSSARY

The other two, slight air and purging fire, Are both with thee, wherever I abide; The first my thought, the other my desire, These present-absent with swift motion slide.

> The other two, slight air and purging fire, are both with Thee, wherever I may be; The first my thought, the other my desire, these are at once here and absent with swift motion passing from one place to another.

For when these quicker elements are gone In tender embassy of love to thee, My life, being made of four, with two alone Sinks down to death, oppress'd with melancholy;

> For when these quicker elements are gone, tenderly surrendered, and sent to Thee, my life is made of four ele-

> ments, water, earth, air, and fire. With two alone, earth and water, my body sinks down to death, oppressed with melancholy.

Until life's composition be recured By those sweet messengers return'd from thee, Who even but now come back again, assur'd Of thy fair health, recounting it to me:

> Life's completeness is restored by those sweet messengers from Thee, that at this very moment recount to me the assurance of their fair, healing nature.

This told, I joy; but then no longer glad, I send them back again, and straight grow sad.

> Receiving this, I am in joy; but then no longer glad, I send the messengers back again, and immediately grow sad.

COMMENTARY

In Sonnet 44, Shakespeare introduces the themes of spiritual thoughts that have no material limitations but are able to "*jump both sea and land*" (Sonnet 44.7) and "*injurious distance*" (Sonnet 44.2); and secondly, material thoughts of the "*dull substance*" of the flesh made of so much "*earth and water.*" (Sonnet 44.1, 11) The latter leads to "*heavy tears*" and makes one earthbound, having to attend "*time's leisure with my moan.*" (Sonnet 44.12, 14)

In Sonnet 45, Shakespeare's focus is on the elements of "*air*" and "*fire,*" neither of which are earthbound, but are of a heavenly nature. Air is "*the first* [which is] *my thought,*" and the second, "*purging fire,*" which cleanses the soul of earthly desires. Thoughts of the spiritual and worldly alternate. "*These present-absent with swift motion slide.*"

The Poet avers that life is made of four elements. When life is composed of "*two alone,*" earth and water, which are elements of the "*flesh*" (Sonnet 44.1), this causes one to sink "*down to death*" and to be "*oppress'd with melancholy.*" The correct balance of "*life's composition*" may only be restored by those swift messengers returned "*from thee.*" These alone give assurance of "*fair health.*" Joy comes to one who sends his thought "*in tender embassy of love.*" Such a person has life restored to equilibrium by the response of "*sweet messengers return'd from thee.*"

All is "*joy*" until the "*swift messengers*" of responding love are sent "*back again.*" This occurs when pure "*thought*" slides "*with swift motion*" back to the "*purging fire*" of "*desire.*" "*This told, I joy; but then no longer glad, I send them back again, and straight grow sad.*"

BIBLICAL PASSAGES SUGGESTED BY SONNET 45

"Then we which are alive and remain shall be caught up together with them in the clouds, to meet the Lord in the air: and so shall we ever be with the Lord." **1 Thess. 4:17**

"Everything that may abide the fire, ye shall make it go through the fire, and it shall be clean: nevertheless it shall be purified with the water of separation: and all that abideth not the fire ye shall make go through the water." **Num. 31:23**

"If any man's work shall be burned, he shall suffer loss: but he himself shall be saved; yet so as by fire." **1 Cor. 3:15**

"That the trial of your faith, being much more precious than of gold that perisheth, though it be tried with fire, might be found unto praise and honor and glory at the appearing of Jesus Christ." **1 Pet. 1:7**

"For by fire and by his sword will the Lord plead with all flesh: and the slain of the Lord shall be many." **Isa. 66:16**

"He sendeth forth his commandment upon earth: his word runneth very swiftly." **Ps. 147.15**

SONNET 46

Mine eye and heart are at a mortal war,
How to divide the conquest of thy sight,
Mine eye my heart thy picture's sight would bar,
My heart mine eye the freedom of that right.
My heart doth plead that thou in him dost lie,
(A closet never pierced with crystal eyes)
But the defendant doth that plea deny,
And says in him thy fair appearance lies.
To 'cide this title is impannelled
A quest of thoughts, all tenants to the heart;
And by their verdict is determined
The clear eye's moiety and the dear heart's part:
As thus, mine eye's due is thine outward part,
And my heart's right thy inward love of heart.

THEME

Which is greater, spiritual vision and insight or divine love? One who feels God as Love prefers it over insight or Wisdom, but both have a rightful place as expressions of Spirit.

GLOSSARY

Mine eye and heart are at a mortal war, How to divide the conquest of thy sight, Mine eye my heart thy picture's sight would bar, My heart mine eye the freedom of that right.

Mine eye and heart are at a mortal war, how to divide the conquest of Thy sight, my eyes (focused on the mundane) prevent my (soulful) heart from seeing the vision of Thee, my heart's earthly desires prevent my (spiritual) eye the rightful privilege of seeing Thee.

My heart doth plead that thou in him dost lie, (A closet never pierced with crystal eyes) But the defendant doth that plea deny, And says in him thy fair appearance lies.

My heart raises the plea that inside of it, Thou art present. (A chamber of devotion never pierced by crystal eyes.) But the accused (the eyes) denies the accusation, and says in him (them) Thy beautiful vision abides.

To 'cide this title is impannelled A quest of thoughts, all tenants to the heart; And by their verdict is determined The clear eye's moiety and the dear heart's part:

To decide which is correct there are impannelled questioning thoughts, all of which naturally inhabit the heart; and, by their verdict, is determined the rightful claim belonging to spiritual sight (eyes) and the just claim of the loving heart.

As thus, mine eye's due is thine outward part, And my heart's right thine inward love of heart.

And so the verdict is rendered: to my eyes belong Thine outward (material) expression; to my heart belongs Thy nature as pure Love.

COMMENTARY

This Sonnet presents the case of which is greater: spiritual vision or inwardly felt divine love? Which has a greater claim: the eyes that can see the material creation and are capable of spiritual perception, or the heart that either desires worldly things or prefers love of the soul? If the heart is searched, the "*tenants*" of love and devotion reach the verdict that to the heart belongs "*thine inward love of heart*," or divine love; and to clear, spiritually-perceptive eyes belongs the manifestation of intuitive pure vision: "*The clear eye's moiety*." Spirit is both Love and Wisdom, feeling and intelligence. In that sacred chamber or "*closet never pierced with crystal eyes*," there abides pure Love, which may be expressed outwardly or felt inwardly as coming from the Spirit. Spiritual vision or insight, when perceived, is greatly uplifting, or it may be a window to the soul's intuition. Spiritual insight, intuition, and vision are themes previously explored in Sonnets 5, 7, 14, 24, 27, and 33. This Sonnet's verdict is reached by the jury impannelled by "*A quest of thoughts, all the tenants to the heart*." When the soulful heart feels divine love, it jealously believes this alone is the correct nature of Spirit. In reality, of course, Spirit is both Love and Divine Intelligence or Wisdom. Neither alone can claim "*title*" to being God's true nature.

BIBLICAL PASSAGES SUGGESTED BY SONNET 46

"But as for them whose heart walketh after the heart of their detestable things and their abominations, I will recompense their way upon their own heads, saith the Lord God." **Ezek. 11:21**

"Afterwards the spirit took me up, and brought me in a vision by the Spirit of God into Chaldea, to them of the captivity. So the vision that I had seen went up from me." **Ezek. 11:24**

"A new heart also will I give you, and a new spirit will I put within you: and I will take away the stony heart out of your flesh, and I will give you an heart of flesh." **Ezek. 36:26**

"But the Lord said unto Samuel, Look not on his countenance, or on the height of his stature; because I have refused him: for the Lord seeth not as man seeth; for man looketh on the outward appearance, but the Lord looketh on the heart." **1 Sam. 16:7**

"The statutes of the Lord are right, rejoicing the heart: the commandment of the Lord is pure, enlightening the eyes." **Ps. 19:8**

"My heart is fixed, O God, my heart is fixed: I will sing and give praise." **Ps. 57:7**

"And I will give them an heart to know me, that I am the Lord: and they shall be my people, and I will be their God: for they shall return unto me with their whole heart." **Jer. 24:7**

"The Lord by wisdom hath founded the earth; by understanding hath he established the heavens." **Prov. 3:19**

"The light of the body is the eye: if therefore thine eye be single, thy whole body shall be full of light." **Matt. 6:22**

SONNET 47

Betwixt mine eye and heart a league is took,
And each doth good turns now unto the other,
When that mine eye is famished for a look,
Or heart in love with sighs himself doth smother,
With my love's picture then my eye doth feast,
And to the painted banquet bids my heart.
Another time mine eye is my heart's guest,
And in his thoughts of love doth share a part.
So either by thy picture or my love,
Thyself away art present still with me;
For thou not farther than my thoughts canst move,
And I am still with them and they with thee;
Or, if they sleep, thy picture in my sight
Awakes my heart, to heart's and eye's delight.

THEME

Spirit is both visible and invisible. The scriptures declare that God may appear as Light or be felt as Love. When one cannot see with "blind eyes," one may still invoke the soul's love in prayer; or when the heart seems empty, it can with loving eyes see the beauty of the Spirit all around. In either instance, the soul is uplifted again into joy.

GLOSSARY

Betwixt mine eye and heart a league is took, And each doth good turns now unto the other, When that mine eye is famished for a look, Or heart in love with sighs himself doth smother,

> Between mine eye and my heart an agreement of mutual assistance is reached, and each now does assist the other: When the eye is starving for a vision, or when the loving heart, full of sighs, is suffocating,

With my love's picture then my eye doth feast, And to the painted banquet bids my heart. Another time mine eye is my heart's guest, And in his thoughts of love doth share a part.

> Seeing a vision of my Beloved, mine eye feasts, and invites the heart to partake of the full cup; another time mine eye is my heart's guest, and in his (heart's) thoughts of love does share a part.

So either by thy picture or my love, Thyself away art present still with me; For thou not farther than my thoughts canst move, And I am still with them and they with thee;

> So either by a vision of Thee, or feeling my heart's love, even in Thy seeming absence, Thou art always present with me; for Thou art no further away than my thoughts, and I am always absorbed within them, and Thy Love within Thee;

Or, if they sleep, thy picture in my sight Awakes my heart, to heart's and eye's delight.

> Or if they sleep, Thy vision in my spiritual sight awakens my heart's love, to the mutual joy of both heart and eyes.

COMMENTARY

Spiritual vision invites the glory of God into one's being and into the inner court ("*closet*") of the heart. (Sonnet 46.6) As expressed in Sonnet 46, the Spirit has both the attributes of Love and Wisdom. The opened eyes are awakened to God's presence as Light, or divine understanding, or Wisdom. The heart is the center of love and feeling. The Lord is described as an omniscient, or all-knowing, Consciousness, and also the source of all Love. It requires divine Intelligence for the universe to continue to operate and also divine Love and Compassion. As divine attributes reflected in man, neither is really in a "*mortal war*" (Sonnet 46.1) unless, and until, the ego intervenes to cloud one's judgment (spiritual sight) or lead one's heart toward material desires instead of unselfish love—"*the dear heart's part.*" (Sonnet 46.12) Sonnet 47 resolves the issue by showing that a cooperative balance restores "*life's composition.*" (Sonnet 45.9) "*Betwixt mine eye and heart a league is took, And each doth good turns now unto the other.*" When one is expressing either divine understanding (spiritual sight) or divine love (heart), God can never be absent. "*For thou not farther than my thoughts canst move.*" "*With my love's picture then my eye doth feast, And to the painted banquet bids my heart. Another time mine eye is my heart's guest, And in his thoughts of love doth share a part.*" What a state of joy and blessing "*to heart's and eye's delight.*"

BIBLICAL PASSAGES SUGGESTED BY SONNET 47

"Afterward he brought me to the gate, even the gate that looketh toward the east:" **Ezek. 43:1**

"For by him were all things created, that are in heaven, and that are in earth, visible and invisible, whether they be thrones, or dominions, or principalities, or powers: all things were created by him, and for him:" **Col. 1:16**

"And the Lord said unto him, I have heard thy prayer and thy supplication, that thou hast made before me: I have hallowed this house, which thou hast built, to put my name there for ever; and mine eyes and mine heart shall be there perpetually." **1 Kings 9:3**

"We have also a more sure work of prophecy; whereunto ye do well that ye take heed, as unto a light that shineth in a dark place, until the day dawn, and the day star arise in your hearts." **2 Pet. 1:19**

"As for me, I will behold thy face in righteousness: I shall be satisfied, when I awake, with thy likeness." **Ps. 17:15**

"For I delight in the law of God after the inward man." **Rom. 7:22**

SONNET 48

How careful was I when I took my way,
Each trifle under truest bars to thrust,
That to my use it might unused stay
From hands of falsehood, in sure wards of trust!
But thou, to whom my jewels trifles are,
Most worthy comfort, now my greatest grief,
Thou best of dearest and mine only care,
Art left the prey of every vulgar thief.
Thee have I not lock'd up in any chest,
Save where thou art not, though I feel thou art,
Within the gentle closure of my breast,
From whence at pleasure thou mayst come and part;
And even thence thou wilt be stol'n, I fear,
For truth proves thievish for a prize so dear.

THEME

The spiritual journey is a double-edged sword. Self-deception and ignorance subtly undermine the path. The goal is difficult to achieve, and one's frailties and fears can steal away victory. By divine Grace one is afforded a guiding Light along the way.

GLOSSARY

How careful was I when I took my way, Each trifle under truest bars to thrust, That to my use it might unused stay From hands of falsehood, in sure wards of trust

> How careful I was when I began my journey, each diversion stowed beneath faithful restraints that it might to my expense remain inaccessible from the grasp of falsehood, in the confines of trusted wardens.

But thou, to whom my jewels trifles are, Most worthy comfort, now my greatest grief, Thou best of dearest and mine only care, Art left the prey of every vulgar thief.

> But Thou, to whom my precious possessions are trifles,

> most valued solace, now greatest grief, Thou dearest of the dear, and all I really care about, art kept out of reach by my common, worldly thoughts.

Thee have I not lock'd up in any chest, Save where thou art not, though I feel thou art, Within the gentle closure of my breast, From whence at pleasure thou mayst come and part;

> Thee I have not locked up in any chest, except for the place it seems Thou are not, though I feel Thou art there. Thou art, within the sweet encasement of my heart, and from where at Thy pleasure Thou mayst come and go;

And even thence thou wilt be stol'n, I fear, For truth proves thievish for a prize so dear.

> And even from there, I am afraid Thou wilt be stolen, for even what seems true may steal away a prize so dear.

COMMENTARY

In Sonnet 26.10, Shakespeare mentions the journey and hopes "*whatsoever star*" that guides his moving, points on him graciously with fair "*aspect.*" In Sonnet 27.11 his thoughts make a zealous pilgrimage to the "*jewel hung in ghastly night.*" On his journey, in Sonnet 34, he travels without his "*cloak*" and is overtaken in his journey, encountering the "*rotten smoke*" of base clouds. (Sonnet 34.2, 4) The path has a contrasting dualistic nature wherein "*Roses have thorns, and silver fountains mud.*" (Sonnet 35.2) But always there is a deep desire to see the Beloved: "*All days are nights to see till I see thee.*" (Sonnet 43.13) The path requires a balance of love and wisdom until "*life's composition be recur'ed.*" (Sonnet 45.9)

In Sonnet 48, our traveler takes every precaution to keep "*Each trifle*" of base thought or desire "*under truest bars.*" Now he travels with his "*cloak,*" and each deceitful imperfection is held in check "*in sure wards of trust.*" But where the traveler may *think* God is, "*Thou art not*"; but with feeling he *knows*: "*I feel thou art, Within the gentle closure of my breast.*" The Lord, however, comes when He chooses, and to receive is an aspect of Grace. Fear shuts out the light of Spirit, and that which one puts one's faith in wrongly "*proves thievish for a prize so dear.*"

BIBLICAL PASSAGES SUGGESTED BY SONNET 48

"Now the serpent was more subtil than any beast of the field which the Lord God had made. And he said unto the woman, Yea, hath God said, Ye shall not eat of every tree of the garden?" **Gen. 3:1**

"He that trusteth in his own heart is a fool: but whoso walketh wisely he shall be delivered." **Prov. 28:26**

"For the thing which I greatly feared is come upon me, and that which I was afraid of is come unto me." **Job 3:25**

"There is no fear in love; but perfect love casteth out fear: because fear hath torment. He that feareth is not made perfect in love." **1 John 4:18**

"Sell that ye have, and give alms; provide yourselves bags which wax not old, a treasure in the heavens that faileth not, where no thief approacheth, neither moth corrupteth." **Luke 12:33**

"And I gave my heart to seek and search out by wisdom concerning all things that are done under heaven: this sore travail hath God given to the sons of man to be exercised therewith." **Eccl. 1:13**

ADDITIONAL REFERENCES

The Nobel laureate poet, Rabindranath Tagore, in his "Thou Art My Life," expresses the seeker's thoughts in Sonnet 48. "Thou art my life, thou art my love, thou art the sweetness which I do seek. In the thought by my love brought, I taste thy name so sweet. Devotee knows how sweet you are. He knows whom you let know."

In *The Conversations and Letters of Brother Lawrence* (Oxford: One World, 1993), Brother Lawrence, a lay brother of the Carmelite Order in Paris who has long been revered for his humility and simple, faith-filled approach to God, expresses the following about God: "We have a God who is infinitely gracious, and knows all our wants. He will come in His own time, and when you least expect it." ("Third Letter," p. 41.) "He disposes of hearts as He pleases" ("Tenth Letter," p. 64).

SONNET 49

Against that time, if ever that time come,
When I shall see thee frown on my defects,
When as thy love hath cast his utmost sum,
Call'd to that audit by advis'd respects;
Against that time when thou shalt strangely pass,
And scarcely greet me with that sun, thine eye,
When love, converted from the thing it was,
Shall reasons find of settled gravity;
Against that time do I ensconce me here
Within the knowledge of mine own desert,
And this my hand against myself uprear,
To guard the lawful reasons on thy part:
To leave poor me thou hast the strength of laws,
Since why to love I can allege no cause.

THEME

In humility, one offers neither self justification, nor alleges self merit, but in faith and surrender yields to the Lord's Will and Justice.

GLOSSARY

Against that time, if ever that time come, When I shall see thee frown on my defects, When as thy love hath cast his utmost sum, Call'd to that audit by advis'd respects;

In preparation for that time (if ever that time come) when I shall see Thee frown on my defects, and at the time when Thy Love has expressed itself to the greatest extent possible, in light of all respects and conditions which called it forth:

Against that time when thou shalt strangely pass, And scarcely greet me with that sun, thine eye, When love, converted from the thing it was, Shall reasons find of settled gravity;

In preparation for that time when Thou shalt pass by like a stranger, and scarcely greet me with the shining Light

> of Thine eye; when love, changed from what it had been, shall find justifications in established precedent;

Against that time do I ensconce me here Within the knowledge of mine own desert, And this my hand against myself uprear, To guard the lawful reasons on thy part:

> In preparation for that time, I do fortify myself within the knowledge of my own deserving merits, and raise my hand solemnly against myself, and to defend the lawful reasons on Thy part.

To leave poor me thou hast the strength of laws, Since why to love I can allege no cause.

> To leave poor me, Thou hast every right, since I can allege no just cause as to why Thou shouldst love me.

COMMENTARY

In Sonnet 48.7 is expressed a great reverence for the "*best of dearest and mine only care.*" One on the spiritual path wants to take every precaution not to lose the One who is the "*most worthy comfort*" (Sonnet 48.6), and yet knowing that God comes when He will, there is fear of losing the Beloved's Grace. "*And even thence thou wilt be stol'n, I fear.*" (Sonnet 48.13)

In Sonnet 49, the fear continues as the Poet believes the time will come when God will "*frown*" upon him and pass him by, as a stranger might, because of his "*defects.*" Shakespeare is, however, resigned to such an event because the Lord can find reasons of "*settled gravity*" and in the "*strength of laws.*" Furthermore, the Poet himself acknowledges the "*audit*" of his "*defects,*" and with his own hands points to his flaws ("*my hand against myself*"). The treatment he receives is his "*own desert.*" Even after receiving much blessing and grace, Shakespeare says of the spiritual aspirant that he may believe, in all humility, that his lack of merit will ultimately cause a loss of the Lord's favor. "*To leave poor me thou hast the strength of laws.*" Brother Lawrence speaks to this time, even after years of having received the great joy and consolation of God's presence: "Such was my beginning; and yet I must tell you that for the first ten years I suffered much: the apprehension that I was not devoted to God as I wished to be, my past sins always present to my mind, and the great unmerited favors which God did me were the matter and source of my sufferings. During this time I fell often, and rose again presently. It seemed to me that the creatures, reason, and God Himself were against me, and faith alone for me. I troubled sometimes with thoughts that to believe I had received such favors was an effect of my presumption, which pretended to be at once where others arrive with difficulty; at other times that it was a willful delusion, and that there was no salvation for me." (*The Conversations and Letters of Brother Lawrence,* "Second Letter," p. 35)

Why does the traveler lose faith or despair in the journey? Why did the freed slaves of Egypt continue to lose faith in spite of the many blessings they received? Perhaps it is a test of one's faith, of one's true willingness or mettle to seek God. Shakespeare, in this Sonnet, expresses the same fear and humility as others who have made, and are still making the spiritual journey.

BIBLICAL PASSAGES SUGGESTED BY SONNET 49

"And the children of Israel said unto them, Would to God we had died by the hand of the Lord in the land of Egypt, when we sat by the flesh pots, and when we did eat bread to the full; for ye have brought us forth into this wilderness, to kill this whole assembly with hunger." **Exod. 16:3**

"And the people thirsted there for water; and the people murmured against Moses, and said, Wherefore is this that thou hast brought us up out of Egypt, to kill us and our children and our cattle with thirst? **Exod. 17:3**

"And thou shalt remember all the way which the Lord thy God led thee these forty years in the wilderness, to humble thee, and to prove thee, to know what was in thine heart, whether thou wouldest keep his commandments, or no." **Deut. 8:2**

"How long wilt thou forget me, O Lord? For ever? How long wilt thou hide thy face from me?" **Ps. 13:1**

"Be patient therefore, brethren, unto the coming of the Lord, Behold, the husbandman waiteth for the precious fruit of the earth, and hath long patience for it, until he receive the early and latter rain. Be ye also patient; stablish your hearts: for the coming of the Lord draweth nigh." **James 5:7-8**

SONNET 50

How heavy do I journey on the way,
When what I seek, my weary travel's end,
Doth teach that ease and that repose to say,
"Thus far the miles are measur'd from thy friend."
The beast that bears me, tired with my woe,
Plods dully on, to bear that weight in me,
As if by some instinct the wretch did know
His rider lov'd not speed, being made from thee:
The bloody spur cannot provoke him on
That sometimes anger thrusts into his hide,
Which heavily he answers with a groan
More sharp to me than spurring to his side,
For that same groan doth put this in my mind:
My grief lies onward, and my joy behind.

THEME

The spiritual journey is sometimes long, but it has much to teach each one along the way. The soul inhabits a mortal body that often suffers the pains of wrongful behavior and no amount of anger or prodding can bring the journey to an end. In despair, it may seem that only more sorrow is ahead, and that the goal is far away.

GLOSSARY

How heavy do I journey on the way, When what I seek, my weary travel's end, Doth teach that ease and that repose to say, "Thus far the miles are measur'd from thy friend."

> How heavy do I journey on my way, when what I seek is my weary travel's end. There I might find comfort and repose which will give me the understanding to say. 'How very long has been the distance you have been from thy friend',

The beast that bears me, tired with my woe, Plods dully on, to bear that weight in me, As if by some instinct the wretch did know His rider lov'd not speed, being made from thee:

> This mortal frame that bears my soul, weary with my sorrow, plods sluggishly on to bear that weight in me. It is as if by some instinct this overburdened body did know that his soulful inhabitant did not love the speed with which it was carried from Thee.

The bloody spur cannot provoke him on That sometimes anger thrusts into his hide, Which heavily he answers with a groan More sharp to me than spurring to his side,

> The bloody spur, sometimes inflicted in anger, cannot provoke him to move more quickly along. He answers mournfully with a groan that is more painful to my soul than spurring to his side.

For that same groan doth put this in my mind: My grief lies onward, and my joy behind.

> For that same groan does bring to my mind, that ahead is more grieving and my joy behind.

COMMENTARY

In the previous sonnets, the Poet revisited the nature of the spiritual path and the tests along the way. Shakespeare seeks his "*weary travel's end*" and sounds a little like Job: "My soul is weary of my life; I will leave my complaint upon myself; I will speak in the bitterness of my soul" (**10:1**); "Wherefore is light given to him that is in misery, and life unto the bitter in soul" (**3:20**); "My days are swifter than a weaver's shuttle, and are spent without hope." (**7:6**)

The body is weary of the long journey, and the traveler is tested by life's travails: "*How heavy do I journey on the way, When what I seek, my weary travel's end. . . . The best that bears me, tired with my woe, Plods dully on, to bear that weight in me.*" No impatience is tolerated along the way. "*The bloody spur cannot provoke him on That sometimes anger thrusts into his hide.*"

One feels the weighty burden expressed in this Sonnet for the long and weary journey. Complaints and groans accompany the way, and sometimes discouragement. "*For that same groan doth put this in my mind: My grief lies onward, and my joy behind.*" "And not only they, but ourselves also, which have the first fruits of the Spirit, even we ourselves groan, within our selves, waiting for the adoption, to wit, the redemption of our body." **(Rom. 8:23)**

But still the traveler moves on.

SONNET 51

Thus can my love excuse the slow offence
Of my dull bearer when from thee I speed:
From where thou art why should I haste me thence?
Till I return, of posting is no need.
O what excuse will my poor beast then find,
When swift extremity can seem but slow?
Then should I spur, though mounted on the wind,
In winged speed no motion shall I know,
Then can no horse with my desire keep pace;
Therefore desire, of perfect'st love being made,
Shall neigh no dull flesh in his fiery race,
But love, for love, thus shall excuse my jade,
Since from thee going he went willful slow,
Towards thee I'll run and give him leave to go.

THEME

The soul is like a charioteer sometimes carried away by the steed of wrong desires. Innately realizing, through conscience and intuition, its directionless error, the intelligently-guided will turns toward Spirit. The incorrect actions of the past are somewhat mitigated by the fact that at least, when moving wrongly, the movement was slow.

GLOSSARY

Thus can my love excuse the slow offence Of my dull bearer when from thee I speed: From where thou art why should I haste me thence? Till I return, of posting is no need.

> Can my love excuse the sluggard offense of this temporal, desirous flesh when from Thee I speed away? From where Thou art, why should I go hastily? Until I turn myself around, I have no need of great speed.

O what excuse will my poor beast then find, When swift extremity can seem but slow? Then should I spur, though mounted on the wind, In winged speed no motion shall I know,

Oh what excuse will this mortal frame find then when maximum speed can seem but slow? Then I should spirit ahead as if mounted on the wind, and in winged speed I am not conscious of my movement at all.

Then can no horse with my desire keep pace; Therefore desire, of perfect'st love being made, Shall neigh no dull flesh in his fiery race, But love, for love, thus shall excuse my jade,

Then no physical vehicle could match the speed of my soul's desire. And that wish of being united with the most perfect Love shall call out not, as material flesh in his fiery race to Thee, but by the impelling force of Love; for Love alone shall excuse the previous slow pace of this sorrowful mortal.

Since from thee going he went willful slow, Towards thee I'll run and give him leave to go.

Since in his going away from Thee, he intentionally went slowly; but to Thee, I will run and give leave for all mortal, worldly things to depart.

COMMENTARY

Sonnet 50 expresses the author's lament and weariness of a life lived incorrectly. The body and mind is "*tired with my woe*" (Sonnet 50.5) bearing the "*weight in me.*" (Sonnet 50.6) The soul, however, depicted as "*His rider*" (Sonnet 50.8), moves "*by some instinct*"(Sonnet 50.7) or intuition and understands that moving away from the spiritual path was wrong and therefore "*lov'd not speed, being made from thee*" (Sonnet 50.8), i.e. of Spirit. It prods along, however, in discouragement, feeling that more "*grief lies onward*" (Sonnet 50.14) and that the joy of "*travel's end*" (Sonnet 50.2) is being left farther behind.

In Sonnet 51, man's inherent spiritual nature and conscience is going in the wrong direction, or at least slowly "*when from thee I speed.*" "*Thus can my love excuse the slow offence Of my dull bearer when from thee I speed, From where thou art why should I haste me thence?*" There is no need for speed in the wrong direction. "*Till I return, of posting is no need.*"

In Sonnet 50, spurring the "*The beast that bears me*" (Sonnet 50.5) was only met with heavy "*groan.*" (Sonnet 50.11) The traveler was weary and discouraged. (See Biblical citations in Sonnet 50.) In Sonnet 51, the rider-as-soul takes command, with willful desire, to be united with the most perfect love of Spirit. "*Then should I spur, though mounted on the wind, in winged speed no motion shall I know.*" Then on eternal wings it is propelled, and all past error is forgiven ("*shall excuse my jade*"). The winged soul flies heavenward in its fiery chariot leaving bodily attachment behind with "*leave to go.*"

BIBLICAL PASSAGES SUGGESTED BY SONNET 51

"Who layeth the beams of his chambers in the waters: who maketh the clouds his chariot: who walketh upon the wings of the wind: Who maketh his angels spirits; his ministers a flaming fire" **Ps. 104:3-4**

"Was the Lord displeased against the rivers? was thine anger against the rivers? was thy wrath against the sea, that thou didst ride upon thine horses and thy chariots of salvation?" **Hab. 3:8**

"At thy rebuke, O God of Jacob, both the chariot and horse are cast into a dead sleep." **Ps. 76:6**

"And it came to pass, as they still went on, and talked, that, behold, there appeared a chariot of fire, and horses of fire, and parted them both asunder; and Elijah went up by a whirlwind into heaven." **2 Kings 2:11**

"But they that wait upon the Lord shall renew their strength; they shall mount up with wings as eagles; they shall run, and not be weary; and they shall walk, and not faint." **Isa. 40:31**

SONNET 52

So am I as the rich, whose blessed key
Can bring him to his sweet up-locked treasure,
The which he will not every hour survey,
For blunting the fine point of seldom pleasure.
Therefore are feasts so solemn and so rare,
Since, seldom coming, in the long year set,
Like stones of worth they thinly placed are,
Or captain jewels in the carcanet.
So is the time that keeps you as my chest,
Or as the wardrobe which the robe doth hide,
To make some special instant special blest
By new unfolding his imprison'd pride.
Blessed are you, whose worthiness gives scope,
Being had, to triumph; being lack'd, to hope.

THEME

Once the sought-after heavenly goal is within reach, every new experience of the soul is dearly treasured. With each new spiritual contact, he feels himself in glory and even while waiting on the Lord, he is ever hopeful.

GLOSSARY

So am I as the rich, whose blessed key Can bring him to his sweet up-locked treasure, The which he will not every hour survey, For blunting the fine point of seldom pleasure.

> So am I as one who is rich with the blessed key that can open the way to the sweet celestial locked-up treasure, which he will not constantly examine, so as to not blunt the rare pleasure perceived by precise one-pointed attention.

Therefore are feasts so solemn and so rare, Since, seldom coming, in the long year set, Like stones of worth they thinly placed are, Or captain jewels in the carcanet.

> And such are as feast days, specially celebrated and regarded, since they come infrequently, as is ordained in the long span of a lifetime. Like precious stones they are infrequently encountered, or as the very most precious gems, they are carefully set in the jeweled necklace.

So is the time that keeps you as my chest, Or as the wardrobe which the robe doth hide, To make some special instant special blest By new unfolding his imprison'd pride.

> So are the special moments which keep you as my heart's treasure, just as in a wardrobe one hides a special garment to make some moment especially blessed, by newly unfolding his imprisoned pride.

Blessed are you, whose worthiness gives scope, Being had, to triumph; being lack'd, to hope.

> Blessed are you whose inherent nature brings one to the goal, which once attained, is triumphant glory, and lacked, is yet hoped for.

COMMENTARY

Sonnet 52 is a marvelous literary sonnet rich with the interplay of words and meanings that exemplify Shakespeare's genius. One key to unlocking this Sonnet is understanding the use of the word "*scope*." The *Oxford English Dictionary* indicates the following definitions of "scope" in Shakespeare's time: (1) "The goal or terminal point of a race, a journey"; (1b) "something aimed at or desired"; (2) "A person who is an object of desire or pursuit"; and also, "T.B. *La Pamaud. Fr. Acad.11*. to God, who is the scope, which we desire and shall one day attain unto."

Sonnet 52 is an important threshold in the Sonnets. The early Sonnets speak of the wisdom of right behavior and the correct use of free will. Reference is made to the beauty of the Spirit, or the purpose and joy in life of developing one's soul nature. The author, through the wisdom of the Sonnets, reveals that he has been on a spiritual journey and has seen the divine light present in the spiritual eye, and felt its divine sweetness ("*love's delight*"). He finds that God encompasses all "*worth and truth.*" "[*B*]*eauty, birth or wealth, or wit, or any of these all, or all, or more.*" (Sonnet 37.4-5) The Lord is beyond the capacity of any poet to express, even under inspiration or "*Muse.*" (Sonnet 38.1)

More alluring than all things, the Divine yet comes when He chooses. "*But here's the joy; my friend and I are one.*" (Sonnet 42.13) How to find and hold on to the Beloved either in one's sight, or heart, or both, is challenging. (Sonnets 46-47) One journeys on to find the "*best of dearest.*" (Sonnet 48.7)

Finally in Sonnet 52, the traveler has received the "*blessed key*" that can bring him to the "*sweet up-locked treasure.*" The key here is spiritual in nature; it does not immediately unlock, but "*Can bring*" the traveler to his "*up-locked treasure.*" Such a key is symbolic of course, and is mentioned in the Bible as "the key of the house of David" that can "open and none shall shut" ("And the key of the house of David will I lay upon his shoulder; so he shall open, and none shall shut; and he shall shut, and none shall open." **Isa. 22:22**) It is referred to also in Matthew and other biblical verses: "And I will give unto thee the keys of the kingdom of heaven: and whatsoever thou shalt bind on earth shall be bound in heaven: and whatsoever thou shalt loose on earth shall be loosed in heaven." (**Matt. 16:19**) "And to the angel of the church in Philadelphia write; these things saith he that is holy, he that is true, he that hath the key of David, he that openeth, and no man shutteth; and shutteth, and no man openeth." **(Rev. 3:7)** The key brings him to his "*up-locked treasure.*" The *Oxford English Dictionary* records the use of "up-locked" in this very Sonnet: "*Up*" signifies celestial, the place which is above. "*Treasure*" is the heavenly kingdom which is the "*travel's end*" (Sonnet 50.2) that has been previously out of reach or *locked* away.

Our traveler does not say how he received the "*blesed key,*" but Isaiah may give a clue: "And an highway shall be there, and a way, and it shall be called The way of holiness; the unclean shall not pass over it; but it shall be for those: the wayfaring men, though fools, shall not err therein" **(Isa. 35:8)**. The place of the sojourner's end is not without, but within the heart. It is the "*dear heart's part*" (Sonnet 46.12), "*the gentle closure of my breast*" (Sonnet 48.11) into which the beloved comes and goes: "*at pleasure thou mayest come and part.*" (Sonnet 48.12) This treasure is kept as the heart's love; it is not analyzed or examined mentally ("*he will not every hour survey*"), for the mind is the slayer of soul, and it can steal away the one-pointed devotional attention, "*For blunting the fine point.*" The treasure is won by the heart, not the mind. "But thou, when thou prayest, enter into thy closet, and when thou hast shut thy door, pray to thy Father which is in secret; and thy Father which seeth thee in secret shall reward thee openly. But when ye pray, use not vain repetitions, as the heathen do: for they think that they shall be heard for their much speaking." **(Matt. 6:6-7)**

The wardrobe which is the closet for the hidden robe is *within.* It makes special moments blest by "*new unfolding his imprison'd pride.*" The Matthew verse's reference to "closet" and "secret" are played upon in the Sonnet as the "*wardrobe*" and "*robe*" which, with the mention of "*jewels,*" has special Biblical significance. "I will greatly rejoice in the Lord, my soul shall be joyful in my God; for he hath clothed me with the garments of salvation, he hath covered me with the robe of righteousness, as a bridegroom decketh himself with ornaments, and as a bride herself with her jewels." **(Isa. 61:10)**

Shakespeare intentionally uses his words to play upon both their secular and spiritual meanings. The robe, as a spiritual mantel, not only brings blessing, but it does so each time that pride, which is both imprisoned in the ego, and imprisoning to the soul, is again and again unfolded and released. The soul's sacred qualities ("*worthiness*") bring one at last to God, the goal of its journey, or "*scope.*" In a triumph of glory, and even when the Lord is absent ("*being lacked*") from the consciousness, "*seldom coming, in the long year set,*" the heart is yet filled with hope. "*Blessed are you, whose worthiness gives scope, Being had, to triumph; being lack'd, to hope.*"

BIBLICAL PASSAGES SUGGESTED BY SONNET 52

"For we are saved by hope: but hope that is seen is not hope: for what a man seeth, why doth he yet hope for? But if we hope for that we see not, then do we with patience wait for it." **Rom. 8:24-25**

SONNET 53

What is your substance, whereof are you made,
That millions of strange shadows on you tend?
Since every one hath, every one, one shade,
And you, but one, can every shadow lend.
Describe Adonis, and the counterfeit
Is poorly imitated after you;
On Helen's cheek all art of beauty set,
And you in Grecian tires are painted new.
Speak of the spring and foison of the year,
The one doth shadow of your beauty show,
The other as your bounty doth appear;
And you in every blessed shape we know.
In all external grace you have some part,
But you like none, none you, for constant heart.

THEME

Of the One Eternal Substance are all things made, yet the world is only a mere shadow of the Creator who shall endure forever.

GLOSSARY

What is your substance, whereof are you made, That millions of strange shadows on you tend? Since every one hath, every one, one shade, And you, but one, can every shadow lend.

> What is your essence, of what are you made, that countless shadowy manifestations are your servitors, since every one has but a single reflection, and You, the Single Essence, can manifest everything that is.

Describe Adonis, and the counterfeit Is poorly imitated after you; On Helen's cheek all art of beauty set, And you in Grecian tires are painted new.

> Describe Adonis, the ideal beauty, and the material world is a poor imitation. On the face of Helen is the paragon of beauty imitated, and you clothed in all the Greek ideals and qualities are newly portrayed.

Speak of the spring and foison of the year, The one doth shadow of your beauty show, The other as your bounty doth appear; And you in every blessed shape we know.

> Speak of springtime and the harvest of the year. The one is but a poor imitation of your true Beauty, the other is a representation of Your endless Bounty, and You in every blessed aspect of creation we recognize.

In all external grace you have some part, But you like none, none you, for constant heart.

> All external manifestations of beauty contain some essence of these, but You, oh Eternal Unique, are ever-changeless Love.

COMMENTARY

"*What is your substance, whereof are you made, That millions of strange shadows on you tend?*" Shakespeare asks the question similarly found in Isaiah: "To whom then will ye liken me, or shall I be equal? saith the Holy One." **(Isa. 40:25)** All created things are but shadows that attend to the Lord ("*That millions of strange shadows on you tend.*") "O Lord, how manifold are thy works! in wisdom hast thou made them all: the earth is full of thy riches." **(Ps. 104:24)** "These wait all upon thee; that thou mayest give them their meat in due season." **(Ps. 104:27)** "Thou sendest forth thy spirit, they are created: and thou renewest the face of the earth." **(Ps. 104:30)** "For by him were all things created, that are in heaven, and that are in earth, visible and invisible, whether they be thrones, or dominions, or principalities, or powers: all things were created by him, and for him: And he is before all things, and by him all things consist." **(Col. 1:16-17)** The play on light and shadows is found in Genesis: "In the beginning God created the heaven and the earth. And the earth was without form, and void; and darkness was upon the face of the deep. And the Spirit of God moved upon the face of the waters. And God said, Let there be light: and there was light. And God saw the light, that it was good: and God divided the light from the darkness." **(Gen. 1:1-4)** God is the eternal "*constant heart,*" but the creation of "*strange shadows*" is only temporary. "Thy kingdom is an everlasting kingdom, and thy dominion endureth throughout all generations." **(Ps. 145:13)** "Heaven and earth shall pass away, but my words shall not pass away" **(Matt. 24:35)** "The grass witherest, the flower fadeth: but the word of our God shall stand for ever." **(Isa. 40:8)** "For we are strangers before thee, and sojourners, as were all our fathers: our days on the earth are as a shadow, and there is none abiding." **(1 Chr. 29:15)**

Sonnet 53 begins a new segment of inquiry and commentary by the author. In previous Sonnets, the focus has been often upon the nature of right and wrong, the soul's development and yearning, the relationship of the soul and Spirit, and the spiritual journey. Having come to this juncture in Sonnet 52, the focus in upcoming Sonnets is more upon the nature of God, or Spirit Itself, and the Divine relationship to His creation and man. Sonnet 54 continues this theme.

SONNET 54

O how much more doth beauty beauteous seem,
By that sweet ornament which truth doth give.
The rose looks fair, but fairer we it deem
For that sweet odour which doth in it live.
The canker-blooms have full as deep a dye
As the perfumed tincture of the roses,
Hang on such thorns, and play as wantonly,
When summer's breath their masked buds discloses:
But, for their virtue only is their show,
They live unwoo'd, and unrespected fade;
Die to themselves. Sweet roses do not so;
Of their sweet deaths, are sweetest odours made:
And so of you, beauteous and lovely youth,
When that shall vade, my verse distils your truth.

THEME

The true Essence and Beauty of all things lies hidden within, unseen by casual observation.

GLOSSARY

O how much more doth beauty beauteous seem, By that sweet ornament which truth doth give. The rose looks fair, but fairer we it deem For that sweet odour which doth in it live.

> Oh how much more does precious inner beauty reflect itself without when truth is uncovered. The rose is fair, but how much more it is appreciated because of its inner fragrance.

The canker-blooms have full as deep a dye As the perfumed tincture of the roses, Hang on such thorns, and play as wantonly, When summer's breath their masked buds discloses:

> The wild canker roses bloom with a fullness of color deep, just as the perfume-tinctured rose; they also are hung with thorns, and play as frivolously, when sum-

mer's wind uncovers their masked buds;

But, for their virtue only is their show, They live unwoo'd, and unrespected fade; Die to themselves. Sweet roses do not so; Of their sweet deaths, are sweetest odours made:

> But their only virtue is their appearance, they live unwoo'd, and fade unrespectfully away, dying unnoticed. Sweet roses do not do so, as their precious fallen petals are the source of a wondrous fragrance.

And so of you, beauteous and lovely youth, When that shall vade, my verse distils your truth.

> As so it is of You, beautiful and lovely Youth, when that essence shall fade, my verse uncovers Your Truth.

COMMENTARY

Here Shakespeare likens the Spirit to the hidden beauty that lies within. As "*truth doth give*" us a clearer picture, that which is the true beauty of Spirit, manifests outwardly, as here in the "*rose.*" As in Sonnet 5, the theme of beauty "*distilled*" is explored. However, Shakespeare is speaking in Sonnet 5 of each man's soul which lies dormant, and whose beauty is wasted ("*bereft*") without "*remembrance* [of] *what it was*," unless it is uncovered, "*distilled*," and allowed to flourish: "*their substance still lives sweet.*" (Sonnet 5.11, 12, 13, 14) In Sonnet 54, as in Sonnet 53, Shakespeare examines the nature of Spirit itself: behind the creation is the Creator, an aspect of which is Beauty in its pure essence. "*O how much more doth beauty beauteous seem, By that sweet ornament which truth doth give.*" People do not appreciate the truth of this, because they do not appreciate "*that sweet odour which doth in it live*," meaning within or behind the physical veil of creation. The use of "*live*" is no accident of poetry. The Poet means life itself, Essence Itself. When one sees only the external, this is what is given value: "*their virtue only is their show.*" People are drawn to the beauty of the "*rose*," but how many see the Creator behind the creation? "*They live unwoo'd, and unrespected fade; Die to themselves. Sweet roses do not so.*" When one looks deeper, and allows the physical to die ("*their sweet deaths*") one's perception penetrates to the Spirit behind, and in this "*truth*" and understanding are "*sweetest odours made.*" Finally, Shakespeare ties together a triple metaphor in his conclusion: the Creator behind the creation which is unseen; the rose, within which lives sweet odour; and the Sonnet verse, with its deeper meaning that must be distilled to reveal truth.

Superficial readings of the "*lovely youth*" Sonnets will fade and give way ("*vade*") to a deeper understanding and a realization of the "shadow sonnet" which lies beneath.

The lack of appreciation (as a "*youth*") of the Spirit behind all nature gives way as well to a deepening, mature understanding and appreciation of that aspect of God which is the pure Beauty behind all physical beauty ("*beauty beauteous*").

These progressions toward a deepening consciousness of Spirit are likened to "*sweet deaths*" of immaturity from which fragrant flowers ("*sweet odours*") of wisdom are made: just as the "*sweet odour*" lives within the rose, so hidden beneath the superficial verse is a deeper meaning or Truth to be distilled: "*my verse distils your truth.*"

BIBLICAL VERSES SUGGESTED BY SONNET 54

"To open the blind eyes, to bring out the prisoners from the prison, and them that sit in darkness out of the prison house." **Isa. 42:7**

"I am the rose of Sharon, and the lily of the valleys." **Song of Sol. 2:1**

"I will praise thee; for I am fearfully and wonderfully made: marvelous are thy works; and that my soul knoweth right well. My substance was not hid from thee, when I was made in secret, and curiously wrought in the lowest parts of the earth." **Ps. 139:14-15**

"As thou knowest not what is the way of the spirit, nor how the bones do grow in the womb of her that is with child: even so thou knowest not the works of God who maketh all" **Eccl. 11:5**

"And should sleep, and rise night and day, and the seed should spring and grow up, he knoweth not how." **Mark 4:27**

"And when he had taken the book, the four beasts and four and twenty elders fell down before the Lamb, having every one of them harps, and golden vials full of odours, which are the prayers of saints." **Rev. 5:8**

"How fair is thy love, my sister, my spouse! How much better is thy love than wine! and the smell of thine ointments than all spices!" **Song of Sol. 4:10**

"While we look not at the things which are seen, but at the things which are not seen: for the things which are seen are temporal; but the things which are not seen are eternal." **2 Cor. 4:18**

SONNET 55

Not marble, nor the gilded monuments
Of princes, shall outlive this powerful rhyme;
But you shall shine more bright in these contents
Than unswept stone, besmear'd with sluttish time.
When wasteful war shall statues overturn,
And broils root out the work of masonry,
Nor Mars his sword nor war's quick fire shall burn
The living record of your memory.
'Gainst death and all-oblivious enmity
Shall you pace forth; your praise shall still find room,
Even in the eyes of all posterity
That wear this world out to the ending doom.
So till the judgment that yourself arise,
You live in this, and dwell in lovers' eyes.

THEME

Throughout all time, the words of truth and praise of all generations shall rest in the Lord; and till the Judgment Day, those who truly love Him, will know Him as their own.

GLOSSARY

Not marble, nor the gilded monuments Of princes, shall outlive this powerful rhyme; But you shall shine more bright in these contents Than unswept stone, besmear'd with sluttish time.

> Not marble, nor gilded monuments of princes shall outlive this powerful rhyme, but You shall shine more bright in these contents than unkempt monuments ravaged by the ages.

When wasteful war shall statues overturn, And broils root out the work of masonry, Nor Mars his sword nor war's quick fire shall burn The living record of your memory.

> When wasteful war shall have overturned statues, and strife has put the masons' work asunder, neither the

sword of Mars nor war's fiery rage shall burn the living record of Your memory.

'Gainst death and all-oblivious enmity Shall you pace forth; your praise shall still find room, Even in the eyes of all posterity That wear this world out to the ending doom.

Against death, and the forces of oblivion shall You march forth in triumph; Your praises still being sung always in the eyes of every generation that inhabit this world until the ending doom.

So till the judgment that yourself arise, You live in this, and dwell in lovers' eyes.

So till the Day of Judgment and your resurrection, You live on, and dwell in lovers' eyes.

COMMENTARY

In Sonnet 54.14 Shakespeare says that his verse "*distils your truth.*" He points out that behind all creation is the Creator, but a maturing consciousness is required to fully appreciate this essence in all things. Sonnet 54 focuses upon the simple enduring Beauty of Nature, while Sonnet 55, in stark contrast, decries the superficial monuments built by man, which inevitably yield to destruction by "*sluttish time.*" In Sonnet 55, Shakespeare declares, as do the scriptures, that the Lord alone is Eternal, and will be praised for all time. Those who are true "*lovers*" of God will keep Him always in their hearts; they have "*eyes*" with which to see Him.

BIBLICAL PASSAGES SUGGESTED BY SONNET 55

"Thy kingdom is an everlasting kingdom, and thy dominion endureth throughout all generations." **Ps. 145:13**

"And this is the will of him that sent me, that every one which seeth the Son, and believeth on him, may have everlasting life: and I will raise him up at the last day." **John 6:40**

"And the Lord direct your hearts into the love of God, and into the patient waiting for Christ." **2 Thess. 3:5**

SONNET 56

Sweet love, renew thy force; be it not said
Thy edge should blunter be than appetite,
Which but today by feeding is allayed,
Tomorrow sharpen'd in his former might.
So, love, be thou, although today thou fill
Thy hungry eyes, even till they wink with fullness,
Tomorrow see again, and do not kill
The spirit of love with a perpetual dullness,
Let this sad int'rim like the ocean be
Which parts the shore, where two contracted new
Come daily to the banks, that, when they see
Return of love, more bless'd may be the view;
Or call it winter, which being full of care,
Makes summer's welcome thrice more wish'd, more rare.

THEME

The aspirant's love for the Lord must be continuous and ever deepening. This ardor brings the longed-for response and blessing.

GLOSSARY

Sweet love, renew thy force; be it not said Thy edge should blunter be than appetite, Which but today by feeding is allayed, Tomorrow sharpen'd in his former might.

> Sweet Love, renew Thy strength that it not be said that Thy power to fulfill is less than the desire to know Thee, which only for today is satisfied by feeding the soul's nature within, but tomorrow is again renewed in all its former strength.

So, love, be thou, although today thou fill Thy hungry eyes, even till they wink with fullness, Tomorrow see again, and do not kill The spirit of love with a perpetual dullness,

> So, love, although today you fill longing eyes until they can drink in no more, tomorrow look again longingly, but

> do not weaken the heavenly flow from the Spirit of Love by yielding to a habitual indifference.

Let this sad int'rim like the ocean be Which parts the shore, where two contracted new, Come daily to the banks, that, when they see Return of love, more bless'd may be the view;

> Let the sad interim between desire and fulfillment be like the ocean which parts the shores upon which young lovers stand, and where daily they stand on opposite banks full of anticipation, and when they see the return of the beloved, are more greatly blest by the sight;

Or call it winter, which being full of care, Makes summer's welcome thrice more wish'd, more rare.

> It is likened to the interim winter season filled with troubles, which makes summer's return so much more wished for, and more cherished.

COMMENTARY

Shakespeare here departs from his treatment of the aspects of Spirit, and focuses on the loving demand of the aspiring devotee for fulfillment. The metaphor of appetite and fulfillment is used as a mundane example in the first 4 lines, but this shifts immediately in lines 5-8 to the "*eyes*" of spiritual vision used by Shakespeare so frequently in the Sonnets. To receive a response, the aspirant's "*eyes*" must be "*hungry*" or desirous of the Lord's loving response. This longing must continue daily ("*Tomorrow see again*") and it must be ever-new, so as to not dissipate ("*do not kill*") the satisfying "*spirit of love*" by a habitual, monotonous demand or indifference ("*a perpetual dullness*"). In other words, to receive a deepening response from the Spirit of Love requires a deepening desire of the soul. "*Sweet love, renew thy force; be it not said Thy edge should blunter be than appetite.*"

The time between yearning and response is a "*sad int'rim.*" What is required is a return "*daily to the banks*" from which the "*hungry eyes . . . two contracted new,*" see the "*Return of love*" in more blest vision than before. The contracting of "*two*" is a coming together. "The light of the body is the eye: If therefore thine eye be single, thy whole body shall be full of light." (**Matt. 6:22**)

The metaphor of winter and summer continues the thought of desire and fulfillment. Winter follows the autumn harvest, and for some, it is a "*sad int'rim*" and "*full of care.*" The seasons change and the longed-for "*summer's welcome*" returns again.

Hungering for God is an important theme in this Sonnet, and Shakespeare says it is a prerequisite to receiving His response.

BIBLICAL PASSAGES SUGGESTED BY SONNET 56

"Blessed are they that keep his testimonies, and that seek him with the whole heart." **Ps. 119:2**

"And thou shalt love the Lord thy God with all thine heart, and with all thy soul, and with all thy might." **Deut. 6:5**

"Then shall ye call upon me, and ye shall go and pray unto me, and I will harken unto you. And ye shall seek me, and find me, when ye shall search for me with all your heart." **Jer. 29:12-13**

"And he will love thee, and bless thee, and multiply thee: he will also bless the fruit of thy womb, and the fruit of thy land, thy corn, and thy wine, and thine oil, the increase of thy kine, and the flocks of thy sheep, in the land which he sware unto thy fathers to give thee." **Deut. 7:13**

SONNET 57

Being your slave, what should I do but tend
Upon the hours and times of your desire?
I have no precious time at all to spend,
Nor services to do, till you require.
Nor dare I chide the world-without-end hour
Whilst I, my sovereign, watch the clock for you,
Nor think the bitterness of absence sour,
When you have bid your servant once adieu.
Nor dare I question with my jealous thought
Where you may be, or your affairs suppose,
But, like a sad slave, stay and think of nought
Save, where you are, how happy you make those.
So true a fool is love that in your will,
Though you do anything, he thinks no ill.

THEME

One who is completely devoted and surrendered to God, thinks often and longingly on the Lord, and knows always that His will is for the best.

GLOSSARY

Being your slave, what should I do but tend Upon the hours and times of your desire? I have no precious time at all to spend, Nor services to do, till you require.

> Being Your devoted servant, what should I do but spend my time in trying to do Your will? I have no important matters to attend to nor service to render except that it be for You.

Nor dare I chide the world-without-end hour Whilst I, my sovereign, watch the clock for you, Nor think the bitterness of absence sour When you have bid your servant once adieu.

> Nor dare I rebuke the seemingly endless hours while I, my Lord, wait impatiently for You; nor dare I think of

> how painful and unpleasant is your absence, when you bid adieu to one who waits so devotedly upon You.

Nor dare I question with my jealous thought Where you may be, or your affairs suppose, But, like a sad slave, stay and think of nought Save, where you are, how happy you make those.

> Nor dare I question with any jealous thought where You may be, nor make suppositions about Your affairs; but like a trustworthy servant, I remain steadfast and think of nothing else but where You are and how happy are those You attend to.

So true a fool is love that in your will, Though you do anything, he thinks no ill.

> So faithful is my love that it is completely and freely surrendered to Your will in all respects.

COMMENTARY

In Sonnet 56, the focus was, as here, on the devotee's love of God. The tone of the Sonnet—with reference to being "*your slave*"—seems servile, but was common in Elizabethan poetic tradition. Here, "*your slave*" means reverent devotee or disciple, one whose will is surrendered to that of the "*sovereign*" upon whose desire the devotee waits. As expressed in previous Sonnets, the time away "*whilst I, my sovereign, watch the clock for you*" is a difficult period ("*absence sour*"). The lover of the Divine "*sovereign*" is not possessive or selfish; for he does not "*question with my jealous thought,*" but remains trustingly "*like a sad slave*" thinking of how happy others are delighting in God's presence ("*how happy you make those*").

The lover of the Lord neither intellectualizes nor second guesses God; but he is actually wise in his fool's love by his complete surrender and devotion. There is nothing God could do to cause enmity to arise in the lover: "*Though you do anything,*" he thinks "*no ill.*"

This carries on the theme of Sonnet 56 of loving God "with all thine heart" (**Deut. 6:5**). "Then shall ye call upon me, and ye shall go and pray unto me, and I will hearken unto you. And ye shall seek me, and find me, when ye shall search for me with all your heart." (**Jer. 29:12-13**)

The theme in Sonnet 57 demonstrates complete surrender of heart and mind, showing that the lover neither permits a "*jealous thought*," nor thinks "*ill*". "*So true a fool is love that in your will, Though you do anything, he thinks no ill.*" Shakespeare is exemplifying how he believes the lover of God obeys the commandment "to love the Lord thy God with all thine heart, and with all thy soul, and with all thy might." **(Deut. 6:5)** Of such a lover of God it is said, "We are fools for Christ's sake, but ye are wise in Christ; we are weak, but ye are strong; ye are honourable, but we are despised." **(1 Cor. 4:10)**

BIBLICAL AND RELATED PASSAGES SUGGESTED BY SONNET 57

"Jesus said unto him, Thou shalt love the Lord thy God with all thy heart, and with all thy soul, and with all thy mind." **Matt. 22:37**

"He that troubleth his own house shall inherit the wind: and the fool shall be servant to the wise of heart." **Prov. 11:29**

St. Frances of Assisi: "The misunderstanding townspeople of Assisi called a youth among them named Francesco Bernardone, 'pazzo,' a pathetic fool. Later in his life, St. Francis was called a 'fool in Christ' who ventured to conquer with the force of love and complete faith in God. His trials, tests, persecutions, and intense physical disease could not deflect his love for God. The last stanza of his famous canticle 'The Praises of the Creatures' (Cantico de lo Frato Sole) reads:

> 'Be Praised my Lord, for sister death
> From whom no man living can escape.
> Alas for those who die in mortal sin,
> But happy they who find themselves within thine will,
> On them the second death can work no harm.'"
>
> (Fulop-Miller, *The Saints that Moved the World* [Salem, N.H.: Ayer Co. Publishers, 1945], p. 245)

SONNET 58

That God forbid that made me first your slave,
I should in thought control your times of pleasure,
Or at your hand the account of hours to crave,
Being your vassal, bound to stay your leisure.
O let me suffer, being at your beck,
The imprisoned absence of your liberty;
And patience, tame to sufferance, bide each check,
Without accusing you of injury.
Be where you list, your charter is so strong,
That you yourself may privilege your time
To what you will; to you it doth belong
Yourself to pardon of self-doing crime.
I am to wait, though waiting so be hell,
Not blame your pleasure, be it ill or well.

THEME

One who is completely devoted and surrendered to God waits patiently for the Lord's response knowing always that His Will is best.

GLOSSARY

That God forbid that made me first your slave, I should in thought control your times of pleasure, Or at your hand the account of hours to crave, Being your vassal, bound to stay your leisure.

> I am made to be Your devoted servant first, and God forbid I should ever think to control the moments with You that are at your pleasure; or should crave from You personally an account of (Your) time, being trustingly devoted to wait for You at Your leisure.

O let me suffer, being at your beck, The imprisoned absence of your liberty; And patience, tame to sufferance, bide each check, Without accusing you of injury.

> Let me persevere, being at your beckoning call, while I feel imprisoned by Your chosen absence; and let my seasoned patience endure Your willful withdrawal, without

accusing You of being unjust.

Be where you list, your charter is so strong, That you yourself may privilege your time To what you will; to you it doth belong Yourself to pardon of self-doing crime.

Be where You will, Your nature is of such power, that time is under Your command to do what You will; to You it does belong, as does pardon for any self-created harm.

I am to wait, though waiting so be hell. Not blame your pleasure, be it ill or well.

I am to wait, though the waiting is like a hell, and not find fault with Your will, be it painful or joyful.

COMMENTARY

Sonnet 58 mirrors the theme found in Sonnet 57: surrendering completely to the Will of God in mind and heart. Sonnet 58 adds that God grants "*patience . . . though waiting so be hell.*" "Out of the depths have I cried unto thee, O Lord. Lord, hear my voice: let thine ears be attentive to the voice of my supplications. . . . My soul waiteth for the Lord more than they that watch for the morning: I say, more than they that watch for the morning." **(Ps. 130:1-2, 6)** This is the refrain of a soul that suffers "*The imprisoned absence of your liberty.*" "Yea, in the way of thy judgments, O Lord, have we waited for thee; the desire of our soul is to thy name, and to the remembrance of thee." **(Isa. 26:8)** This is one whose patience is "*tame to sufferance*" and yet surrenders "*to what you will.*"

As Brother Lawrence says in his third letter of *The Practice of the Presence of God:* "He will come in His own time, and when you least expect it: thank Him with me for the favors He does you, particularly the fortitude and patience which He gives you in your afflictions." These Bible passages, and Brother Lawrence's words, are reflective of those who, like Shakespeare, have trodden the same spiritual ground and have had to endure the patient waiting upon God's will.

SONNET 59

If there be nothing new, but that which is
Hath been before, how are our brains beguiled,
Which, laboring for invention, bear amiss
The second burthen of a former child.
O that record could with a backward look,
Even of five hundred courses of the sun,
Show me your image in some antique book,
Since mind at first in character was done.
That I might see what the old world could say
To this composed wonder of your frame;
Whether we are mended, or whether better they,
Or whether revolution be the same.
O sure I am the wits of former days,
To subjects worse have given admiring praise.

THEME

Life and mankind, as recorded in history, apparently change little over the centuries. "The thing that hath been, it is that which shall be; and that which is done is that which shall be done: and there is no new thing under the sun." **(Eccl. 1:9)** Those whose works are inspired by the mundane are soon forgotten.

GLOSSARY

If there be nothing new, but that which is Hath been before, how are our brains beguiled, Which, laboring for invention, bear amiss The second burthen of a former child.

> If there is really nothing new today, except that which history has recorded before, how much then do we deceive ourselves. While we try so hard to be uniquely original, we simply re-enact the worldly drama which has already transpired before.

O that record could with a backward look, Even of five hundred courses of the sun, Show me your image in some antique book, Since mind at first in character was done.

If only I could see how in ancient times You were first conceived and recorded in some ancient text.

That I might see what the old world could say To this composed wonder of your frame; Whether we are mended, or whether better they, Or whether revolution be the same.

If only I might read what those in ancient times might have recorded in response to Your wondrously ordered scheme of things, perhaps I could judge better whether we have learned and evolved over time, or whether the ancients knew better, or whether in the course of time, nothing has really changed.

O sure I am the wits of former days, To subjects worse have given admiring praise.

Oh, I am quite certain that the learned men of ancient times were also prone incorrectly to waste their praise on less worthy topics of concern.

COMMENTARY

In Sonnet 59, Shakespeare changes the focus from the immediately preceding Sonnets. Here he relates how people fool themselves into believing that they are somehow greater or better than those who lived before. "*If there is nothing new . . . how are our brains beguiled.*"

"But thou art the same, and thy years shall have no end." **(Ps. 102:27)**

Shakespeare wonders whether, if he could see some "*antique book*" of ancient days when mankind first contemplated ("*Since mind at first in character was done*") the Divine scheme, ("*what the old world could say To this composed wonder of your frame*") if he could judge "*Whether we are mended, or whether better they, Or whether revolution be the same.*" Events in creation are repeated, but mankind has not completely uncovered the history of past ages. "For, behold, I create new heavens and a new earth: And the former shall not be remembered, nor come into mind." **(Isa. 65:17)** Shakespeare is certain, however, that even the supposed learned of old, whose focus is mundane, would have produced works lacking in wisdom. Uninspired works, whether of ancient times, or

Shakespeare's day, do nothing to advance men spiritually. "*O sure I am the wits of former days, To subjects worse have given admiring praise.*" The product of such pundits is quickly forgotten. "Thou hast heard, see all this; and will not ye declare it? I have shewed thee new things from this time, even hidden things, and thou didst not know them." **(Isa. 48:6)**

SONNET 60

Like as the waves make towards the pebbled shore,
So do our minutes hasten to their end;
Each changing place with that which goes before,
In sequent toil all forwards do contend.
Nativity, once in the main of light,
Crawls to maturity, wherewith being crowned,
Crooked eclipses 'gainst his glory fight,
And Time that gave doth now his gift confound.
Time doth transfix the flourish set on youth,
And delves the parallels in beauty's brow,
Feeds on the rarities of nature's truth,
And nothing stands but for his scythe to mow.
And yet to times in hope my verse shall stand,
Praising thy worth, despite his cruel hand.

THEME

Birth, life, and death are the ineluctable destiny of man held captive by Time. Nothing is enduring over time, except that which is tied to the changeless, that is, Truth and Spirit.

GLOSSARY

Like as the waves make towards the pebbled shore, So do our minutes hasten to their end; Each changing place with that which goes before, In sequent toil all forwards do contend.

> Like waves which move endlessly towards the pebbled varied shores, so do our brief moments on this earth hasten toward their end. As one life ends, another takes its place, in constant movement and striving one after the other.

Nativity, once in the main of light, Crawls to maturity, wherewith being crowned, Crooked eclipses 'gainst his glory fight, And Time that gave doth now his gift confound.

> The newborn sees its first light, crawls to the crowning

glory of maturity, often subject to misfortunes along the way, and then Time ravages the gift of life it previously bestowed.

Time doth transfix the flourish set on youth, And delves the parallels in beauty's brow, Feeds on the rarities of nature's truth, And nothing stands but for his scythe to mow.

Time pointedly depletes the bloom of youth, and digs wrinkles into the once beautiful brow, feeding on the most beauteous of nature's perfect creations, and nothing stands which time's scythe does not cut down.

And yet to times in hope my verse shall stand, Praising thy worth, despite his cruel hand.

And yet, for the hopeful future generations, my verse shall still remain, praising Thy works, despite time's seemingly cruel hand.

COMMENTARY

In Sonnet 59, Shakespeare looks at time and creation. He pointedly states that works of man that focus on the mundane are soon forgotten. In Sonnet 60, he moves from the character of the creation to individual beings who are born, grow, and die in each generation, all subject to Time. In Sonnet 59, there is nothing "*new under the sun.*" In spite of "*the wits*" who may believe that their talents deserve "*admiring praise*," their works could not endure the test of time. (Sonnet 59.14) Shakespeare, however, believes, as he stated in Sonnet 19, that "*my verse shall stand.*"

Sonnet 60 likens men's lives to waves which advance "*towards the pebbled shore*" and "*hasten to their end.*" Birth, or "*Nativity*," begins the life process; then, in maturity, it is crowned, only to be depleted by that tyrant Time, which once gave life and now destroys it ("*now his gift confound*"). No matter what ravages Time's "*scythe*" may do, Shakespeare foresees that his works will stand through succeeding ages. "*And yet to times in hope my verse shall stand . . . despite his cruel hand.*" This is in contrast to the lesser verse of "*the wits of former days*" referred to in Sonnet 59.13. The implication is that Shakespeare's verse is not shallow like that which gives "*admiring praise*" to the mundane, but is founded on "*praising thy worth*," which is to say, praise of the works of God. Sonnet 59 makes reference to the Biblical verse found in Ecclesiastes 1:9, and its summary line that "*there is no new thing under the sun*." In Sonnet 60, we read the line "*Crooked eclipses 'gainst his glory fight*." Ecclesiastes answers concerning these "*Crooked eclipses*," meaning periodic misfortunes in life: "I have seen all the works that are done under the sun; and, behold, all is vanity and vexation of spirit. That which is crooked cannot be made straight: and that which is wanting cannot be numbered." **(Eccl. 1:14-15)** While man is enmeshed in vanity like the "*wits of former days*," (Sonnet 59.13) his life is subject to "*Crooked eclipses*" that cannot be made straight. For the egotist, there is no future. His days are numbered because "that which is wanting cannot be numbered."

On what basis does Shakespeare claim that his verse will stand for all time? He accepts without judgment the Divine plan and praises all the works of God, even those apparent cruelties wrought by Time. The depth and wisdom of Shakespeare's verse touches his readers on a profound level, and it is this which shall sustain it. The overarching theme here is that to be enduring, it is necessary to change allegiance from the mundane aspects of creation ("*subjects worse*" [Sonnet 59.14]) to the Creator ("*thy worth*").

BIBLICAL PASSAGES SUGGESTED BY SONNET 60

"Whoso keepeth the commandment shall feel no evil thing: And a wise man's heart discerneth both time and judgment." **Eccl. 8:5**

"And they that be wise shall shine as the brightness of the firmament; and they that turn many to righteousness as the stars forever and ever." **Dan. 12:3**

"Heaven and earth shall pass away, but my words shall not pass away." **Matt. 24:35**

"Concerning thy testimonies, I have known of old that thou hast founded them for ever." **Ps. 119:152**

SONNET 61

Is it thy will thy image should keep open
My heavy eyelids to the weary night?
Dost thou desire my slumbers should be broken,
While shadows like to thee do mock my sight?
Is it thy spirit that thou send'st from thee
So far from home into my deeds to pry,
To find out shames and idle hours in me,
The scope and tenour of thy jealousy?
O no, thy love, though much, is not so great.
It is my love that keeps mine eye awake;
Mine own true love that doth my rest defeat,
To play the watchman ever for thy sake.
For thee watch I whilst thou dost wake elsewhere,
From me far off, with others all too near.

THEME

Being truly awake means to forego the sleep of ignorance of our own true spiritual nature and then to choose to do good and loving things.

GLOSSARY

Is it thy will thy image should keep open, My heavy eyelids to the weary night? Dost thou desire my slumbers should be broken, While shadows like to thee do mock my sight?

> Is it Thy wish that the prospect of seeing Thine image should keep my tired eyes open into the long night? Dost Thou want my sleep to be broken while shadowy images I believe to be of Thee mock my sight?

Is it thy spirit that thou send'st from thee, So far from home into my deeds to pry, To find out shames and idle hours in me, The scope and tenour of thy jealousy?

> Is it some part of Thy Spirit that Thou does send out far from the center of Thyself to pry into my deeds and discover what shames are the fruit of my egotistical pursuits that is the aim and purpose of Thy jealousy?

O no, Thy love, though much, is not so great. It is my love that keeps mine eye awake; Mine own true love that doth my rest defeat, To play the watchman ever for thy sake.

> O no, Thy love, though much, is not so great in that respect. It is my own love for Thee which keeps my eye awake for Thee; my own deepest love and devotion that keeps sleep away; my love is ever vigilant, seeking the sight of Thee.

For thee watch I whilst thou dost wake elsewhere, From me far off, with others all too near.

> Ever will I watch for Thee, while Thou dost appear elsewhere, seemingly far from me, but near and dear to others who perceive Thee.

COMMENTARY

Shakespeare returns again to the themes of Sonnets 57 and 58 in the sense of watching and waiting upon the Beloved's return. By sleeping, in ignorance, one risks missing out on the chance to see the Beloved. But one is tested: "*shadows like to thee do mock my sight.*" Yet one is to "Give not sleep to thine eyes, nor slumber to thine eyelids." **(Prov. 6:4)** If one sleeps, one will miss out. "How long wilt thou sleep, O sluggard? When wilt thou arise out of thy sleep?" **(Prov. 6:9)**

Shakespeare knows that the Lord is scripturally described as a jealous God, and so feels, out of guilt, for the "*shames and idle hours in* [him]," that somehow God is watching and judging him. This is unlike the "*watchman ever for thy sake*" in line 12, who is the devotee. There are two "*parties*" in this Sonnet being addressed. One is Spirit being watched for, and the other is the awakening ego self, which feels shame and which expresses a love that is "*not so great.*" The ego may be much in terms of "*human loving*," but it is not "*great*" in expressing love of the soul. This spiritually expressive soul-self is "*my love that keeps mine eye awake.*" And Shakespeare reiterates—so that we are not amiss in thinking this to be the love of the soul—that this is "*Mine own true love.*" This is the individual soul nature being addressed in the following from Matthew: "Watch ye therefore: for ye know not when the master of the house cometh. . . . Lest coming suddenly, he find you sleeping."

(Mark 13:35-36)

Shakespeare then states that others who have been watchful are rewarded. "[*T*]*hou dost wake elsewhere, From me far off, with others all too near.*" They are the ones of which it is said: "And that, knowing the time, that now it is high time to awake out of sleep: for now is our salvation nearer than when we believed." **(Rom. 13:11)** "Love not sleep, lest thou come to poverty; open thine eyes, and thou shalt be satisfied with bread." **(Prov. 20:13)**

Shakespeare's words, expressing a universal theme, have been echoed by other spiritually-oriented poets. In his "Gitanjali" poems the Nobel Laureate, Rabindranath Tagore, pours out his heart's devotion in speaking of the Lord.

> This is my delight, thus to wait and watch at the wayside where shadow chases light and the rain comes in the wake of the summer.
>
> Messengers, with tidings from unknown skies, greet me and speed along the road. My heart is glad within, and the breath of the passing breeze is sweet.
>
> From dawn till dusk I sit here before my door, and I know that of a sudden the happy moment will arrive when I shall see.
>
> In the meanwhile I smile and I sing all alone. In the meanwhile the air is filling with the perfume of promise.

Like the unabashed spiritual poetry of Tagore, the deeper meaning of Shakespeare's Sonnet is a canticle of prayer that the soul whispers of one who journeys to the Divine.

SONNET 62

Sin of self-love possesseth all mine eye,
And all my soul, and all my every part;
And for this sin there is no remedy,
It is so grounded inward in my heart.
Methinks no face so gracious is as mine,
No shape so true, no truth of such account;
And for myself mine own worth do define,
As I all other in all worths surmount.
But when my glass shows me myself indeed,
Beated and chopped with tanned antiquity,
Mine own self-love quite contrary I read,
Self so self-loving were iniquity.
'Tis thee, myself, that for myself I praise,
Painting my age with beauty of thy days.

THEME

All that is good and beautiful within is part of the soul's nature given to each one as a child of God. Identified with the ego, however, the soul can be overcome with delusive worldly desires and self-love.

GLOSSARY

Sin of self-love possesseth all mine eye, And all my soul, and all my every part; And for this sin there is no remedy, It is so grounded inward in my heart.

The sin of self-love completely blinds my vision, and corrupts my soul, into the core of my being; there is no remedy for the base foundation of material desire implanted within me as the selfish ego.

Methinks no face so gracious is as mine, No shape so true, no truth of such account; And for myself mine own worth do define, As I all other in all worths surmount.

There is no face with as much grace as the one I see. No body as true, and no account of this evaluation to belie my own; and I alone define my own self worth seeing that in every way it surpasses all others.

But when my glass shows me myself indeed, Beated and chopped with tanned antiquity, Mine own self-love quite contrary I read, Self so self-loving were iniquity.

> But when I am able to clearly see with understanding the true image of my soul's nature, which was previously hidden from my perception by life's disturbing circumstances and trials, it is in stark contrast to the iniquity of that narcissistic, ego-centered man I was.

'Tis thee, myself, that for myself I praise, Painting my age with beauty of thy days.

> It is Thee (my true soul-self) that I am truly praising and not my ego-identified self. I am adorning my old age with the ever-youthful beauty of the Spirit.

COMMENTARY

In Sonnet 61, Shakespeare reflects upon he who forsakes his sleep of ignorance and begins, out of wisdom and love, to be watchful over his spiritual life and to keep faith with his soul nature, which is of God.

In Sonnet 62, Shakespeare, with his characteristic ingenuity, uses double meanings, juxtaposing the little ego self and the greater self, which is the soul. In a sense, he is having a heart-to-heart conversation between his ego-self and his higher nature, the soul. He begins with what seems to be a berating exposition of his sinful, narcissistic nature, which is of such depth and vanity that it cannot be separated from the core of his being. "*Sin of self-love possesseth all mine eye, And all my soul, and all my every part; And for this sin there is no remedy, It is so grounded inward in my heart.*" The sensually-bent ego is a part of man's nature and takes hold in "*all my every part.*"

Shakespeare continues by elucidating upon the attributes of this "*self-love.*" These qualities encompass a belief in unsurpassable beauty, form, and virtue. He has been his own yardstick by which all others are measured. "*And for myself mine own worth do define, As I all other in all worths surmount.*" These statements are reminiscent of the following Biblical verse: "Vanity of vanities, saith the Preacher, vanity of vanities;

all is vanity." **(Eccl. 1:2)** The double meaning of the second quatrain, is that he is referring, on the one hand to a narcissistic evaluation of an egotist, and on the other, to qualities of his soul. Those of the soul are the ones which truly "*define*" and "*surmount*" all other lesser, or egoistical aspects of his nature.

In the next quatrain, we see what the wise introspective nature sees ("*when my glass shows me myself indeed*"). This glass is a reflection in which the soul mirrors the Spirit. The Poet is not looking through his "glass darkly" but with clear perception. (See Commentary Sonnet 3) The result is realization of spiritual Truth: that self-loving, in the sense of the ego or little self, is plainly sinful. "*Self so self-loving were iniquity.*" But in line 13, "*myself*" is the true self, the image of God in man, and it is the ego which is the pseudo-self. The Poet's realization of these truths came apparently after being "*Beated and chopped with tanned antiquity.*" Wisdom eventually followed the trial or beatings of life, and like raw leather going through the tanning process, it eventually shines with a fine luster.

In the final couplet, Shakespeare says that all of this praise of self is not for the little ego-self, but "'*Tis thee* (myself) . . . *that for myself I praise.*" The real self is the soul that possesses the earlier-described qualities of Beauty and Truth and is the true paragon by which the lesser ego-self is to be compared. "*As I all other in all worths surmount.*"

Finally Shakespeare, as in earlier sonnets, reflects upon the ever-youthful, rejuvenating effects of keeping one's focus upon the Truth and Beauty of the soul and Spirit. "*Painting my age with beauty of thy days.*" This reflects the wisdom taught by many saints and mystics including St. Augustine and Walter Hilton.

BIBLICAL PASSAGE SUGGESTED BY SONNET 62

"And saying, Sirs, why do ye these things? We also are men of like passions with you, and preach unto you that ye should turn from these vanities unto the living God, which made heaven, and earth, and the sea, and all things that are therein." **Acts 14:15**

SONNET 63

Against my love shall be, as I am now,
With Time's injurious hand crushed and o'erworn,
When hours have drained his blood and filled his brow
With lines and wrinkles; when his youthful mourn
Hath travelled on to age's steepy night,
And all those beauties whereof now he's king
Are vanishing or vanished out of sight,
Stealing away the treasure of his spring.
For such a time do I now fortify
Against confounding age's cruel knife,
That he shall never cut from memory
My sweet love's beauty, though my lover's life.
His beauty shall in these black lines be seen,
And they shall live, and he in them still green.

THEME

Spiritual writings and poems will endure the passing of ages moving from periods of spiritual awareness to the darker ages.

GLOSSARY

Against my love shall be, as I am now, With Time's injurious hand crushed and o'erworn, When hours have drained his blood and filled his brow With lines and wrinkles; when his youthful mourn

> In preparation for a time when the Beauty of my Beloved shall be perceived as I am now, broken and worn out by Time's injurious hand; when the passing years have sapped his life blood and filled his forehead with lines and wrinkles; when he mourns his lost youth

Hath travelled on to age's steepy night, And all those beauties whereof now he's king, Are vanishing or vanished out of sight, Stealing away the treasure of his spring.

> Has traveled precipitously with age into the darkness, and all those beauties over which he now reigns are vanishing

> or have completely disappeared from sight, stealing away the previous treasure of his vibrant springtime.

For such a time do I now fortify Against confounding age's cruel knife, That he shall never cut from memory My sweet love's beauty, though my lover's life.

> For such a time of darkness do I now fortify against Time's ruinous and savage scythe, so that the passing ages shall never erase the sweet memory of my soul's inner Beauty, though such remembrance no longer pervades men's consciousness.

His beauty shall in these black lines be seen, And they shall live, and he in them still green.

> The beauty of the Spirit shall ever be recognized in these dark lines, and they shall endure, and the true nature of the Spirit described in them shall ever flourish.

COMMENTARY

Throughout the ages, man has ever oscillated between periods of growth and spiritual renaissance and ages of darkness and spiritual forgetfulness. "*When hours have drained his blood and filled his brow With lines and wrinkles; when his youthful mourn Hath travelled on to age's steepy night.*" The Greeks made reference to four ages, described as gold, silver, bronze, and iron. To prepare for such dark times, awakened souls have fortified mankind by preserving spiritual truths in sacred words and writing until the coming again of more enlightened ages. "*For such a time do I now fortify.*" It is recorded that during the Dark Ages monasteries were built, sometimes on inaccessible mountain ledges, to preserve sacred texts and wisdom. Skillfully hiding the Dead Sea scrolls in concealed caves assured their preservation for millennia.

In Sonnet 62, Shakespeare reveals in the final couplet that it is "*thee*" and not "*myself I praise.*" (Sonnet 62.13) Sonnet 63 refers to remembrance of the same spiritual self that is "*cut from memory*" by "*confounding age's cruel knife.*" "[C]*onfounding age's*" refers to centuries and not just the advancing age of one person's life. Even when men forget the spiritual message of Shakespeare's Sonnets, their essential "*beauty*" shall endure in the written "*black lines*" of his poetry. In them "*His*

(Spirit's) *beauty*" shall be recognized, "*seen*," and be as rejuvenating as the spring season "*and he in them still green*."

In Sonnet 61, Shakespeare refers to mankind, who sleeps in ignorance and needs to be awakened and vigilant. In Sonnet 62, Shakespeare refers to man steeped in the sin of selfishness and self-love, reminiscent of "vanity of vanities . . . all is vanity," quoting from **Eccl. 12:8**. Both in Sonnets 61 and 62, man must be perseverant and introspective in order to develop a consciousness of his spiritual, innately-loving nature: "*Mine own true love*." (Sonnet 61.11) One must continue to grow in self-awareness ("*my glass shows me myself indeed*" [Sonnet 62.9]) to keep his spiritual consciousness evolving with age. "*Painting my age with beauty of thy days*." (Sonnet 62.14)

In Sonnet 63, Shakespeare refers to the dark ages when men are generally steeped in spiritual ignorance, not to mention a lack of true self-awareness and understanding. "[*W*]*hen his youthful morn Hath travelled on to age's steepy night*." In this "*steepy night*" man's consciousness generally has plunged into darkness. As mentioned above, the Greeks referred to this dark period as the iron age of man.

Shakespeare states that mankind must be fortified against such dark periods by preserving spiritual truths during its "*youthful morn*." In the lines "*My sweet love's beauty, though my lover's life*," Shakespeare refers to the beauty of Spirit that outlives the physical "*life*." Shakespeare implies that there are those in every age who, no matter what the outward circumstances, are still able to see the timeless, spiritual beauty in his verse. "*His beauty shall in these black lines be seen, And they shall live, and he in them still green*."

BIBLICAL PASSAGES SUGGESTED BY SONNET 63

"Remember now thy Creator in the days of thy youth, while the evil days come not, nor the years draw nigh, when thou shall say, I have no pleasure in them." **Eccl. 12:1**

"The grass withereth, the flower fadeth: but the word of our God shall stand for ever." **Isa. 40:8**.

SONNET 64

When I have seen by Time's fell hand defaced
The rich proud cost of outworn buried age,
When sometime lofty towers I see down-razed,
And brass eternal slave to mortal rage;
When I have seen the hungry ocean gain
Advantage on the kingdom of the shore,
And the firm soil win of the watery main,
Increasing store with loss, and loss with store;
When I have seen such interchange of state,
Or state itself confounded to decay;
Ruin hath taught me thus to ruminate,
That Time will come and take my love away.
This thought is as a death, which cannot choose
But weep to have that which it fears to lose.

THEME

Fear is a limiting quality of ego consciousness which shuts out the light of the Spirit. It is very human to fear the loss of love until one is so ensconced in faith and Spirit that one has a "joy no man taketh" away.

GLOSSARY

When I have seen by Time's fell hand defaced, The rich proud cost of outworn buried age, When sometime lofty towers I see down-razed, And brass eternal slave to mortal rage;

When I have seen the savage hand of Time deface the proud and costly things of antiquity now buried; and when I see the formerly lofty towers leveled to the ground, and even the resilient brass yield completely to human devastation;

When I have seen the hungry ocean gain, Advantage on the kingdom of the shore, And the firm soil win of the watery main, Increasing store with loss, and loss with store;

And when I have seen the seas encroach successfully

> where the shore once reigned supreme, and likewise when I see the reverse, where land now is set upon the ocean's previous domain, increasing ocean where once was land, and land where once was seas;

When I have seen such interchange of state, Or state itself confounded to decay; Ruin hath taught me thus to ruminate, That Time will come and take my love away.

> And when I have indeed seen such exchange of conditions, or when the universal structure itself seems wasted into decay; such ruin wrought by Time has taught me to ponder thus, that Time will eventually steal my dearest Love from me.

This thought is as a death, which cannot choose, But weep to have that which it fears to lose.

> This thought is like a horrible death which casts me into an inconsolable state of weeping for fear of my loss.

COMMENTARY

Sonnet 64 has deep symbolism on several levels. In Sonnet 63, Shakespeare refers to the passing of ages from periods of spiritual ignorance to those of higher consciousness when readers can appreciate the "*beauty . . . in these black lines*." (Sonnet 63.13) In Sonnet 64, while again Time is a theme, it refers both to destruction of physical structures and to acquisition and deterioration on the spiritual plane. The earthy material is represented in "*lofty towers*" and "*brass*." The oceans, however, are symbolic of the "*living waters*" of the Spirit. ("For my people have committed two evils; they have forsaken me the fountain of living waters, . . ." **(Jer. 2:13)** The "*firm soil*" is the material as opposed to spiritual. During alternating periods of time, like those in Sonnet 63 of darkness and higher awareness, mankind flourishes in higher golden ages with living waters when "*the hungry ocean gain*[s] *Advantage on the kingdom of the shore*" and is steeped in materialism when the "*firm soil win of the watery main*." Time has then "*travelled on to age's steepy night*." (Sonnet 63.5)

Again, as in Sonnets 61, 62, and 63, Shakespeare addresses both

Spirit, as the inner soul, and the worldly-oriented ego nature. In Sonnet 61.7, guilt for the speaker's "*shames*" led him to believe that Spirit, instead of being an all-loving and forgiving God, was somehow judging him. It is the ego-self's doubt and guilt that places a limitation on man's ability to express his spiritual nature.

In Sonnet 64, Shakespeare, aware of the changing nature of all things, entertains the thought that, perhaps there will come a day when Time will take away either his love for God or God's love for him. "*That Time will come and take my love away.*" It is hard to imagine that for one who in Sonnet 57 waits "*Upon the hours*" (Sonnet 57.2) for God, or who is a faithful "*watchman*" in Sonnet 61.12, could be presented by such fearful thoughts. Shakespeare incorrectly reasons that if things can be "*confounded to decay*" then perhaps the Love for and from God could end, even though such a "*thought is as a death.*" Just as doubt and "*shames*" in Sonnet 61.7 limited the intellect's power to discern Truth, the same is true of fear: it corrupts man's innate capacity to see and express Truth.

A second interpretation on another level of meaning in Sonnet 64 is found in the soul's addressing the Spirit. Again fear is the limiting factor. Shakespeare is fearful that as Time defaces and ruins all things, that perhaps the very focus of his life which is the "*scope*" (Sonnet 52.13) and aim of his adoration, the Lord, may be removed or taken away from him. Such a thought is not just "*as a death*" but reduces him to weeping. The disciples of Christ were also filled with fear and sorrow at the thought of losing their Master. "And ye now therefore have sorrow: but I will see you again, and your heart shall rejoice, and your joy no man taketh from you." **(John 16:22)**

The sentiments expressed by Shakespeare in this Sonnet are very human and understandable. They are evidenced in man's experiences generally, and of those on a sacred spiritual journey who hold most dear their precious, awakened love for God.

SONNET 65

Since brass, nor stone, nor earth, nor boundless sea,
But sad mortality o'ersways their power,
How with this rage shall beauty hold a plea,
Whose action is no stronger than a flower?
O how shall summer's honey breath hold out
Against the wrackful siege of batt'ring days,
When rocks impregnable are not so stout,
Nor gates of steel so strong, but Time decays?
O fearful meditation, where, alack,
Shall time's best jewel from Time's chest lie hid?
Or what strong hand can hold his swift foot back?
Or who his spoil of beauty can forbid?
O none, unless this miracle have might,
That in black ink my love may still shine bright.

THEME

Love and Beauty are eternal qualities of the Spirit which cannot be touched by the passage of Time. One should try to see these qualities both in the Infinite, and as they are expressed by man, in the timeless spiritual messages expressed in writings meant to uplift mankind.

GLOSSARY

Since brass, nor stone, nor earth, nor boundless sea, But sad mortality o'ersways their power, How with this rage shall beauty hold a plea, Whose action is no stronger than a flower?

> Since neither brass, nor stone, nor earth, nor boundless oceans have sufficient power to stand against the determined force of Time, how can Beauty whose nature is encased in the delicate flower, have any hope of winning out against Time?

O how shall summer's honey breath hold out Against the wrackful siege of batt'ring days, When rocks impregnable are not so stout, Nor gates of steel so strong, but Time decays?

> Oh how shall the sweet summer breezes hold out against the ruinous onslaught of battering days, when impregnable boulders and gates of steel lack sufficient strength to stop the decays of Time?

O fearful meditation, where, alack, Shall Time's best jewel from Time's chest lie hid? Or what strong hand can hold his swift foot back? Or who his spoil of beauty can forbid?

> Oh what a dreadful contemplation! Where, alas, can there be some timeless jewel that can escape Time's sepulcher? Or what mighty hand can leash the sure tread of Time, or who can restrain Time's injury to Beauty?

O none, unless this miracle have might, That in black ink my love may still shine bright.

> Oh none, unless this miracle has might enough in these written words to illuminate forever the true nature of my love expressed therein.

COMMENTARY

In Sonnet 65, Shakespeare carries on the theme of Time's destructive nature as found in Sonnets 63 and 64. He is insisting to the reader that there is a timeless message to be found in his words written in "*black ink*." The implication is that there is a light which "*may still shine bright*" in the darkness of "*these black lines*." (Sonnet 63.13)

What is "*Time's best jewel*" that is impervious to Time itself? It is Light which shines like a jewel; for in the beginning, before all created things which are subject to "*time decays*," was Light. "Let there be light." **(Gen. 1:3)**

If one can recognize in Shakespeare's "*black lines*" (Sonnet 63.13) the true meaning which is shining through them, he uncovers the timeless message and nature of his love, "*my love.*" (Sonnet 64.12) It is, of course, his love of God. "For God, who commanded the light to shine out of darkness, hath shined in our hearts, to give the light of the knowledge of the glory of God in the face of Jesus Christ."**(2 Cor. 4:6)**

Beyond Time is immortality and salvation. In Sonnet 64, there is fear expressed that either Shakespeare's love will be worn down by Time, or that the Goal of his adoration will somehow be put beyond his reach. In Sonnet 65, this fear is put to rest. "The Lord is my light and my salvation; whom shall I fear? The Lord is the strength of my life; of whom shall I be afraid?" **(Ps. 27:1)**

SONNET 66

Tired with all these, for restful death I cry,
As, to behold desert a beggar born,
And needy nothing trimmed in jollity,
And purest faith unhappily forsworn,
And gilded honour shamefully misplaced,
And maiden virtue rudely strumpeted,
And right perfection wrongfully disgraced,
And strength by limping sway disabled,
And art made tongue-tied by authority,
And folly, doctor-like, controlling skill,
And simple truth miscalled simplicity,
And captive good attending captain ill.
Tired with all these, from these would I be gone,
Save that to die, I leave my love alone.

THEME

No matter what the outer circumstances or conditions, what we truly are is reflected in what we do or do not do in response to these. Life is full of seeming injustices and incongruities, but mortal man in his ego-consciousness cannot judge the Creator or the creation because he truly lacks the wisdom to comprehend it all.

GLOSSARY

Tired with all these, for restful death I cry, As, to behold desert a beggar born, And needy nothing trimmed in jollity, And purest faith unhappily forsworn,

> I am beaten down by these injustices, and cry out for the respite of death. I am weary of seeing someone of merit born without position and no chance of success, and some morally depraved humbug decked out in lavish finery, and one of purest fidelity unhappily dismissed,

And gilded honour shamefully misplaced, And maiden virtue rudely strumpeted, And right perfection wrongfully disgraced, And strength by limping sway disabled,

> And golden rank shamefully allotted to the undeserving, and maiden virginity rudely prostituted, and genuine perfection wrongfully disgraced, and authority by half-hearted rule left incapable of administration,

And art made tongue-tied by authority, And folly, doctor-like, controlling skill, And simple truth miscalled simplicity, And captive good attending captain ill.

> And the arts silenced by authority, and ignorant, false pundits put in charge of true intellect, and innocent truth labeled stupidity, and the truly good made to serve the purely evil.

Tired with all these, from these would I be gone, Save that to die, I leave my love alone.

> Tired with all these, from these I seek a final exit, except that in dying, I would be abandoning Love.

COMMENTARY

Sonnet 66 is reflective of Job in the Bible who is weary with the many tests placed upon him. "My soul is weary of my life. . . ." **(Job 10:1)** Seeing life's travails makes one weary of life. "Therefore I hated life; because the work that is wrought under the sun is grievous unto me: for all is vanity and vexation of spirit." **(Eccl. 2:17)**

Similarly, Shakespeare calls out for release in "*restful death.*" He tires of life's seeming iniquities. "[*G*]*ilded honour* (is) *shamefully misplaced*" and "*right perfection wrongfully disgraced.*" Ecclesiastes goes on: "Folly is set in great dignity, and the rich sit in low place." **(Eccl. 10:6)** ("*And captive good attending captain ill*"). "I have seen servants upon horses, and princes walking as servants upon the earth." **(Eccl. 10:7)** "And who knoweth whether he shall be a wise man or a fool? yet shall he have rule over all my labour wherein I have laboured, and wherein I have shewed myself wise under the sun. This is also vanity. Therefore I went about to cause my heart to despair of all the labour which I took under the sun." **(Eccl. 2:19-20)**

In all of life's seeming incongruities, man is ill-equipped to render superlative judgments on life's conditions unless he possesses the soul's spiritually-endowed Wisdom to understand. "Who is as the wise man? and who knoweth the interpretation of a thing? a man's wisdom maketh his face to shine, and the boldness of his face shall be changed. I counsel thee to keep the king's commandment, and that in regard of the oath of God. Be not hasty to go out of his sight: stand not in an evil thing; for he doeth whatsoever pleaseth him. Where the word of a king is, there is power: and who may say unto him, What doest thou?" **(Eccl. 8:1-4)** One who is "*Tired with all these*" and "*from these . . . would be gone*," shows a lack of true Wisdom. The ways of God are a mystery to man. "As thou knowest not what is the way of the spirit, nor how the bones do grow in the womb of her that is with child: even so thou knowest not the works of God who maketh all." **(Eccl. 11:5)**

So what is the answer to this conundrum? "Let us hear the conclusion of the whole matter: Fear God, and keep his commandments: for this is the whole duty of man. For God shall bring every work into judgment, with every secret thing, whether it be good, or whether it be evil." **(Eccl. 12:13-14)** Choosing death or other escapes from life's travails weakens one spiritually. This is tantamount to abandoning one's soul, and this is the meaning of "*I leave my love alone*," in the final line of the Sonnet. "Whosoever keepeth the commandment shall feel no evil thing: and a wise man's heart discerneth both time and judgment." **(Eccl. 8:5)**

SONNET 67

Ah wherefore with infection should he live,
And with his presence grace impiety,
That sin by him advantage should achieve,
And lace itself with his society?
Why should false painting imitate his cheek
And steal dead seeming of his living hue?
Why should poor beauty indirectly seek
Roses of shadow, since his rose is true?
Why should he live, now Nature bankrupt is,
Beggared of blood to blush through lively veins?
For she hath no exchequer now but his,
And, proud of many, lives upon his gains.
O him she stores, to show what wealth she had
In days long since, before these last so bad.

THEME

Whether life is full of deceitfulness expressed by others, or whether we deceive ourselves steeped in ego consciousness, a time will come for mankind when goodness will prevail, and a time will come for redemption in each individual life if we open the treasure hidden in our own soul.

GLOSSARY

Ah wherefore with infection should he live, And with his presence grace impiety, That sin by him advantage should achieve, And lace itself with his society?

> Why should a man's soul have to endure such infection, and why does he, with his inherently spiritual nature, give in to wickedness that falsely portrays sin as good, thereby perversely affecting others in his society?

Why should false painting imitate his cheek And steal dead seeming of his living hue? Why should poor beauty indirectly seek Roses of shadow, since his rose is true?

> Why should cosmetic cover up be able to imitate spiri-

tual goodness and by such lifeless artifice put on the appearance of being genuine? Why should those of falseness seek deceitfully to portray truly beautiful qualities when there is only one true Essence?

Why should he live, now Nature bankrupt is, Beggared of blood to blush through lively veins? For she hath no exchequer now but his, And, proud of many, lives upon his gains.

Of what purpose is the continuation of the spiritual self when Nature's creation itself appears bankrupt, drained of the living Essence that formerly provided sustenance to mankind? For Nature has now no treasure but that of Spirit, and many are those filled with pride who now live upon gains deceitfully acquired.

O him she stores, to show what wealth she had In days long since, before these last so bad.

Oh how Spirit keeps in store her treasure trove, to show future generations what true wealth She has produced, in ages long past, before these times of evil.

COMMENTARY

In Sonnet 66, the Poet cries out in despair for so many apparent injustices and immoralities of the times and says that "*for restful death I cry.*" (Sonnet 66.1) He concludes, however, that to choose death, or some other escape would be wrong. This would be a betrayal of his soul ("*save that to die, I leave my love alone*" [Sonnet 66.14]).

Now in Sonnet 67, Shakespeare, as the Poet, has a new complaint: the soul of man, viewing the passing spectacle (as the despairing poet did not choose a spiritual death in Sonnet 66), must "*live*" viewing the sight of deceitful persons who falsely pretend to imitate qualities of the soul, such as Truth, Beauty, Love, and Kindness, only to see such sinful behavior weave itself into the fiber of society. "*That sin by him advantage should achieve, And lace itself with his society.*"

These deceivers that imitate truth are known in the history of man. "For they that are such serve not our Lord Jesus Christ, but their own belly; and by good words and fair speeches deceive the hearts of the simple." **(Rom. 16:18)** These deceivers by "*false painting imitate his cheek.*" "For such are false apostles, deceitful workers, transforming themselves into the apostles of Christ." **(2 Cor. 11:13)**

In the horrifically-portrayed time of spiritual darkness, the evildoers, of course, do not have the last word. Nature or Spirit "*stores*" to show future generations that goodness was before and will come again. "He that sitteth in the heavens shall laugh: the Lord shall have them in derision." **(Ps. 2:4)**

Shakespeare's Sonnet has a dual interpretation. The first is macrocosmic. As for mankind and the ages, there will always be deceivers and "false apostles" but "*Nature*" or God "*stores*" spiritual wealth in those who have world missions for mankind, like Christ and the saints and sages whose lives are recorded in various religions. These figures fill the centuried pages of scriptural literature banishing discouragement and despair as well as suppressing evil.

The second interpretation of the Sonnet is microcosmic, for each one individually. There are times in every life when deceit or falseness may overtake an individual. Why does the soul continue on, or as Shakespeare states, "*wherefore with infection should he live.*" In Sonnet 62, there is a description of two alternating states: that of human, materialistic, ego-consciousness, and that of soul awareness. Sonnets 63, 64, and 65 refer to changing ages of time, but these can also be interpreted as changing phases of an individual's life. The common thread is the interplay of the soul, the reflection of the Spirit in man, and the worldly-attached ego. Man may be rescued in times of spiritual forgetfulness by God or by spiritual upliftment, whether from the "*beauty in these black lines*" (Sonnet 63.13) or some other source of strength. Times are never so "*bankrupt*" that the Spirit, or the power in one's own soul, does not have a "*store*" of power to show "*what wealth she had*" before these difficult periods that are "*so bad.*"

So whether on the larger universal plane of mankind, or in our individual varied experiences, faith and never giving in to despair by leaving "*love alone,*" will get us through difficult times. Goodness is the inner wealth of Spirit which will come repeatedly. "Know therefore that the Lord thy God, he is God, the faithful God, which keepeth covenant and mercy with them that love him and keep his commandments to a thousand generations." **(Deut. 7:9)**

SONNET 68

Thus in his cheek the map of days outworn,
When beauty lived and died as flowers do now,
Before these bastard signs of fair were born,
Or durst inhabit on a living brow;
Before the golden tresses of the dead,
The right of sepulchers, were shorn away,
To live a second life on second head;
Ere beauty's dead fleece made another gay.
In him those holy antique hours are seen,
Without all ornament, itself and true,
Making no summer of another's green,
Robbing no old to dress his beauty new;
And him as for a map doth Nature store,
To show false Art what beauty was of yore.

THEME

While the soul and Spirit are clothed in pure Beauty, the self-centered ego in man puts on a false show of decadent raiment. Eventually the power of Truth and Beauty to store treasure in every heart will awaken those lost in forgetfulness of Spirit and show them the way home.

GLOSSARY

Thus in his cheek the map of days outworn, When beauty lived and died as flowers do now, Before these bastard signs of fair were born, Or durst inhabit on a living brow;

> For this reason, the entire perfection of His Spiritual nature serves as the epitome of ages past, when the Beauty of the Spirit, as flowers do now, existed perfectly before these false tokens of beauty were worn, or dared to reside upon the forehead of the living;

Before the golden tresses of the dead, The right of sepulchers, were shorn away, To live a second life on second head; Ere beauty's dead fleece made another gay.

> Before expensive hairpieces were bought from the sepulcher, after being shorn from the dead to live a second life on a second head; before it was the curls of the dead that spruced up another.

In him those holy antique hours are seen, Without all ornament, itself and true, Making no summer of another's green, Robbing no old to dress his beauty new;

> In His Being is seen the blessedness of ages without embellishment, purity always, true and changeless, needing no adornment from another to cause it to blossom, nor clothing itself in worn garments to dress up Beauty's perfection;

And him as for a map doth Nature store, To show false Art what beauty was of yore.

> Nature holds as its treasure for all time this guiding light to show false practitioners what the true Nature of Spirit has been from time immemorial.

COMMENTARY

In Sonnet 68, Shakespeare contrasts two meanings of Beauty: the first is that of all Perfection or Beauty in Spirit, which has been for all time. "*Thus in his cheek the map of days outworn.*" This Beauty is pure as the "*flowers.*" The second reference is to false beauty, which is vanity of the ego. As in preceding Sonnets, there is the interplay of soul or Spirit ("*beauty*") and the ego, a "*bastard sign*" or false token of beauty or vanity.

Outwardly embellished bodies, with wigs and raiment made from the dead, give only the appearance of beauty ("*bastard signs of fair*"). "Woe unto you, scribes and Pharisees, hypocrites! For ye are like unto whited sepulchers, which indeed appear beautiful outward, but are within full of dead man's bones, and of all uncleanness." **(Matt. 23:27)** There is a similar picture of vanity and falseness, as seen in Sonnets 66 and 67, now carried over to Sonnet 68. In Sonnet 68, the only true Beauty to seek after is found in the realm of the Spirit. "One thing have I desired of the Lord, that will I seek after; that I may dwell in the house of the Lord all the days of my life, to behold the beauty of the Lord, and to enquire in his temple." **(Ps. 27:4)**

Shakespeare's use of "*shorn*" and "*fleece*" bring to mind the imagery of sheep. Coupled with reference to the sepulcher, one cannot escape the similarity of these lines with the following: "Like sheep they are laid in the grave; death shall feed on them; and the upright shall have dominion over them in the morning; and their beauty shall consume in the grave from their dwelling." **(Ps. 49:14)**

Shakespeare uses hair and clothing alternately as symbols for vanity or spirituality. The message is clear, however: "Whose adorning let it not be that outward adorning of plaiting the hair . . . or of putting on of apparel; but let it be the hidden man of the heart, in that which is not corruptible, even the ornament of a meek and quiet spirit, which is in the sight of God of great price." **(1 Pet. 3:3-4)**

In the final couplet, spiritual Beauty is always kept ready ("*doth Nature store*") to show the way ("*as for a map*") to those lost in "*false Art.*" Those who wear "*dead fleece*" are like lost sheep who need to be guided home. "He shall feed his flock like a Shepherd: he shall gather the lambs with his arm, and carry them in his bosom, and shall gently lead those that are young." **(Isa. 40:11)** For those whose lives are made of beauty and purity, this has been the case since time immemorial ("*what beauty was of yore.*")

SONNET 69

Those parts of thee that the world's eye doth view,
Want nothing that the thought of hearts can mend.
All tongues, the voice of souls, give thee that due,
Uttering bare truth, even so as foes commend.
Thy outward thus with outward praise is crowned;
But those same tongues that give thee so thine own,
In other accents do this praise confound
By seeing farther than the eye hath shown.
They look into the beauty of thy mind,
And that, in guess, they measure by thy deeds;
Then, churls, their thoughts, although their eyes were kind,
To thy fair flower add the rank smell of weeds.
But why thy odour matcheth not thy show,
The solve is this, that thou dost common grow.

THEME

God is simple and complete as a flower. Man cannot appraise His Light nor add a penny to His goldmine of Wisdom. Mankind's attempts to do so are ill-conceived and misguided.

GLOSSARY

Those parts of thee that the world's eye doth view, Want nothing that the thought of hearts can mend. All tongues, the voice of souls, give thee that due, Uttering bare truth, even so as foes commend.

> Thy creation is spread before all the world's gaze. There is no lack of perfection, so man's deepest thoughts cannot improve upon it. All men who speak or write of Thee with true heartfelt emotions give Thee proper due, uttering the simplest truths, even as enemies in spite of themselves must give praise.

Thy outward thus with outward praise is crowned; But those same tongues that give thee so thine own, In other accents do this praise confound By seeing farther than the eye hath shown.

Thy Nature is crowned with outward praise; but those same tongues that pay homage, in different ways nullify their former outward praises by focusing attention beyond the simple truths that the eye has shown.

They look into the beauty of thy mind, And that in guess they measure by thy deeds; Then, churls, their thoughts, although their eyes were kind, To thy fair flower add the rank smell of weeds.

They look for Beauty inherent in what they believe is godly thought, and they guess at the true nature of Thy Being, drawing inferences from Thy outward creation; then, these misguided men, although in thought they believed that they were perceiving and praising kindly, only succeeded in demeaning the Divine Perfection of Nature's flower by adding the foul-smelling weeds of their own puny appraisal.

But why thy odour matcheth not thy show, The solve is this, that thou dost common grow.

But why does the perfume of Thy Presence seems incongruous with Thine outward creation? The solution is this, that Thou art made common through the tawdry, and misguided appraisal of ignorant men.

COMMENTARY

There is nothing lacking in the Divine Perfection, and no man by his own thoughts can add anything to improve upon it: "*Want nothing that the thought of hearts can mend.*" Trying to fathom God is fruitless: "He hath made everything beautiful in his time: also he hath set the world in their heart, so that no man can find out the work that God maketh from the beginning to the end." **(Eccl. 3:11)**

Sonnet 69 is in contrast to Sonnet 67 in a pointed way. In Sonnet 67, Shakespeare is commenting on the "*false apostles*" and deceivers. In Sonnet 69, the Poet says that even those who are well-meaning in their opinions about the nature of the Spirit ("*although their eyes were kind*") only "*confound*" and confuse people by their common thoughts, which are like the "*rank smell of weeds*" in the presence of a "*fair flower.*" "For

I bear them record that they have a zeal of God, but not according to knowledge. For they being ignorant of God's righteousness, and going about to establish their own righteousness, have not submitted themselves unto the righteousness of God." **(Rom. 10:2-3)**

The result is that God is lowered in a sense, or made "*common,*" by those who are "*churls*" judging the Divine by limited human standards ("*in guess they measure by thy deeds*") and not by the infinite yardstick of Wisdom, of which they have no true knowledge.

SONNET 70

That thou art blamed shall not be thy defect,
For slander's mark was ever yet the fair;
The ornament of beauty is suspect,
A crow that flies in heaven's sweetest air.
So thou be good, slander doth but approve
Thy worth the greater, being wooed of time;
For canker vice the sweetest buds doth love,
And thou present'st a pure unstained prime.
Thou hast passed by the ambush of young days,
Either not assailed, or victor being charged;
Yet this thy praise cannot be so thy praise,
To tie up envy evermore enlarged.
If some suspect of ill masked not thy slow,
Then thou alone kingdoms of hearts shouldst owe.

THEME

The pure of heart see only purity, while those who have a sense of their own flaws (or lack of perfection) project these upon others, including the Spirit.

GLOSSARY

That thou art blamed shall not be thy defect, For slander's mark was ever yet the fair; The ornament of beauty is suspect, A crow that flies in heaven's sweetest air.

That Thou art blamed is not because of any defect in Thee, but because Purity has always been the target of slanderers; the outward appearance of Beauty leads some to suspect deeper flaws, like seeing a black crow that flies in purest realms of the heavens.

So thou be good, slander doth but approve Thy worth the greater, being wooed of time; For canker vice the sweetest buds doth love, And thou present'st a pure unstained prime.

Thou art goodness and slander just confirms Thy worth

> even more over time. Cancerous vices seek out the pure and the good, especially such a pure example of perfection as Thou art.

Thou hast passed by the ambush of young days, Either not assailed, or victor being charged; Yet this thy praise cannot be so thy praise, To tie up envy evermore enlarged.

> Thou hast escaped the wiles of foolish and unwise days of youth, either through never coming under the attack of temptations or through being assailed in Thy victorious stance. But even the fact that Thou hast remained pure, is not sufficient to fend off envious slanderers, whose numbers ever increase.

If some suspect of ill masked not thy slow, Then thou alone kingdoms of hearts shouldst owe.

> If there did not exist the suspicious notion that some inherent flaw exists in Thy nature, then Thou alone would reign supreme in the kingdom of hearts.

COMMENTARY

In Sonnet 67, Shakespeare writes about intentional deceivers. Sonnet 69 gives a description of those who speak out, not from malice, but with the motive of displaying knowledge where they are truly ignorant. They purport to improve upon the perfection of a flower but add only "*the rank smell of weeds.*" (Sonnet 69.12)

In Sonnet 70, the perfection of soul and Spirit is the target of slander. "*For slander's mark was ever yet the fair.*" "O ye sons of men, how long will ye turn my glory into shame? How long will ye love vanity, and seek after leasing?" **(Ps. 4:2)**

Man is not capable of judging perfection, as he cannot comprehend it. "And the light shineth in darkness; and the darkness comprehended it not." **(John 1:5)** Man fears what he does not understand and becomes suspicious of it. "*The ornament of beauty is suspect.*" His slander is born of fear and suspicion. "For I have heard the slander of many; fear was on every side; while they took counsel together against me, they devised to take away my life." **(Ps. 31:13)**

Shakespeare, in this Sonnet, speaks of the purity found in both the Spirit and in man's soul. Not only is the Lord assailed by vanity and lies about His Glory, but His reflection, the soul in man, must endure the "*canker vice*" that loves to feed on "*sweetest buds*," especially those of "*a pure unstained prime*." Because of his awareness, even subconsciously, of his faults or lack of perfection, he projects those on to others. "*For slander's mark was ever yet the fair*." Equally as harmful is he of dark faults, who has difficulty in believing in the innate goodness within himself, others, and the creation around him. What he sees is "*A crow that flies in heaven's sweetest air*." "That only which we have within, can we see without. If we meet no gods, its because we harbour none." (Ralph Waldo Emerson, *Essays*, XVII. Worship) "They endure no light, themselves being obscure." (Percy B. Shelley, "The Sensitive Plant")

One deeper theme in Sonnet 70 is that ignorance of one's own innate perfection turns one into a slanderer. "Unto the pure all things are pure: but unto them that are defiled and unbelieving is nothing pure; but even their mind and conscience are defiled." (**Titus 1:15**) If one through belief in self worth and Spirit could cease being "*suspect of ill*," then the light would shine through, and that which was "*masked*" would be revealed. The result would be that Spirit, and belief in one's own spiritual worth, would reign over the kingdom of men's hearts. "*Then thou alone kingdoms of hearts shouldst owe*."

BIBLICAL PASSAGE SUGGESTED BY SONNET 70

"A new heart also will I give you, and a new spirit will I put within you: and I will take away the stony heart out of your flesh, and I will give you an heart of flesh." **Ezek. 36:26**

SONNET 71

No longer mourn for me when I am dead
Than you shall hear the surly sullen bell
Give warning to the world that I am fled
From this vile world, with vilest worms to dwell.
Nay, if you read this line, remember not
The hand that writ it; for I love you so,
That I in your sweet thoughts would be forgot,
If thinking on me then should make you woe.
O if, I say, you look upon this verse,
When I perhaps compounded am with clay,
Do not so much as my poor name rehearse,
But let your love even with my life decay.
Lest the wise world should look into your moan,
And mock you with me after I am gone.

THEME

Persecution arises for those who love one who has passed on but is still being derided unjustly.

GLOSSARY

No longer mourn for me when I am dead Than you shall hear the surly sullen bell Give warning to the world that I am fled From this vile world, with vilest worms to dwell.

> No longer mourn for me when I am dead when you shall hear the stern, solemn bell give warning to the world that I have fled from this vile world, to dwell with even more vile worms of the ground.

Nay, if you read this line, remember not The hand that writ it; for I love you so, That I in your sweet thoughts would be forgot, If thinking on me then should make you woe.

> Nay, if you read this line of verse, do not remember the hand that wrote it; for I love you so deeply, that I in your sweet thoughts would be forgotten, if thinking of

my passing would cause you sorrow.

O if, I say, you look upon this verse, When I perhaps compounded am with clay, Do not so much as my poor name rehearse, But let your love even with my life decay.

> Oh if, (I say), you at some time look at this sonnet when I (perhaps) have been long returned to the dust of the earth, do not so much as repeat my insignificant name, but let your love for me fade away as my life has done.

Lest the wise world should look into your moan, And mock you with me after I am gone.

> Lest the supposed pundits of the world pry into the cause of your sorrow, and cast derision upon you after I am gone because of your association with me.

COMMENTARY

The Poet feels that there will be those after his passing who, through lack of understanding ("*the wise world*") will continue to deride his name. As for those who persist in their love for him, he declares that they should not even utter his name ("*Do not so much as my poor name rehearse*") lest they be subject to mockery. It is an unselfish sentiment of the Poet, and is consistent with earlier Sonnets in which he states that Love and Beauty in his verse "*shall live*" (Sonnet 63.14) and his own love for the Spirit "*in black ink . . . may still shine bright.*" (Sonnet 65.14) It is unimportant that he personally be remembered, but only that his message live on.

There is also a reminiscence of Biblical passages on the subject of those who are persecuted for their adherence to love of Truth. "Blessed are ye, when men shall revile you, and persecute you, and shall say all manner of evil against you falsely, for my sake." **(Matt. 5:11)** Shakespeare is certain of the longevity of the love shining through his verse, and there is the suggestion that the "*wise world*" is like the "*churls*" (Sonnet 69.11) and the "*slander*[er]*'s*," (Sonnet 70.2) who will attack or "*mock*" the one who loves or appreciates Shakespeare's verse simply because it lacks understanding of their true meaning and quality.

SONNET 72

O lest the world should task you to recite,
What merit lived in me that you should love
After my death, dear love, forget me quite,
For you in me can nothing worthy prove;
Unless you would devise some virtuous lie,
To do more for me than mine own desert,
And hang more praise upon deceased I,
Than niggard truth would willingly impart:
O lest your true love may seem false in this,
That you for love speak well of me untrue,
My name be buried where my body is,
And live no more to shame nor me nor you.
For I am shamed by that which I bring forth,
And so should you, to love things nothing worth.

THEME

To thine own self be true. Acting or speaking falsely, even out of love, is wrong.

GLOSSARY

O lest the world should task you to recite, What merit lived in me that you should love After my death, dear love, forget me quite, For you in me can nothing worthy prove;

> O lest the pundits should take you to task and impose upon you the burden of defending what merit you found in me that impels you to continue in your love after I am gone, dear one; then completely forget about me because you will find in me no evidence with which to prove my worth;

Unless you would devise some virtuous lie, To do more for me than mine own desert, And hang more praise upon deceased I, Than niggard truth would willingly impart:

> Unless you would concoct some tale of my virtues, which would afford me more than my personal worth merits,

and hang greater praise upon me after I have left this world than stingy truth sayers would willingly bestow:

O lest your true love may seem false in this, That you for love speak well of me untrue, My name be buried where my body is, And live no more to shame nor me nor you.

O lest your true love may seem to have lowered itself by engaging in any falsehoods, namely, that out of your love, you speak well of me through fabrication; it is better to let my name be buried in the grave where my body lay, and live no more to shame neither you nor me:

For I am shamed by that which I bring forth, And so should you, to love things nothing worth.

For I am ashamed by what I do, and so should you feel shame, to love things that have no worth.

COMMENTARY

In Sonnet 71, the writer counsels his loving admirer(s) to read his verse, but not focus on who he was in life, lest they have to suffer mockery from those who may be derisive of the Poet or his life. In Sonnet 72, the Poet states in effect that his life was shameful and that to defend his memory, his admirer might be tempted to "*devise some virtuous lie.*" He does not wish this, lest such falsity would only serve to bring shame to his "*dear love.*" His counsel is to be "*true to thyself*" and remain pure. To speak falsely, even out of love, is wrong, and shames the Beloved just as much as those who act or speak falsely as has been addressed in Sonnets 67, 69, and 70.

BIBLICAL PASSAGE SUGGESTED BY SONNET 72

"God forbid: yea, let God be true, but every man a liar; as it is written, that thou mightest be justified in thy sayings, and mightest overcome when thou art judged. But if our unrighteousness commend the righteousness of God, what shall we say? Is God unrighteous who taketh vengeance? (I speak as a man) God forbid: for then how shall God judge the world? For if truth of God hath more abounded through my lie unto his glory; why yet am I also judged as a sinner?" **Rom. 3: 4-7**

SONNET 73

That time of year thou mayst in me behold,
When yellow leaves, or none, or few, do hang
Upon those boughs which shake against the cold,
Bare ruin'd choirs, where late the sweet birds sang.
In me thou see'st the twilight of such day,
As after sunset fadeth in the west,
Which by and by black night doth take away,
Death's second self, that seals up all in rest.
In me thou see'st the glowing of such fire,
That on the ashes of his youth doth lie,
As the deathbed whereon it must expire,
Consum'd with that which it was nourish'd by.
This thou perceiv'st, which makes thy love more strong,
To love that well which thou must leave ere long.

THEME

The body may ebb away toward death, but this process does not touch the soul that in old age may glow with the fire of Wisdom gained through battles during the stages of youthful ignorance and error.

GLOSSARY

That time of year thou mayst in me behold, When yellow leaves, or none, or few, do hang Upon those boughs which shake against the cold, Bare ruin'd choirs, where late the sweet birds sang.

> Thou mightest see in my age something like the later seasons of the year when yellowed leaves, or none, or few, are still hanging upon those boughs that shake against the cold, barren-word manuscript pages, where lately was read and recited the sweet song of my soul's outpourings.

In me thou see'st the twilight of such day, As after sunset fadeth in the west, Which by and by black night doth take away, Death's second self, that seals up all in rest.

> In my body thou seest a life that is as the twilight of the day that remains after the sunset in the western sky; but which soon loses its glimmer to the black night, Death's final sleep, that lays all to rest.

In me thou see'st the glowing of such fire, That on the ashes of his youth doth lie, As the deathbed whereon it must expire, consum'd with that which it was nourish'd by.

> In my being thou seest the glow of that kind of fire, that stands on top of the extinguished ashes of ignorance of my youth; and from this forgotten, dead part of my being it must depart, completely consumed by the fire of Wisdom by which it was nourished.

This thou perceiv'st, which makes thy love more strong, To love that well which thou must leave ere long.

> All of this thou perceivest, which only increases the depth of thy love, to love with great constancy that which thou must leave before long.

COMMENTARY

The Poet's physical form is aging and even his writing has waned ("*Bare ruin'd choirs*") where once the pages were filled with songs of the soul ("*where late the sweet birds sang*"). "The flowers appear on the earth; the time of the singing of birds is come." **(Song of Sol. 2:12)** "Our soul is escaped as a bird out of the snare of the fowlers." **(Ps. 124:7)**

Shakespeare uses "*in me*" in lines 5 and 9, to mean the physical form and soul, respectively. The body is taken away by death's sleep. "*Death's second self.*" The soul, however, in line 9 is seen "*glowing of such fire.*" This "*fire*" is the fire of Wisdom which consumes the ignorance that is characteristic of unknowing "*youth.*" "My heart was hot within me, while I was musing the fire burned: then spake I with my tongue." **(Ps. 39:3)** "Then I said, I will not make mention of him, nor speak any more in his name. But his word was in mine heart as a burning fire shut up in my bones." **(Jer. 20:9)**

The soul, being full of the fire of Wisdom ("*glowing of such fire*"), is released from the "*death bed*" of the physical form that it must transcend: "*consum'd with that which it was nourish'd.*"

The entire process of the soul's liberation and "*glowing of such fire*" is perceived as a gratifying and gracious process which, in gratitude, strengthens the faith and love of any who would witness or experience such an event. "*This thou perceiv'st, which makes thy love more strong, To love that well which thou must leave ere long.*"

The theme of the Sonnet is that of the declining physical body, the soul's songs, Wisdom born out of the ignorance that is being consumed; and the human soul, alive with the glow of Wisdom, which is now thankful to God for a graceful exit from life.

BIBLICAL PASSAGE SUGGESTED BY SONNET 73

"And let the peace of God rule in your hearts, to the which also ye are called in one body; and be ye thankful. Let the word of Christ dwell in you richly in all wisdom; teaching and admonishing one another in psalms and hymns and spiritual songs, singing with grace in your hearts to the Lord." **Col. 3:15-16**

SONNET 74

But be contented when that fell arrest,
Without all bail shall carry me away,
My life hath in this line some interest,
Which for memorial still with thee shall stay.
When thou reviewest this, thou dost review
The very part was consecrate to thee,
The earth can have but earth, which is his due;
My spirit is thine, the better part of me:
So then thou hast but lost the dregs of life,
The prey of worms, my body being dead,
The coward conquest of a wretch's knife,
Too base of thee to be remembered,
The worth of that is that which it contains
And that is this, and this with thee remains.

THEME

The true value of one's life is the spiritual legacy that it has left behind. This memorial is a reflection of what was received from God, the One to whom all souls return in the end.

GLOSSARY

But be contented: when that fell arrest, Without all bail shall carry me away, My life hath in this line some interest, Which for memorial still with thee shall stay.

> But be contented: when the hand of death from which there is no release shall carry me away, my soul's essence will continue to be reflected in these Sonnets as a memorial to the soul and Spirit, in which it has its place.

When thou reviewest this, thou dost review The very part was consecrate to thee, The earth can have but earth, which is his due; My spirit is thine, the better part of me.

> When Thou dost make a judgment of these Sonnets, Thou dost see that their very essence was consecrated to

Thee: the earth can have but the dust, which is its due; my soul, which is the essence of my being, is Thine.

So then thou hast but lost the dregs of life, The prey of worms, my body being dead; The coward conquest of a wretch's knife, Too base of thee to be remembered,

So really thou hast only lost the worthless physical remains, the food for worms, when my body is dead; the virtueless conquest of the blow struck by death's scythe is of little worth to be remembered by Thee.

The worth of that is that which it contains And that is this, and this with thee remains.

The true worth of the physical body is the spiritual essence within it. What it contains is my soul, which ever has its place in Thee.

COMMENTARY

As with previous sonnets, Shakespeare is addressing both man and the Spirit, and the diverse lines are a rich admixture of metaphors relating to God, soul, and man. Sonnet 74 is almost a prayer of consecration of his work and soul to God, as well as of his physical form returning as dust to the earth. It has already been recognized by Kerrigan (*The Sonnets and A Lover's Complaint* [London: Penguin, 1986]) that Sonnets 71-74 have Biblical overtones, especially **Job 17:11-15**: "My days are past, my purposes are broken off, even the thoughts of my heart. They change the night into day: the light is short because of darkness. If I wait, the grave is mine house: I have made my bed in the darkness. I have said to corruption, Thou art my father: to the worm, Thou art my mother, and my sister. And where is now my hope? As my hope, who shall see it?"

As for Shakespeare, his purposes are not broken off. His spiritual essence lives on in the Sonnets. As for his hope, "*this with thee remains.*"

SONNET 75

So are you to my thoughts as food to life,
Or as sweet-season'd showers are to the ground;
And for the peace of you I hold such strife
As 'twixt a miser and his wealth is found.
Now proud as an enjoyer, and anon
Doubting the filching age will steal his treasure;
Now counting best to be with you alone,
Then bettered that the world may see my pleasure;
Sometime all full with feasting on your sight,
And by and by clean starved for a look,
Possessing or pursuing no delight,
Save what is had or must from you be took.
Thus do I pine and surfeit day by day
Or gluttoning on all, or all away.

THEME

Life's true treasure is being immersed in God, but there is a constant battle or strife between man's soul and his self-centered ego. Winning this battle requires that he desire spiritual treasures with the same zeal and longing that a miser has for his wealth.

GLOSSARY

So are you to my thoughts as food to life, Or as sweet-season'd showers are to the ground; And for the peace of you I hold such strife As 'twixt a miser and his wealth is found.

> You are to my thoughts what food is to my body, or as the nourishing seasonal rains are to the earth; and I struggle to hold onto the peace that you bring to my soul with the same vehemence as a miser who longs for his gold.

Now proud as an enjoyer, and anon Doubting the filching age will steal his treasure; Now counting best to be with you alone, Then better'd that the world may see my pleasure;

> Presently there is satisfaction in obtaining the object of

> enjoyment, and soon there arises some fear that at any moment this treasure will be stolen. There arises the thought that the best of all is to be alone in Thy presence, then I think how much better it would be if the world could perceive and understand the true nature of my joy.

Sometime all full with feasting on your sight, And by and by clean starved for a look, Possessing or pursuing no delight, Save what is had or must from you be took.

> At one moment filled and overflowing with the majestic sight of You, and soon thereafter utterly hungering for just a glimmer; neither owning nor pursuing any earthly delight, save what is possessed or must be coaxed from You.

Thus do I pine and surfeit day by day Or gluttoning on all, or all away.

> So it is that alternately I pine, or am completely filled, from one day to the next; or suffusing myself completely in your Being, or I am totally bereft of any joy.

COMMENTARY

Shakespeare declares that man is not just a body, but is essentially the soul. As the body requires food, so the soul must be "*nourish'd*" (Sonnet 73.12) by thoughts and actions that are spiritually enriching. "*So are you to my thoughts as food to life.*" There is a battle between the desires of the body and the self-centered ego, on the one hand, and the nature of the higher self, or soul, on the other. (See commentary to Sonnet 141.)

To achieve victory ("*for the peace of you*") one must strive with the same fervent desire that a miser has for his treasure. "*I hold such strife As 'twixt a miser and his wealth is found.*" Always in the back of the miser's thoughts is the longed-for treasure. There are many battles in which victory may be temporarily won. "*Now proud as an enjoyer.*" Then fear ("*Doubting*") arises that the thieving desires of the ego "*will steal his treasure.*" The greatest "*treasure*" is to be immersed in the Spirit. "*Now counting best to be with you alone.*" (See also Sonnet 29.13-14.) Yet even better is that others may see and understand and desire the same. "*Then bettered that the world may see my pleasure.*"

Such is man's ineluctable fate, alternately to "*pine*" and surfeit day by day. "*Thus do I pine and surfeit day by day.*" But here again is a double meaning so characteristic of Shakespeare. In one sense he pines for lack of his spiritual treasure, while losing the same by surfeiting himself in material pursuits. In Sonnet 146, Shakespeare writes: "*Then, soul, live thou upon thy servant's loss, And let that pine to aggravate thy store; Buy terms divine in selling hours of dross; Within be fed, without be rich no more.*" By allowing the material desires to "*pine*," he may then receive such that his "cup runneth over," or he is "*surfeit*[ed] *day by day.*" This is accomplished by keeping his thoughts and actions centered upon the Spirit and spiritual pursuits. "*So are you to my thoughts as food to life. . . .*"

BIBLICAL PASSAGES SUGGESTED BY SONNET 75

"Yea, if thou criest after knowledge, and liftest up thy voice for understanding; If thou seekest her as silver, and searchest for her as for hid treasures; then shalt thou understand the fear of the Lord, and find the knowledge of God." **Prov. 2:3-5**

"But if from thence thou shalt seek the Lord thy God, thou shalt find him, if thou seek him with all thy heart and with all thy soul." **Deut. 4:29**

SONNET 76

Why is my verse so barren of new pride,
So far from variation or quick change?
Why with the time do I not glance aside
To new-found methods and to compounds strange?
Why write I still all one, ever the same,
And keep invention in a noted weed,
That every word doth almost tell my name,
Showing their birth, and where they did proceed?
O know, sweet love, I always write of you,
And you and love are still my argument;
So all my best is dressing old words new,
Spending again what is already spent:
For as the sun is daily new and old,
So is my love still telling what is told.

THEME

The Divine is all things, "*still all one, ever the same,*" and yet it manifests and expresses Itself in infinite, exhaustless variety.

GLOSSARY

Why is my verse so barren of new pride, So far from variation or quick change? Why with the time do I not glance aside To new-found methods and to compounds strange?

> Why is my verse plain and lacking in prideful, novel splendor, so distant from the clever variations and excessive style changes seen in today's poetry? Why do I not join in with the fashion of writing that looks to new-found ways of expression and uses strange compound phraseology?

Why write I still all one, ever the same, And keep invention in a noted weed, That every word doth almost tell my name, Showing their birth, and where they did proceed?

> Why do I write always, and ever the same, and keep my

> thoughts along a predictably recognizable theme, such that every word almost reveals my name, showing their origins, and from where they have descended?

O know, sweet love, I always write of you, And you and love are still my argument; So all my best is dressing old words new, Spending again what is already spent:

> Oh know, sweet Love, I always write of You, and You and love are my constant theme; so my every effort is in discovering Thy changeless ways to express diversity in new ways, and from energies already spent, there arises a limitless font from which I can draw again:

For as the sun is daily new and old, So is my love still telling what is told.

> For as the rising sun is ever the same, but always new, so is my love continually telling what it has already expressed in endless ways.

COMMENTARY

Shakespeare is criticizing the new fashion ("*new-found methods*") of his contemporaries who, out of "*new pride*," are more interested in entertaining with their "*compounds strange*" than in using verse to express lofty themes. The most revered poetry is meant to awaken and expand the higher consciousness in man by stimulating the subtler realms of thought.

Shakespeare himself keeps his writing "*still all one, ever the same.*" He states that "*you and love are still my argument,*" an ever constant theme. The Lord and the author's constant love of Him are the center of his life, and his verse attempts in ever diverse ways to express this anew. "*So all my best is dressing old words new.*" The sun is the same and "*daily new,*" and Spirit, the Changeless, or "*old*" never ceases to reveal itself, in nature, and through the limitless font of the Poet's ingenuity to express it. In this sense, every *word* of the Poet expresses his soul's themes, and thus "*doth almost tell my name, Showing their birth, and where they did proceed.*" Their source is in the Poet's soul, and the expression or "*name*" is of the Spirit or God imprinted on his soul.

Just as Shakespeare's soul expresses Spirit, so also in Creation "*every word doth almost tell my name*" because man is sustained "by every word that proceedeth out of the mouth of the Lord" (**Deut. 8:3**) All "things" are created by the spoken word of God (**Gen. 1:3-15**), and it is then that every aspect of Creation, which is an expression of God, "*dost almost tell my name.*" In this sense, Shakespeare is saying that all created things are a *part* of Spirit, a manifestation which only partly (or "*almost*") reveals the Divine "*name*" behind all creation, "*Showing their birth, and where they did proceed.*"

BIBLICAL PASSAGES SUGGESTED BY SONNET 76

"Now there are diversities of gifts, but the same spirit. And there are differences of administrations, but the same Lord. . . . But the manifestation of the Spirit is given to every man to profit withal. For to one is given by the Spirit the word of wisdom; to another the word of knowledge by the same Spirit. . . . To another divers kinds of tongues; to another the interpretation of tongues." **1 Cor. 12:4-5, 7-8, 10.**

"Lift up your eyes on high, and behold who hath created these things. . ." **Isa. 40:26**

"Hear, O Israel: The Lord our God is one Lord." **Deut. 6:4**

SONNET 77

Thy glass will show thee how thy beauties wear,
Thy dial how thy precious minutes waste;
The vacant leaves thy mind's imprint will bear,
And of this book this learning mayst thou taste.
The wrinkles which thy glass will truly show
Of mouthed graves will give thee memory;
Thou by thy dial's shady stealth mayst know
Time's thievish progress to eternity.
Look! what thy memory cannot contain,
Commit to these waste blanks, and thou shalt find
Those children nurs'd, deliver'd from thy brain,
To take a new acquaintance of thy mind.
These offices, so oft as thou wilt look,
Shall profit thee and much enrich thy book.

THEME

Honest introspection can uproot faults and bad habits and help one to lead a more positive and fulfilling life.

GLOSSARY

Thy glass will show thee how thy beauties wear, Thy dial how thy precious minutes waste; The vacant leaves thy mind's imprint will bear, And of this book this learning mayst thou taste.

A little self-reflection or introspection will truly reveal the nature of your beautiful qualities, the manner in which you spend your time, how you waste precious moments; the empty pages of your life reflect the character of your thoughts, and from this manuscript of your life, you may be more fully instructed.

The wrinkles which thy glass will truly show Of mouthed graves will give thee memory; Thou by thy dial's shady stealth mayst know Time's thievish progress to eternity.

The defects of character and egotistical pursuits which

are the highway to a sorry grave will, by your honest introspection, be brought to remembrance; you will see how your life over time, and imperceptibly so, has moved ever closer to its eternal end.

Look! what thy memory cannot contain, Commit to these waste blanks, and thou shalt find Those children nurs'd, deliver'd from thy brain, To take a new acquaintance of thy mind.

Once you exercis an honest introspection, and then determine to fill the empty pages of your life with new and positive thoughts, these will take hold of your consciousness and give you a clear direction.

These offices, so oft as thou wilt look, Shall profit thee and much enrich thy book.

This process of inner reflection, and repeated introspection, will enrich your character and bring fulfillment to your life.

COMMENTARY

In Sonnet 70, Shakespeare comments upon those who are judgmental of others but apparently oblivious to their own faults. In Sonnet 77, Shakespeare states that a little reflection on one's life will reveal how the "*precious minutes*" are wasted as a result of wrong thoughts and actions. "*The vacant leaves thy mind's imprint will bear.*" By an honest introspection, one will begin to see the "truth" about one's life. "*The wrinkles which thy glass will truly* show." He then will want to change his behavior and thoughts in order to follow a more positive direction. This new course taken ("*those children nurs'd*") will refresh and renew the mind ("*take a new acquaintance*") that will ultimately lead to greater happiness and a richer life. "*These offices . . . Shall profit thee, and much enrich thy book.*"

Shakespeare, of course, is analogizing our life to a script or book which each one of us is writing for himself by the choices of thought and action being expressed. We can choose empty pages or "*vacant leaves,*" which lead slowly to the awaiting grave of emptiness, or a profitable and enriching life: "*profit thee and much enrich thy book.*" Thoughts are a powerful force in our life.

James Allen, in his *As A Man Thinketh*, clearly expounds upon the link between one's thoughts and the results in life that inexorably flow from such thinking. This theme is further described in the following passages:

BIBLICAL PASSAGES SUGGESTED BY SONNET 77

"For as he thinketh in his heart, so is he." **Prov. 23:7**
"But let a man examine himself, and so let him eat of that bread and drink of that cup." **1 Cor. 11:28**

"Thou hypocrite, first cast out the beam out of thine own eye; and then shalt thou see clearly to cast out the mote out of thy brother's eye." **Matt. 7:5**

"Wherefore doth a living man complain, a man for the punishment of his sins? Let us search and try our ways, and turn again to the Lord." **Lam. 3:39-40**

"Examine yourselves, whether ye be in the faith; prove your own selves. Know ye not your own selves, how that Jesus Christ is in you, except ye be reprobates?" **2 Cor. 13:5**

SONNET 78

So oft have I invok'd thee for my Muse,
And found such fair assistance in my verse,
As every alien pen hath got my use,
And under thee their poesy disperse.
Thine eyes, that taught the dumb on high to sing,
And heavy ignorance aloft to fly,
Have added feathers to the learned's wing,
And given grace a double majesty.
Yet be most proud of that which I compile,
Whose influence is thine, and born of thee.
In others' works thou dost but mend the style,
And arts with thy sweet graces graced be;
But thou art all my art, and dost advance
As high as learning my rude ignorance.

THEME

To accomplish the highest skill in one's work or "*art*" one should turn to the Divine as a source of help and inspiration.

GLOSSARY

So oft have I invok'd thee for my Muse, And found such fair assistance in my verse, As every alien pen hath got my use, And under thee their poesy disperse.

So very often I have invoked Thee as a source of inspiration for my poetry, and found the constancy of Thy beautiful presence aiding the composition of my verse. Now other writers copy my style, and they make use of Thee in publishing their works.

Thine eyes, that taught the dumb on high to sing, And heavy ignorance aloft to fly, Have added feathers to the learned's wing And given grace a double majesty.

Thine eyes which have given song to the speechless and have caused the ignorant to take flight with wisdom, have added grace to those already gifted in their poetry, making their expression doubly majestic.

Yet be most proud of that which I compile, Whose influence is thine, and born of thee. In others' works thou dost but mend the style, And arts with thy sweet graces graced be;

Nevertheless, place the highest value on my compositions, whose source and power is derived from Thee. In the works of others, references to Thee embellish their wanting style, and all great works are graced by the majestic font which flows from Thee;

But thou art all my art, and dost advance As high as learning my rude ignorance.

But Thou art all my learning and artful skill, and dost elevate my ignorance to a true state of knowing.

COMMENTARY

Shakespeare makes it clear that the true source of his skill, and major influence upon his life and work, is God alone. "*So oft have I invok'd thee for my Muse . . . thou art all my art.*" In Sonnet 76, we find Shakespeare stating clearly that the Spirit permeates all of his "*art*": "*why write I still all one, ever the same, . . . O know, sweet love, I always write of you.*" (Sonnet 76.5, 9) In Sonnet 78, Shakespeare comments upon those "*alien*" writers who use spiritual themes merely as an embellishment to their poetry. But to those already spiritually attuned, the Divine adds "*feathers to the learned's wing*" and has "*given grace a double majesty.*" The only truly valuable poetic works, says Shakespeare, are those which are influenced by and elevated above the ordinary ("*heavy ignorance*") and by those "*Whose influence is thine.*" Such a spiritual influence advances "*As high as learning my rude ignorance.*"

Those works of art, drama, music, and poetry that touch the heart and uplift the consciousness, are those which endure. In these we find an ever-new depth and expression. Shakespeare's works are infused with a "*double majesty,*" and are ever fresh and new for those who over the centuries have been positively affected by them.

BIBLICAL PASSAGES SUGGESTED BY SONNET 78

"But there is a spirit in man: and the inspiration of the Almighty giveth them understanding." **Job 32:8**

"Give instruction to a wise man, and he will be yet wiser: teach a just man, and he will increase in learning." **Prov. 9:9**

"And he hath put a new song in my mouth. . . . Blessed is that man that maketh the Lord his trust." **Ps. 40:3, 4**

SONNET 79

Whilst I alone did call upon thy aid,
My verse alone had all thy gentle grace;
But now my gracious numbers are decay'd,
And my sick Muse doth give another place.
I grant, sweet love, thy lovely argument
Deserves the travail of a worthier pen;
Yet what of thee thy poet doth invent
He robs thee of, and pays it thee again.
He lends thee virtue, and he stole that word
From thy behavior; beauty doth he give,
And found it in thy cheek; he can afford
No praise to thee but what in thee doth live.
Then thank him not for that which he doth say,
Since what he owes thee thou thyself dost pay.

THEME

When one calls upon God for aid in all things, then what is produced is endowed with a gentle grace from the all-giving Hand.

GLOSSARY

Whilst I alone did call upon thy aid, My verse alone had all thy gentle grace; But now my gracious numbers are decay'd, And my sick Muse doth give another place.

I alone called upon Thee for aid in composing my verse, and it alone was the full expression of Thy gentle grace; but now my graceful verses are fewer in number, and whatever poetic skill I possessed has now declined and now allows another to take my place.

I grant, sweet love, thy lovely argument Deserves the travail of a worthier pen; Yet what of thee thy poet doth invent He robs thee of, and pays it thee again.

I admit, sweet Love, that a theme based upon Thy loving qualities deserves the efforts of a poet of worthier skill; and yet whatever quality of Thine the poet expresses, he has taken from Thy nature and only recites what he has borrowed from Thee.

He lends thee virtue, and he stole that word From thy behavior; beauty doth he give, And found it in thy cheek; he can afford No praise to thee but what in thee doth live.

He expounds on Thy virtue, but he gives only expression to what he sees already is Thy nature; and about Beauty too he writes, but again, this Thou hast already written across the firmament; he can give no original expression to praise Thee, but what is already apparent for all to see.

Then thank him not for that which he doth say, Since what he owes thee thou thyself dost pay.

So such a one deserves no credit for what he expresses, since he only gives Thee Thy due from the vastness of Thine own treasure.

COMMENTARY

Shakespeare carries on the theme of Sonnet 78 in which the product of one's "*travail*" is only unique when one first acknowledges and receives aid from God, who is the only true Giver and Originator in the Universe. Those who merely recite the obvious, write without adding anything original. "[*H*]*e can afford No praise to thee but what in thee doth live.*" In Sonnet 78, "*Thine eyes*" are what carried the Poet's art "*As high as learning.*" Here, praise is given where praise is due. In Sonnet 79, the unenlightened Poet who "*robs thee*" is not the beneficiary of "*sweet graces*" (Sonnet 78.12) and so "*thank him not for that which he doth say.*"

BIBLICAL PASSAGE SUGGESTED BY SONNET 79

"Verily, verily, I say unto you, He that entereth not by the door into the sheepfold, but climbeth up some other way, the same is a thief and a robber." **John 10:1**

SONNET 80

O how I faint when I of you do write,
Knowing a better spirit doth use your name,
And in the praise thereof spends all his might,
To make me tongue-tied, speaking of your fame.
But since your worth (wide as the ocean is)
The humble as the proudest sail doth bear,
My saucy bark (inferior far to his)
On your broad main doth wilfully appear.
Your shallowest help will hold me up afloat,
Whilst he upon your soundless deep doth ride;
Or, being wrack'd, I am a worthless boat,
He of tall building and of goodly pride:
Then if he thrive and I be cast away,
The worst was this, my love was my decay.

THEME

Man has a dual nature, ever competing for dominance, the higher spiritual self or soul, and the lower, self-centered ego nature.

GLOSSARY

O how I faint when I of you do write, Knowing a better spirit doth use your name, And in the praise thereof spends all his might, To make me tongue-tied, speaking of your fame!

> I am devotionally overcome when writing of You, knowing that my higher self gives expression to Your sacred Name. Giving praise with my all mind and might, leaves me speechless in wonderment.

But since your worth (wide as the ocean is) The humble as the proudest sail doth bear, My saucy bark, inferior far to his, On your broad main doth wilfully appear.

> Your boundless nature upholds the most humble and most proud. My presumptuous ego-nature, far below my soul's grandeur, tries to assert its perversity across the

scope of your vast horizon.

Your shallowest help will hold me up afloat, Whilst he upon your soundless deep doth ride; Or, being wrack'd, I am a worthless boat, He of tall building and of goodly pride:

> Even the least part from the vast main of Your nature will keep the ego afloat in the shallows, or cause it to shipwreck in the mire of worthless selfish pursuits, while the soul seeker, stalwart and strong in his magnificence, moves surely and silently in the depths of deep peace and tranquility.

Then if he thrive and I be cast away, The worst was this, my love was my decay.

> If the soul's nature thrives at the expense of the lower ego nature, the very worst is that my love of the Spirit spelled the end of my ego self.

COMMENTARY

In the Sonnets Shakespeare often makes reference to man's conflicting natures of soul and ego. In Sonnet 39 we read: "*O how thy worth with manners may I sing, When thou art all the better part of me.*" (Sonnet 39.1-2) As G. Blakemore Evans points out in his edited edition of *The Sonnets* (Cambridge: Cambridge University Press, 1996), "*better part*" refers to the soul, citing Golding's translation from Ovid's *Metamorphoses* XV, 875 (commentary on Sonnet 39, p. 149). In Sonnet 74, Shakespeare expresses it thus: "*My spirit is thine, the better part of me.*"(Sonnet 74.8) Man's soul and selfish ego are further described in Sonnet 144.2 as the "*two spirits.*" One is "*the better angel*" and the other is "*the worser spirit.*" (Sonnet 144.3, 4)

In Sonnet 80 we have the analogy of two boats, the "*humble*" and the proud. Shakespeare does not condemn either, but merely points out that one remains in the shallows simply "*afloat,*" while the other, majestic and strong ("*He of tall building and of goodly pride*") courses the profound depths of life. "*Whilst he upon your soundless deep doth ride.*"

If the soul's nature wins out ("*thrive*") the worst that can happen is that the shallow boat of "*saucy bark (inferior far to his)*" will decay.

In many Sonnets we see the metaphor played out wherein the soul triumphs if the right spiritual course is followed. For example: Sonnet 5.13-14, "*flowers distill'd . . . their substances still lives sweet*"; Sonnet 6.13-14, "*Be not self-will'd, for thou art much too fair, To be death's conquest*"; Sonnet 146.9, 12-14, "*Then, soul, live thou upon they servant's loss . . . Within be fed, without be rich no more. . . . So shalt thou feed on Death, . . . there's no more dying then,*" and many others.

BIBLICAL PASSAGES SUGGESTED BY SONNET 80

"O Lord, how manifold are thy works! in wisdom hast thou made them all: the earth is full of thy riches. So is this great and wide sea, wherein are things creeping innumerable, both small and great beasts." **Ps. 104:24-25**

"They that go down to the sea in ships, that do business in great waters; These see the works of the Lord, and his wonders in the deep." **Ps. 107:23-24**

SONNET 81

Or I shall live your epitaph to make,
Or you survive when I in earth am rotten;
From hence your memory death cannot take,
Although in me each part will be forgotten.
Your name from hence immortal life shall have,
Though I, once gone, to all the world must die,
The earth can yield me but a common grave,
When you entombed in men's eyes shall lie.
Your monument shall be my gentle verse,
Which eyes not yet created shall o'er-read;
And tongues to be your being shall rehearse,
When all the breathers of this world are dead,
You still shall live, such virtue hath my pen,
Where breath most breathes, even in the mouths of men.

THEME

The greatest monument and testimonial epitaph of one's life is found in those things that reflect the soul's nature, that eternal part of one's being that is revered throughout all time.

GLOSSARY

Or I shall live your epitaph to make, Or you survive when I in earth am rotten; From hence your memory death cannot take, Although in me each part will be forgotten.

> Whether I live long enough to complete this verse as an ever-living memorial to You, or whether You ("*the better part of me*" [Sonnet 39.2]) are remembered when my earthly flesh has long rotted away for all time, Your memory cannot be effaced by death although all that was of me (the ego self) will long-since be forgotten.

Your name from hence immortal life shall have, Though I, once gone, to all the world must die, The earth can yield me but a common grave, When you entombed in men's eyes shall lie.

Your name from this time and evermore shall be, though I, once dead, must be forgotten by all the world; this earthly, material world can give me only a common grave, while you are immortalized in the depths of men's hearts;

Your monument shall be my gentle verse, Which eyes not yet created shall o'er-read; And tongues to be your being shall rehearse, When all the breathers of this world are dead,

My humble verse is the monument to the soul's victory, which shall be read over and again by future generations and be spoken of repeatedly by voices yet to be heard, when all who draw breath in this world breathe no more.

You still shall live, such virtue hath my pen, Where breath most breathes, even in the mouths of men.

You, the better part of me and source of all inspiration for my writing, shall have life; wherever the breath of Spirit enlivens men's souls, and also in those who recite this verse.

COMMENTARY

Shakespeare, as noted in the commentary to Sonnet 80, often refers to the soul nature as the "*better spirit*" (Sonnet 80.2) and "*the better part of me.*" (Sonnet 39.2)

In Sonnet 18.13-14, Shakespeare says "*So long as men can breathe, or eyes can see, So long lives this, and this gives life to thee.*" In that Sonnet, Shakespeare is praising the Beauty of Spirit to be appreciated by men who can "*breathe*" or have "*eyes*" that see.

In Sonnet 81, Shakespeare also makes reference to "*immortal life,*" "*breath,*" and "*men's eyes.*" Here, however, his attention is not on the overarching Spirit, but upon expressions of the soul, that part of man that has "*immortal life.*" As men recognize the deeper spiritual themes in Shakespeare's "*gentle verse,*" it will be appreciated for the immortal Truth and Beauty it contains. Long after the author's death ("*when I in earth am rotten*") he will be remembered for the "*immortal*" nature of his writing, which drew its power and inspiration from the Spirit: "*such virtue hath my pen.*" "According as his divine power hath given unto us all things that pertain unto life and godliness, through the knowledge of him that hath called us to glory and virtue." **(2 Pet. 1:3)**

In the commentary to Sonnet 72, we see that the author, in reference to his ego self, says in lines 13-14: "*I am shamed,*" as it "*bring*[s] *forth . . . things nothing worth.*" In Sonnet 80, the selfish ego is referred to as a "*worthless boat.*" It is not self-effacement, but true humility that impels this gentle author to credit divine "*virtue*" with his literary achievement. He is contented that "*My name be buried where my body is*" (Sonnet 72.11) and that "*in me* [the ego] *each part will be forgotten*" in a "*common grave.*"

In lines 8, 12, and 14 Shakespeare makes references to "*men's eyes*" and "*breath*" in varying contexts. "*When you entombed in men's eyes shall lie*" means that those who see and appreciate the spiritual qualities, take them deeply to heart, and hold them fast within. Such spiritually-appreciated verse, when "*entombed*" within, has a resurrecting quality. There is a play of words: that which is "*entombed,*" normally refers to death, but here it has the contrasting power to give "*immortal life.*" "*When all the breathers of this world are dead*" in line 12 has a double meaning: first, as those alive in the author's time pass on. It also has the meaning that the "*gentle verse,*" like all eternal Truth, continues on until mankind breathes no more. It thus has the quality of Spirit and "*immortal life.*" Certainly, dead men who do not breathe cannot with "*tongues . . . rehearse.*" But persons who experience deeper states of ecstasy can certainly "*rehearse.*" They, like the author, as described in earlier Sonnets, see the spiritual Light, and in higher states of consciousness may experience breathlessness where the body appears lifeless, as has been recorded in the lives of saints such as St. Teresa of Avila. "I protest by your rejoicing which I have in Christ Jesus our Lord, I die daily." **(1 Cor. 15:31)** "In whose hand is the soul of every living thing, and the breath of all mankind." **(Job 12:10)**

"*Where breath most breathes, even in the mouths of men,*" has both a spiritual meaning, and a mundane interpretation. "And the Lord God formed man of the dust of the ground, and breathed into his nostrils the breath of life; and man became a living soul." **(Gen. 2:7)** "*Where breath most breathes*" in Sonnet 81, is in the soul of man. As long as a man utters spiritual Truths ("*even in the mouths of men*") his soul "*shall* *live*." Such is the power of the Spirit that is breathed into the souls of receptive hearts, and also expressed outwardly by the Poet ("*such virtue hath my pen*").

SONNET 82

I grant thou wert not married to my Muse,
And therefore mayst without attaint o'erlook
The dedicated words which writers use
Of their fair subject, blessing every book.
Thou art as fair in knowledge as in hue,
Finding thy worth a limit past my praise;
And therefore art enforc'd to seek anew
Some fresher stamp of the time-bettering days.
And do so, love; yet when they have devised
What strained touches rhetoric can lend,
Thou truly fair wert truly sympathized
In true plain words by thy true-telling friend;
And their gross painting might be better us'd,
Where cheeks need blood; in thee it is abus'd.

THEME

The source of all beauty and eloquence is the Spirit, whose vastness cannot be captured by any one individual. Those who are not truly imbued with Truth fail in the attempt to move us with their shallow rhetoric.

GLOSSARY

I grant thou wert not married to my Muse, And therefore mayst without attaint o'erlook The dedicated words which writers use Of their fair subject, blessing every book.

> I grant that Thou hast never been married only to my verse, and therefore may be found in the devotional themes of other writers without my feeling unappreciated, as every book that dedicates its theme to Thy Beauty is blessed.

Thou art as fair in knowledge as in hue, Finding thy worth a limit past my praise; And therefore art enforc'd to seek anew Some fresher stamp of the time-bettering days.

Thou art all Beauty and Eloquence; whose nature is beyond my capacity to praise in verse; and so Thou art constrained to seek new poets who may give fresh expression to Thy nature in days to come.

And do so, love; yet when they have devised What strained touches rhetoric can lend, Thou truly fair wert truly sympathized In true plain words by thy true-telling friend;

Do so, Beloved, yet I think when they have strained to contrive their rhetoric, it will be apparent that Thou were truly apprehended and represented in the simple verse of the one who is Thy real Truth-revealing friend.

And their gross painting might be better us'd, Where cheeks need blood; in thee it is abus'd.

And others, while attempting grossly to add their pale touches, abuse nature's canvas of Thy perfect Beauty.

COMMENTARY

In Sonnet 81.9, Shakespeare states that his "*gentle verse*" will stand as a monument of expression to the Divine. In Sonnet 82, he makes it clear that the Spirit cannot be captured by one individual, even him. "*Finding thy worth* [is] *a limit past my praise.*" As future ages ("*time-bettering days*") see new expressions of verse, Shakespeare declares that poets then will be those who fail miserably to express what in their hearts they do not truly apprehend. "As thou knowest not what is the way of spirit, . . . even so thou knowest not the works of God who maketh all." **(Eccl. 11:5)** Shakespeare states that his "*true plain words*" are those of a "*true-telling friend.*" In his Sonnets, Shakespeare declares repeatedly that the source of his inspiration and understanding is the Lord. (See Sonnet 78.13.) "Drunk with the bliss of singing I forget myself and call thee friend who are my Lord," wrote the Nobel Laureate poet, Rabindranath Tagore. "But there is a spirit in man: and the inspiration of the Almighty giveth them understanding." **(Job 32:8)**

SONNET 83

I never saw that you did painting need,
And therefore to your fair no painting set;
I found, or thought I found, you did exceed
The barren tender of a poet's debt:
And therefore have I slept in your report,
That you yourself, being extant, well might show
How far a modern quill doth come too short,
Speaking of worth, what worth in you doth grow.
This silence for my sin you did impute,
Which shall be most my glory being dumb;
For I impair not beauty being mute,
When others would give life, and bring a tomb.
There lives more life in one of your fair eyes,
Than both your poets can in praise devise.

THEME

All of one's talent and ability is from the Spirit. For one to comment on another's lesser abilities is to show pride. Silence is golden, while the Spirit itself speaks volumes of illumination and is always the true teacher of life and beauty.

GLOSSARY

I never saw that you did painting need, And therefore to your fair no painting set; I found, or thought I found, you did exceed The barren tender of a poet's debt:

> It never occurred to me to try to embellish Your incomparable nature, therefore this was never attempted; I understand, or thought I did, that Your vast nature was beyond all the ability You gave this poor poet to tender living verse.

And therefore have I slept in your report, That you yourself, being extant, well might show How far a modern quill doth come too short, Speaking of worth, what worth in you doth grow.

> And therefore I have been silent in reporting on the

shortcomings of others works in "new-found methods," (Sonnet 76.4) knowing that Thy vast and omnipresent nature will be the most worthy instruction on the shallow composition of others who attempt to describe what value is present in Thy limitless vastness.

This silence for my sin you did impute, Which shall be most my glory being dumb; For I impair not beauty being mute, When others would give life, and bring a tomb.

You imputed sin for my silence, but my silence is golden and does more to show Your Beauty, than others whose attempts at life-giving inspiration bring only emptiness.

There lives more life in one of your fair eyes, Than both your poets can in praise devise.

There is more infinitude in only a part of Thine all-seeing, and seen nature, than poets both shallow and enlightened could ever devise to praise.

COMMENTARY

Shakespeare acknowledges his limitations. His verse as an expression of his love, never attempts, in an egotistical sense, to overstep its boundaries. "*I never saw that you did painting need.*" Shakespeare acknowledges that for all his poetic ability, he owes a "*poet's debt.*" He could not metaphorically take a beautiful plant ("*fair*") and graft or "*set*" anything that could add to its beauty. As for those who wrote with a "*modern quill,*" such as those in Sonnet 76 who pen with "*new-found methods*" in "*compounds strange*" (Sonnet 76.4), Shakespeare declares that he prefers "*being mute.*" Nature itself, "*being extant,*" might well show that lesser poets "*come too short.*" Silence, says Shakespeare, "*shall be most my glory.*" In other words, instead of being the judge over another's works, which would reflect pride, Shakespeare allows others' work to find their way to the "*tomb*" in their futile attempt to "*give life.*" Life, or Spirit itself, needs no embellishment from any poet, as the light it casts from one part ("*in one of your fair eyes*") is beyond anything "*your poets can in praise devise.*"

In Sonnet 82.12, Shakespeare refers to himself as "*thy true-telling friend.*" As for certain other poets, he refers to their product as "*gross painting*" in which the Spirit "*is abus'd.*" (Sonnet 82.13, 14) In Sonnet 83, Shakespeare states that "*I slept in your report*" and was "*mute*" as regards the manner in which the "*modern quill doth come too short.*" It seems a contradiction for Shakespeare to declare that he will remain "*mute*" while at the same time pointing out the "*gross painting*" (Sonnet 82.13), which can only "*bring a tomb.*" The explanation is that Shakespeare says "*you yourself, being extant, well might show*" what "*worth . . . doth grow.*" Spirit is the true author as regards the subject of "*beauty.*"

Shakespeare states that his verse reflects his constant theme of love for the Divine. "*I always write of you, And you and love are still my argument.*" (Sonnet 76.9-10) Those who become awakened or enlightened by their own self-effort, or by introspection perhaps, as noted in Sonnet 77, learn about the true nature of beauty, "*worth,*" and "*life.*"

As already related in several other Sonnet commentaries, Shakespeare makes reference to the single spiritual eye. This is the deeper meaning of the phrase, "*There lives more life in one of your fair eyes.*" The singular light of the spiritual eye becomes the true teacher, as it is a portal to higher states of wisdom and consciousness. Intuitive knowledge or wisdom, imparted in this light of Truth, is instructive beyond anything "*your poets can in praise devise.*"

BIBLICAL PASSAGE SUGGESTED BY SONNET 83

"I will instruct thee and teach thee in the way which thou shalt go: I will guide thee with mine eye." **Ps. 32:8**

SONNET 84

Who is it that says most, which can say more
Than this rich praise, that you alone are you,
In whose confine immured is the store
Which should example where your equal grew?
Lean penury within that pen doth dwell,
That to his subject lends not some small glory;
But he that writes of you, if he can tell
That you are you, so dignifies his story.
Let him but copy what in you is writ,
Not making worse what nature, made so clear,
And such counterpart shall fame his wit,
Making his style admired everywhere.
You to your beauteous blessings add a curse,
Being fond on praise, which makes your praises worse.

THEME

The Lord is the Sole Unique in and beyond the Universe. He is the Source of all and the Treasure House from which all of value proceeds.

GLOSSARY

Who is it that says most, which can say more Than this rich praise, that you alone are you, In whose confine immured is the store Which should example where your equal grew?

> There is no greater statement of truth and praiseworthy verse than that You alone are You, in whose Consciousness alone is kept the only Source of anything that can be a representation of your equal.

Lean penury within that pen doth dwell, That to his subject lends not some small glory; But he that writes of you, if he can tell That you are you, so dignifies his story.

> It is a poor writer who is unable to lend some small glory to his subject. But he who writes of You, truly knowing

> that You are You, is able to ring dignity to his story.

Let him but copy what in you is writ, Not making worse what nature, made so clear, And such counterpart shall fame his wit, Making his style admired everywhere.

> Let him but copy Truth in its exact nature, not placing his own words above what nature, made so clear, and he shall reap fame and admiration everywhere for his wit and wisdom.

You to your beauteous blessings add a curse, Being fond on praise, which makes your praises worse.

> Divine Justice, however, will diminish the fame of anyone who becomes proud of the flattery and admiration heaped upon him.

COMMENTARY

In Sonnet 83 Shakespeare states unequivocally that the Spirit is Infinite: beginningless and endless. No one can even begin in verse or otherwise to capture and articulate anything except that Spirit "*being extant, well might show.*" (Sonnet 83.6) In Sonnet 84, Shakespeare says, on one level, that there is nothing more to say, my Lord, than this: "*That you are you.*" "Hear, O Israel: The Lord our God is one Lord." **(Deut. 6:4)** "Unto thee it was shewed, that thou mightest know that the Lord he is God; there is none else beside him." **(Deut. 4:35)**

This is also reminiscent of "And God said unto Moses, I AM THAT I AM: and he said, Thus shalt thou say unto the children of Israel, I AM hath sent me unto you." **(Exod. 3:14)** The realization of the Poet is that he understands "*that you alone are you.*" This understanding, however, is not within the grasp of the "*barren tender of a poet's debt*" (Sonnet 83.4), but only in the "*equal*" that is securely within the Being of Spirit ("*in whose confine immured is the store*"). On another level, Shakespeare declares that one who understands that his soul is a part of Spirit knows "*that you alone,*" Spirit, "*are you,*" the soul. Such a person has the knowledge that in his soul "*is the store*" or treasure house, where Spirits "*equal grew.*" "Know ye not that ye are the temple of God, and that the Spirit of God dwelleth in you." **(1 Cor. 3:16)** "I have said Ye are gods;

and all of you are children of the most High." **(Ps. 82:6)**

Shakespeare goes on to say that only a writer who can tell "*that you are you*" is able to express something which "*dignifies his story.*" Shakespeare applauds the writer of deeper spiritual understanding who truly realizes that he, as a soul, is a part of the Spirit and writes from that depth. "[*H*]*is story*" is not just the writing, but the biography of one who is creating from a deeper level of comprehension. A poet who can clearly express deeper truths and is "*Not making worse what nature made so clear,*" shall be admired everywhere.

In the final couplet, again on two interpretative levels, Shakespeare expresses an admonition to one who becomes prideful of his work. On the one hand, the "*curse*" is a pronouncement of divine law: "When pride cometh, then cometh shame: but with the lowly is wisdom." **(Prov. 11:2)** In Sonnet 83.4 Shakespeare realizes he is not the doer of great works, but his is the "*barren tender of a poet's debt.*" On another level is the "*glory*" of silence. "*Which shall be most my glory, being dumb.*" (Sonnet 83.10) One who is "*fond on praise*" is not humble, but brings on his own "*curse . . . which makes your praises worse.*" "Woe unto them that are wise in their own eyes, and prudent in their own sight!" **(Isa. 5:21)**

So in Sonnet 83.11 we see the "*mute*" Shakespeare who, while in the state of "*being dumb*" (Sonnet 83.10) is lowly with wisdom, as the proverb above states. Sonnet 84 contrasts the writer who also "*dignifies his story*" with some understanding of the nature of Spirit, but who in the end succumbs to adulation, finding that to his once "*beauteous blessings*" is added a "*curse.*" "*You to your beauteous blessings add a curse, Being fond on praise, which makes your praises worse.*"

SONNET 85

My tongue-tied Muse in manners holds her still,
Whilst comments of your praise, richly compil'd,
Reserve their character with golden quill,
And precious phrase by all the Muses fil'd.
I think good thoughts, while others write good words,
And, like unlettered clerk, still cry "Amen"
To every hymn that able spirit affords,
In polish'd form of well-refined pen.
Hearing you prais'd, I say, "'tis so, 'tis true,"
And to the most of praise add something more;
But that is in my thought, whose love to you,
(Though words come hindmost) holds his rank before,
Then others for the breath of words respect,
Me for my dumb thoughts, speaking in effect.

THEME

Those in popular favor who attribute their art to questionable divine inspiration are only lauded by those who are equally shallow.

GLOSSARY

My tongue-tied Muse in manners holds her still, Whilst comments of your praise, richly compil'd, Reserve their character with golden quill, And precious phrase by all the Muses fil'd.

> My own silent muse remains discretely withheld in silence, while the profusely composed praise of You flows lavishly from the most refined golden quill.

I think good thoughts, while others write good words, And, like unlettered clerk, still cry 'Amen' To every hymn that able spirit affords In polish'd form of well-refined pen.

> I myself keep my good thoughts to myself, while others write good words and are like an unlearned church sexton who, with rote repetition to every hymn says "*Amen,*" to every hymn inspired by an able spirit and written in the

polished form of a well-refined pen.

Hearing you prais'd, I say, "'tis so, 'tis true," And to the most of praise add something more; But that is in my thought, whose love to you, (Though words come hindmost) holds his rank before,

When I hear such praise of You, I say "it is so, it is true," and to the most exalted praise I add something greater, but only in my silent thoughts, whose love for you takes all precedent over my words.

Then others for the breath of words respect, Me for my dumb thoughts, speaking in effect.

While others in wordy praises go on interminably, I, in my silent thought, speak most truly.

COMMENTARY

In Sonnet 83.14, Shakespeare states that the Spirit is beyond what "*your poets in praise devise.*" In Sonnet 84, there are those whose work is "*admired everywhere*" but who "*being fond on praise*" are truly shallow and are depreciated for their pride in the eyes of the Divine Judge. (Sonnet 84.12, 14) They are like the "*unlettered clerk*" who neither understands the work admired nor the author of the verse.

Shakespeare states that his praise is even greater. It "*is in my thought, whose love of you*" takes precedent over words which "*come hindermost.*" As for all the "*good words*" of others, they are merely an "*unlettered*" expression. Without thinking they say "*'Amen' To every hymn that able spirit affords.*" Shakespeare says it is his humble ("*dumb*") silent thoughts of love that are truly "*speaking.*"

As to this section of the Sonnets, many writers interpret these as Shakespeare's comments on a rival poet or poets. For my own part, I believe Shakespeare might well have been above critiquing other writers, but he, too, was human. For all his good spiritual qualities, Shakespeare, like most, was probably not perfected in wisdom. As a deeper lesson to those who create works, Shakespeare says that they should avoid being fond of praise and must not be so egotistical as to suggest they are divinely inspired by some "*able spirit.*" In such circumstance, it is better to remain "*tongues-tied,*" holding one's praise "*still,*" than to give expression by rote like an "*unlettered clerk.*" As for Shakespeare, he states: ". . . *in my thought, whose love to you, (Though words come hindmost) holds his rank before.*"

BIBLICAL PASSAGES SUGGESTED BY SONNET 85

"Through thy precepts I get understanding: therefore I hate every false way." **Ps. 119:104**

"The heart of him that hath understanding seeketh knowledge: but the mouth of fools feedeth on foolishness." **Prov. 15:14**

"Thus saith the Lord God; Woe unto the foolish prophets, that follow their own spirit, and have seen nothing!" **Ezek. 13:3**

SONNET 86

Was it the proud full sail of his great verse,
Bound for the prize of all too precious you,
That did my ripe thoughts in my brain inhearse,
Making their tomb the womb wherein they grew?
Was it his Spirit, by Spirits taught to write
Above a mortal pitch, that struck me dead?
No, neither he, nor his compeers by night
Giving him aid, my verse astonished.
He, nor that affable familiar ghost
Which nightly gulls him with intelligence,
As victors of my silence cannot boast,
I was not sick of any fear from thence.
But when your countenance filled up his line,
Then lack'd I matter, that enfeebled mine.

THEME

All is Spirit. When the ego steps aside, all is perceived as One and the same, no part better than any other.

GLOSSARY

Was it the proud full sail of his great verse, Bound for the prize of all too precious you, That did my ripe thoughts in my brain inhearse, Making their tomb the womb wherein they grew?

> Was the puffed and full-blown pride of his grand verse, aimed at the prize of Your nature, always beyond reach, that silenced my thoughts from outward expression and kept them locked within the tomb of my mind wherein they were nurtured?

Was it his Spirit, by Spirits taught to write Above a mortal pitch, that struck me dead? No, neither he, nor his compeers by night Giving him aid, my verse astonished.

> Was it his lively mind, taught by some phantasmagorical spirit to write in a manner high above us mortals that si-

lenced my tongue from outward expression? No, neither he, nor his nocturnal visitors silenced my verse.

He, nor that affable familiar ghost Which nightly gulls him with intelligence, As victors of my silence cannot boast, I was not sick of any fear from thence.

Neither he, nor his amiable familiar that by night plies him with false erudition, can claim victory for my silence as I was never fearful of them.

But when your countenance filled up his line, Then lack'd I matter, that enfeebled mine.

But when I saw your face imbedded in his verse, then I gave no further thought to the matter, nor was I concerned that my verse was in any way diminished by his.

COMMENTARY

In Sonnet 86, Shakespeare sums up this group of his Sonnets in which he seems to comment upon the "*Lean penury*" (Sonnet 84.5) and pride of another poet.

It is entirely possible that the "*others*" in Sonnet 83.12 may be other writers, but that "*both your poets*" (83.14) are really the "*better spirit*" of Sonnet 80.2, or the soul; and that the other one, full of "*proud full sail,*" is only the ego's self-centered nature. History records that in the early spiritual journey of St. Anthony, he was plagued nightly by wanton demons. These manifestations are really the demons of the ego that persistently battle the soul for dominance. Throughout this group of Sonnets, we see Shakespeare "*dumb*" and "*mute*" (Sonnet 83.10, 11) while the ego "*counterpart shall fame his wit.*" (Sonnet 84.11) Whether this is Shakespeare's "*worser spirit,*" (Sonnet 144.4) or another poet, in the end, is of no consequence. Shakespeare comes to the realization that when God is intoned in any lines, whether of the wise, or not, His name is still sweet, His inspiration is to be respected and praised.

BIBLICAL PASSAGES SUGGESTED BY SONNET 86

"But there is a spirit in man: and the inspiration of the Almighty giveth them understanding." **Job 32:8**

"The rich and the poor meet together: the Lord is the maker of them all." **Prov. 22:2**

"How sweet are thy words unto my taste! yea, sweeter than honey to my mouth." **Ps. 119:103**

SONNET 87

Farewell, thou art too dear for my possessing,
And like enough thou know'st thy estimate,
The charter of thy worth gives thee releasing;
My bonds in thee are all determinate.
For how do I hold thee but by thy granting,
And for that riches where is my deserving?
The cause of this fair gift in me is wanting,
And so my patent back again is swerving.
Thy self thou gav'st, thy own worth then not knowing,
Or me, to whom thou gav'st it, else mistaking;
So thy great gift, upon misprision growing,
Comes home again, on better judgment making.
Thus have I had thee, as a dream doth flatter,
In sleep a king but, waking, no such matter.

THEME

Man in his ordinary, egocentric consciousness does not have the capacity to fully understand the Lord's grace and judgments, but upon waking from his soul's ignorance, he begins to comprehend his place as a child of God.

GLOSSARY

Farewell, thou art too dear for my possessing, And like enough thou know'st thy estimate, The charter of thy worth gives thee releasing; My bonds in thee are all determinate.

> Thou art beyond my ability to apprehend, and only Thou alone can know Thine Infinitude: Thy boundless omnipresence is Thy measurelessness; And my place in Thee is by Thee determined.

For how do I hold thee but by thy granting And for that riches where is my deserving? The cause of this fair gift in me is wanting, And so my patent back again is swerving.

> What I receive from Thee is by Thy grace alone, and

where is there merit in me to receive such riches? The reason for Thy grace I find wanting in me, and so I fear Thy grant to me is swerving toward revocation.

Thy self thou gav'st, thy own worth then not knowing, Or me, to whom thou gav'st it, else mistaking; So thy great gift, upon misprision growing, Comes home again, on better judgment making.

Thyself, Thou didst give completely, but I through error, not fully realizing Thy bounty, thought there was a mistake in Thy grace to me. But now, with the benefit of better understanding, I comprehend Thy nature, and that Thy gift to me is irrevocably given.

Thus have I had thee, as a dream doth flatter, In sleep a king but, waking, no such matter.

So I have been like an ignorant dreamer who is deceived into believing himself a king, but who, on waking, fully comprehends how things really are.

COMMENTARY

The boundless infinitude of Spirit is beyond man's comprehension. "[*T*]*hou art too dear for my possessing*." Each one is a child of the Divine. It is through His grace that one receives, neither always understanding the Lord's motivations, nor fully seeing what in us seems to merit Divine gifts. "*And for that riches where is my deserving? The cause of this fair gift in me is wanting*." Self-doubt occludes the gift of the light of understanding and causes one to waver on the path. "*And so my patent back again is swerving*."

With a deeper understanding of one's relationship with the heavenly Beloved, the way is again made more clear, or "*Comes home again, on better judgement making*."

Man often sleeps in ignorance of his true spiritual nature as a child of God. One in a dream may fancy himself a king, and on waking be struck with the true reality. "*Thus have I had thee, as a dream doth flatter, In sleep a king but, waking, no such matter*." Scripture states that as children of God we are truly gods and kings in this world of the Lord's creation, but for the most part, we do not comprehend that reality.

BIBLICAL PASSAGES SUGGESTED BY SONNET 87

"It is the glory of God to conceal a thing: but the honour of kings is to search out a matter." **Prov. 25:2**

"Behold, what manner of love the Father hath bestowed upon us, that we should be called the sons of God: therefore the world knoweth us not, because it knew him not." **1 John 3:1**

"For the grace of God that bringeth salvation hath appeared to all men." **Titus 2:11**

"That being justified by his grace, we should be made heirs according to the hope of eternal life." **Titus 3:7**

"O the depth of the riches both of the wisdom and knowledge of God! how unsearchable are his judgments, and his ways past finding out!" **Rom. 11:33**

"Beloved, now are we the sons of God, and it doth not yet appear what we shall be: but we know that, when he shall appear, we shall be like him; for we shall see him as he is." **1 John 3:2**

SONNET 88

When thou shalt be disposed to set me light,
And place my merit in the eye of scorn,
Upon thy side against myself I'll fight,
And prove thee virtuous, though thou art forsworn.
With mine own weakness being best acquainted,
Upon thy part I can set down a story
Of faults concealed, wherein I am attainted;
That thou in losing me shalt win much glory.
And I by this will be a gainer too;
For bending all my loving thoughts on thee,
The injuries that to myself I do,
Doing thee vantage, double-vantage me.
Such is my love, to thee I so belong,
That for thy right, myself will bear all wrong.

THEME

By circumstances and soulful introspection, one learns to uproot inner weaknesses as these come to light. By all-surrendering love to God, one glorifies the heavenly Father and purifies one's soul of dross.

GLOSSARY

When thou shalt be disposed to set me light, And place my merit in the eye of scorn, Upon thy side against myself I'll fight, And prove thee virtuous, though thou art forsworn.

> When it is Thy will to deflate my ego, by exposing my true nature before the eye of scorn, I will fight my lying ego and acclaim Thy virtue in correcting my errors.

With mine own weakness being best acquainted, Upon thy part I can set down a story Of faults concealed, wherein I am attainted; That thou in losing me shalt win much glory.

> I am well acquainted with my inner weakness, and to further the growth of my spiritual being, I will confess the errors that become apparent so that the ego's hold

may be loosened and my soul may regain its glory.

And I by this will be a gainer too; For bending all my loving thoughts on thee, The injuries that to myself I do, Doing thee vantage, double-vantage me.

My soul's gain, by focusing all my loving thoughts on the Spirit, shall be a loss to the earthbound ego. But this loss will bring happiness to my life and even greater benefit to my soul.

Such is my love, to thee I so belong, That for thy right, myself will bear all wrong.

So great is my love for Thee, to whom I devote myself completely, that to do Thy will alone, I will expose and correct all my ego's faults.

COMMENTARY

Shakespeare understands the nature of the battle between the soul and the ego (see Sonnet 144). When circumstances hold the ego's faults up to the light of truth ("*place my merit in the eye of* scorn"), it seeks to justify itself by saying it is not so ("[*T*]*hou art forsworn*"). The path to wisdom, Shakespeare says, is to admit one's faults and fight the ego's defenses. "*Upon thy side against myself I'll fight.*" By taking stock of the ego ("*set down a story*"), one can uproot "*faults concealed,*" and thereby loosen the ego's hold on the soul ("*losing me*") and "*win much glory.*" Shakespeare says that by "*bending all my loving thoughts on thee,*" the only "*injuries*" are to the egocentric self. This then gives "*double-vantage*" to the soul seeking to free itself from the fetters of the earthbound ego. Shakespeare declares that it is by all-surrendering love for God ("*Such is my love, to thee I belong*") that he is able and most willing to "*fight*" all wrong "*within himself.*"

BIBLICAL PASSAGES SUGGESTED BY SONNET 88

"Behold, happy is the man whom God correcteth: therefore despise not thou chastening of the Almighty." **Job 5:17**

"My son, despise not the chastening of the Lord; neither be weary of his correction: For whom the Lord loveth he correcteth; even as a father the son in whom he delighteth. Happy is the man that findeth wisdom, and the man that getteth understanding." **Prov. 3:11-13**

SONNET 89

Say that thou didst forsake me for some fault,
And I will comment upon that offence.
Speak of my lameness, and I straight will halt,
Against thy reasons making no defence.
Thou canst not, love, disgrace me half so ill,
To set a form upon desired change,
As I'll myself disgrace; knowing thy will,
I will acquaintance strangle and look strange,
Be absent from thy walks, and in my tongue,
Thy sweet beloved name no more shall dwell,
Lest I, too much profane, should do it wrong,
And haply of our old acquaintance tell.
For thee, against myself I'll vow debate,
For I must ne'er love him whom thou dost hate.

THEME

One desirous of uprooting egotistical faults must not make excuses for engaging in wrongful conduct. Deceit is uprooted by truth. Temptation is defeated by a mind fixed upon affirmative vows or prayers, while eschewing incorrect actions and wrong habits.

GLOSSARY

Say that thou didst forsake me for some fault, And I will comment upon that offence. Speak of my lameness, and I straight will halt, Against thy reasons making no defence.

> Suppose that Thou didst forsake me because of my own faults, I immediately would comment upon my shortcoming, admit my error, and make no defense against Thy just action.

Thou canst not, love, disgrace me half so ill, To set a form upon desired change, As I'll myself disgrace; knowing thy will, I will acquaintance strangle, and look strange;

> The moment that Thou, Love, allow my faults to come

to light, I myself, seeing the disgrace, and knowing Thy Will, will distance myself from my former bad acquaintances and habits.

Be absent from thy walks, and in my tongue, Thy sweet beloved name no more shall dwell, Lest I, too much profane, should do it wrong, And haply of our old acquaintance tell.

If I feel that Thou dost no more walk with me, I will not utter Thy sweet beloved name, lest I, who am profane, speak wrongly; and perhaps disclose the nature of our relationship.

For thee, against myself I'll vow debate, For I must ne'er love him whom thou dost hate.

For Thee, I will even combat temptations by making affirmative vows, for I must never love that which to Thee is hateful.

COMMENTARY

Shakespeare gives some suggestion on how one is to act in the face of one's faults or bad habits. He states that if circumstances "*Speak of my lameness*," he will make "*no defence*" against the consequence ("*thou didst forsake me*") or the wisdom ("*thy reasons*") of their being a negative result of engaging in the wrongful conduct.

Shakespeare says he will straight away, upon recognizing the "*desired change*," go in the opposite direction and become estranged to his old ways. "*I will acquaintance strangle and look strange*."

The third quatrain of Sonnet 89 has two levels of interpretation. In the first, addressing the ego, Shakespeare implies that his old haunts shall know him no more. "*Be absent from thy walks*." He will not even give voice to his old "loves." "[*I*]*n my tongue, Thy sweet beloved name no more shall dwell*." He understands that even speaking about his old ways could be injurious. "*Lest I, too much profane, should do it wrong*."

The second interpretation is that Shakespeare is addressing the Lord. "*Be absent from thy walks*" means that Shakespeare feels the Lord is no longer walking with him, spiritually speaking. This is because of "*some fault*." The Poet will "*no more*" speak "*Thy sweet beloved name*," stating that due to his "*offence*," he is "*too much profane.*" In such a sinful or "*profane*" state, he feels that he cannot address the Lord properly but would "*do it wrong.*" Further, he would be speaking to the "*sweet beloved*" as if the "*old acquaintance*" or relationship still existed, hearkening back to a time when he did not feel "*that thou didst forsake me for some fault.*" The Poet, with "*loving thoughts on thee*" (Sonnet 88.10) would, out of reverence, and feeling "*too much profane,*" refrain from either uttering "*thy sweet beloved name,*" or referring to the "*old acquaintance.*"

The way to defeat wrong behavior and thoughts is by positive affirmations and prayerful vows ("*I'll vow debate*"), keeping the mind away from old temptations that it used to "*love*" and remembering that these are hateful to the well-being of the soul. "*For I must ne'er love him whom thou dost hate.*"

There is also a play on Bible passages found in the Book of Job. Job is complaining of being forsaken and an outcast. "He hath put my brethren far from me, and mine acquaintance are verily estranged from me." (**Job 19:13**) In Sonnet 89, the Poet says, "*I will acquaintance strangle and look strange.*" It is one's faults and bad habits that cause one to feel as if "*thou didst forsake me.*" It is each person who must change and become estranged from his old "*acquaintance*" of bad habits and temptations.

BIBLICAL PASSAGES SUGGESTED BY SONNET 89

"Depart from evil, and do good; seek peace, and pursue it." **Ps. 34:14**

"Ye that love the Lord, hate evil." **Ps. 97:10**

"Let love be without dissimulation. Abhor that which is evil; cleave to that which is good." **Rom. 12:9**

SONNET 90

Then hate me when thou wilt, if ever, now;
Now, while the world is bent my deeds to cross,
Join with the spite of fortune, make me bow,
And do not drop in for an after-loss:
Ah do not, when my heart hath 'scaped this sorrow,
Come in the rearward of a conquered woe;
Give not a windy night a rainy morrow,
To linger out a purpos'd overthrow.
If thou wilt leave me, do not leave me last,
When other petty griefs have done their spite,
But in the onset come: so shall I taste
At first the very worst of fortune's might,
And other strains of woe, which now seem woe,
Compar'd with loss of thee will not seem so.

THEME

Harmful egotistical habits, desires, and actions inevitably lead to grief. The worst punishment, however, is the fear of heavenly judgment, a smiting conscience, and loss of mental peace.

GLOSSARY

Then hate me when thou wilt, if ever, now; Now, while the world is bent my deeds to cross, Join with the spite of fortune, make me bow, And do not drop in for an after-loss:

> If ever Thou wilt show hate for my faults, do it while worldly circumstances are bent on thwarting my actions. Add Thy force to that of misfortune, and bring me to my knees. Do not delay until my final ruin, and then add more by Thy punishing disdain.

Ah do not, when my heart hath 'scaped this sorrow, Come in the rearward of a conquered woe; Give not a windy night a rainy morrow, To linger out a purpos'd overthrow.

> And do not, when I have some emotional relief from

> woeful circumstances, come from behind, and pounce again. That is like a stormy night which gives way to a rainy morrow, and merely elongates the sorrow of inevitable defeat.

If thou wilt leave me, do not leave me last, When other petty griefs have done their spite, But in the onset come: so shall I taste At first the very worst of fortune's might,

> If I will not have Thy support, leave me now, not at the end, when puny emotional griefs, have done their worst. If ill fortune is to be my destiny, come with the first troubling winds that blow, that I might taste the worst of bitter times at the onset.

And other strains of woe, which now seem woe, Compar'd with loss of thee will not seem so.

> And the painful experiences, which now seem like a source of grief, compared to the loss of Thee, will seem inconsequential.

COMMENTARY

Shakespeare, as the speaker, acknowledges that his worldly life and fortunes have turned against him. "*The world is bent my deeds to cross.*" The loss of peace and God's grace, as a result of egotistical action, would be even more devastating than any "*spite of fortune.*" Shakespeare says that if the Lord is to abandon him because of his perceived sinful conduct, that this punishment or "*hate*" come quickly and not after the adversity of worldly circumstances that he has been dealt. "[*D*]*o not drop in for an after-loss.*" The worst of all the losses that he says can come ("*the very worst of fortune's might*") would be if "*thou wilt leave me.*"

When one engages in wrongful conduct, the conscience is the first to smite one; and afterward there is a loss of peace and security. Shakespeare says that if this loss of peace would come "*in the onset,*" one might learn more quickly that, "*Compar'd with loss of thee,*" other "*petty griefs*" will not seem so "*woeful.*" In this way, wrongful thoughts and actions are conquered "*in the onset,*" and one may be able to escape "*a rainy morrow*" and the "*strains of woe*" that otherwise would befall one. As for Shakespeare, there could be no loss to compare with that which would befall him without his "*sweet love*" (Sonnet 76.9). "*And other strains of woe, which now seem woe, Compar'd with the loss of thee will not seem so.*"

BIBLICAL PASSAGES SUGGESTED BY SONNET 90

"What man is he that feareth the Lord? him shall he teach in the way that he shall choose." **Ps. 25:12**

"Cast me not away from thy presence; and take not thy holy spirit from me." **Ps. 51:11**

"The sacrifices of God are a broken spirit: a broken and contrite heart, O God, thou wilt not despise." **Ps. 51:17**

"But your iniquities have separated between you and your God, and your sins have hid his face from you, that he will not hear." **Isa. 59:2**

"For when they shall say peace and safety; then sudden destruction cometh upon them, as travail upon a woman with child; and they shall not escape." **1 Thess. 5:3**

SONNET 91

Some glory in their birth, some in their skill,
Some in their wealth, some in their body's force,
Some in their garments, though new-fangled ill,
Some in their hawks and hounds, some in their horse;
And every humour hath his adjunct pleasure,
Wherein it finds a joy above the rest,
But these particulars are not my measure;
All these I better in one general best.
Thy love is better than high birth to me,
Richer than wealth, prouder than garments' cost,
Of more delight than hawks or horses be;
And having thee, of all men's pride I boast:
Wretched in this alone, that thou mayst take
All this away, and me most wretched make.

THEME

The only lasting and worthwhile joy of man, greater than any earthly possession, is love of the Divine.

GLOSSARY

Some glory in their birth, some in their skill, Some in their wealth, some in their body's force, Some in their garments, though new-fangled ill, Some in their hawks and hounds, some in their horse;

> Some people glory in their family heritage, some in their ability, some in their wealth, some in their bodily strength, some in their fine tailored, new-fangled garments, some in their hawks and hounds, some in their horses.

And every humour hath his adjunct pleasure, Wherein it finds a joy above the rest: But these particulars are not my measure; All these I better in one general best.

> And each person's temperament has its indulgent pleasure that gives some joy above other interests. But these pleasures of others have no meaning for me, as there is

one above all that I find best.

Thy love is better than high birth to me, Richer than wealth, prouder than garments' cost, Of more delight than hawks or horses be; And having thee, of all men's pride I boast:

Thy Love is better than high birth to me; a treasure beyond material wealth, more precious than costly garments, more delightful than hawks or horses could ever be; and having Thee, I have something greater than any man's physical possession.

Wretched in this alone, that thou mayst take All this away, and me most wretched make.

Only one thing could bring me sorrow: that Thou mayest take all this joy from me, making me the most wretched of men.

COMMENTARY

In Sonnet 91, Shakespeare compares the earthly prides and pleasures of men in their "*birth . . . skill . . . wealth . . . garments*" etc., to one thing alone that is superior to all the rest: "*Thy love*" which is "*better . . . richer . . . prouder* [and] *of more delight.*" The only true loss would be, not of possessions or skill or high birth, but that "*thou mayest take all this* [love] *away.*" This Sonnet is reminiscent of Sonnet 66.13 in which the Poet asserts that, of life's frivolities, he is "*Tir'd with all these.*" The mundane has no value in the life of one who has "*Thy love,*" which is "[*r*]*icher than wealth.*" In other words, love of the Divine, in the Poet's heart, is a treasure beyond all earthy possessions.

BIBLICAL PASSAGES SUGGESTED BY SONNET 91

"For ye had compassion of me in my bonds, and took joyfully the spoiling of your goods, knowing in yourselves that ye have in heaven a better and an enduring substance." **Heb. 10:34**

"I love them that love me; and those that seek me early shall find me. Riches and honour are with me; yea, durable riches and righteousness. My fruit is better than gold." **Prov. 8:17-19**

SONNET 92

But do thy worst to steal thyself away,
For term of life thou art assured mine,
And life no longer than thy love will stay,
For it depends upon that love of thine.
Then need I not to fear the worst of wrongs,
When in the least of them my life hath end.
I see a better state to me belongs
Than that which on thy humour doth depend.
Thou canst not vex me with inconstant mind,
Since that my life on thy revolt doth lie.
O what a happy title do I find
Happy to have thy love, happy to die!
But what's so blessed-fair that fears no blot?
Thou mayst be false, and yet I know it not.

THEME

In the temporal world, men wrongfully put their faith in things which, when lost, provide misery. One whose happiness is fixed in the Spirit is never deluded or vexed by fear of material losses.

GLOSSARY

But do thy worst to steal thyself away, For term of life thou art assured mine, And life no longer than thy love will stay, For it depends upon that love of thine.

> But do the worst of all things by hiding Thyself from me, for life itself is real so long as I am assured that Thou art with me, as my life's only sustenance is Thy love.

Then need I not to fear the worst of wrongs, When in the least of them my life hath end. I see a better state to me belongs, Than that which on thy humour doth depend.

> I do not fear the loss of material things which to some, the slightest loss, means complete disaster; to me belongs a more lasting treasure not dependent upon the whim of ego.

Thou canst not vex me with inconstant mind, Since that my life on thy revolt doth lie. O what a happy title do I find, Happy to have thy love, happy to die!

> Thou canst not disturb my peace by a restless mind, since my life is sustained by revolt against worldly things. Oh what joy is mine, happy in the Lord's love, and happy to be dead to the mundane pleasures of life!

But what's so blessed-fair that fears no blot? Thou mayst be false, and yet I know it not.

> But what is it in life that seems so perfect and yet gives us trepidation at the thought of losing it. Thou mayest seem hidden in Thine imperfect creation, but to me Thou art ever present.

COMMENTARY

In the previous Sonnet Shakespeare stated that some people find their glory and pride in status or possessions, while he, on the other hand, finds all he needs in a loving, devotional relationship with the Lord. Only the loss of this spiritual treasure could bring wretchedness. In Sonnet 92, Shakespeare carries on the theme, but points out that the Spirit is hidden behind the delusive seeming of the world. "*But do thy worst to steal thyself away.*" For Shakespeare, his true existence is "*assured*" as long as "*thy love will stay.*" While some are devastated by fear of "*the worst of wrongs,*" meaning that some material thing may be taken away ("*when in the least of them my life hath end*"), Shakespeare will not be disturbed. "*Thou canst not vex me by inconstant mind.*" It is those whose happiness is dependent upon "*birth . . . skill . . . wealth*" and other worldly things who are vexed by a restless mind. They do not see that it is the Lord who is secreted behind the veil of His creation. "All the world's a stage, and all the men and women merely players." (*As You Like It*, II.vii.139-140) "We are such stuff as dreams are made on." (*The Tempest*, IV.i.156-157) These lines of Shakespeare reflect the falseness of this world upon which most people depend for happiness. It is as foolish as a stage actor who plays the part of a king who loses his kingdom and who feels his "*life hath end*[ed]." Shakespeare says that the Lord may be hidden behind the veil of his "*false*" creation, but that he is not fooled. "*Thou mayest be false, yet I know it not.*"

BIBLICAL PASSAGES SUGGESTED BY SONNET 92

"While we look not at the things which are seen, but at the things which are not seen: for the things which are seen are temporal; but the things which are not seen are eternal." **2 Cor. 4:18**

"I have seen all the works that are done under the sun; and, behold, all is vanity and vexation of spirit." Eccl. **1:14**

SONNET 93

So shall I live, supposing thou art true,
Like a deceived husband; so love's face
May still seem love to me, though alter'd new:
Thy looks with me, thy heart in other place.
For there can live no hatred in thine eye,
Therefore in that I cannot know thy change.
In many's looks the false heart's history
Is writ in moods and frowns, and wrinkles strange,
But heaven in thy creation did decree
That in thy face sweet love should ever dwell;
Whate'er thy thoughts or thy heart's workings be,
Thy looks should nothing thence but sweetness tell.
How like Eve's apple doth my beauty grow,
If thy sweet virtue answer not thy show.

THEME

Creation is outwardly alluring and attractive, but one's life must be lived such that worldly activities reflect the inner grace of one's developing soul along its journey toward the Spirit.

GLOSSARY

So shall I live, supposing thou art true, Like a deceived husband; so love's face May still seem love to me, though alter'd new: Thy looks with me, thy heart in other place.

> I will live in this world acting as if all is real and true, just as a deceived husband, seeing the outward expression of love in his wife's face, believes she still loves him, although her love is really elsewhere. The outer appearance is one of a loving nature, but the heart's desires are not correspondingly present.

For there can live no hatred in thine eye, Therefore in that I cannot know thy change. In many's looks the false heart's history Is writ in moods and frowns, and wrinkles strange,

> In the eye of the Spirit, no ugliness can exist in creation; my limited understanding of the things of this world is such that I cannot perceive Thy true nature. In many aspects of life, one can, by introspection and understanding, discern that in egotistical moods, negative attitudes, and imperfections in the emotional make-up, desires of the heart have led many along falsely.

But heaven in thy creation did decree That in thy face sweet love should ever dwell; Whate'er thy thoughts or thy heart's workings be, Thy looks should nothing thence but sweetness tell.

> But it is a heavenly decree that as part of the creation, man should be lured by the attractions of this seemingly sweet world. But whatever your thoughts or heart's desires and emotional attachments may be, your true nature within and without should always reveal the inner sweetness of your soul.

How like Eve's apple doth my beauty grow, If thy sweet virtue answer not thy show.

> Oh how my attachments to this world of false appearances will grow if my life's outer activities do not reflect the inner grace of the Spirit that touches my soul.

COMMENTARY

In Sonnet 92, Shakespeare says that he understands "all the world's a stage," and that we are like actors in a drama. He is not fooled by the delusive seeming, but keeps the polestar of his vision upon the Spirit. In Sonnet 93, Shakespeare says that he is going to play along with the drama of life as if it were real. "*So shall I live, supposing thou art true.*" It is necessary that one plays one's "part" well, while not being completely taken in by the drama. In other words, one must keep one's feet on the ground, but one's eyes heavenward. Shakespeare lives in the visible world, but his love is secreted elsewhere. "*Thy looks with me, thy heart in other place.*"

Life has its beauty, for "*there can live no hatred in thine eye,*" meaning that there can be no ugliness in creation as God has envisioned and made it to be; and He is an immanent aspect of its manifestation. However, one is enjoined to look more deeply to understand man's misplaced attachment to worldly things. "*In many's looks the false heart's history is writ in moods and frowns, and wrinkles strange.*"

The makeup of this world is such that man is made to struggle against worldly attachments toward spiritual perfection. "*But heaven in thy creation did decree that in thy face sweet love should ever dwell.*" No matter how we live and carry on our life, it must be reflective of the inner spiritual nature of our being. "*What e'er thy thoughts or thy hearts workings be, thy looks should nothing thence but sweetness tell.*" If one's behavior appears virtuous, but the heart's desires are selfish and materially-oriented, one is likely to go the way of Eve who succumbed to the wiles of the serpent, and while enjoying the apple, plunged from Eden.

BIBLICAL PASSAGES SUGGESTED BY SONNET 93

"And when the women saw that the tree was good for food, and that it was pleasant to the eyes, and a tree to be desired to make one wise, she took of the fruit thereof, and did eat, and gave also unto her husband with her; and he did eat." **Gen. 3:6**

"Better is the sight of the eyes than the wandering of the desire: this is also vanity and vexation of spirit." **Eccl. 6:9**

SONNET 94

They that have power to hurt, and will do none,
That do not do the thing they most do show,
Who, moving others, are themselves as stone,
Unmoved, cold, and to temptation slow;
They rightly do inherit heaven's graces,
And husband nature's riches from expense;
They are the lords and owners of their faces,
Others but stewards of their excellence.
The summer's flower is to the summer sweet,
Though to itself it only live and die,
But if that flower with base infection meet,
The basest weed outbraves his dignity:
For sweetest things turn sourest by their deeds;
Lilies that fester smell far worse than weeds.

THEME

Those who are most prominent before the eyes of the world, and who are an example to others, are under the highest duty to act rightly and justly, not just in appearance, but in essence.

GLOSSARY

They that have power to hurt, and will do none, That do not do the thing they most do show, Who, moving others, are themselves as stone, Unmoved, cold, and to temptation slow;

> Those who have power to hurt, but no personal will to do anything good, do not truly do in their own lives what they outwardly pretend. Such persons have great influence over others' lives but are themselves stone cold and unmoved. They are not easily swayed or tempted to do positive things in their own lives.

They rightly do inherit heaven's graces, And husband nature's riches from expense; They are the lords and owners of their faces, Others but stewards of their excellence.

> They rightly are the inheritors of moral and intellectual graces, and are stewards over nature's abundance bound to keep it from waste; they are solely responsible and accountable for their outward appearances and behavior as examples before the world, while others who play no public role, are stewards in this short life of their own inner excellence, the soul.

The summer's flower is to the summer sweet, Though to itself it only live and die, But if that flower with base infection meet, The basest weed outbraves his dignity:

> The summer flower contributes its beauty for the short term of its blooming, even though it lives and dies unnoticed by the world. But, if that which flowers before the world are men of power and apparent excellence, who act in a base and corrupt manner, then even the most common among men surpass them in worth and excellence before the heavenly Judge.

For sweetest things turn sourest by their deeds; Lilies that fester smell far worse than weeds.

> When the most beautiful among us are corrupt in their deeds and actions, they are truly the most sour to our taste and liking, just as festering lilies smell far worse than weeds.

COMMENTARY

In Sonnet 93, Shakespeare tell us creation is imbued with temptations, and that it is man's duty by "*decree*"(Sonnet 93.9) that he should overcome worldly allurements. To put on "*love's face*" (Sonnet 93.2) while the "*heart* [is] *in other place*" (Sonnet 93.4), only further ensnares the soul, as with "*Eve's apple.*"(Sonnet 93.13)

In Sonnet 94, Shakespeare directs his comments towards those who have power, influence, and authority over the lives and well-being of others. These are the lords, monarchs, clergy, and others in places of public trust. They put on an outward show of propriety and piety ("*they most do show*") but are themselves as "*stone, unmoved, cold, and to temptation slow.*" There is a sarcastic and ironic use of the word "*temptation*," which normally implies being tempted toward sin, but in this case, it refers to those who are "*slow*" to be tempted toward doing good.

These persons are meant to play an essential role in this world. They have been given "*heaven's graces*" and are responsible for "*husband*[ing] *nature's riches from expense.*" Since they are before the public view, and are born to serve mankind, they have a higher duty to perform in life because they influence the behavior of others. If people see their leaders misbehaving, they too will feel that it is acceptable to act improperly.

But, it is the innate spiritual part within each one that is truly the "*excellence.*" Every person has a role to play in this world, just as "*the summer's flower is to the summer sweet.*" The world has beauty in nature, and every flower has its place or role even if "*to itself it only live and die.*" Although it may go unnoticed by man, it, like the sparrow "shall not fall on the ground without your Father." **(Matt. 10:29)**

When important persons of influence and position are seemingly like one of the "*sweetest things*," but are really like a summer flower with "*base infection*," they "*turn sourest by their deeds.*" The most humble people who have no influence over others, but who are proper "*stewards of their excellence*," are like spiritual stars that outshine the others. "*The basest weed outbraves his dignity.*"

BIBLICAL PASSAGES SUGGESTED BY SONNET 94

"And when thou prayest, thou shalt not be as the hypocrites are: for they love to pray standing in the synagogues and in the corners of the streets, that they may be seen of men. Verily I say unto you, They have their reward." **Matt. 6:5**

"Give them according to their deeds, and according to the wickedness of their endeavors: give them after the work of their hands; render to them their desert." **Ps. 28:4**

"For a bishop must be blameless, as the steward of God; not self-willed, not soon angry, not given to wine, no striker, not given to filthy lucre; . . . Holding fast the faithful word as he hath been taught, that he may be able by sound doctrine both to exhort and to convince the gainsayers." **Titus 1:7, 9**

"And the Lord said, Who then is that faithful and wise steward, whom his lord shall make ruler over his household. . . . Blessed is that servant, whom his lord when he cometh shall find so doing. Of a truth I say unto you, that he will make him ruler over all that he hath. But and if that servant say in his heart, My lord delayeth his coming; and shall begin to beat the men-servants and maidens, and to eat and drink, and to be drunken; The lord of that servant will come in a day when he looketh not for him, . . . and will cut him in sunder, and will appoint him his portion with the unbelievers." **Luke 12:42-46**

"Woe to the crown of pride, . . . whose glorious beauty is a fading flower, which are on the head of the fat valleys of them that are overcome with wine!" **Isa. 28:1**

"But the meek shall inherit the earth; and shall delight themselves in the abundance of peace." **Ps. 37:11**

SONNET 95

How sweet and lovely dost thou make the shame
Which, like a canker in the fragrant rose,
Doth spot the beauty of thy budding name!
O in what sweets dost thou thy sins enclose!
That tongue that tells the story of thy days,
Making lascivious comments on thy sport,
Cannot dispraise but in a kind of praise;
Naming thy name blesses an ill report.
O, what a mansion have those vices got
Which for their habitation chose out thee,
Where beauty's veil doth cover every blot
And all things turn to fair that eyes can see!
Take heed, dear heart, of this large privilege:
The hardest knife ill us'd doth lose his edge.

THEME

Man is endowed with free will. Temptations are like poison honey that promise sweetness, but deliver death. The power of wisdom-guided discrimination is lost if not properly exercised.

GLOSSARY

How sweet and lovely dost thou make the shame, Which, like a canker in the fragrant rose, Doth spot the beauty of thy budding name! O in what sweets dost thou thy sins enclose!

> How attractive and inviting are sinful temptations which, like a blight within the fragrant rose, tarnishes beauty even before it can fully blossom! Oh, in how many ways do outward temptations hide the shackling sins within.

That tongue that tells the story of thy days, Making lascivious comments on thy sport, Cannot dispraise but in a kind of praise; Naming thy name blesses an ill report.

> Those who tell stories of your exploits (making light of your lascivious behavior) say nothing bad of you, but in

fact, praise you and your reputation, praising what is really a life ill-lived.

O, what a mansion have those vices got, Which for their habitation chose out thee, Where beauty's veil doth cover every blot, And all things turn to fair that eyes can see!

Oh what a bodily habitation do those vices possess, which you, of your own free will, have chosen; and the delusive beauty of outward appearances hides the "*base infection*" (Sonnet 94.11) within.

Take heed, dear heart, of this large privilege: The hardest knife ill us'd doth lose his edge.

Man's free will is an important aspect of his being, so take heed of what you seek as your heart's desire. The sword of soul-endowed free will is double-edged and will lose the sharpness of its discriminative powers if ill used.

COMMENTARY

In Sonnet 94 Shakespeare addresses those who outwardly appear virtuous, but who inwardly are steeped in materialism and sinful pursuits. They are like "*Lilies that fester* [and] *smell far worse than weeds.*" (Sonnet 94.14)

In Sonnet 95, Shakespeare addresses the individual who is endowed with free will, a "*large privilege.*" No matter what reputation one carries, one's shameful conduct is "*like a canker in the fragrant rose*" of the soul. One's corporal being or "*mansion*" is inhabited by destructive vices that are like an infection within one's spiritual being. "*O, what a mansion have those vices got which for their habitation chose out thee.*" Notice that it is each person's use of free will that causes the "*blot.*" The apparent attractiveness of wrong desires is "*where beauty's veil doth cover every blot,*" since attractions are like the serpent of poison honey that delivers death in coils of sweetness. "*O in what sweets dost thou thy sins enclose!*" Sensual eyes go after desires of the heart, which each one creates for oneself. "*How sweet and lovely dost thou make the shame.*" By continuing to choose wrongfully, one is failing to "[*t*]*ake heed, dear heart, of this large privilege*" of free will. Wisdom and discrimination, which are inherent qualities of the soul, must correctly guide one's free will. It is a double-edged sword that either utilizes its discriminative powers to cut through the veils of ignorance and chooses wisely; or is "*ill us'd*" and loses its inherent soul-guiding ability. "*The hardest knife ill us'd doth lose his edge.*" Notice that Shakespeare says the knife loses "*his edge.*" He personifies this soul-guided power of discrimination as belonging to each "*dear heart,*" endowed with the "*large privilege*" of free will.

BIBLICAL PASSAGES SUGGESTED BY SONNET 95

"And the spirit of the Lord shall rest upon him, the spirit of wisdom and understanding, the spirit of counsel and might, the spirit of knowledge and of the fear of the Lord." **Isa. 11:2**

"And whatsoever mine eyes desired I kept not from them, I withheld not my heart from any joy. . . . Then I looked on all the works that my hands had wrought, and on the labor that I had labored to do; and, behold, all was vanity and vexation of spirit, and there was no profit under the sun." **Eccl. 2:10-11**

"But these, as natural brute beasts, made to be taken and destroyed, speak evil of the things that they understand not; and shall utterly perish in their own corruption; And shall receive the reward of unrighteousness, as they that count it pleasure to riot in the day time. Spots they are and blemishes, sporting themselves with their own deceivings while they feast with you." **2 Pet. 2:12-13**

"While they promise them liberty, they themselves are the servants of corruption: for of whom a man is overcome, of the same is he brought in bondage." **2 Pet. 2:19**

SONNET 96

Some say thy fault is youth, some wantonness,
Some say thy grace is youth and gentle sport;
Both grace and faults are lov'd of more and less:
Thou mak'st faults graces that to thee resort.
As on the finger of a throned queen
The basest jewel will be well esteem'd:
So are those errors that in thee are seen
To truths translated and for true things deemed.
How many lambs might the stern wolf betray,
If like a lamb he could his looks translate!
How many gazers mightst thou lead away,
If thou wouldst use the strength of all thy state?
But do not so; I love thee in such sort,
As, thou being mine, mine is thy good report.

THEME

On the field of human existence, man must deal with the forces of good and evil. A person may be pulled in one direction or another from time to time, but the inherent goodness of the soul, and the grace of the Divine, will eventually bring each of God's children to the heavenly home.

GLOSSARY

Some say thy fault is youth, some wantonness, Some say thy grace is youth and gentle sport; Both grace and faults are lov'd of more and less: Thou mak'st faults graces that to thee resort.

> Some men criticize the faults of others and may attribute these to immature or irresponsible behavior, while others simply see such conduct as the harmless and charming frivolity of the young at heart. In general, whether some behavior is considered a sin, or fault, or accepted as charming frivolity, many people are wont to engage in such egotistical pursuits. But for those who turn to the Lord, their sins or faults are remedied through grace.

As on the finger of a throned queen The basest jewel will be well esteem'd: So are those errors that in thee are seen To truths translated and for true things deemed.

> On the finger of the reigning queen, the basest jewel will be admired. Blots of wrong behavior in man are viewed by the Lord with understanding compassion. The Lord only sees the divinity in man's soul, and thus faults are changed to graces, and wrongful conduct is bent toward the way of Truth.

How many lambs might the stern wolf betray, If like a lamb he could his looks translate! How many gazers mightst thou lead away, If thou wouldst use the strength of all thy state?

> How many gentle folk could the merciless wolf of ravenous temptations lead astray, if Satan could make sin appear to be even more attractive. And how many more who look to Thee could be converted and be lead away from sin, if Thou wouldst use the heavenly power of Thine Omnipotence?

But do not so; I love thee in such sort, As, thou being mine, mine is thy good report.

> But do not do so. I understandingly love Thy nature, and Thy grant of free will to man, and my wish is that my own life speak out as a good example of all of Thy graces to mankind.

COMMENTARY

Sonnet 96 concludes this group of the Sonnets, which deal with the battle of the soul and the selfish ego and man's use of free will.

In Sonnet 96, Shakespeare points out that people have differing views on egotistical pursuits. To some it is the "*fault*" or sin of youth, or just plain "*wantonness.*" To others engaging in frivolity it is just a "*gentle sport*" and the charm or "*grace*" of immaturity. In either case, people are wont and love to engage in worldly actions "*more and less.*" These are the tempting desires of the heart in which mankind engages. From the point of view of the Spirit, the Poet asserts that the Lord sees only the soul's goodness in his children. Wrongful conduct is like "*the basest jewel*" upon the "*finger*" of the majestic soul, which Shakespeare calls the "*throned queen.*" Sins of man are "*errors*" of conduct or thoughts, which by the grace of God are changed to truths. "*So are those errors that in thee are seen to truths translated and for true things deemed.*"

In the nature of man, the battle is between the soul and the ego. Shakespeare refers to the "*lamb*" and "*wolf,*" which represent, in one sense, the human battle within each of us but is in a larger cosmic sense the battle between God, or Christ as the "Lamb of God," and Satan, who is called the "*stern wolf*" who will "*betray.*"

Shakespeare says that the Lord could dissuade or "*lead away*" straying mankind from temptation: "*If Thou wouldst use the strength of all thy state.*" But, the Poet says that he is content in the heavenly plan: "*I love Thee in such sort.*" "*As, Thou being mine, mine is thy good report,*" "And it is enough that I am Thine and Thou art mine, and that it is the example of my life which gives testimony to Thy Grace."

BIBLICAL PASSAGES SUGGESTED BY SONNET 96

"There is an evil which I have seen under the sun, and it is common among men." **Eccl. 6:1**

"For who knoweth what is good for man in this life, all the days of his vain life which he spendeth as a shadow? for who can tell a man what shall be after him under the sun?" **Eccl. 6:12**

"For sin shall not have dominion over you: for ye are not under the law, but under grace." **Rom. 6:14**

"The wolf and the lamb shall feed together, and the lion shall eat straw like the bullock: and dust shall be the serpent's meat. They shall not hurt nor destroy in all my holy mountain, saith the Lord." **Isa. 65:25**

"The next day John seeth Jesus coming unto him, and saith, Behold the Lamb of God, which taketh away the sin of the world." **John 1:29**

"And all mine are thine, and thine are mine; and I am glorified in them. And now I am no more in the world, but these are in the world, and I come to thee. Holy Father, keep through thine own name those whom thou hast given me, that they may be one, as we are." **John 17:10-11**

SONNET 97

How like a winter hath my absence been
From thee, the pleasure of the fleeting year!
What freezings have I felt, what dark days seen!
What old December's bareness everywhere!
And yet this time remov'd was summer's time,
The teeming autumn, big with rich increase,
Bearing the wanton burden of the prime,
Like widow'd wombs after their lords' decease:
Yet this abundant issue seem'd to me
But hope of orphans and unfather'd fruit;
For summer and his pleasures wait on thee,
And, thou away, the very birds are mute:
Or, if they sing, 'tis with so dull a cheer,
That leaves look pale, dreading the winter's near.

THEME

In almost every spiritual journey there is what is termed "the dark night of the soul." It is a testing period, yet it holds hidden promise. While it is upon the devotee, all may seem bleak and barren, waiting upon the Lord whose absence is keenly felt.

GLOSSARY

How like a winter hath my absence been From thee, the pleasure of the fleeting year! What freezings have I felt, what dark days seen! What old December's bareness everywhere!

> My absence from Thee, in contrast to the days of fleeting seasons past, is like a freezing barren winter of days filled only with darkness!

And yet this time remov'd was summer's time, The teeming autumn, big with rich increase, Bearing the wanton burden of the prime, Like widow'd wombs after their lords' decease:

> Yet this dark time was in reality a growing period, which held the promise of a rich harvest. It yet bore the seeds of

> days in my prime that were laced still with the burden of my wantonness, like a womb made fertile by a lord who now is absent.

Yet this abundant issue seem'd to me But hope of orphans and unfather'd fruit, For summer and his pleasures wait on thee, And, thou away, the very birds are mute:

> So much promise was there before of the budding fruit of my devotion, which now is like the hope of an orphan, and a child who is born without the father's presence. Because the joys of resplendent seasons past wait upon Thee alone, and Thou now absent, I cannot hear even the sweat songs of birds.

Or, if they sing, 'tis with so dull a cheer, That leaves look pale, dreading the winter's near.

> Or if there is singing, it gives but dull cheer, and even the leaves seem pale dreading the return of the dark night.

COMMENTARY

Interestingly, Shakespeare states "*how like a winter hath my absence been.*" It is not the absence of the Beloved, but "*my absence,*" which suggests the "*time remov'd*" is occasioned by the devotee himself. It is a period of "*freezings*" and "*dark days seen.*" In earlier Sonnets, Shakespeare sees the "*gracious light*" (Sonnet 7.1), but here only "*dark days.*" The dark night of the soul is a test by God of the devotee's patience, and unselfish love and devotion. As seen in Sonnet 27, Shakespeare describes "*looking on darkness,*" which by his "*soul's imaginary sight . . . presents thy shadow*" and "*makes black night beauteous.*" (Sonnet 27.8-10, 12) But the Lord will come when He will. In Sonnet 57, the Poet says: "*Being your slave, what should I do but tend upon the hours and times of your desire? . . . Nor I dare I chide the world-without-end hour whilst I, my sovereign, watch the clock for you, . . . When you have bid your servant once adieu.*" (Sonnet 57.1-2, 5-6, 8). Also, in Sonnet 58.5-8, Shakespeare laments: "*O, let me suffer, being at your beck, Th' imprison'd absence of your liberty, and patience, tame to sufferance, bide each check, without accusing you of injury.*"

The periods of "*absence*" in Sonnets 57 and 58 are understood as a test of "*patience*" and continued devotion without protest. In Sonnet 97, it is "*my absence*" about which Shakespeare is speaking. It is a time when the devotee's mettle is tested, and it carries the promise of being "*summer's time*." The seed is planted, but it seems gloomily to be within "*widow'd wombs*." This dark time seems more severe than those absences described in Sonnets 57 and 58, but still the Poet's pronouncement: "*For summer and his pleasures wait on thee*."

BIBLICAL PASSAGES SUGGESTED BY SONNET 97

"Out of the depths have I cried unto thee, O Lord. Lord, hear my voice: let thine ears be attentive to the voice of my supplications. . . . My soul waiteth for the Lord more than they that watch for the morning: I say, more than they that watch for the morning." **Ps. 130:1-2, 6**

"Yea, in the way of thy judgments, O Lord, have we waited for thee; the desire of our soul is to thy name, and to the remembrance of thee." **Isa. 26:8**

"Therefore night shall be unto you, that ye shall not have a vision." **Mic. 3:6**

"Thus hath the lord God shewed unto me: and behold a basket of summer fruit. Behold the days come, saith the Lord God, that I will send a famine in the land, not a famine of bread, nor a thirst for water, but of hearing the words of the Lord." **Amos 8:1, 11**

"By night on my bed I sought him whom my soul loveth: I sought him, but I found him not. I will rise now . . . and in the broad ways I will seek him whom my soul loveth: I sought him but I found him not. The watchmen that go about the city found me: to whom I said, Saw ye whom my soul loveth? It was but a little that I passed from them, but I found him whom my soul loveth: I held him, and would not let him go." **Song of Sol. 3:1-4**

Here we see in the Song of Songs, and previous passages, that a dark night comes to test the devotee. It is the persistence of the devotee, in spite of the Divine absence, that causes him to seek until he again finds "Him whom my soul loveth" (**Song of Sol. 3:2**).

SONNET 98

From you have I been absent in the spring,
When proud-pied April, dressed in all his trim,
Hath put a spirit of youth in everything,
That heavy Saturn laugh'd and leap'd with him.
Yet nor the lays of birds, nor the sweet smell
Of different flowers in odour and in hue,
Could make me any summer's story tell,
Or from their proud lap pluck them where they grew:
Nor did I wonder at the lily's white,
Nor praise the deep vermilion in the rose;
They were but sweet, but figures of delight,
Drawn after you, you pattern of all those.
Yet seem'd it winter still, and, you away,
As with your shadow I with these did play.

THEME

All the world and its beauty is just a shadow, a manifestation of God. In the dark night of the soul, nothing will give solace but God alone.

GLOSSARY

From you have I been absent in the spring, When proud-pied April, dressed in all his trim, Hath put a spirit of youth in everything, That heavy Saturn laugh'd and leap'd with him.

> I have been absent from You in the spring when April is dressed in proud floral fantasy and the youthful spirit of renewal is such that even grave Saturn laughed and leapt high in celebration of the season.

Yet nor the lays of birds, nor the sweet smell Of different flowers in odour and in hue, Could make me any summer's story tell, Or from their proud lap pluck them where they grew:

> Nevertheless, neither songs of birds, nor flowers of myriad fragrances and hues could incite me to write of summer's lush flowering; nor did I wish to pluck them up

from their place upon nature's lap.

Nor did I wonder at the lily's white, Nor praise the deep vermilion in the rose; They were but sweet, but figures of delight, Drawn after you, you pattern of all those.

> Neither was I moved to marvel at the lily's white, or the roses deep vermilion. They were merely sweet; merely shadows of true Beauty drawn in Your likeness. You are the only flower from which these manifestations are drawn.

Yet seem'd it winter still, and, you away, As with your shadow I with these did play.

> For me, it was still the darkness of winter with You away,
> but as You with Your shadows, did I with nature play.

COMMENTARY

Sonnet 98 continues the theme of the dark night of the soul. Clearly nothing, not even the manifest beauty of nature, a "*proud-pied April, dresse'd in all his trim . . . nor the lays of birds, nor the sweet smell of different flowers*" can satisfy the seeker who looks for the Creator alone, and who thus can never be satisfied with His manifestation in Nature.

In Sonnet 61.4, Shakespeare speaks of "*shadows* [that] *like to thee do mock my sight.*" The material manifestations cannot satisfy the longings of the soul. "*Yet seem'd it winter still, and, you away, as with your shadow I with these did play.*"

BIBLICAL PASSAGES SUGGESTED BY SONNET 98

"The heavens declare the glory of God; and the firmament sheweth his handywork." **Ps. 19:1**

"Canst thou by searching find out God? Canst thou find out the Almighty unto perfection?" **Job 11:7**

SONNET 99

The forward violet thus did I chide:
Sweet thief whence didst thou steal thy sweet that smells,
If not from my love's breath? The purple pride
Which on thy soft cheek for complexion dwells
In my love's veins thou hast too grossly dyed.
The lily I condemned for thy hand,
And buds of marjoram had stol'n thy hair;
The roses fearfully on thorns did stand,
One blushing shame, another white despair;
A third, nor red nor white, had stol'n of both,
And to his robbery had annex'd thy breath,
But, for his theft, in pride of all his growth
A vengeful canker eat him up to death.
More flowers I noted, yet I none could see
But sweet or colour it had stol'n from thee.

THEME

All of creation, in its different aspects, is a manifestation of the Divine. Such is the case with the beauty of the flowers and their sweet fragrances, which suggest the infinite Beauty and Sweetness of the Lord himself.

GLOSSARY

The forward violet thus did I chide: Sweet thief whence didst thou steal thy sweet that smells, If not from my love's breath? The purple pride Which on thy soft cheek for complexion dwells

> I chided the presumptuous violet: Sweet thief, from where did you steal that fragrance if not from my love's breath? And the prideful purple which coats your soft petals

In my love's veins thou hast too grossly dyed. The lily I condemned for thy hand, And buds of marjoram had stol'n thy hair; The roses fearfully on thorns did stand,

> Is found in my love's veins. I condemned the lily's whiteness as being an invention of Nature's hand, and buds of marjoram had stolen Thy hair. The roses, in fear of stealing Thy beauty, stand atop of stems,

One blushing shame, another white despair; A third, nor red nor white, had stol'n of both, And to his robbery had annex'd thy breath, But, for his theft, in pride of all his growth A vengeful canker eat him up to death.

> One in red-faced shame, another, white in despair; a third, neither red nor white, had stolen a mixture from both, and added to the robbery the sweet fragrance from Thy breath. But for its transgression in having pride for all its growth, a vengeful canker takes deadly retribution upon it.

More flowers I noted, yet I none could see But sweet or colour it had stol'n from thee.

> Many more flowers, yet I could see none that had not stolen their fragrance or color from Thee.

COMMENTARY

This Sonnet continues the theme of Sonnet 98 in which the color and fragrance of the lily and rose are "*drawn after you, you pattern of all those.*" (Sonnet 98.12) The flowers' beauty and fragrance suggest the Lord, as a shadow suggests a solid figure, but they did not reveal Him.

In Sonnet 99, the lily is a "*sweet thief*" of its fragrance, and the rose has committed "*his robb'ry*" to achieve its color and fragrance. Inherent in Creation, however, is the dual nature of things: pleasure and pain, life and death, joy and sorrow, beauty and ugliness. The only changeless One is the Lord, hence, the rose "*for his theft in pride*" must suffer "*a vengeful canker* [to] *eat him up to death.*" This is the ever-changing duality of the material world where beauty alternates with deformity.

BIBLICAL PASSAGE SUGGESTED BY SONNET 99

"The heavens declare the glory of God; and the firmament sheweth his handywork." **Ps. 19:1**

SONNET 100

Where art thou, Muse, that thou forget'st so long
To speak of that which gives thee all thy might?
Spend'st thou thy fury on some worthless song,
Darkening thy power to lend base subjects light?
Return, forgetful Muse, and straight redeem
In gentle numbers time so idly spent;
Sing to the ear that doth thy lays esteem,
And gives thy pen both skill and argument.
Rise, resty Muse, my love's sweet face survey,
If Time have any wrinkle graven there;
If any, be a satire to decay,
And make Time's spoils despised everywhere.
Give my love fame faster than Time wastes life;
So thou prevent'st his scythe and crooked knife.

THEME

During the "dark night of the soul," the introspective devotee calls for the silent Voice within to reveal the imperfections in his nature that have impeded his perceptions of Truth.

GLOSSARY

Where art thou, Muse, that thou forget'st so long To speak of that which gives thee all thy might? Spend'st thou thy fury on some worthless song, Darkening thy power to lend base subjects light?

> Where art Thou, Muse, that Thou hast for so long forgotten to speak of that from which Thou dost receive all of Thy power? Hast Thou spent Thy fury on some worthless lines, depleting Thy power, lending it to base subjects?

Return, forgetful Muse, and straight redeem In gentle numbers time so idly spent; Sing to the ear that doth thy lays esteem, And gives thy pen both skill and argument.

> Return immediately, forgetful Muse, and redeem in no-

> ble verse the time frivolously wasted in idleness. Sing Thy song to ears that hear gratefully, and give Thy servant's pen wise and worthy themes.

Rise, resty Muse, my love's sweet face survey, If Time have any wrinkle graven there; If any, be a satire to decay, And make Time's spoils despised everywhere.

> Arise, my indolent Muse, take stock of any imperfection on the face of my love, to see if time has placed any graven imperfection there. If any be found, show the ineffectual power of Time to destroy. Make Truth supreme and ignorance despised everywhere.

Give my love fame faster than Time wastes life; So thou prevent'st his scythe and crooked knife.

> Give my Love enduring fame more quickly than Time can waste life away. Keep Time in check, preventing the operation of its deadly and depreciating hand.

COMMENTARY

In Sonnet 97 Shakespeare lamented how "*like a winter hath my absence been from thee, . . . what freezings have I felt, what dark days seen!*" (Sonnet 97.1-4). In Sonnet 98.13, the Poet feels that with "*you away*" it "*yet seem'd . . . winter still.*" The outward creation was still visible, but only as a "*shadow*" (Sonnet 98.14) of the Creator.

The Sonnets generally express the author's spiritual thoughts and perceptions in myriad ways. Shakespeare declares in Sonnet 76.9-10: "*O, know, sweet love, I always write of you, and you and love are still my argument.*" In Sonnet 100, Shakespeare calls upon the "*Muse . . . to speak of that which gives thee all thy might.*" The source of power and "*might*" of the Poet's "*Muse*" is Divine inspiration. While Shakespeare suffers because of this "*absence . . . like widow'd wombs*" (Sonnet 97.1, 8), he begins to question his "*Muse*": "*Spend'st thou thy fury on some worthless song. . . ?*" Shakespeare is being introspective about the loss of his Muse's poetic inspiration. The source of his inspiration is, of course, his love and inward perceptions of the Lord. In effect, he is asking himself whether there is something lacking in his own nature; or whether he himself has been musing, even unconsciously, "*on some worthless song*" that has deprived him of the "*light*," and thus darkened his power "*to lend base subjects light.*"

Shakespeare's reference to "*my love's sweet face*" has a dual meaning. The first is the face of the Divine, Shakespeare's true love. Time plays upon creation and ravages it with "*his scythe and crooked knife.*" Time is described as "*a satire to decay*" because in reality, while the creation seems to be fraught with change and death, the Creator is ever changeless and timeless.

In its second meaning, "*my love's sweet face*" refers to Shakespeare's own love for God. During his "*absence*," and the lack of inspiration from the Muse, he wonders if his idle "*graven*" wanderings have put a "*wrinkle*" upon the face of his "*sweet love.*" (Sonnet 76.9) Shakespeare asks that should such a "*wrinkle*" of imperfection infect his nature, that it be corrected by a savage attack upon the delusive unreality that Time could ever spoil a pure, "sweet *love*" that is changeless. Shakespeare says, "*Sing to the ear that doth thy lays esteem.*" Shakespeare's prayer is that he again hear the inner voice of the Spirit, which will give his "*love fame faster than time wastes life.*"

BIBLICAL PASSAGES SUGGESTED BY SONNET 100

"He that hath ears to hear, let him hear." **Matt. 11:15**

"What profiteth the graven image that the maker thereof hath graven it; the molten image, and a teacher of lies, that the maker of his work trusteth therein, to make dumb idols?" **Hab. 2:18**

"Oh that my words were now written! oh that they were printed in a book! That they were graven with an iron pen and lead in the rock for ever! For I know that my redeemer liveth, and that he shall stand at the latter day upon the earth." **Job 19:23-25**

SONNET 101

O truant Muse, what shall be thy amends
For thy neglect of truth in beauty dyed?
Both truth and beauty on my love depends;
So dost thou too, and therein dignified.
Make answer, Muse: wilt thou not haply say,
"Truth needs no colour, with his colour fix'd;
Beauty no pencil, beauty's truth to lay;
But best is best, if never intermix'd"?
Because he needs no praise, wilt thou be dumb?
Excuse not silence so, for 't lies in thee
To make him much outlive a gilded tomb
And to be prais'd of ages yet to be.
Then do thy office, Muse; I teach thee how
To make him seem long hence as he shows now.

THEME

Even though the Divine is Perfection itself, and beyond the ability of mere words to express in terms of beauty or truth, still such expressions are needed to inspire mankind to rise above human attachment to "*gilded*" tombs of materialism.

GLOSSARY

O truant Muse, what shall be thy amends For thy neglect of truth in beauty dyed? Both truth and beauty on my love depends; So dost thou too, and therein dignified.

> O absent Muse, in what way shalt Thou make amends for Thy neglect in expressing Truth infused with pure Beauty? Truth and Beauty have their source in my Divine Beloved as does my muse whose inspiration is thereby dignified.

Make answer, Muse: wilt thou not haply say, "Truth needs no colour, with his colour fix'd; Beauty no pencil, beauty's truth to lay; But best is best, if never intermix'd"?

In answer, Muse, would you perhaps say, "Truth needs nothing added to it as it is already perfect. Beauty needs no glorious words to express its inherent truths; and Perfection remains such without reference to Truth or Beauty"?

Because he needs no praise, wilt thou be dumb? Excuse not silence so, for 't lies in thee To make him much outlive in gilded tomb And to be prais'd of ages yet to be.

Because the Divine is beyond praise, wilt Thou be silent? Don't use such an excuse for silence, for it is Thine obligation to express His eternal nature, which outlives every desired material thing, and to praise Him for ages and generations yet to come.

Then do thy office, Muse; I teach thee how To make him seem long hence as he shows now.

Do your duty, Muse. I will instruct Thee how to express His eternal nature, which is beyond the finite material creation of today.

COMMENTARY

During the period of Shakespeare's seeming inability to write his "*eternal lines*," he has lamented his "*absence*" (Sonnet 97.1) and in Sonnet 100 looked within to see if upon his "*love's sweet face*" (Sonnet 100.9) some wrinkle of imperfection might be "*graven there*." In Sonnet 101, the Poet, by way of some possible defense for the "*truant Muse*," states that the Divine is already Perfection itself, and that "*truth needs no colour, with his colour fix'd; Beauty no pencil, beauty's truth to lay*." In other words, what more is needed of the Poet than to love and seek the Divine. Trying to express Him in mere words is incorrect as "*best is best, if never intermix'd. . . . he needs no praise*."

In spite of the Poet's love and appreciation of the Divine, mankind is yet steeped in materialism and worships its "*gilded*" tombs. The inspired words of truth, and expressions of beauty by the Poet, encourage mankind to look beyond the material seeming, or the "*show*" of creation; and to look to perceive the One from whence all Truth and

Beauty are derived. "*Both truth and beauty on my love depends.*" As always, Shakespeare's "*love*" is the Divine Beloved. "*O, know, sweet love, I always write of you.*" (Sonnet 76.9)

BIBLICAL PASSAGES SUGGESTED BY SONNET 101

"Great is the Lord, and greatly to be praised; and his greatness is unsearchable." **Ps. 145:3**

"My praise shall be of thee in the great congregation: I will pay my vows before them that fear him." **Ps. 22:25**

"I will make thy name to be remembered in all generations: therefore shall the people praise thee for ever and ever." **Ps. 45:17**

"The heart of the wise teacheth his mouth, and addeth learning to his lips." **Prov. 16:2**

SONNET 102

My love is strengthen'd, though more weak in seeming;
I love not less, though less the show appear:
That love is merchandiz'd whose rich esteeming
The owner's tongue doth publish everywhere.
Our love was new, and then but in the spring,
When I was wont to greet it with my lays;
As Philomel in summer's front doth sing,
And stops her pipe in growth of riper days:
Not that the summer is less pleasant now
Than when her mournful hymns did hush the night,
But that wild music burthens every bough,
And sweets grown common lose their dear delight.
Therefore, like her, I sometime hold my tongue,
Because I would not dull you with my song.

THEME

Spiritually-inspired love that is very profound ceases to express itself in outward forms. Out of humility, it maintains a reverent silence.

GLOSSARY

My love is strengthen'd, though more weak in seeming; I love not less, though less the show appear: That love is merchandiz'd whose rich esteeming The owner's tongue doth publish everywhere.

> My love is stronger, though it seems less. I love not less, though I do not write of Thee as much. The idea of love is sold as a commodity by those who publish whatever words fall from their tongues.

Our love was new, and then but in the spring, When I was wont to greet it with my lays; As Philomel in summer's front doth sing, And stops her pipe in growth of riper days:

> When my love for Thee burst forth like springtime, I was wont to declare it in my poetry. The nightingale in early summer sings beautifully, but quiets its song as the

season ripens:

Not that the summer is less pleasant now Than when her mournful hymns did hush the night, But that wild music burthens every bough, And sweets grown common lose their dear delight.

> It is not that summer is less beautiful now than when her mournful tunes did sooth the night, but only that the incessant music began to burden the boughs. And when lovely songs become common, they lose their sweet essence.

Therefore, like her, I sometime hold my tongue, Because I would not dull you with my song.

> Therefore, like her, I sometimes utter not a sound, because I would not depreciate your Beauty with my ordinary song.

COMMENTARY

In Sonnet 101, Shakespeare chides his muse for not inspiring new ways to express his songs, which will "*make him much outlive a gilded tomb.*" (Sonnet 101.11) In Sonnet 102, however, our Poet first states, "*my love is strengthen'd.*" This is an essential aspect of the Sonnet's deeper meaning. There are those who have "*merchandiz'd*" or cheapened love by publishing "*everywhere*" whatever the "*owner's tongue*" can sell. Shakespeare, when "*love was new . . . in the spring,*" was "*wont to greet it with my* [his] *lays*" or Sonnets. In other words, his poetry was the natural and spontaneous outpouring of a heart filled with love.

The lovely song of the nightingale is heard in early summer and ceases as the summer matures. Incessant, "*wild music,*" however is like love poetry that is "*merchandiz'd.*" The sweet essence grows to be "*common*" or unworthy as the songs "*lose their dear delight.*" Here the meaning is that true expressions of love are infused with the power to give joy, while the commonplace burdens the listener ("*burthens every bough*").

The dear Poet humbly preferred to hold his "*tongue,*" and not be like those who "*publish everywhere,*" rather than make the song to his beloved something "*common.*" So in answer to the demand for his muse to "*do thy office*" in Sonnet 101.13, Shakespeare declares his "*love is strengthen'd*" whether expressed in poetic lines ("*lays*") or not.

A true loving relationship needs no outward "*show*" as it blossoms in the sunshine of "*riper days*."

An additional commentary by the fourteenth century Christian mystic, Walter Hilton: "The greatest scholar on Earth cannot with all his wit imagine what this opening of the spiritual eye is, or fully declare it with his tongue, for it cannot be acquired by study or through human toil alone, but principally by the grace of the Holy Spirit, together with the work of man. I am afraid to speak of it at all, for I feel myself ignorant; it goes beyond my experience, and my lips are unclean. This opening of the spiritual eye is that luminous darkness and rich nothing that I spoke of before, and it may be called purity of spirit and spiritual rest, inward stillness and peace of conscience. . ." (*The Scale of Perfection*, trans. Clark & Dorward [New York: Paulist Press, 1991], p. 280).

BIBLICAL PASSAGES SUGGESTED BY SONNET 102

"He that speaketh in an unknown tongue edifieth himself; but he that prophesieth edifieth the church." **1 Cor. 14:4**

"To the end that my glory may sing praise to thee, and not be silent. O Lord my God, I will give thanks unto thee for ever." **Ps. 30:12**

"A time to rend, and a time to sew; a time to keep silence, and a time to speak." **Eccl. 3:7**

SONNET 103

Alack what poverty my Muse brings forth,
That having such a scope to show her pride,
The argument, all bare, is of more worth
Than when it hath my added praise beside.
O, blame me not, if I no more can write!
Look in your glass, and there appears a face
That over-goes my blunt invention quite,
Dulling my lines and doing me disgrace.
Were it not sinful then, striving to mend,
To mar the subject that before was well?
For to no other pass my verses tend
Than of your graces and your gifts to tell;
And more, much more, than in my verse can sit,
Your own glass shows you when you look in it.

THEME

There is nothing to compare with the beauty of the Spirit reflected in the soul of man, which is made in the image of God. Words are insufficient to describe what the soul experiences when the light of the spiritual eye is opened.

GLOSSARY

Alack what poverty my Muse brings forth, That having such a scope to show her pride, The argument, all bare, is of more worth Than when it hath my added praise beside.

> How little my Muse brings forth, even though she has such power to show off her splendor. But the object of my attention, in its pure state, is a Treasure to which my words can add no value.

O, blame me not, if I no more can write! Look in your glass, and there appears a face That over-goes my blunt invention quite, Dulling my lines and doing me disgrace.

> I am blameless for being unable to write more. Look at

Your reflection, the soul within, which mirrors the Spirit. Its purity surpasses my capacity for poetic expression, making my verse dull in comparison, bringing me disgrace for attempting to capture its beauty with mere words.

Were it not sinful then, striving to mend, To mar the subject that before was well? For to no other pass my verses tend Than of your graces and your gifts to tell;

Wouldn't it be a sin to try and improve on something that is already perfect? My only goal has been to put into verse the flawless Beauty and Grace of the Spirit.

And more, much more, than in my verse can sit, Your own glass shows you when you look in it.

And more, much more than any words can find expression in my verse, is the Light of the Spirit that is reflected in your soul, when you look within.

COMMENTARY

Sonnets 100 and 101 spoke of the muse that was silent. Sonnet 102.1, however, clearly states that Shakespeare's "*love is strengthen'd*" as his love's expression is now less in words than in silent "*song*." (Sonnet 102.14)

Sonnet 103 continues to explain that the "*argument*" or subject of his "*verse*" is, in its pure state, of greater worth than any words can praise. "*The argument, all bare, is of more worth Than when it hath my added praise beside.*"

The lines "*look in your glass, and there appears a face,*" refers to looking into the spiritual eye to see the soul's essence, which is made in the image of God. This thought is expanded upon in Sonnet 104 with the line, "*when first your eye I eyed,*" (Sonnet 104.2) which will be discussed below.

The beauty of the soul, a reflection of the Spirit, is beyond description in mere words. "*That over-goes my blunt invention quite, Dulling my lines and doing me disgrace.*"

By "*doing me* [him] *disgrace,*" Shakespeare means that an attempt to express the inexpressible soul in words is similar to Sonnet 102, wherein "*the owner's tongue doth publish everywhere,*" and "*love is merchandiz'd.*"

While our Poet states that his intention has always been to express the wondrous grace of Spirit ("*For to no other pass my verses tend Than of your graces and your gifts to tell*") he clearly acknowledges that "*your own glass shows you when you look in it*," much, much more than any words can express. Verse sits in silent awe when one peers into the reflection of the Ineffable. As to the lines in Sonnet 104, "*your eye I eyed*," G. Blakemore Evans states in his commentary: "Behind Shakespeare's 'eye' figure may lie two neo-Platonic concepts: (1) the eye as the window of the soul; (2) the beautiful soul in the beautiful body."

BIBLICAL PASSAGE SUGGESTED BY SONNET 103

"For now we see through a glass, darkly; but then face to face: now I know in part; but then shall I know even as also I am known." **1 Cor. 13:12**

SONNET 104

To me, fair friend, you never can be old,
For as you were when first your eye I eyed,
Such seems your beauty still. Three winters cold
Have from the forests shook three summers' pride,
Three beauteous springs to yellow autumn turn'd
In process of the seasons have I seen,
Three April perfumes in three hot Junes burn'd,
Since first I saw you fresh, which yet are green.
Ah yet doth beauty, like a dial hand,
Steal from his figure, and no pace perceiv'd:
So your sweet hue, which methinks still doth stand,
Hath motion, and mine eye may be deceiv'd:
For fear of which, hear this, thou age unbred:
Ere you were born was beauty's summer dead.

THEME

Only the Spirit is eternal, changeless Beauty. Individual perception must be free of egotistical expression and pride if it is to even begin to perceive the Light that emanates from the Spirit.

GLOSSARY

To me, fair friend, you never can be old, For as you were when first your eye I eyed, Such seems your beauty still. Three winters cold Have from the forests shook three summers' pride,

> To me, precious Beloved, you are ever-new. Your perfect Beauty radiates into the stillness of my being now, as it did when first my spiritual eye was opened unto You. It was the lingering pride within the midst of my being that closed my eye to You through three long winters of my soul's dark night.

Three beauteous springs to yellow autumn turn'd In process of the seasons have I seen, Three April perfumes in three hot Junes burn'd, Since first I saw you fresh, which yet are green.

> Three beautiful springs turned to yellow autumns. I have seen the seasons change with the perfume of spring consumed in the summer's heat. Throughout, You alone have remained ever-fresh, ever-constant.

Ah yet doth beauty, like a dial hand, Steal from his figure, and no pace perceiv'd: So your sweet hue, which methinks still doth stand, Hath motion, and mine eye may be deceiv'd:

> Beauty imperceptibly changes with the passage of time, stealing from Mother Nature her bright face; likewise, Your sweet beauty seems Immutable in the stillness of my spiritual sight, but perhaps my eye is deceived.

For fear of which, hear this, thou age unbred: Ere you were born was beauty's summer dead.

> I am in awe of the ineffable visions and say to all unborn generations: "Hear me this: Before the Creator, there is no beauty that truly exists."

COMMENTARY

In Sonnet 104, Shakespeare is speaking at the metaphysical level of Christian mystics and saints before the seventeenth century.

Once the spiritual eye is opened, the beholder longs to continue in its captivating sweetness. In Sonnet 102, the Poet states: "*Our love was new, and then but in the spring . . . I was wont to greet it with my lays.*" (Sonnet 102.5, 6).

Shakespeare's "*spring*" refers to the first blossoming or opening of the spiritual eye. The newly entranced devotee bursts into song, delighted over the vision, of "*April perfumes*" expressed in Sonnet 104.

The scriptures warn, however, that spiritual realization can make one prideful. This results in the loss of spiritual perception and vision. As it has been stated by saints: "When the ego steps in, God steps out." So now pride is met with emptiness or "*winters cold*". "*Three winters cold Have from the forests shook three summers' pride.*"

God has not departed, but His Light has been occluded by the sin of pride. The Lord is the same: "*For as you were when first your eye I eyed, Such seems your beauty still.*"

The outward beauties of nature are only manifestations of the unchangeable Spirit. "*They were but sweet, but figures of delight, Drawn after you, you pattern of all those.*" (Sonnet 98.11- 12) "*In process of the seasons,*" Beauty changes the face of nature very slowly. Spiritual sight sees the "*sweet hue*" of the Spirit, whose "*seasons*" "*yet are green.*" In other words, it is the creation that changes, and the Spirit that is changeless. In its changelessness, however, the spiritual aspirant is ever enthralled by the "newness" of the depth of Love, Sweetness, and Wisdom that is experienced. In comparison, the beauty of summer is "dead" or lifeless. In the material universe, "*sweets grown common lose their dear delight.*" (Sonnet 102.12) In the realm of the immortal Spirit, Beauty is "*green*" when first "*eyed*" and remains "*fresh*" now, and will throughout ages of unborn generations: "*thou age unbred.*"

"Unwise are those people . . . [who by] vanities hinder the grace that God gives them." "The cause of all this [vanity] is secret pride and presumption in themselves. For example, having felt a little grace they regard it so far superior to any other that they fall into vain glory, and in this way they lose it." (Walter Hilton, *The Scale of Perfection*, p. 100)

BIBLICAL PASSAGES SUGGESTED BY SONNET 104

"Thou hast set all the borders of the earth: thou hast made summer and winter." **Ps. 74:17**

"For all that is in the world, the lust of the flesh, and the lust of the eyes, and the pride of life, is not of the Father, but is of the world." **1 John 2:16**

"Thy kingdom is an everlasting kingdom, and thy dominion endureth throughout all generations." **Ps. 145:13**

"Pride goeth before destruction, and an haughty spirit before a fall." **Prov. 16:18**

SONNET 105

Let not my love be call'd idolatry,
Nor my beloved as an idol show,
Since all alike my songs and praises be
To one, of one, still such, and ever so.
Kind is my love today, tomorrow kind,
Still constant in a wondrous excellence;
Therefore my verse, to constancy confin'd,
One thing expressing, leaves out difference.
"Fair, kind, and true," is all my argument,
"Fair, kind, and true," varying to other words,
And in this change is my invention spent,
Three themes in one, which wondrous scope affords.
"Fair, kind, and true" have often liv'd alone,
Which three till now never kept seat in one.

THEME

If a person would be idolatrous or worshipful toward anything, then it must be toward the one eternal Beloved in whom all Beauty, Sweetness, and Truth are merged.

GLOSSARY

Let not my love be call'd idolatry, Nor my beloved as an idol show, Since all alike my songs and praises be To one, of one, still such, and ever so.

> My Love can never be called idolatry, and my Beloved is not the idol of material creation, since all my songs and praises are dedicated to the Eternal One, now and forever One.

Kind is my love today, tomorrow kind, Still constant in a wondrous excellence; Therefore my verse, to constancy confin'd, One thing expressing, leaves out difference.

> In one expression, my Love is sweetness now and always, a perpetual, constant, and wondrous Presence. Therefore, my verse is unwavering and constant in its theme to the

one beloved, eternal Unity.

"Fair, kind, and true," is all my argument, "Fair, kind, and true," varying to other words, And in this change is my invention spent, Three themes in one, which wondrous scope affords.

Beauty, Sweetness, and Truth is my All. No matter what synonyms or variations I use, all powers of my expression are exhausted. Three themes in one afford an infinite variety and scope to my inventive thoughts.

"Fair, kind, and true" have often liv'd alone, Which three till now never kept seat in one.

Beauty, Sweetness, and Truth have often been expanded upon as separate themes, all three of which, to me, are indivisibly rooted in the One.

COMMENTARY

In Shakespeare's time, the Biblical commandments were taken seriously. The commandment to "worship no other god" (**Exod. 34:14**) or "idols" (**Lev. 26:1**) enjoined against religious worship to "false gods" as well as "any graven image, or any likeness of any thing that is in heaven above, or that is in the earth beneath." (**Exod. 20:4**) In the literal sense this meant, of course, not to worship idols. In a deeper sense, however, man is not to engage in vainglorious pursuits, or go after the selfish desires of the heart. "And the cares of this world, and the deceitfulness of riches, and the lusts of other things entering in, choke the word, and it becometh unfruitful." (**Mark 4:19**) Shakespeare is clearly and emphatically declaring in Sonnet 105: "*Let not my love be call'd idolatry, Nor my beloved as an idol show.*" His love is not to be found in the "*show*" of the material world, or in idolizing any one individual in his verse. The "*beloved*" is the One to whom all "*songs and praises be.*" This is often repeated by Shakespeare, as expressed for example in Sonnet 76: "*O, know, sweet love, I always write of you, And you and love are still my argument.*" (Sonnet 76.9)

In Sonnet 105, Shakespeare states that his "*beloved*" has been and is "*still constant in a wondrous excellence.*" Every variation in the wording, "*Fair, kind, and true,*" or Beauty, Sweetness, and Truth, and every manner of thought and "*invention*" on these themes affords "*wondrous scope*" for "*songs and praises.*"

The realization for Shakespeare, whose "*eye*" first "*eyed*" (Sonnet 104.2) the Beloved in a beauteous spring when he was wont to greet the Spirit with his "*lays*" (Sonnet 102.6) is that the Eternal is One, and all qualities and attributions are "*kept seat,*" meaning that they are rooted in the "*One.*"

BIBLICAL PASSAGES SUGGESTED BY SONNET 105

"Thou shalt not make unto thee any graven image, or any likeness of any thing that is in heaven above, or that is in the earth beneath, or that is in the water under the earth." **Exod. 20:4**

"Know therefore this day, and consider it in thine heart, that the Lord he is God in heaven above, and upon the earth beneath: there is none else." **Deut. 4:39**

"Hear, O Israel: The Lord our God is one Lord: And thou shalt love the Lord thy God with all thine heart, and with all thy soul, and with all thy might." **Deut. 6:4-5**

SONNET 106

When in the chronicle of wasted time
I see descriptions of the fairest wights,
And beauty making beautiful old rhyme,
In praise of ladies dead and lovely knights,
Then, in the blazon of sweet beauty's best,
Of hand, of foot, of lip, of eye, of brow,
I see their antique pen would have expressed
Even such a beauty as you master now.
So all their praises are but prophecies
Of this our time, all you prefiguring;
And for they look'd but with divining eyes,
They had not skill enough your worth to sing:
For we, which now behold these present days,
Have eyes to wonder, but lack tongues to praise.

THEME

As man progresses, he endeavors to see the spiritual Essence in creation, but until his "*divining eyes*" of conjecture are opened to spiritual vision, he will still be unable to profoundly express Truth from the depths of his being.

GLOSSARY

When in the chronicle of wasted time I see descriptions of the fairest wights, And beauty making beautiful old rhyme, In praise of ladies dead and lovely knights,

> When I look into the annals of even the best writers, I see how they attempted to beautify with lovely verse, old rhyme in praise of dead maidens and gallant knights,

Then, in the blazon of sweet beauty's best, Of hand, of foot, of lip, of eye, of brow, I see their antique pen would have expressed Even such a beauty as you master now.

> Then in the outward portrayal of Nature's perfect creation of the human form of hand, foot, lip, of brow, I see their ancient writing might have expressed some aspect

> of Beauty that your creation manifests.

So all their praises are but prophecies Of this our time, all you prefiguring; And for they look'd but with divining eyes, They had not skill enough your worth to sing:

> All of their praises foretell of this time when aspects of Your nature are much written about, and although they looked at Beauty, they did not truly see with divine inspiration, and they were lacking in scope to capture Your beauty in verse.

For we, which now behold these present days, Have eyes to wonder, but lack tongues to praise.

> But we in our time have a true desire to perceive. Our eyes look in wonderment, but our hearts lack intuitive comprehension to sing Thy praise.

COMMENTARY

Shakespeare pointedly states that even the best writers have spent their efforts "*In praise of ladies dead and lovely knights.*" "*Lovely knights*" had the fine qualities of chivalry, dedicating their lives to doing good and noble deeds. Their sense of honor, respect, and loyalty are also admiral aspects of spiritual expression in people generally.

To Shakespeare, the perfect beauty of Nature is, in one aspect, demonstrated in the human form. Even a hand, a foot, lip, eye, or brow possessed by the "*ladies dead and lovely knights*" is a part of God's masterful expression, man made in His image. The "*fairest wights*" were unable to see the Creator behind the creation.

In any case, their "*antique*" verse was a precursor of a time when writers would set out to more directly express spiritual themes, such as Truth and Beauty. "*So all their praises are but prophecies Of this our time, all you prefiguring.*" Although the "*fairest wights*" looked for the higher spiritual qualities with "*divining eyes,*" they lacked the capacity to recognize the Spirit behind all virtuous qualities in man. "*They had not skill enough your worth to sing.*"

As for Shakespeare's own time, he declares that there is some interest in perceiving the spiritual qualities manifest in nature and mankind, but there is yet lacking a depth of intuitive understanding to give voice to the marvels of creation and its Creator. "*For we, which now behold these present days, Have eyes to wonder, but lack tongues to praise.*"

Perhaps Shakespeare is being a bit judgmental of the work of others. This Sonnet may be evidence of the "*pride*" (Sonnet 104.4) that was assaulted by "*three winters cold*" in Sonnet 104.3.

BIBLICAL PASSAGES SUGGESTED BY SONNET 106

"To whom then will ye liken God? or what likeness will ye compare unto him?" **Isa. 40:18**

"Open thou mine eyes, that I may behold wondrous things out of thy law." **Ps. 119:18**

"My lips shall utter praise, when thou hast taught me thy statutes. My tongue shall speak of thy word: for all thy commandments are righteousness." **Ps. 119:171-172**

"And in that day shall the deaf hear the words of the book, and the eyes of the blind shall see out of obscurity, and out of darkness." **Isa. 29:18**

"Charity never faileth: but whether there be prophecies, they shall fail; whether there be tongues, they shall cease; whether there be knowledge, it shall vanish away. For we know in part, and we prophesy in part. But when that which is perfect is come, then that which is in part shall be done away." **1 Cor. 13:8-10**

SONNET 107

Not mine own fears, nor the prophetic soul
Of the wide world dreaming on things to come,
Can yet the lease of my true love control,
Suppos'd as forfeit to a confin'd doom.
The mortal moon hath her eclipse endur'd,
And the sad augurs mock their own presage,
Incertainties now crown themselves assur'd,
And peace proclaims olives of endless age.
Now with the drops of this most balmy time
My love looks fresh, and Death to me subscribes,
Since, spite of him, I'll live in this poor rhyme,
While he insults o'er dull and speechless tribes:
And thou in this shalt find thy monument,
When tyrants' crests and tombs of brass are spent.

THEME

With Divine reassurance and peace, man overcomes all, even the fear of death.

GLOSSARY

Not mine own fears, nor the prophetic soul Of the wide world dreaming on things to come, Can yet the lease of my true love control, Suppos'd as forfeit to a confin'd doom.

> No fear of mine, or the supposed prophets of the world, who are dreamers, can ever convince me that my love for you will end with the death of this physical body.

The mortal moon hath her eclipse endur'd, And the sad augurs mock their own presage, Incertainties now crown themselves assur'd, And peace proclaims olives of endless age.

> This changing mortal body has come through its dark time, and previous gloomy predictions now mock their false prophecy. Uncertainty is now crowned with assurance and deepest inner peace proclaims my soul's immortality.

Now with the drops of this most balmy time My love looks fresh, and Death to me subscribes, Since, spite of him, I'll live in this poor rhyme, While he insults o'er dull and speechless tribes:

> Today I am suffused with the balm of peace and security. My love of the Spirit is fresh and renewed, and death itself submits to me; and to spite him, I will live in my humble verse, while death closes forever the mouths of the silent, unenlightened masses.

And thou in this shalt find thy monument, When tyrants' crests and tombs of brass are spent.

> And Thou in my verse shall find Thy monument, when the insignias and common tombs of unbelievers have long since gone to dust.

COMMENTARY

This Sonnet hearkens back to Sonnet 104 where the Poet's endurance of the dark night of the soul is described thus: "*Three winters cold Have from the forests shook three summers' pride.*" His spiritual vision is impaired ("*mine eye may be deceiv'd*" [Sonnet 104.12]) and he is insecure and is stricken with "*fear.*" (Sonnet 104.13)

We discover in Sonnet 107 that Shakespeare has come through his ordeal. His own fears led him to believe that his "*true love*" was "*Suppos'd as forfeit to a confin'd doom.*" The "*confin'd doom*" refers to his soul within his bodily frame. His fear was that death would defeat him. We see in Sonnet 146.11 that by living in "*terms divine* [and] *in selling hours of dross*" the soul triumphs over Death. In Sonnet 107, the frail body or "*mortal moon hath her eclipse endur'd.*" The soul in perfect communion with the Spirit is said to reflect the spiritual light, just as the moon reflects the sun's light. The "*eclipse*" is again a reference to the dark night of the soul wherein the Light of the Spirit had been cut off.

In Sonnet 107, the Poet's fears are dispelled: "*Incertainties now crown themselves assur'd.*" Death is again overcome. "*So shalt thou feed on Death.*" (Sonnet 146.13) Those who are "*tyrants*" and who live without spiritual expression ("*dull and speechless tribes*") find that death will triumph over them, and their lives, like "*tombs of brass are spent.*"

BIBLICAL PASSAGES SUGGESTED BY SONNET 107

"Having the understanding darkened, being alienated from the life of God through the ignorance that is in them, because of the blindness of their heart:" **Eph. 4:18**

"And God shall wipe away all tears from their eyes; and there shall be no more death, neither sorrow, nor crying, neither shall there be any more pain: for the former things are passed away." **Rev. 21:4**

"Thou wilt keep him in perfect peace, whose mind is stayed on thee: because he trusteth in thee." **Isa. 26:3**

SONNET 108

What's in the brain, that ink may character,
Which hath not figur'd to thee my true spirit?
What's new to speak, what new to register,
That may express my love, or thy dear merit?
Nothing, sweet boy; but yet, like prayers divine,
I must each day say o'er the very same;
Counting no old thing old, thou mine, I thine,
Even as when first I hallowed thy fair name.
So that eternal love in love's fresh case
Weighs not the dust and injury of age,
Nor gives to necessary wrinkles place,
But makes antiquity for aye his page;
Finding the first conceit of love there bred,
Where time and outward form would show it dead.

THEME

The relationship of the true devotee with the Divine cannot be expressed in words or thought, but is experienced as an ever-new, fresh relationship that defies Time or Death.

GLOSSARY

What's in the brain, that ink may character, Which hath not figur'd to thee my true spirit? What's new to speak, what new to register, That may express my love, or thy dear merit?

> What is in thought that words may adequately express that which truly portrays the true nature of my soul? What may I say or write that is new, or that expresses my love, or Thy sweet nature?

Nothing, sweet boy; but yet, like prayers divine, I must each day say o'er the very same; Counting no old thing old, thou mine, I thine, Even as when first I hallowed thy fair name.

> Nothing, sweet Divine child, and yet, like devotional prayers, I am compelled to repeat my daily invocations,

> wherein repeating that "Thou art mine and I am Thine," it is as fresh and new as when first I spoke Thy Holy Name.

So that eternal love in love's fresh case Weighs not the dust and injury of age, Nor gives to necessary wrinkles place, But makes antiquity for aye his page;

> Thus the love of the Spirit is ever encased anew in my soul, untouched by the injurious passage of Time that inflicts man with the infirmities of old age, but instead puts Time in its rightful place as the servant of the Spirit.

Finding the first conceit of love there bred, Where time and outward form would show it dead.

> Finding Love's eternal essence first endowed by God in my soul where Time's passage, and outward bodily aging, would show it dead.

COMMENTARY

Man in thought alone cannot conceive the character of "*thee my true spirit.*" Nor can he with words describe love of the Spirit or its Nature. "*What's new to speak, what new to register, That may express my love, or thy dear merit?*"

Saints and mystics proclaim that constant remembrances of God, or Christ, as Savior, or child ("*sweet boy*"), turn's man's consciousness toward the Divine. Man then develops a sweet, ever-new rapport with God: "*like prayers divine, I must each day say o'er the very same; Counting no old thing old, thou mine, I thine, Even as when first I hallowed thy fair name.*"

The relationship with the Divine is ever new, and never grows old. "*So that eternal love in love's fresh case Weighs not the dust and injury of age.*" The passage of time, and its injurious effects upon man, is a common theme of the Poet in his Sonnets. "*Time's scythe*" (Sonnet 12.13) and "*crooked knife.*" (Sonnet 100.14) Time, however, is a relative aspect of creation and only a servant of the Creator who "*makes antiquity for aye his page.*"

Within the soul of man, love is embossed as an eternal spark of the Divine. The outward physical form must suffer the infirmities of old age and death, but the devotee who takes shelter within, finds victory over Time and Death. "*So shalt thou feed on Death, that feeds on men, And Death once dead, there's no more dying then.*" (Sonnet 146.13)

BIBLICAL PASSAGES SUGGESTED BY SONNET 108

"For which cause we faint not; but though our outward man perish, yet the inward man is renewed day by day." **2 Cor. 4:16**

"But they that wait upon the Lord shall renew their strength; they shall mount up with wings as eagles; they shall run, and not be weary; and they shall walk, and not faint." **Isa. 40:31**

"And have put on the new man, which is renewed in knowledge after the image of him that created him." **Col. 3:10**

SONNET 109

O never say that I was false of heart,
Though absence seem'd my flame to qualify,
As easy might I from myself depart
As from my soul, which in thy breast doth lie:
That is my home of love: if I have ranged,
Like him that travels I return again;
Just to the time, not with the time exchang'd,
So that myself bring water for my stain.
Never believe, though in my nature reign'd
All frailties that besiege all kinds of blood,
That it could so preposterously be stain'd,
To leave for nothing all thy sum of good;
For nothing this wide universe I call,
Save thou, my rose; in it thou art my all.

THEME

Man journeys through life engaging in all manner of egoistical behavior, but eventually he must return to his heavenly home, realizing that only there can he find everything of true worth and goodness.

GLOSSARY

O never say that I was false of heart, Though absence seem'd my flame to qualify, As easy might I from myself depart As from my soul, which in thy breast doth lie:

> Never say that I was acting with a false heart. Though my being away seemed to diminish the warmth of my devotion, I could no more leave myself as leave my soul, which belongs completely to Thee.

That is my home of love: if I have ranged, Like him that travels I return again; Just to the time, not with the time exchang'd, So that myself bring water for my stain.

> Within your keeping is my home and refuge. If I have wandered like a traveler, return I must, just as if no time

had passed or stolen my true love; the result of which is that I am bathed clean in healing waters of devotion.

Never believe, though in my nature reign'd All frailties that besiege all kinds of blood, That it could so preposterously be stain'd, To leave for nothing all thy sum of good;

Never believe, though my nature has been inflicted so with every frailty that attacks men of all paths and ranks, that I might be afflicted as to leave the total sum of all Thy Goodness for the little that this world offers.

For nothing this wide universe I call, Save thou, my rose; in it thou art my all.

Yes, I callest the entire creation a nothing, except for Thou, my perfect rose of love; in which I find my all.

COMMENTARY

In Sonnet 108, Shakespeare says that in his soul is "*the first conceit of love there bred.*" In Genesis, it is declared that man was made in the image of God. (**Gen. 1:27**) From the "*first,*" or beginning of creation, the spark of Divine Love was infused into man's soul.

In life one may engage in "*all frailties,*" but none can ever from his true self "*depart.*" Like the prodigal son, one must eventually journey home. "*Like him that travels, I return again.*" Clearly Shakespeare refers to his soul in this Sonnet in stating: "*As easy might I from myself depart As from my soul, which in thy breast doth lie.*" The soul of man resides for a time in bodily form, but it "*doth lie*" eternally in the Spirit.

The Poet understands that the world and egotistical pleasures are counted as "*nothing*" against "*all thy sum of good.*" What can the universe offer to one who recognizes Divine Love, symbolized as the "*rose*"? In the constancy of such precious love the Poet proclaims: "*thou art my all.*"

BIBLICAL PASSAGES SUGGESTED BY SONNET 109

"For thus saith the Lord God, the Holy One of Israel; In returning and rest shall ye be saved; in quietness and in confidence shall be your strength." **Isa. 30:15**

"Come, let us return unto the Lord: for he hath torn, and he will heal us; he hath smitten, and he will bind us up." **Hos. 6:1**

"I am the rose of Sharon, and the lily of the valleys." **Song of Sol. 2:1**

"Jesus answered and said unto her, If thou knewest the gift of God, and who it is that saith to thee, Give me to drink; thou wouldest have asked of him, and he would have given thee living water." **John 4:10**

SONNET 110

Alas 'tis true I have gone here and there,
And made myself a motley to the view,
Gor'd mine own thoughts, sold cheap what is most dear,
Made old offences of affections new.
Most true it is that I have look'd on truth
Askance and strangely; but, by all above,
These blenches gave my heart another youth,
And worse essays prov'd thee my best of love.
Now all is done, have what shall have no end,
Mine appetite I never more will grind
On newer proof, to try an older friend,
A god in love, to whom I am confin'd.
Then give me welcome, next my heaven the best,
Even to thy pure and most most loving breast.

THEME

Heavenly Grace can turn one's life around such that worldly desires fall away in favor of a spiritually-inspired life.

GLOSSARY

Alas 'tis true I have gone here and there, And made myself a motley to the view, Gor'd mine own thoughts, sold cheap what is most dear, Made old offences of affections new.

> Alas! It is true, I have gone here and there acting like a fool for everyone to see, sacrificed precious thoughts and that which is dear for meaningless sense pleasures, and then repeated my offenses over again.

Most true it is that I have look'd on truth Askance and strangely; but, by all above, These blenches gave my heart another youth, And worse essays prov'd thee my best of love.

> It is also true that I have looked at truth askance as though it was a distant stranger; but by the Grace of all that is above, my deviations from Truth cleared a path within

> me that reawakened my heart. I clearly saw my reprehensible conduct as unworthy, and that in Thee alone was proof of true Love.

Now all is done, have what shall have no end, Mine appetite I never more will grind On newer proof, to try an older friend, A god in love, to whom I am confin'd.

> Now my spent youth and fruitless wanderings are over: never again will my sensual cravings be whetted with fresh desires that test the constancy of my one true longing, for God, to whom I confine all my desires.

Then give me welcome, next my heaven the best, Even to thy pure and most most loving breast.

> Next to coming into heaven, the best would be if Thou wouldst welcome me now to Thy pure and loving breast.

COMMENTARY

In Sonnet 109.9-10, the Poet confesses that "*in my nature reign'd all frailties that besiege all kinds of blood.*" His confessions, reminiscent perhaps of St. Augustine, continue in Sonnet 110. Our Poet has traveled from "*here and there*" playing the "*motley*" fool in the eyes of many.

His better and higher reason was ignored ("*Gor'd mine own thoughts*"), and he "*sold cheap what is more dear.*" He made "*offences of affections new*" by perhaps entering into new situations of loves and degrading them and himself. There is the sense that in selling "*what is most dear,*" he refers to his very soul.

But "*by all above,*" the Poet is awakened and given a new life. ("*These blenches gave my heart another youth.*") "*All above*" is a reference to heavenly Grace, which puts an end to his wanderings "*here and there.*" He realized that his behavior was like poorly written "*essays.*"

This realization *"Prov'd thee my best of love . . . A god in love, to whom I am confin'd.*" His old haunts would know him no more. "*Mine appetite I never more will grind.*"

One can dream of Grace or "*heaven,*" but being welcomed into "[*T*]*hy pure and most loving breast*" is the best of all.

BIBLICAL PASSAGES SUGGESTED BY SONNET 110

"My brethren, count it all joy when ye fall into divers temptations; Knowing this, that the trying of your faith worketh patience; . . . Blessed is the man that endureth temptation; for when he is tried, he shall receive the crown of life, which the Lord hath promised to them that love him." **James 1:2-3, 12**

"All the labor of man is for his mouth, and yet the appetite is not filled" **Eccl. 6:7**

"For what is a man profited, if he shall gain the whole world, and lose his own soul? Or what shall a man give in exchange for his soul?" **Matt. 16:26**

"Whom have I in heaven but thee? And there is none upon earth that I desire beside thee. My flesh and my heart faileth: but God is the strength of my heart, and my portion for ever. For, lo, they that are far from thee shall perish: thou hast destroyed all them that go a whoring from thee. But it is good for me to draw near to God: I have put my trust in the Lord God, that I may declare all thy works." **Ps. 73:25-28**

SONNET 111

O for my sake do you with Fortune chide,
The guilty goddess of my harmful deeds,
That did not better for my life provide
Than public means which public manners breeds.
Thence comes it that my name receives a brand,
And almost thence my nature is subdu'd
To what it works in, like the dyer's hand:
Pity me, then, and wish I were renew'd;
Whilst, like a willing patient, I will drink
Potions of eisell 'gainst my strong infection;
No bitterness that I will bitter think,
Nor double penance, to correct correction.
Pity me, then, dear friend, and I assure ye
Even that your pity is enough to cure me.

THEME

Wrong habits, which are deeply-ingrained, are like an affliction to the soul, resulting in dire consequences. Only a strong willingness to change, and Divine Grace, provide a remedy.

GLOSSARY

O for my sake do you with Fortune chide, The guilty goddess of my harmful deeds, That did not better for my life provide Than public means which public manners breeds.

> O for my sake, do you wish Fortune to punish those harmful deeds I have done under the influence of my dominating egoistical demands? These mean and lowly things, which are habitually practiced by the public, produced in my life the bitter results that could be expected.

Thence comes it that my name receives a brand, And almost thence my nature is subdu'd To what it works in, like the dyer's hand: Pity me, then, and wish I were renew'd

> Because of my transgressions, my name is branded. My

habits, so ingrained by repetition, like the ink on a dyer's hand, almost completely subdue my better nature. Have pity on me and grant that I be renewed.

Whilst, like a willing patient, I will drink Potions of eisell 'gainst my strong infection; No bitterness that I will bitter think, Nor double penance, to correct correction.

Like an eager patient I will drink medicinal potions to combat the strong infection that plagues my soul; I will not resent the remedy nor reject double portions of penance to oust the offending habits.

Pity me, then, dear friend, and I assure ye Even that your pity is enough to cure me.

Have pity on me, then, dear Friend, and I assure You that Your soothing pity is enough to cure me.

COMMENTARY

In Sonnet 109, Shakespeare makes reference to his "*stain*" and "*all frailties*" that in his "*nature reigned.*" Sonnet 110 describes how the author "*sold cheap what is most dear*" and repeated his old habits again and again ("*made old offences of affections new*").

Sonnet 111 describes the author's reckoning as he reaps what his sinful conduct has sown. But his ill fortune was by the Hand of God, which chides in order to awaken. "*O, for my sake do you with Fortune chide.*"

Shakespeare blames the "*guilty goddess*" for being the instigator of his "*harmful deeds.*" This "*guilty goddess*" is like "*the worser spirit a woman coloured ill*" of Sonnet 144. The repetition of worldly habits, the mean behavior of persons in general, became firmly rooted and resulted in him almost completely subduing his better nature. "*Thence comes it that my name receives a brand, and almost thence my nature is subdu'd.*" Worldly, egotistically-centered habits become ingrained like the inks of "*the dyer's hand.*" In Sonnet 62, Shakespeare says that "*for this sin there is no remedy, It is so grounded inward in my heart.*"

The realization that a "*remedy*" is needed comes from the awakening blows of Fortune's chiding, whereby the Poet's "*name receives a brand.*"

While in Sonnet 62, Shakespeare says "*there is no remedy*" for "*this sin*," Sonnet 111 suggests that "*a willing patient*" who would ingest "*potions of eisell 'gainst my strong infection*," and even do "*double penance*," has a chance to "*correct correction*," and turn the tide of ill fortunes.

With all manner of willingness to accept his "*bitter*" medicine, and the chidings of Fortune, our Poet sees his ultimate cure in the pity or grace of his ever-constant, dear Friend, the Lord. "*Pity me, then, dear friend, and I assure ye Even that your pity is enough to cure me.*"

BIBLICAL PASSAGES SUGGESTED BY SONNET 111

"For which cause we faint not; but though our outward man perish, yet the inward man is renewed day by day." **2 Cor. 4:16**

"My friends scorn me: but mine eye poureth out tears unto God." **Job 16:20**

"My strength is dried up like a potsherd; and my tongue cleaveth to my jaws; and thou hast brought me into dust of death." **Ps. 22:15**

"Heal me, O Lord, and I shall be healed; save me, and I shall be saved: for thou art my praise." **Jer. 17:14**

"For they being ignorant of God's righteousness, and going about to establish their own righteousness, have not submitted themselves unto the righteousness of God." **Rom. 10:3**

"For whom the Lord loveth he chasteneth, and scourgeth every son whom he receiveth." **Heb. 12:6**

SONNET 112

Your love and pity doth the impression fill
Which vulgar scandal stamped upon my brow,
For what care I who calls me well or ill,
So you o'er-green my bad, my good allow?
You are all-the-world, and I must strive
To know my shames and praises from your tongue;
None else to me, nor I to none alive,
That my steel'd sense or changes right or wrong.
In so profound abysm I throw all care
Of other's voices, that my adder's sense
To critic and to flatterer stopped are.
Mark how with my neglect I do dispense.
You are so strongly in my purpose bred,
That all the world besides methinks are dead.

THEME

Healing Divine Love and Grace can so change a person that the common voices of critic and flatterer are as nothing to one who seeks only to hear the inner voice of soul-guided intuition.

GLOSSARY

Your love and pity doth the impression fill Which vulgar scandal stamped upon my brow; For what care I who calls me well or ill, So you o'er-green my bad, my good allow?

> Your love and pity heal the wounds that malicious scandals stamped across my brow. Besides, why should I care who speaks well or ill of me so long as you are renewing my spirit and inciting me to good actions?

You are all-the-world, and I must strive To know my shames and praises from your tongue; None else to me, nor I to none alive, That my steel'd sense or changes right or wrong.

> You are all the world to me, and I must strive to know my shames and praises from Your inner voice, which

> speaks to me. There is no one else for me, nor do I live for any other. It is only You who can influence my hardened senses to change either toward right or wrong.

In so profound abysm I throw all care Of other's voices, that my adder's sense To critic and to flatterer stopped are. Mark how with my neglect I do dispense:

> Into the deepest abyss I consign all concerns of what others say, and I turn a deaf ear to critic and flatterer alike. Take heed of how it is that with such indifference I dispense with care or concern over other's voices.

You are so strongly in my purpose bred, That all the world besides methinks are dead.

> You are so much embedded in my being and purpose that it is as if all the rest of the world is dead to me.

COMMENTARY

The plea for "*pity*" from the "*dear friend*," and its curative powers in Sonnet 111, have taken hold. In Sonnet 112, the scar "*branded*" upon the Poet's brow by the "*vulgar scandal*" finds healing by the Lord's Love and Pity. "*Your love and pity doth the impression fill Which vulgar scandal stamped upon my brow.*" Although marked by scandal, spiritual renewal has made the Poet indifferent to whomever "*calls me* [him] *well or ill.*" The Poet has turned away from his life of "*harmful deeds*" (Sonnet 111.2) and allows goodness to pour in. "*So you o'er-green my bad, my good allow.*"

Only the Lord's inner counsel will the Poet hear: He is "*all-the-world*" to him. Throughout the Sonnets, Shakespeare has enunciated that the Lord is the only theme of his verse and the center of his life. (Sonnet 76.10: "*You and love are still my argument*"; Sonnet 78.12: "*But thou art all my art*"; Sonnet 105.4: "*To one, of one, still such, and ever so*"; Sonnet 108.7: "*Thou mine, I thine.*")

Shakespeare, resigned in complete faith to the Lord, determines to utterly tune out the voices of both "*critic*" and "*flatterer.*" This he is able to do because his life's purpose is one-pointedly centered upon God. "*Mark how with my neglect I do dispense; You are so strongly in my purpose bred, That all the world besides methinks are dead.*" Essentially, the Poet has turned a deaf ear to the worldly voices, who are as if dead to him. He only hears the soul's inner voice and is receptive to the Lord's soothing Grace and Wisdom.

BIBLICAL PASSAGES SUGGESTED BY SONNET 112

"Their poison is like the poison of a serpent: they are like the deaf adder that stoppeth her ear; Which will not hearken to the voice of charmers, charming never so wisely." **Ps. 58:4-5**

"Where is the wise? where is the scribe? where is the disputer of this world? hath not God made foolish the wisdom of this world?" **1 Cor. 1:20**

"Truly my soul waiteth upon God: from him cometh my salvation. He only is my rock and my salvation; he is my defense; I shall not be greatly moved. How long will ye imagine mischief against a man? ye shall be slain all of you: as a bowing wall shall ye be, and as a tottering fence. They only consult to cast him down from his excellency: they delight in lies: they bless with their mouth, but they curse inwardly. My soul, wait thou only upon God; for my expectation is from him. He only is my rock and my salvation: he is my defense; I shall not be moved. In God is my salvation and my glory: the rock of my strength, and my refuge, is in God." **Ps. 62:1-7**

SONNET 113

Since I left you, mine eye is in my mind,
And that which governs me to go about
Doth part his function and is partly blind,
Seems seeing, but effectually is out;
For it no form delivers to the heart
Of bird, of flower, or shape which it doth latch,
Of his quick objects hath the mind no part,
Nor his own vision holds what it doth catch:
For if it see the rud'st or gentlest sight,
The most sweet favour or deformed'st creature,
The mountain or the sea, the day or night,
The crow or dove, it shapes them to your feature.
Incapable of more, replete with you,
My most true mind thus maketh mine untrue.

THEME

Enraptured in the highest states of ecstasy, one perceives all creation as one complete whole made in Truth of spiritual essence and light.

GLOSSARY

Since I left you, mine eye is in my mind, And that which governs me to go about Doth part his function and is partly blind, Seems seeing, but effectually is out;

> Since I left my deepest blissful meditation of Thee, my consciousness is still enthralled. My conscious mind still partly functions to keep my body going, but it is also in part still enraptured. Although my eyes see the physical world, my mind takes no conscious notice.

For it no form delivers to the heart Of bird, of flower, or shape which it doth latch, Of his quick objects hath the mind no part, Nor his own vision holds what it doth catch:

> My mind sees the birds, flowers, and shapes, but my heart is unmoved by them. My mind is not absorbed in the activities of everyday life, but remains aloof.

For if it see the rud'st or gentlest sight, The most sweet favour or deformed'st creature, The mountain or the sea, the day or night, The crow or dove, it shapes them to your feature.

> Whether the eye sees the rudest or gentlest sight or the sweetest or most deformed creature, the mountain, or the sea, or the day, or night, the crow, or dove, it still cognizes them all as being essentially formed of spiritual light and essence.

Incapable of more, replete with you, My most true mind thus maketh mine untrue.

> My true intuitive consciousness can do no other than be totally engrossed in Thee as the true Essence of all things; and this belies the unreality of what my physical eyes see as real.

COMMENTARY

Sonnet 113 is deeply symbolic. It describes what saints and mystics experience in higher states of consciousness. Such states are called ecstatic union in religious literature. "*Since I left you, mine eye is in my mind.*" This reference is to the elevated state of consciousness that is experienced when higher ecstatic union or super-conscious experience gives way to ordinary waking consciousness. It was recorded in the life of St. Teresa of Avila, as with many other saints and mystics, that in states of ecstasy the individual remains in an immobile, trance-like state, often accompanied by cessation of breath and heartbeat. Even after the ecstatic union gives way to the ordinary consciousness of the mind, the saintly individual still feels enraptured.

In the life of St. Francis of Assisi we read: "[The] ecstatic exuberance which was a fundamental trait of his character enabled him to burst forth in a childlike delight for no other reason than that he was one of God's creatures. The road he pursued was just a straight and dusty white road with fields on either side. But he who walked on it was filled with ecstatic joy and able to see the beauty of all things, the delicate splendor of every leaf and blade of grass, and he sensed the tender love of the father who had created it all. And suddenly he grew aware of the oneness pervading all things through the oneness of their common

Creator, and his soul overflowed with a feeling of brotherhood with all created things. A sensation of love overcame him, stronger than any he had ever sensed before, a sensation of brotherly love for earth and cloud, for leaf and blade of grass, for everything under the sun." (Fulop-Miller, *The Saints that Moved the World*, p. 226)

In St. Francis' perception there was a "oneness pervading all things." In Sonnet 113, the Poet's physical sight of the eyes "*doth part his function and is partly blind, Seems seeing, but effectually is out.*" He sees forms and shapes "*of bird, of flower, of shape which it doth latch; of his quick objects hath the mind no part, nor his own vision holds what it doth catch.*"

While the eyes see the physical realm, the higher consciousness sees the Essence beneath and behind. "*The most sweet favour or deformed'st creature, The mountain or the sea, the day or night, The crow or dove, it shapes them to your feature.*"

Like St. Francis, "he grew aware of the oneness pervading all things". Shakespeare, in his ineffable perceptions, says he was "*Incapable of more, replete with you, My most true mind thus maketh mine untrue.*" The ordinary conscious mind is "*untrue*" as it is unaware of the Spirit in all created things. Once the ecstatic state is experienced, the sense of completeness overtakes the limitations of physical consciousness.

Again, as for St. Francis, "all along his way he sang and prayed, and it was always the same thanksgiving addressed to the Creator for the great gift of being part of the Creation." (p. 226) The significance of Sonnet 113 is that it tells us that Shakespeare, who many times describes the sight of his spiritual eye in the Sonnets, also experienced states of ecstatic consciousness. That Shakespeare is one of the special brotherhood and sisterhood who have experienced such ecstatic states is not surprising, given the deep spiritual understanding and wisdom found in his Sonnets and other writings. How deeply or how often Shakespeare had such super-consciousness experiences remains yet a mystery.

SONNET 114

Or whether doth my mind being crown'd with you,
Drink up the monarch's plague, this flattery?
Or whether shall I say mine eye saith true,
And that your love taught it this alchemy,
To make of monsters and things indigest
Such cherubins as your sweet self resemble,
Creating every bad a perfect best,
As fast as objects to his beams assemble?
O 'tis the first, 'tis flattery in my seeing,
And my great mind most kingly drinks it up:
Mine eye well knows what with his gust is 'greeing,
And to his palate doth prepare the cup:
If it be poison'd, 'tis the lesser sin
That mine eye loves it and doth first begin.

THEME

The higher states of intuitive consciousness cognize the Truth and spiritual Essence within the material world. The physical eyes do not truly see what is real given that the bodily senses are only finite. The intuitive consciousness is soul-guided and beyond finite sensual experience. It is able, therefore, to guide one's perceptions from the worldly towards the heavenly.

GLOSSARY

Or whether doth my mind being crown'd with you, Drink up the monarch's plague, this flattery? Or whether shall I say mine eye saith true, And that your love taught it this alchemy,

> I want to understand if my mind in states of higher consciousness consumes the sin of pride, or whether my eye sees what is real because of Your Love's alchemy, which has transformed me.

To make of monsters and things indigest Such cherubins as your sweet self resemble, Creating every bad a perfect best, As fast as objects to his beams assemble?

> Is it this transformation that causes one to see monsters and inanimate objects as sweet cherubim resembling You, and which turns every ugly thing into something perfect as fast as the beams of light assemble and coalesce into form?

O 'tis the first, 'tis flattery in my seeing, And my great mind most kingly drinks it up: Mine eye well knows what with his gust is 'greeing, And to his palate doth prepare the cup:

> Oh, I see it is the lower, sensual mind that perceives the ordinary, and my higher consciousness that dispels the ego-centered visions. My eye knows what the mind desires to see and serves it a cup to its liking, whether sensual or spiritual.

If it be poison'd, 'tis the lesser sin That mine eye loves it and doth first begin.

> If the mind is poisoned by sensuality, my eye is less sinful for loving what it sees. The eye may, at other times, perceive the true Essence, as opposed to the sensual, and thereby turn the consciousness away from temptation toward the spiritual.

COMMENTARY

Sonnet 113 clearly states that the higher intuitive consciousness, or super-conscious mind, cognizes the essential Reality of all creation. Shakespeare says that "*My most true mind thus maketh mine eye untrue.*" In Sonnet 114, Shakespeare poses the question of whether the mind truly sees or whether "*your love*"—meaning God's Love and Grace—taught the eye to see "*monsters*" as "*cherubins.*"

The conclusion is that the mind in the super-conscious state is the center of perception. If the eye sees that which "*'tis flattery in my seeing,*" it is because this is what the sensual mind desires. "*Mine eye well knows what with his gust is 'greeing.*" In response to the mind's "*palate,*" the eye will "*prepare the cup.*" If the mind is sensuous, the eye will seek sensuality. If the mind is spiritually bent, it will be "*crown'd*" with spiritual food, "*crown'd with you.*"

The eye cannot be faulted for what it sees. If it sees "*monsters*" it is the fault of the alluring desires of the senses. In essence therefore the sin of the eye is "*the lesser sin.*" "*If it be poison'd, 'tis the lesser sin That mine eye loves it and doth first begin.*" Once the mind is above worldly temptations, the love of Divine Grace will prepare the cup that transforms the ordinary into the spiritual.

BIBLICAL PASSAGE SUGGESTED BY SONNET 114

"While we look not at the things which are seen, but at the things which are not seen: for the things which are seen are temporal; but the things which are not seen are eternal." **2 Cor. 4:18**

SONNET 115

Those lines that I before have writ do lie,
Even those that said I could not love you dearer,
Yet then my judgment knew no reason why
My most full flame should afterwards burn clearer.
But reckoning Time, whose million'd accidents
Creep in 'twixt vows, and change decrees of kings,
Tan sacred beauty, blunt the sharp'st intents,
Divert strong minds to the course of alt'ring things;
Alas why, fearing of Time's tyranny,
Might I not then say, "Now I love you best,"
When I was certain o'er incertainty,
Crowning the present, doubting of the rest?
Love is a babe; then might I not say so,
To give a full growth to that which still doth grow.

THEME

Love is infinite as God is infinite. The spiritual aspirant knows that its limits cannot be grasped or circumscribed by trying to present an assessment of its nature.

GLOSSARY

Those lines that I before have writ do lie, Even those that said I could not love you dearer, Yet then my judgment knew no reason why My most full flame should afterwards burn clearer

> The words that I penned before are not completely true, even those that said I could not love you more dearly. I did not know, nor did I have reason to understand, that my deepest love could burn ever more brightly and profoundly.

But reckoning Time, whose million'd accidents Creep in 'twixt vows, and change decrees of kings, Tan sacred beauty, blunt the sharp'st intents, Divert strong minds to the course of alt'ring things;

> But Time has a way of changing the course of things un-

expectedly. It alters vows made and judgments decreed, and changes one's perception of sacred beauty. It thwarts even the most determined intentions, diverting the plans of the strong-willed minds toward an altered course.

Alas! why, fearing of Time's tyranny, Might I not then say, "Now I love you best," When I was certain o'er incertainty, Crowning the present, doubting of the rest?

So, respecting how Time changes the firmest resolutions I could say: "Now I love you best," as I did before when I was certain beyond doubt of my love. Today I may crown my love with highest homage knowing that it yet might grow in the future.

Love is a babe; then might I not say so, To give a full growth to that which still doth grow.

Love after all is not static but may grow as I have seen. It would therefore be incorrect to circumscribe my love in a finite way when its potential is to reach infinite proportions.

COMMENTARY

Sonnet 113 describes the ecstatic state of communion in which the Poet says that in that rapturous experience he is "*incapable of more, replete with you.*" In Sonnet 115, Shakespeare realizes that the higher states of consciousness are not finite, but increase in intensity. "*Yet then my judgment knew no reason why my most full flame should afterwards burn clearer.*" Saints have described how their perceptions of the Spirit grow in intensity and deepen over time.

It is not correct to state finalities when "*reckoning time*" is known to change even everyday worldly events. ("*Creep in 'twixt vows, and change decrees of kings.*") If the course of human events is alterable, how much more dynamic is love, a quality of the soul.

The Bible reports that "God is Love." To human minds, uncomprehending of the Spirit, the consciousness is like a "*babe,*" dowered with the potential for infinite expression. "*Love is a babe: then might I not say so, to give full growth to that which still doth grow.*"

BIBLICAL PASSAGES SUGGESTED BY SONNET 115

"And we have known and believed the love that God hath to us. God is love; and he that dwelleth in love dwelleth in God, and God in him." **1 John 4:16**

"Hast thou not known? hast thou not heard, that the everlasting God, the Lord, the Creator of the ends of the earth, fainteth not, neither is weary? there is no searching of his understanding." **Isa. 40:28**

"Then I beheld all the work of God, that a man cannot find out the work that is done under the sun: because though a man labor to seek it out, yet he shall not find it; yea further; though a wise man think to know it, yet shall he not be able to find it." Eccl. **8:17**

SONNET 116

Let me not to the marriage of true minds
Admit impediments. Love is not love
Which alters when it alteration finds,
Or bends with the remover to remove.
O no, it is an ever-fixed mark,
That looks on tempests and is never shaken;
It is the start to every wand'ring bark,
Whose worth's unknown, although his height be taken.
Love's not Time's fool, though rosy lips and cheeks
Within his bending sickle's compass come;
Love alters not with his brief hours and weeks,
But bears it out even to the edge of doom.
If this be error, and upon me prov'd,
I never writ, nor no man ever lov'd.

THEME

True love comes from the Divine, and God's Love is ever the most true and constant beyond all human praise or limitation.

GLOSSARY

Let me not to the marriage of true minds Admit impediments. Love is not love Which alters when it alteration finds, Or bends with the remover to remove.

> Let it never be said that in the union of true minds Love is not true and constant, or that it wavers in its expression in difficult times or goes astray with unforeseen circumstance bent upon altering it.

O no, it is an ever-fixed mark, That looks on tempests and is never shaken; It is the start to every wand'ring bark, Whose worth's unknown, although his height be taken.

> O no, it is the polestar that guides through every storm and hearkens to wandering souls but is never shaken. Its true worth is beyond appraisal, although many have attempted its description and measures.

Love's not Time's fool, though rosy lips and cheeks Within his bending sickle's compass come; Love alters not with his brief hours and weeks, But bears it out even to the edge of doom.

> True Love is unaffected by Time, but lovers of merely worldly beauty have been swept away like a brief harvest caught in the sickle's blade. True Love is not affected by Time's hours and passing seasons, but endures and outlasts all until the last day.

If this be error, and upon me prov'd, I never writ, nor no man ever lov'd.

> If I have erred in my declaration, and this is proved against me, then nothing I ever wrote is true, and no man has ever loved.

COMMENTARY

It is interesting how in Sonnet 115 Shakespeare describes his ever-changing, deepening experience of Love. As Sir Walter Scott has said: "Love rules the court, the grove, and men below, and saints above: For love is heaven and heaven is love." ("Lay of the Last Minstrel," Canto IV) Sonnet 116 is a declaration that God's Love is the only true constant in a world of change: "*it is an ever-fixed mark.*" This Love is unalterable, and the saving grace of wandering souls. It "*is never shaken; it is the star to every wand'ring bark.*"

The constancy and nature of Divine Love is beyond human appraisal and beyond the reality of "*Time's tyranny.*" (Sonnet 115.9) Love's "*worth's* [are] *unknown, although his height be taken.*"

So deep is Shakespeare's conviction about Love, that he believes that if he is wrong, his life's work is meaningless and love has never touched the heart of any man. "*If this be error and upon me proved, I never writ, nor no man ever lov'd.*"

BIBLICAL PASSAGES SUGGESTED BY SONNET 116

"For the mountains shall depart, and the hills be removed; but my kindness shall not depart from thee, neither shall the covenant of my peace be removed, saith the Lord that hath mercy on thee." **Isa. 54:10**

"Now before the feast of the passover, when Jesus knew that his hour was come that he should depart out of this world unto the Father, having loved his own which were in the world, he loved them unto the end." **John 13:1**

SONNET 117

Accuse me thus: that I have scanted all
Wherein I should your great deserts repay,
Forgot upon your dearest love to call,
Whereto all bonds do tie me day by day;
That I have frequent been with unknown minds,
And given to time your own dear-purchas'd right;
That I have hoisted sail to all the winds
Which should transport me furthest from your sight.
Book both my wilfulness and errors down,
And on just proof surmise accumulate;
Bring me within the level of your frown,
But shoot not at me in your waken'd hate;
Since my appeal says I did strive to prove
The constancy and virtue of your love.

THEME

The Lord is forgiving of man's sins greater than "seventy times seven" because the Lord God understands the difficult temptations of life, which ever test the constancy of his children.

GLOSSARY

Accuse me thus: that I have scanted all Wherein I should your great deserts repay, Forgot upon your dearest love to call, Whereto all bonds do tie me day by day;

> Accuse me of the following: That I have utterly failed to repay the many benefactions that have come to me, and I have forgotten to acknowledge your deepest expressions of Love, which are daily flowing to me and binding my heart with countless solicitudes.

That I have frequent been with unknown minds, And given to time your own dear-purchas'd right; That I have hoisted sail to all the winds Which should transport me furthest from your sight.

> And I have frequented the company of worldly-think-

ing persons, and wasted time in idle pursuits instead of spending precious hours in communion with Thee; and I have expended energies in worthless pursuits that have carried me far from your sacred presence.

Book both my wilfulness and errors down, And on just proof surmise accumulate; Bring me within the level of your frown, But shoot not at me in your waken'd hate;

You should dutifully record my willfulness and sins, and on just proof and other evidence that You might accumulate, bring me within the purview of your harshest decree. But do not immediately execute judgment as a result of Your awakened knowledge and disapproval of my actions.

Since my appeal says I did strive to prove The constancy and virtue of your love.

Since, by way of defense, I state that my actions were meant only to prove the gracious constancy and forgiving nature of Your Love.

COMMENTARY

Sonnet 116 is a complete avowal of the constancy of Love in all circumstances as it "*bears out even to the edge of doom.*" Man will test the Lord by his own inconstancy, in spite of the many blessings that flow to him. "*I have scanted all wherein I should your great deserts repay.*" Sonnet 117 sets out a list of the Poet's ungracious actions, which transport him far from the spiritual life ("*transport me farthest from your sight*"). This is reminiscent of Sonnet 110.3 where the Poet states that he "*sold cheap what is most dear.*"

Life is both a testament of man's constancy in love, and the Lord's ever-loving, forgiving, and constant nature toward His children. Love for the worldly, as opposed to the spiritual, is one of life's battles. Joys are appreciated more because of the sorrows faced by mankind. Shakespeare says to the Lord that He is correct to "*Bring me within the level of your frown, But shoot not at me in your waken'd hate.*" He goes on to state that he, a sinner, by his actions "*strive*[s] *to prove the constancy and virtue of your love.*"

According to E.M.W. Tillyard, Elizabethans were very conscious of the theological themes of sin and salvation, and there are "few references to the Pauline scheme of redemption" in the works of "sonneteers and dramatists" (*The Elizabethan World Picture* [New York: Vintage, 1964], p. 18). Shakespeare, however, declares that to him, God is a God of love. He therefore pulls together the theme of Sonnet 116 on the constancy of the Love of God toward Man, and the proof of such in Sonnet 117 wherein the inconstancy of man is ever forgiven by God.

BIBLICAL PASSAGES SUGGESTED BY SONNET 117

"Who is a God like unto thee, that pardoneth iniquity, and passeth by the transgression of the remnant of his heritage? he retaineth not his anger for ever, because he delighteth in mercy." **Mic. 7:18**

"And the Lord passed by before him, and proclaimed, The Lord, The Lord God, merciful and gracious, longsuffering, and abundant in goodness and truth." **Exod. 34:6**

"The Lord hath appeared of old unto me, saying, Yea, I have loved thee with an everlasting love: therefore with loving kindness have I drawn thee." **Jer. 31:3**

SONNET 118

Like as, to make our appetites more keen,
With eager compounds we our palate urge;
As, to prevent our maladies unseen,
We sicken to shun sickness when we purge;
Even so, being full of your ne'er-cloying sweetness,
To bitter sauces did I frame my feeding;
And, sick of welfare, found a kind of meetness
To be diseas'd, ere that there was true needing.
Thus policy in love, to anticipate
The ills that were not, grew to faults assured,
And brought to medicine a healthful state,
Which, rank of goodness, would by ill be cured;
But thence I learn, and find the lesson true,
Drugs poison him that so fell sick of you.

THEME

Unhealthy practices of bodily purging may show a lack of faith. Once a spiritual aspirant feels the sweetness of the Lord's response, he should drop doubts and fears of bodily illness, relying more upon his faith for a cure to the true sickness within.

GLOSSARY

Like as, to make our appetites more keen, With eager compounds we our palate urge; As, to prevent our maladies unseen, We sicken to shun sickness when we purge;

To whet an appetite we often use pungent mixtures to incite the desires of the palate. To prevent illnesses from occurring, we use compounds to purge our bodies in order to rid it of imagined impurities.

Even so, being full of your ne'er-cloying sweetness, To bitter sauces did I frame my feeding; And, sick of welfare, found a kind of meetness To be diseas'd, ere that there was true needing.

In the same way, even though I was filled with your never-surfeited sweetness, I still used harsh methods upon my healthy body to purge it of what I thought might cause it to be made ill by the sickness of mortal sins.

Thus policy in love, to anticipate The ills that were not, grew to faults assured, And brought to medicine a healthful state, Which, rank of goodness, would by ill be cured;

This method of purgation, in the cause of preserving love and preventing imagined ills, resulted in my falling victim to the improper remedy. Foolishly, I was seeking a cure for a most healthy state: Namely that I was completely filled with Your gracious goodness, which if I were ill would have cured me in any case.

But thence I learn, and find the lesson true, Drugs poison him that so fell sick of you.

So I truly learned and find the lesson to be true, that false preventative practices are poison because they show that one has fallen from one's faith and trust in You.

COMMENTARY

In Shakespeare's time people did not generally understand proper ways to prevent illness or to cure it. Purgation, Shakespeare declares, resulted in more harm to the body. "*The ills that were not, grew to faults assured.*" Shakespeare was filled with the sweetness of God's presence, which never grew old or tiring, "*being full of your ne'er-cloying sweetness.*" Saints and mystics often describe their relationship with God as being one of sweetness. The fear of reverting to "*old offences*" (Sonnet 110.4) might have caused some to use harmful purges. Shakespeare, however, relates in Sonnet 107.1, 3) that "*not mine own fears, nor the prophetic soul of the wide world . . . can yet the lease of my true love control.*" In Sonnet 118, Shakespeare seems to comment on practices that others use. This he believes shows a lack of faith that "*grew to faults assured.*" Doubt and lack of faith in God's grace and goodness is itself an "*ill*" to be cured for the spiritual aspirant who "*so fell sick of you.*" This means that one is "*sick*" who has fallen from this faith in God. This disease is one of the soul and not the body. If Shakespeare is true to his belief in Sonnet

117, then even the spiritually sick will find a cure in "*the constancy and virtue of your* [God's] *love.*" (Sonnet 117.14)

BIBLICAL PASSAGES SUGGESTED BY SONNET 118

"My meditation of him shall be sweet: I will be glad in the Lord." **Ps. 104:34**

"And he that doubteth is damned if he eat, because he eateth not of faith: for whatsoever is not of faith is sin." **Rom. 14:23**

"And the Lord will take away from thee all sickness, and will put none of the evil diseases of Egypt, which thou knowest, upon thee; but will lay them upon all them that hate thee." **Deut. 7:15**

"And he said unto her, Daughter, thy faith hath made thee whole; go in peace, and be whole of thy plague." **Mark 5:34**

"Thou wilt keep him in perfect peace, whose mind is stayed on thee; because he trusteth in thee." **Isa. 26:3**

SONNET 119

What potions have I drunk of Siren tears,
Distill'd from limbecks foul as hell within,
Applying fears to hopes, and hopes to fears,
Still losing when I saw myself to win!
What wretched errors hath my heart committed,
Whilst it hath thought itself so blessed never!
How have mine eyes out of their spheres been fitted,
In the distraction of this madding fever!
O benefit of ill! Now I find true
That better is by evil still made better;
And ruin'd love, when it is built anew,
Grows fairer than at first, more strong, far greater.
So I return rebuked to my content,
And gain by ill thrice more than I have spent.

THEME

A wretched, unhappy way of life can bring one to one's knees and be the prod that incites a true understanding of where true happiness is to be found.

GLOSSARY

What potions have I drunk of Siren tears, Distill'd from limbecks foul as hell within, Applying fears to hopes, and hopes to fears, Still losing when I saw myself to win!

> I have consumed poisons from alluring sirens whose draughts are distilled liquors from the sewers of hell on earth. My expectant hopes for a better life were washed away by my fears; and as often as I raised my hopes, expecting to win over my fears, I found myself losing when I thought to win.

What wretched errors hath my heart committed, Whilst it hath thought itself so blessed never! How have mine eyes out of their spheres been fitted, In the distraction of this madding fever!

> My wayward heart committed despicable acts while it saw itself blessed with good fortune. Chasing lustfully after a sinful life blurred my true vision and distracted me from a better course of conduct.

O benefit of ill! Now I find true That better is by evil still made better; And ruin'd love, when it is built anew, Grows fairer than at first, more strong, far greater.

> I learned after all that positive lessons can come from such a destructive lifestyle. Likewise, a ruined loving relationship, once renewed and rebuilt, can grow more beautiful on its new secure foundation.

So I return rebuked to my content, And gain by ill thrice more than I have spent.

> Rebuked by a life of error, I return eagerly to the true source of my happiness, and my gain is threefold more than I suffered in my life of wretched errors.

COMMENTARY

In Sonnet 111, Shakespeare shows how wrong habits are deeply ingrained and are hard to dislodge. The Poet's willingness to "*drink potions of eisell*" and seek the "*pity*" of Divine Grace provided a remedy (Sonnet 111.10, 13). In Sonnet 109, the Poet refers to his "*frailties*," and in Sonnet 110 reminds us that he repeated "*old offences*."

In Sonnet 119, we find the Poet again committing "*wretched errors*." In Sonnet 111, the Poet willingly would do "*double penance*" to dislodge harmful habits, but saw his cure assured by his faith in the "*pity*" of his "*dear friend*," which we know from other Sonnets to be the Lord. Unlike Sonnet 111, however, Sonnet 119 finds that the Poet is awakened by the "*benefit of ill*." The prod to conscience alone seems enough: "*I return rebuk'd to my content*." Apparently, the "*potions*" of "*Siren tears*" did not so deeply derange the Poet's sense of direction that he was able to "*build anew*" his temporarily "*ruined love*."

The proverb, "a word to be wise is sufficient" seems to apply. The irresistible attraction of Shakespeare's "*content*," the source of his true happiness in Spirit, was able to bring him eagerly back again.

There is an interesting contrast also between Sonnet 119 and Sonnet 111. In Sonnet 111, the "*harmful deeds*" committed resulted in the Poet's name receiving "*a brand.*" The remedies of "*potions of eisell*" and "*double penance*" coupled with the "*pity*" of Divine Grace were "*enough to cure me* [him]." We are uncertain of the "*harmful deeds*" committed in Sonnet 111. In Sonnet 119, however, the conduct is described as "*wretched errors*" of the heart, and consumption of "*Potions . . . distill'd from limbecks foul as hell within.*" So strong were the "*errors*" that the Poet's normal footing and perspective were impaired, and he seemed to have lost his way entirely. "*How have mine eyes out of their spheres been fitted, In the distraction of this madding fever!*" The lifestyle described in Sonnet 119 seems to be far more ruinous than the "*harmful deeds*" of Sonnet 111, which were habitually ingrained "*Like the dyer's hand*" (Sonnet 111.7). Sonnet 111, however, seems to have required more serious remedies than the simple "*rebuke*" described in 119.

It would seem that once habituated bad habits are uprooted and removed, and the "*willing patient*" (Sonnet 111.9) is set firmly on course, a return to the depths of "*wretched errors*" is insufficient to totally derail the traveler from his chosen journey toward the Spirit. It is as if the mind, once set firmly on the right path, has an innate strength or power to overcome occasional setbacks. Certainly the determination to "*build anew*" a "*ruined love*" shows a better grounding than the Poet possessed in Sonnet 111.

To be able to declare that there is a "*benefit of ill*" demonstrates perhaps a more profound understanding and centering than is seen in the "*willing patient*" in Sonnet 111.

BIBLICAL PASSAGES SUGGESTED BY SONNET 119

"A fool despiseth his father's instruction; but he that regardeth reproof is prudent." **Prov. 15:5**

"Happy is the man that findeth wisdom, and the man that getteth understanding." **Prov. 3:13**

"But now, after that ye have known God, or rather are known of God, how turn ye again to the weak and beggarly elements, whereunto ye desire again to be in bondage?" **Gal. 4:9**

"Behold, happy is the man whom God correcteth: therefore despise not thou the chastening of the Almighty" **Job 5:17**

"For our light affliction, which is but for a moment, worketh for us a far more exceeding and eternal weight of glory." **2 Cor. 4:17**

"Now no chastening for the present seemeth to be joyous, but grievous: nevertheless afterward it yieldeth the peaceable fruit of righteousness unto them which are exercised thereby." **Heb. 12:11**

SONNET 120

That you were once unkind befriends me now,
And for that sorrow, which I then did feel,
Needs must I under my transgression bow,
Unless my nerves were brass or hammered steel.
For if you were by my unkindness shaken,
As I by yours, y' have passed a hell of time;
And I, a tyrant, have no leisure taken
To weigh how once I suffer'd in your crime.
O, that our night of woe might have remember'd
My deepest sense, how hard true sorrow hits,
And soon to you, as you to me, then tender'd
The humble salve which wounded bosoms fits!
But that your trespass now becomes a fee;
Mine ransoms yours, and yours must ransom me.

THEME

One's transgressions have an effect on both man and God. One's sins are punished, but once one is reconciled with the Lord, one is set free and the Lord is, in a sense, freed from requiring punishment.

GLOSSARY

That you were once unkind befriends me now, And for that sorrow, which I then did feel, Needs must I under my transgression bow, Unless my nerves were brass or hammered steel.

> The previous circumstances for which I suffered and blamed You, I understand now were really a kindness on Your part. My need is now to respond humbly for Your beneficent chastisement; and so it is, unless my heart were hardened like brass or steel.

For if you were by my unkindness shaken, As I by yours, y' have passed a hell of time; And I, a tyrant, have no leisure taken To weigh how once I suffer'd in your crime.

> For if You were shaken by my unkindness, as I was by

> Yours, You would have experienced a hellish time; and I, like a tyrant, would not have taken the time to reflect on how once I suffered under the weight of Your offense.

O, that our night of woe might have remember'd My deepest sense, how hard true sorrow hits, And soon to you, as you to me, then tender'd The humble salve which wounded bosoms fits!

> It would have been best if our dark time of woe would have awakened in my innermost being the reality of how deeply true sorrow strikes. But as soon as I tended You, and You me, the proper healing ready, this salve of humility, would restore all.

But that your trespass now becomes a fee; Mine ransoms yours, and yours must ransom me.

> But now your offense becomes that which frees me, and my freedom, won through humility, releases me, and your grant of freedom from my offense, releases me.

COMMENTARY

In Sonnet 119, the Poet reflects upon how he received a "*benefit of ill.*" He turned from evil ways ever more resolved to "*build anew.*" The Poet then returned to his "*content*" after being "*rebuked.*" (Sonnet 119.9, 11, 13, 14)

In Sonnet 120, Shakespeare now comments, in a metaphysical sense, on how he suffered during the time of his "*transgression.*" He says the Lord was "*once unkind,*" referring most likely to chastisement when he was "*rebuked.*" (Sonnet 119.13) Now our Poet says he is befriended and must respond by bowing in humility. "*And for that sorrow, which I then did feel, Needs must I under my transgression bow.*"

It is as if Shakespeare is saying: Only a cold, unfeeling person whose prideful conscience is like "*hammered steel*" could fail to respond positively. You, Lord, as the Father, must have in a sense suffered by "*my unkindness.*"

This "*unkindness*" refers to the Poet's "*transgression.*" Again Shakespeare is saying: As an unfeeling person, I did not take the time to reflect upon how I suffered during your "*crime.*" The "*crime*" is either the Lord's rebuke or the Lord's "*absence*" from the Poet. In Sonnet 33.11, Shakespeare writes: "*But, out, alack, He was but one hour mine, The region cloud hath mask'd him from me now.*" Also in Sonnet 39, "*O absence, what a torment wouldst thou prove.*" As soon as the proper "*humble salve*" is applied "*that sorrow, which I then did feel*" is resolved, and the Lord is again one who "*befriends.*" This salve is humility, which destroys the pride that is a common trait of an unfeeling "*tryant.*" "*And soon to you, as you to me, then tender'd The humble salve which wounded bosoms fits!*"

In the legal sense, a "*fee*" means either a penalty or complete title and ownership. The language in the Sonnet that says "*your trespass now becomes a fee*" means that the Lord's unkindness was like an offense or crime. When one commits a "*transgression*" or sin, Divine Law deals the appropriate punishment. However, like in Sonnet 119, where there is a "*benefit of ill,*" the Lord's "*unkind*" response in Sonnet 120 caused the Poet to realize that he must bow in humility for his transgressions. "*Needs must I under my transgression bow.*" It is the act of contrition or humility that delivers the Poet. He may then receive "*a fee,*" meaning a complete release and restoration to wholeness. Humility paves the way to forgiveness, and the Lord is freed from the requirement to impose a punishment: "*your trespass now becomes a fee; Mine ransoms yours, and yours must ransom me.*" The Bible states that the Lord, to redeem man, sacrifices what is dear to him. "Even as the Son of man came not to be ministered unto, but to minister, and to give his life a ransom of many." **(Matt. 20:28)**

BIBLICAL PASSAGES SUGGESTED BY SONNET 120

"But he was wounded for our transgressions, he was bruised for our iniquities; the chastisement of our peace was upon him; and with his stripes we are healed. All we like sheep have gone astray; we have turned every one to his own way; and the Lord hath laid on him the iniquity of us all." **Isa. 53:5-6**

"By humility and the fear of the Lord are riches, and honor, and life." **Prov. 22:4**

"Whosoever therefore shall humble himself as this little child, the same is greatest in the Kingdom of heaven." **Matt. 18:4**

"The Lord is nigh unto them that are of a broken heart; and saveth such as be of a contrite spirit. Many are the afflictions of the righteous; but the Lord delivereth him out of them all." Ps. **34:18-19**

"The sacrifices of God are a broken spirit; a broken and a contrite heart, O God, thou wilt not despise." **Ps. 51:17**

"For thus saith the high and lofty One that inhabiteth eternity, whose name is Holy; I dwell in the high and holy place, with him also that is of a contrite and humble spirit, to revive the spirit of the humble, and to revive the heart of the contrite ones. For I will not contend for ever, neither will I be always wroth; for the spirit should fail before me, and the souls which I have made." **Isa. 57:15-16**

SONNET 121

'Tis better to be vile than vile esteemed,
When not to be receives reproach of being;
And the just pleasure lost, which is so deemed
Not by our feeling, but by others' seeing.
For why should others' false adulterate eyes
Give salutation to my sportive blood?
Or on my frailties why are frailer spies,
Which in their wills count bad what I think good?
No, I am that I am, and they that level
At my abuses reckon up their own;
I may be straight though they themselves be bevel;
By their rank thoughts my deeds must not be shown;
Unless this general evil they maintain,
All men are bad and in their badness reign.

THEME

Many believe that man is inherently a sinful being and judge themselves and others unjustly by that standard.

GLOSSARY

'Tis better to be vile than vile esteemed, When not to be receives reproach of being; And the just pleasure lost, which is so deemed, Not by our feeling, but by others' seeing.

It is better to be vile than to be thought to be so when one is not. The satisfaction of having a good reputation is lost, not by our own self appraisal, but by feeling misjudged by others.

For why should others' false adulterate eyes Give salutation to my sportive blood? Or on my frailties why are frailer spies, Which in their wills count bad what I think good?

Why should other corrupt people hail me as one of their own? Or why should more depraved people than I judge my conduct and believe that what I esteem is evil?

No, I am that I am, and they that level, At my abuses reckon up their own; I may be straight though they themselves be bevel; By their rank thoughts my deeds must not be shown;

> No, I am what I am, and they that heap abuses upon me are really judging by the standard of evil within themselves. I may be virtuous though they are of wanton character, and my deeds must not be judged by their rank thoughts.

Unless this general evil they maintain, All men are bad and in their badness reign.

> Unless it is true, as they say, that all men are inherently evil; and they reign supreme in their belief and judgment of others.

COMMENTARY

In Sonnet 119 we see the admission of the Poet that he engaged in "*wretched errors*," but after being "*rebuked*," he returns to his "*content*" or centering on the spiritual path. (Sonnet 119.5, 13) Sonnet 120 reminds us that the laws of God operate upon man, who has free will to act or commit whatever "*transgression*" he so desires. In a sense, both the Creator and His children are bound by the Heavenly ordinances, until some "*humble salve*" is applied to the "*wounded bosom.*" (Sonnet 120.3, 12) We see that the Lord, to redeem man, gives Christ as "a ransom." (**Matt. 20:28**) As stated often in the Bible, the Lord is compassionate and merciful, but He is also the Judge and Lawgiver.

In Sonnet 121, the Poet shows that men set themselves up as judges over others' alleged "*vile*" conduct. Often their evaluation is incorrect because they judge others by the evil thoughts in themselves. "Think but how vile a spectacle it were to view thy present trespass in another. Men's faults do seldom to themselves appear; Their own transgressions partially they smother." (*The Rape of Lucrece*, 631-634)

This Sonnet is in contrast to Sonnet 120, in which conduct and punishment are determined by Divine decree and not by the opinion of men. Our Poet will not be daunted, however, and insists on being judged not by "*frailer spies*" with "*false adulterate eyes.*" "*No, I am that I am, and they that level at my abuses reckon up their own.*"

This is, of course, reminiscent of the Biblical verse Exodus: "And God said unto Moses, I AM THAT I AM: and he said, Thus shalt thou say unto the children of Israel, I AM hath sent me unto you". **(Exod. 3:14)** In a sense, Shakespeare is saying that men not only judge others by their own "*rank thoughts*" but judge God also by their own reckoning. These "*frailer spies*" chose to see man as inherently sinful, having fallen from grace since Adam. They argue for this as the way of things: "*Unless this general evil they maintain, all men are bad and in their badness reign.*" Shakespeare baulks against such a condemnation saying that "*By their rank thoughts my deeds must not be shown.*" Men are imprisoned or limited by their own thoughts and beliefs: "for there is nothing either good or bad, but thinking makes it so." (*Hamlet*, II.ii.239-241)

Shakespeare declares that unless one is free of "*adulterate eyes*," one should not set oneself up as judge over another. "They say unto him, Master, this woman was taken in adultery, in the very act. . . . What sayest thou? . . . He that is without sin among you, let him first cast a stone at her." **(John 8:4, 5, 7)**

BIBLICAL PASSAGES SUGGESTED BY SONNET 121

"Hearken unto me, ye that know righteousness, the people in whose heart is my law; fear ye not the reproach of men, neither be ye afraid of their revilings." **Isa. 51:7**

"All unrighteousness is sin: and there is a sin not unto death. We know that whosoever is born of God sinneth not; but he that is begotten of God keepeth himself, and that wicked one toucheth him not. And we know that we are of God, and the whole world lieth in wickedness." **1 John 5:17-19**

"I said therefore unto you, that ye shall die in your sins: for if ye believe not that I am he, ye shall die in your sins." **John 8:24**

SONNET 122

Thy gift, thy tables, are within my brain
Full charactered with lasting memory,
Which shall above that idle rank remain,
Beyond all date, even to eternity,
Or, at the least, so long as brain and heart
Have faculty by nature to subsist;
Till each to raz'd oblivion yield his part
Of thee, thy record never can be missed.
That poor retention could not so much hold,
Nor need I tallies thy dear love to score;
Therefore to give them from me was I bold,
To trust those tables that receive thee more:
To keep an adjunct to remember thee
Were to import forgetfulness in me.

THEME

Ordinary human memory and feeling are limited, but once touched by soulful realization, no reminder of man's Divine origin is required.

GLOSSARY

Thy gift, thy tables, are within my brain, Full charactered with lasting memory, Which shall above that idle rank remain, Beyond all date, even to eternity,

> Thy gift, the memory of all Thou hast given to me is fully etched in my consciousness for all time, and shall remain ever above the commonplace.

Or, at the least, so long as brain and heart, Have faculty by nature to subsist; Till each to razed oblivion yield his part Of thee, thy record never can be missed.

> Or at least so long as my heart and brain have, by their nature, faculty to exist. Until oblivion causes my heart and mind to cease having a separate part in Thee, the remembrance of you will always be at the forefront of my consciousness.

That poor retention could not so much hold, Nor need I tallies thy dear love to score; Therefore to give them from me was I bold, To trust those tables that receive thee more:

> The ordinary mental faculty could not hold all of what Thou art, and I do not need to keep an account of the innumerable ways Thy dear Love hast penetrated into my being. Therefore to record in my verse Thy gifts was bold. It is best to trust my mind and heart to receive all that Thou art to me.

To keep an adjunct to remember thee Were to import forgetfulness in me.

> To keep a helpful reminder of any sort would imply that I was forgetful of Thee.

COMMENTARY

Sonnet 122 is a declaration by Shakespeare that all he has received spiritually from the Lord is indelibly etched on his consciousness. "*Thy gift, thy tables, are within my brain full charactered with lasting memory.*" Experiences of the mundane will perish, while those of the soul remain "*even to eternity.*"

Shakespeare qualifies his declaration by stating that the memorial of "*Thy gift* [and] *thy tables*" will be in his mind and heart, or consciousness and feeling, as long as they are not erased, "*so long as brain and hearth have faculty by nature to subsist, till each to raz'd oblivion yield his part.*" The individualized soul of man is said to exist eternally until it is finally merged again into the Spirit on the Day of Judgment.

There is no material way to adequately express and record one's inner spiritual experiences. Since these experiences are indelibly etched upon the consciousness, there is no need to physically record them. "*That poor retention could not so much hold, nor need I tallies thy dear love to score.*"

To set down in all his works the depth of the "*gift*" and all the wisdom he received was bold. "*Therefore to give them from me was I bold.*" Heart and mind, love and consciousness are more pure repositories upon which to record spiritual enlightenment. "*To trust those tables that receive thee more.*"

Using lines of verse or writing as a "*table*" or memorial of spiritual wisdom and experiences is to imply that Shakespeare might have needed such a record so as not to forget the Divine. "*To keep an adjunct to remember thee were to import forgetfulness in me.*" This is clearly not the case for one whose life was centered upon reverence and remembrance of the Lord. "*O, know, sweet love, I always write of you, and you and love are still my argument.*" (Sonnet 76.9-10)

BIBLICAL PASSAGES SUGGESTED BY SONNET 122

"And the Lord said unto Moses, Come up to me into the mount, and be there: and I will give thee tables of stone, and a law, and commandments which I have written; that thou mayst teach them." **Exod. 24:12**

"Neither can they die any more: for they are equal unto the angels; and are the children of God, being the children of the resurrection." **Luke 20:36**

"Then shall the dust return to the earth as it was: and the spirit shall return unto God who gave it." **Eccl. 12:7**

"And these words, which I command thee this day, shall be in thine heart." **Deut. 6:6**

"Therefore judge nothing before the time, until the Lord come, who both will bring to light the hidden things of darkness, and will make manifest the counsels of the hearts: and then shall every man have praise of God." **1 Cor. 4:5**

"For we must all appear before the judgment seat of Christ; that every one may receive the things done in his body, according to that he hath done, whether it be good or bad." **2 Cor. 5:10**

SONNET 123

No, Time, thou shalt not boast that I do change:
Thy pyramids built up with newer might
To me are nothing novel, nothing strange;
They are but dressings of a former sight.
Our dates are brief, and therefore we admire
What thou dost foist upon us that is old,
And rather make them born to our desire,
Than think that we before have heard them told.
Thy registers and thee I both defy,
Not wondering at the present nor the past,
For thy records and what we see doth lie,
Made more or less by thy continual haste.
This I do vow, and this shall ever be;
I will be true, despite thy scythe and thee.

THEME

The world is like a stage, ever costuming itself in different landscapes; but the abiding theme for man is to be spiritually constant in a world of change.

GLOSSARY

No, Time, thou shalt not boast that I do change: Thy pyramids built up with newer might To me are nothing novel, nothing strange; They are but dressings of a former sight.

> No! Time, you will never boast that I ever change. Your pyramids built anew are neither novel nor foreign. They are merely the dressing of old into new costumes.

Our dates are brief, and therefore we admire what thou dost foist upon us that is old, And rather make them born to our desire, Than think that we before have heard them told.

> Our lives on earth are brief, and therefore we admire what is put before us on the landscape of life. We make them fit our desired purpose never recognizing that they

are the same mundane thing that has always been.

Thy registers and thee I both defy, not wondering at the present nor the past, For thy records and what we see doth lie, made more or less by thy continual haste.

All of your recorded history and, thee, oh Time, I defy them both, not finding novelty in what is present or past: for your pageant and all we see, is a lie, made more or less by thy "*thievish progress to eternity.*" (Sonnet 77.8)

This I do vow, and this shall ever be; I will be true, despite thy scythe and thee.

This I do vow, and this shall ever be: I will be true and constant despite thy withering scythe and thee.

COMMENTARY

In Sonnet 116, we read: "*Love's not Time's fool, though rosy lips and cheeks within his bending sickle's compass come; Love alters not with his brief hours and weeks, but bears it out even to the edge of doom.*" (Sonnet 116.9-11) In that Sonnet we see that the constancy of God's Love is ever with man. In Sonnet 123, it is Shakespeare who says "*I will be true.*"

Shakespeare often uses the themes of time, death, and the impermanency and illusion of what seems to be real in this world. "*The lily's white . . . the rose,*" and "*figures of delight*" are all in realty a manifestation of the Divine. "*Drawn after you, you pattern of all those.*" (Sonnet 98.12) All things upon the earth are a "*shadow*" of the heavenly. "*As with your shadow I with these did play.*" (Sonnet 98.14)

In the march of time, all things pass "Swift as a shadow, short as any dream, Brief as the lightning in the collied night. That, in a spleen, unfolds both heaven and earth." (*A Midsummer's Night's Dream*, I.i.144-146)

We are "such stuff as dreams are made on" says Shakespeare. "The gorgeous palaces, the solemn temples, the great globe itself, Yea, all which it inherit, shall dissolve." (*The Tempest*, IV.i.148-156)

While men may believe this world to be unique, it is like a continuous play of familiar themes played out in new costumes. "*To me are nothing novel, nothing strange; They are but dressings of a former sight. . . . [W]e admire what thou dost foist upon us that is old, and rather make them born to our desire than think that we before have heard them told.*"

"All the world's a stage" and we are merely the players, while Time marches on in its "continual haste" (*As You Like It*, II.vii.139-142). As for Shakespeare, he is neither daunted nor deterred by the "*show*" of time: "*this huge stage presenteth nought but shows*." (Sonnet 15.3) In Sonnet 105.5-6 he writes: "*kind is my love today, tomorrow king, still constant in a wondrous excellence*." In Sonnet 123, Shakespeare reaffirms his "*vow*" to "*be true*" no matter what events or changes come upon the world's landscape. "*This I do vow, and this shall ever be; I will be true, despite thy scythe and thee*." (Sonnet 123.13-14)

BIBLICAL PASSAGES SUGGESTED BY SONNET 123

"The thing that hath been, it is that which shall be; and that which is done is that which shall be done: and there is no new thing under the sun. Is there any thing whereof it may be said, See, this is new? it hath been already of old time, which was before us. There is no remembrance of former things; neither shall there by any remembrance of things that are to come with those that shall come after." **Eccl. 1:9-11**

"Truly my soul waiteth upon God: from him cometh my salvation. He only is my rock and my salvation; he is my defense; I shall not be greatly moved." **Ps. 62:1-2**

"In God is my salvation and my glory: the rock of my strength, and my refuge, is in God. Trust in him at all times; ye people, pour out your heart before him: God is a refuge for us. Surely men of low degree are vanity, and men of high degree are a lie: to be laid in the balance, they are altogether lighter than vanity." **Ps. 62:7-9**

"For we are strangers before thee, and sojourners, as were all our fathers: our days on the earth are as a shadow, and there is none abiding." **1 Chron. 29:15**

"Whereas ye know not what shall be on the morrow. For what is your life? It is even a vapor, that appeareth for a little time, and then vanisheth away." **James 4:14**

SONNET 124

If my dear love were but the child of state,
It might for fortune's bastard be unfathered,
As subject to time's love or to time's hate,
Weeds among weeds, or flowers with flowers gather'd.
No, it was builded far from accident;
It suffers not in smiling pomp, nor falls
Under the blow of thralled discontent,
Whereto th'inviting time our fashion calls:
It fears not policy, that heretic,
Which works on leases of short-numb'red hours,
But all alone stands hugely politic,
That it nor grows with heat, nor drowns with showers.
To this I witness call the fools of time,
Which die for goodness, who have liv'd for crime.

THEME

A life built on a solid spiritual foundation is unaffected by the changing tides of fortune; furthermore, it is a beacon that calls one's brothers back to a spiritual way of life.

GLOSSARY

If my dear love were but the child of state, It might for fortune's bastard be unfathered, As subject to time's love or to time's hate, Weeds among weeds, or flowers with flowers gather'd.

> If my precious love were but a child of circumstance, it might be subject to the whims of fortune like an orphan, as likely to receive capricious time's love one moment and hate the next, either weeds among weeds or flowers among flowers gathered.

No, it was builded far from accident; It suffers not in smiling pomp, nor falls Under the blow of thralled discontent, Whereto th' inviting time our fashion calls:

> No, my dear love was built from deliberate care not ac-

> cident. It is not diminished by hypocrisy, nor falls away at the blow of overwhelming discontent, as is commonly seen in the way of life we see nowadays.

It fears not policy, that heretic, Which works on leases of short-numb'red hours, But all alone stands hugely politic, That it nor grows with heat, nor drowns with showers.

> My love is unafraid of the heretical realms of politics that most influences those whose lives of importance are numbered in whimsical hours. But singularly, my love remains complete and fixed in its course, neither enhanced by the warmth of good tides, nor drowned by the flood of misfortune.

To this I witness call the fools of time, Which die for goodness, who have liv'd for crime.

> Let my way of life bear witness and invite those who have been time's fools to die in a state of grace who previously lived for crime.

COMMENTARY

Sonnet 123 established that the Poet's life was built upon a vow to be true despite any change wrought by Time. In Sonnet 124, Shakespeare compares his "*dear love*" to that of others, which are "*subject to time's love, or to time's hate.*" Shakespeare's love is not like that of hypocritical courtiers that rise and fall with the changing whims of circumstance. "*No, it was builded far from accident; it suffers not in smiling pomp, nor falls under the blow of thralled discontent.*" In contrast, Shakespeare's "*dear love*" is "*hugely politic.*" Politic can mean wisely directed, or like the poles of the earth that are fixed in their place and direction, never altering or changing.

Shakespeare's love and life bear witness to a life well-lived and invite his wayward fellows to escape the fetters of whimsical fortune and receive spiritual grace. "*To this I witness call the fools of time, which die for goodness, who have liv'd for crime.*"

BIBLICAL PASSAGES SUGGESTED BY SONNET 124

"Therefore whosoever heareth these sayings of mine, and doeth them, I will liken him unto a wise man, which built his house upon a rock." **Matt. 7:24**

"Yet ye say, The way of the Lord is not equal. Hear now, O house of Israel; Is not my way equal? are not your ways unequal? When a righteous man turneth away from his righteousness, and committeth iniquity, and dieth in them; for his iniquity that he hath done shall he die. Again, when the wicked man turneth away from his wickedness that he hath committed, and doeth that which is lawful and right, he shall save his soul alive. Because he considereth, and turneth away from all his transgressions that he hath committed, he shall surely live, he shall not die." **Ezek. 18:25-28**

"Come and hear, all ye that fear God, and I will declare what he hath done for my soul." **Ps. 66:16**

"And ye also shall bear witness, because ye have been with me from the beginning." **John 15:27**

SONNET 125

Were't aught to me I bore the canopy,
With my extern the outward honouring,
Or laid great bases for eternity,
Which prove more short than waste or ruining?
Have I not seen dwellers on form and favour
Lose all and more by paying too much rent,
For compound sweet forgoing simple savour,
Pitiful thrivers, in their gazing spent?
No, let me be obsequious in thy heart,
And take thou my oblation, poor but free,
Which is not mixed with seconds, knows no art,
But mutual render, only me for thee.
Hence, thou suborned informer! A true soul
When most impeached stands least in thy control.

THEME

A true, devoted soul has left behind the fetters of a life filled with egotistical pursuits and pleasures, which engulf men still tempted by such allurements.

GLOSSARY

Were't aught to me I bore the canopy, With my extern the outward honouring, Or laid great bases for eternity which prove more short than waste or ruining?

> What importance would it be to me if I received the outward honor of bearing the royal canopy, or laid foundations meant to last for eternity, but which prove to be as ephemeral as all things subject to ruin by waste or time?

Have I not seen dwellers on form and favour lose all and more by paying too much rent, For compound sweet forgoing simple savour, Pitiful thrivers, in their gazing spent?

> Have I not seen those who live by courtly favors and outward pomp, lose all and themselves by paying a high price for short-lived gratification, and adulterated plea-

sures while foregoing a simple, virtuous way of live? They are hangers-on who gawk unprofitability upon the superficial aspects of life.

No, let me be obsequious in thy heart, And take thou my oblation, poor but free, Which is not mixed with seconds, knows no art, But mutual render, only me for thee.

No, let me be completely devoted in Thy heart. Accept Thou my oblation, simple but freely rendered, which is not tainted by recondite motivations, and is without deception. It is a mutual exchange, only me for Thee.

Hence, thou suborned informer! A true soul when most impeached stands least in thy control.

Get away from me, you false ways of the wayward ego! A true soul, when most challenged, stands firm and completely out of the selfish ego's control.

COMMENTARY

Sonnet 125 echoes the sentiments of Sonnets 66 and 91. In Sonnet 66, our Poet asserts that he is "*tired*" with all the hypocrisy and "*folly*" he sees in society. "*From these would I be gone.*" (Sonnet 66.13) In Sonnet 91, Shakespeare states that "*glory in birth . . . wealth . . . garments*" (Sonnet 91.1-3) and every other kind of "*adjunct pleasure*" (Sonnet 91.5) are not his "*measure.*" (Sonnet 91.7) "*Thy Love is better than high birth to me, richer than wealth, prouder than garments' cost . . . and having Thee, of all men's pride I boast.*" (Sonnet 91.9-10, 12)

Shakespeare declares repeatedly that "*my spirit is thine, the better part of me*" (Sonnet 74.8), and stands firm and fixed upon the Lord. "*But all alone stands hugely politic.*" (Sonnet 124.11)

In Sonnet 108, Shakespeare declares: "*counting no thing old, thou mine, I thine, even as when first I hallowed thy fair name.*" (Sonnet 108.7-8) It is no surprise then that Shakespeare in his constancy would shun the temptations of a superficial life "*which prove*[s] *more short than waste or ruining.*" (Sonnet 125.4) Shakespeare is not interested in external honors, but offers the Lord his "*oblation, poor but free, which is not mixed with seconds, knows no art ,but mutual render, only me for thee.*"

It is the ego, which he calls the "*suborned informer*," that tries to ensnare the soul. But "*a true soul*" when assailed by temptation, remains fixed and aloof, out of the reach of egoistical temptations. "*A true soul when most impeached stands least in thy control.*" This is the soul of Sonnet 124 that "*all alone stands hugely politic.*" (Sonnet 124.11) The Poet's soul was made "*better*" and learned from "*wretched errors.*" In Sonnet 125, our poet stands firmly out of reach of the "*frailties*" (Sonnet 121.7) that previously assailed him. His soul is "*true*" and surrendered to the Lord, upon whom he waits.

BIBLICAL PASSAGES SUGGESTED BY SONNET 125

"My soul, wait thou only upon God; for my expectation is from him." **Ps. 62:5**

"Behold, as the eyes of servants look unto the hand of their masters, and as the eyes of a maiden unto the hand of her mistress; so our eyes wait upon the Lord our God, until that he have mercy upon us." **Ps. 123:2**

"If thou return to the Almighty, thou shalt be built up, thou shalt put away iniquity far from thy tabernacles." **Job 22:23**

"There hath no temptation taken you but such as is common to man: but God is faithful, who will not suffer you to be tempted above that ye are able; but will with the temptation also make a way to escape, that ye may be able to bear it." **1 Cor. 10:13**

"Because thou hast kept the word of my patience, I also will keep thee from the hour of temptation, which shall come upon all the world, to try them that dwell upon the earth" **Rev. 3:10**

"Hearken, my beloved brethren, Hath not God chosen the poor of this world rich in faith, and heirs of the kingdom which he hath promised to them that love him?" **James 2:5**

SONNET 126

O thou, my lovely boy, who in thy power
Dost hold Time's fickle glass, his sickle hour;
Who hast by waning grown, and therein show'st
Thy lovers withering as thy sweet self grow'st;
If Nature, (sovereign mistress over wrack),
As thou goest onwards, still will pluck thee back,
She keeps thee to this purpose, that her skill
May time disgrace and wretched minutes kill.
Yet fear her, O thou minion of her pleasure,
She may detain, but not still keep, her treasure!
Her audit, though delayed, answer'd must be,
And her quietus is to render thee.

THEME

Man's soul journeys toward its apotheosis, and along the way is tempted by good and evil as this is the nature of creation. Ultimately a soul must answer in judgment for all of man's individual actions.

GLOSSARY

O thou, my lovely boy, who in thy power dost hold Time's fickle glass, his sickle hour; Who hast by waning grown, and therein show'st Thy lovers withering as thy sweet self grow'st;

> Oh my beautiful soul, who in thy power can withstand the vagaries of time, its destructive scythe, and passing hours; you have by resisting evil grown, and thereby have shown your previous heart's desires to have withered away as your true spiritual essence has grown.

If Nature, (sovereign mistress over wrack), As thou goest onwards, still will pluck thee back, She keeps thee to this purpose, that her skill may time disgrace and wretched minutes kill.

> If Nature and her laws govern all creation, of which time is a part, you will be tempted by evil to turn away from the spiritual path. In the nature of things, she seeks to

hold you to her purpose so that ruinous time and the wretched days of life may be overcome.

Yet fear her, O thou minion of her pleasure, She may detain, but not still keep, her treasure!

Yet fear her, you who are the plaything of her whimsical pleasure. She may distract you for a while, but still not ultimately claim you as her treasure.

Her audit, though delayed, answer'd must be, And her quietus is to render thee.

Her final account, though delayed, must be answered, and her final task is to settle all accounts and render a judgment of thee.

COMMENTARY

Sonnet 126 is a transition sonnet that somewhat thematically divides the Sonnets which come before with those following.

The literal interpretation of many of the first 125 Sonnets is that they are concerned with a young man or person of the Poet's acquaintance. Those following are generally believed to reflect a relationship of the Poet with a "*dark lady.*"

In a deeper interpretation of the Sonnets as set out herein, the first 125 sonnets generally involve the nature of the soul in its journey homeward toward the Spirit. The Poet's thoughts on the nature of his soul and its relations with the Divine are of central importance.

In Sonnets 126 to the end, the theme generally involves the soul in its battles with the ego rather than its relationship with the Divine. In Sonnet 126, it is the "*Nature*" or characteristic of creation to be a battleground in which good and evil ever alter in supremacy in order to win over the soul. "*As thou goest onwards, still will pluck thee back, She keeps thee to this purpose*". And in the first quatrain of Sonnet 126 we see that the "*lovely boy,*" this divine child, "*hast by waning grown, and therein show'st Thy lovers withering as thy sweet self grow'st.*" This "*lovely boy*" is the "little child" of the scriptures who brings peace between the "wolf" and "the lamb" **(Isa. 11:6)**. The "*lovely boy*" is one of the children who are sacred to God. "But Jesus said, Suffer little children, and forbid them not, to come unto me: for such is the Kingdom of heaven." **(Matt. 19:14)**

In Sonnet 146 we see how it is a soul that chooses to eschew a wasteful existence by giving up the desires of the heart ("*Thy lovers*"), which grows in power, even over death. "*Then, soul, live thou upon they servant's loss, And let that pine to aggravate thy store; Buy terms divine in selling hours of dross; Within be fed, without be rich no more.*" (Sonnet 146.9-12) In Sonnet 126, "*thy sweet self grow'st*" because the Poet has chosen a life of acquiring "*terms divine*" and was fed "*within.*" The "*sweet self*" is the soul.

Those who feed the desires of the ego will diminish the soul's power. "*But thou, contracted to thine own bright eyes, Feed'st thy lights's flame with self-substantial fuel, Making a famine where abundance lies.*" (Sonnet 1.5-7) The result of feeding the ego's desires, the things the ego loves, is that it makes a famine where an abundance of soul should exist. As a result, "*when nature calls thee to be gone, what acceptable audit canst thou leave?*" (Sonnet 4.12) We see in Sonnet 126 that Nature, "*Her audit, though delayed, answer'd must be.*"

The basic theme of Sonnet 126 connects those Sonnets that came before with those that are to follow. The soul that succeeds in steady progress toward the Spirit will have the "*power*" over "*Time's fickle glass.*" It even has power over Death. "*So shalt thou feed on Death, that feeds on men, And Death once dead, there's no more dying then.*" (Sonnet 146.13-14; see notes therein) All along the way, the soul must do battle with evil and temptations in life. "*As thou goest onwards,* [Nature] *still will pluck thee back.*" Even so, if one commits "*wretched errors*" (Sonnet 119.5), it is necessary to learn from one's mistakes and go on with new determination. "*That better is by evil still made better; And ruin'd love, when it is built anew, Grows fairer than at first, more strong, far greater.*" (Sonnet 119.10-12)

All along one must "*fear her,*" "*Nature, (sovereign mistress over wrack)*": each one is a "*minion of her pleasure,*" until the time of "*her audit . . . and quietus*" when a final judgment is rendered.

BIBLICAL PASSAGES SUGGESTED BY SONNET 126

"In the day when God shall judge the secrets of men by Jesus Christ according to my gospel." **Rom. 2:16**

"For we must all appear before the judgment seat of Christ; that every one may receive the things done in his body, according to that he hath done, whether it be good or bad." **2 Cor. 5:10**

"There hath no temptation taken you but such as is common to man: but God is faithful, who will not suffer you to be tempted above that ye are able; but will with the temptation also make a way to escape, that ye may be able to bear it." **1 Cor. 10:13**

"Blessed is the man that endureth temptation: for when he is tried, he shall receive the crown of life, which the Lord hath promised to them that love him." **James 1:12**

"Of old hast thou laid the foundation of the earth: and the heavens are the work of thy hands." **Ps. 102:25**

"And out of the ground made the Lord God to grow every tree that is pleasant to the sight, and good for food; the tree of life also in the midst of the garden, and the tree of knowledge of good and evil." **Gen. 2:9**

"That ye may be the children of your Father which is in heaven: for he maketh his sun to rise on the evil and on the good, and sendeth rain on the just and on the unjust." **Matt. 5:45**

SONNET 127

In the old age black was not counted fair,
Or if it were, it bore not beauty's name;
But now is black beauty's successive heir,
And beauty slandered with a bastard's shame:
For since each hand hath put on Nature's power,
Fairing the foul with Art's false borrow'd face,
Sweet beauty hath no name, no holy bower,
But is profan'd, if not lives in disgrace.
Therefore my mistress' eyes are raven black,
Her eyes so suited, and they mourners seem
At such who, not born fair, no beauty lack,
Sland'ring creation with a false esteem:
Yet so they mourn, becoming of their woe,
That every tongue says beauty should look so.

THEME

There are those in every age who glorify or justify sinful conduct, calling it proper. They are the ones who should mourn that the beauty of their souls is waning by such indulgence.

GLOSSARY

In the old age black was not counted fair, Or if it were, it bore not beauty's name; But now is black beauty's successive heir, And beauty slandered with a bastard's shame:

> In an earlier age, sinful ("*black*") conduct was not considered virtuous, or if it was acceptable, it would never be called righteous. But now in these times, sin is the common apparent heir of what was spiritually pure, and being virtuous is now derided as if it bore the shame of an illegitimate child.

For since each hand hath put on Nature's power, Fairing the foul with Art's false borrow'd face, Sweet beauty hath no name, no holy bower, But is profan'd, if not lives in disgrace.

> Now man with his two hands has usurped the natural law, making sin appear as though it were virtuous, and spiritual perfection is no more respected, nor has it a sacred place in men's hearts or sanctuaries, but is profaned or at least lives in disgrace.

Therefore my mistress' eyes are raven black, Her eyes so suited, and they mourners seem At such who, not born fair, no beauty lack, Sland'ring creation with a false esteem:

> Therefore, my mistress' eyes of false love see evil and darkness, as is suited to egoistical ways. And yet, they seem to mourn because the physical eyes can be essentially beautiful, but not when they only see the dark side of life; and esteeming it, they ignore the essential Beauty in creation.

Yet so they mourn, becoming of their woe, That every tongue says beauty should look so.

> Still those sinful, ego-centered eyes put on a mourner's appearance, but it is common for people to declare that these are the picture of real beauty.

COMMENTARY

In Sonnet 126 the Poet praised the "*power*" of the "*lovely boy*" that "*Dost hold Time's fickle glass.*" It is by the "*waning*" of the ego's "*lovers*" (those inherent temptations in creation) that the soul's "*sweet self grow'st.*" (Sonnet 126.1, 2, 3, 4)

It is inherent in creation, as stated in Sonnet 126, for "*Nature*" to try and "*pluck thee back.*" (Sonnet 126.5, 6) In other words, there is a battle between ego and soul, good and evil, or God and Satan which ever alternates in supremacy either to win souls back to their heavenly abode, or to continue through temptations to interest men in worldly allurements.

In Sonnet 127, Shakespeare refers to a previous time or age when sinful conduct would not be called virtuous. "*In the old age black was not counted fair.*" The Greeks labeled the changing eras of mankind as the golden, silver, bronze, and iron ages. In the golden age, there was spiritual enlightenment. The Bible is full of stories of either mankind's ventures into sin, or opposite times of spiritual glory.

In Sonnet 126, "*Nature*" keeps her "*audit.*" In Sonnet 127, "*black*" would never be "*counted fair*" in such a spiritual accounting. The time of which Shakespeare speaks in Sonnet 127 is one in which the ego's self-centered desires predominate. The beautiful, soul child, or "*lovely boy*" of Sonnet 126, is called a "*bastard*" in Sonnet 127 by those who loved "*black*" as "*beauty's successive heir.*" In Shakespeare's day, a bastard, or illegitimate child could never receive an inheritance from his true parents.

Sonnet 127, in a wider interpretation, may refer to the philosophy of humanism winning men's hearts during the Renaissance. Before the Renaissance, in the Middle Ages, the Poet refers to concepts and themes in art, architecture, and literature that were centered upon spiritual ideas and ideals, not upon the worldly attributes of men. "*For since each hand hath put on Nature's power, Fairing the foul with Art's false borrow'd face.*"

On the level of each man, or the Poet himself, he speaks of a true "*love*" (Sonnet 100.13) and says to her "*thou art all my art.*" (Sonnet 78.13) This was his love of the Spirit. In Sonnet 125, he says that his is "*a true soul*" (Sonnet 125.13) with a "*dear love.*" (Sonnet 124.1) The offspring of such a pure love is a "*lovely boy*" (Sonnet 126.1) or Divine child, meaning the soul within.

In Sonnet 127, there is no true child or "*heir*" in an age where "*black*" predominates over "*beauty.*" "*But now is black beauty's successive heir.*" There is no "*dear love*" (Sonnet 124.1) in the Spirit, but only a false "*mistress*" whose offspring can only be called a "*bastard.*" This mistress is the dominating ego that yields to worldly temptations. She is "*The worser spirit a woman, colour'd ill. To win me soon to hell, my female evil Tempteth my better angel from my side.*" (Sonnet 144.4-6) Both "*spirits*" in Sonnet 144 are "*both from me, both to each friend.*" (Sonnet 144.11) They are the inherent ego and soul within each one of us in creation. (See Commentary to Sonnet 144)

The raven in Shakespeare's day was a harbinger of evil. "*Therefore my mistress' eyes are raven black*" means that those who pursue sinful ways, do not see the good in the world around them. They are "*sland'ring creation with a false esteem.*"

Sonnet 126 sets up the "*Nature*" of creation in which good and evil, and ego and soul, battle for predominance. In Sonnet 127, the "*mistress*" in charge seems to be the "*(sovereign mistress over wrack)*" of Sonnet 126.5. It is interesting that Shakespeare used parenthesis around "*(sovereign mistress over wrack)*" in Sonnet 126, so that this "*mistress*" in Sonnet 127 can be interpreted as having the new position of "*beauty's successive heir.*" This "*mistress*" struggles against the true "*dear love*" (Sonnet 124.1) and "*Nature*" (Sonnet 126.5), keeping her "*audit*" as she must; it is her duty "*to render thee.*" (Sonnet 126.11-12) It will be Nature's judgment and not that of "*every tongue*" to determine true "*beauty.*" It will be that of the soul, not that of the false mistress ego.

It is also pertinent to reference the works of St. Bernard of Clairvaux and his Sermons on the Bible verses in the Song of Songs. Sermon 25 is entitled "Why the Bride is Black but Beautiful." In several sermons written by the saintly Bernard, he makes reference to the bride of the Song of Songs. This bride is also the human soul which, in the sensually-oriented human body, is tinged with the blackness of sin until it is "married" to the bridegroom Spirit.

The concept of the unperfected soul as a dark image is also found in the works of the fourteenth century English mystic, Walter Hilton. A soul, while in the body, is exposed to all manner of sin or temptation, explains Hilton. Shakespeare in his works touches on the seven "deadly sins." In the next Sonnet, 128, the sin of envy is discussed. Hilton states that on deep reflection a person sees his sinful nature. What is it?. " Indeed, nothing but a dark and painful image of your own soul. . . . If you look at it plainly, this image is all wrapped up in black stinking clothes of sin, such as pride, envy, wrath, accidie [laziness], covetousness, gluttony and lechery." (*The Scale of Perfection*, p. 124)

Many of the spiritual themes found in the Sonnets are also mentioned by Walter Hilton. There is an argument to make that he may well be added as a proper candidate for "Mr. W.H.", the begetter of Shakespeare's Sonnets.

Finally, we read from St. Augustine: "The eyes love fair and varied forms, and bright and soft colors. Let not these occupy my soul; let God rather occupy it, who made these lights, very good indeed, yet it is He my good, not they. These seductions of the eyes I resist, lest my feet wherewith I walk upon Thy way be ensnared; and I lift up mine invisible eyes to Thee . . ." (*Confessions of St. Augustine*, trans. Edward

Pusey [New York: Barnes & Noble, 2003], p. 241).

BIBLICAL PASSAGES SUGGESTED BY SONNET 127

"Woe unto them that call evil good, and good evil; that put darkness for light, and light for darkness; that put bitter for sweet and sweet for bitter." **Isa. 5:20**

"The earth mourneth and fadeth away, the world languisheth and fadeth away, the haughty people of the earth do languish." **Isa. 24:4**

"I am black, but comely, O ye daughters of Jerusalem, as the tents of Kedar, as the curtains of Solomon. Look not upon me, because I am black, because the sun hath looked upon me: my mother's children were angry with me; they made me the keeper of the vineyards; but mine own vineyard have I not kept." **Song of Sol. 1:5-6**

"To open their eyes, and to turn them from darkness to light, and from the power of Satan unto God, that they may receive forgiveness of sins, and inheritance among them which are sanctified by faith that is in me." **Acts 26:18**

SONNET 128

How oft, when thou, my music, music play'st,
Upon that blessed wood whose motion sounds
With thy sweet fingers, when thou gently sway'st
The wiry concord that mine ear confounds,
Do I envy those jacks that nimble leap,
To kiss the tender inward of thy hand,
Whilst my poor lips, which should that harvest reap,
At the wood's boldness by thee blushing stand!
To be so tickled, they would change their state
And situation with those dancing chips,
O'er whom thy fingers walk with gentle gait,
Making dead wood more blest than living lips.
Since saucy jacks so happy are in this,
Give them thy fingers, me thy lips to kiss.

THEME

Within man there is good and evil, represented respectively as the soul and the sense-oriented ego. Envy plays upon man to tempt him from the Spirit, and in God's Grace man is eventually purified. For those who long for God alone, only the Divine kiss of Love will satisfy.

GLOSSARY

How oft, when thou, my music, music play'st, Upon that blessed wood whose motion sounds With thy sweet fingers, when thou gently sway'st The wiry concord that mine ear confounds,

> How often, when You, who are my divine music, play upon the divine essence of my soul within and move my being into a sweet harmony that overwhelms my hearing ears.

Do I envy those jacks that nimble leap, To kiss the tender inward of thy hand, Whilst my poor lips, which should that harvest reap, At the wood's boldness by thee blushing stand!

> Do I envy those that jump about to kiss the tender essence

of thy hand, while my unworthy physical lips, which by right should reap the harvest, at the audaciousness of the envious part of me, now stand shamefaced.

To be so tickled, they would change their state And situation with those dancing chips, O'er whom thy fingers walk with gentle gait, Making dead wood more blest than living lips.

To be so tickled and tricked by envy, my earthly lips would change their blest state with those excited yearnings, over which the Divine Hand passes with gentle grace, purifying my worldly desires, making them more blest than the desires of my lips for sensual experiences.

Since saucy jacks so happy are in this, Give them thy fingers, me thy lips to kiss.

Since the common desires of the ego are happy in being slowly purified by your grace, give them such, but I desire only to be swept away by the Divine kiss.

COMMENTARY

Shakespeare is at his best when his metaphors and use of words on several levels suggest various interpretations.

Sonnet 128 is usually interpreted as a lover who watches his beloved play upon a virginal, an early keyed version of a piano. This lover wishes he could be the keys or "*jacks*" being touched by "*sweet fingers*" so that he can "*leap*" up and touch the "*tender inward of thy* [beloved's] *hand.*" The lover's lips are filled with envy that the jacks are "*tickled*," but they are left unsatisfied. "*Whilst my poor lips, which should that harvest reap, At the wood's boldness by thee blushing stand.*"

In the final quatrain we are led to believe that the "*poor lips*," heretofore unsatisfied, "*would change their state And situation with those dancing chips, O'er whom thy fingers walk with gentle gait.*" The lips then could feel the touch of those "*sweet fingers*" and be "*tickl'd*" as the "*jacks*" (now called the "*dancing chips*"). In the *Oxford English Dictionary* (OED), we see that "dancing" has the meaning of being fickle or following one's desires.

The envious "*poor lips*" believe the keys being touched are more "*blest*" than the lover's lips left unsatisfied as they "*blushing stand.*"

Finally in the ending couplet, the lover states that the "*saucy jacks*" should be given their due ("*Give them thy fingers*"), but the lover wants the kiss of the beloved, which was his deep desire all along.

On a deeper level, the interpretation follows thus: In the first quatrain, it is the beloved of the Poet being spoken of. In the Sonnets, his beloved is the Lord, who is "*my music.*" There is also the play on the word "*Muse.*" In Sonnet 100.1, he says: "*Where art thou, Muse, . . .?*" Those who are filled with divine music are spiritually touched (see below).

The word "*wood*" is defined several ways in the OED. It is the essence of a person. In *Love's Labour's Lost* Shakespeare uses "wood" in this manner, referring to the "wood" divine or inner nature of a person (IV.iii.249). The OED also indicates a meaning of "wood" as a song or sound or poetry that inspires. So in the first quatrain, it is the Lord whose "*sweet fingers*" play upon the soul or inner nature ("*blessed wood*") and creates the divine, enthralling "*music,*" or poetic sound that overwhelms the hearing with its beauty. "When I consider thy heavens, the work of thy fingers, the moon and the stars, which thou hast ordained." **(Ps. 8:3)**

"*The wiry concord that mine ear confounds.*" This is the holy song to one who can hear. "Blessed is the people that know the joyful sound." **(Ps. 89:15)**

In the second quatrain, Shakespeare introduces the villain of sorts. This is "*envy.*" What is envied are "*those jacks that nimble leap to kiss the tender inward of thy hand.*" Envy is one of the seven deadly sins and belongs to the ego. This "*envy*" may be one of the "*wretched errors*" referred to in Sonnet 119.5. In Sonnet 119.7-8, we read: "*How have mine eyes out of their spheres been fitted, In the distraction of this madding fever.*" One can imagine that our Poet is jealous of those who "*leap*" to kiss the "*tender inward*" of the Divine hand. In other words, the envious ego sees itself as at least as deserving as those "*jacks,*" or common fellows who seem to be reaping a better "*harvest.*" "For I was envious at the foolish, when I saw the prosperity of the wicked." **(Ps. 73:3)**

For Shakespeare, one might imagine his possible envy over those "*jacks*" or courtiers who would "*nimble leap*" for the best favor of the Queen's hand. "*To kiss the tender inward of thy hand.*" In a spiritual sense, however, the meaning is different. It is true that our Poet has been enthralled by the "*music*" that is so overwhelmingly sweet to his ear ("*The wiry concord that mine ear confounds*"). But envy, or ego, desires more; it wants the sweetest essence of the Divine hand. The ego is not content with its due but sees itself better, just like the "*saucy jacks*" who leap with "*boldness*" or audacity. They do not wait upon the Lord's grace, but want it all.

This Sonnet's theme is also reflected in the writing of St. Bernard of Clairvaux. In his sermons on the Song of Songs, St. Bernard says: "After receiving that favor, and even the pardon of your offences in the kissing of the feet, you became restless again. Instead of being satisfied with mercy so wonderful, you became eager for great familiarity; with renewed insistence you demanded and obtained the second grace, the kiss of the hand with its endowment of virtues both many and great" (Sermon 9, 1). "The favors I have received are far above what I deserve, but they are less than what I long for. It is desire that drives me on, not reason. . . . Please do not accuse me of presumption if I yield to this impulse of love. My shame indeed rebukes me, but love is stronger than all" (Sermon 9, 2).

"*Whilst my poor lips, which should that harvest reap, At the wood's boldness by thee blushing stand.*"

"So foolish was I, and ignorant: I was as a beast before thee." **(Ps. 73:22)** Upon awakening from the error of envy, what could our Poet do but stand mute before the Lord in shamefaced repentance. "*At the wood's* [jack's] *boldness by the blushing stand.*"

His "*poor lips*" were those he had perceived as not getting their due. They would change place with those "*jacks*" who seem to be getting the better part of the Divine hand. The lips want to be tickled and would change places with the "*dancing chips*," those that are the fickle, excited desires of the ego. In the OED, "tickled" also means to be "tricked." The human ego is lured or tricked into wanting to trade places with those they perceive as receiving more."Their eyes stand out with fatness: they have more than heart could wish." **(Ps. 73:7)**

As described by saints and mystics and in Scriptural writings, the ego needs to be purified of all "sin," including *envy*, in order to progress toward perfection. As the ego is purified of dross, it becomes the pure soul within man, untainted by sense or worldly temptations. Our Poet in Sonnet 119, with a simple rebuke, returned to his "*content*," meaning a purer state of being.

"This is an evil among all things that are done under the sun, that there is one event unto all: yea, also the heart of the sons of men is full of evil, and madness is in their heart while they live, and after that they go to the dead. For to him that is joined to all the living there is hope: for a living dog is better than a dead lion. For the living know that they shall die: but the dead know not any thing, neither have they any more a reward; for the memory of them is forgotten. Also their love, and their hatred, and their envy, is now perished." **(Eccl. 9:3-6)**

Man must undergo a purification from all base, egotistical desires and temptations, including envy. It is the Divine Hand that through Grace delivers man. Man's "*dead wood*" or egotistical nature can change, and if it does, it is better than "*living lips*" that still have fleshly desires.

"Take, O, take those lips away, that so sweetly were forsworn; And those eyes, the break of day, Lights that do mislead the morn; But my kisses bring again, bring again; Seals of love, but seal'd in vain, seal'd in vain." (*Measure For Measure*, IV.i.1-6)

He who is changed is "joined to all the living." **(Eccl. 9:4)**

There are two types of fingers described in the Bible. There are those of man, which do vain things, and the fingers of God. **(Isa. 58:9**, see below)

"When I consider thy heavens, the work of thy fingers, the moon and the stars, which thou hast ordained;" **(Ps. 8:3)** It is the hand of God that delivers man in the end.

"Send thine hand from above; rid me, and deliver me out of great waters, from the hand of strange children." **(Ps. 144:7)**

"The hand that hath made you fair hath made you good." (*Measure For Measure*, III.i.180-181)

In the final couplet, it says that "*saucy jacks*" are happy in their situation as "*dancing chips.*" In one meaning, Shakespeare is saying give them the purification of "*thy fingers*," which means they must be chided for envy. The original Q version of the Sonnet in line 14 says "*their*" fingers not "*thy*" fingers as often emendated. One may interpret the final couplet as meaning that "*saucy jacks*" or common desires should be left with the vain works of "*their fingers.*"

As for Shakespeare, whose soul-desire "*all alone stands hugely politic*" (see Sonnet 124.11), he desires only the true love of God. He has given up the desire for earthly pleasures and seeks only "*thy lips to kiss.*" "Let him kiss me with the kisses of his mouth: for thy love is better than wine." **(Song of Sol. 1:2)**

BIBLICAL PASSAGE SUGGESTED BY SONNET 128

"Then shalt thou call, and the Lord shall answer; thou shalt cry, and he shall say, Here I am. If thou take away from the midst of thee the yoke, the putting forth of the finger, and speaking vanity." **Isa. 58-59**

SONNET 129

Th' expense of spirit in a waste of shame
Is lust in action; and till action, lust
Is perjured, murderous, bloody, full of blame,
Savage, extreme, rude, cruel, not to trust;
Enjoyed no sooner but despised straight;
Past reason hunted; and no sooner had,
Past reason hated, as a swallowed bait,
On purpose laid to make the taker mad:
Mad in pursuit, and in possession so;
Had, having, and in quest to have, extreme;
A bliss in proof, and proved, a very woe,
Before, a joy proposed, behind, a dream.
All this the world well knows; yet none knows well
To shun the heaven that leads men to this hell.

THEME

Lust, like all sins, is tinged with the promise of sweetness but is like a poisoned honey that once imbibed is lethal to the Spirit in man.

GLOSSARY

Th' expense of spirit in a waste of shame Is lust in action; and till action, lust Is perjured, murderous, bloody, full of blame, Savage, extreme, rude, cruel, not to trust;

> Lust in lascivious consummation, or in its contemplation, is a waste to man's inner spirit, leaving him woeful and in shame. Lust engenders lies, murder, and injury. It is froth with blame, and is savage and extreme in its cruelty and lack of morality, and is never to be trusted.

Enjoyed no sooner but despised straight; Past reason hunted; and no sooner had, Past reason hated, as a swallowed bait, On purpose laid to make the taker mad:

> Lustful action is no sooner enjoyed than immediately despised. It is beyond the limit of human reason, and served

up without rationality. It is hatred beyond reason, like bait once swallowed. It is a lure and temptation that inflicts the partaker with madness.

Mad in pursuit, and in possession so; Had, having, and in quest to have, extreme; A bliss in proof, and proved, a very woe, Before, a joy proposed; behind, a dream.

It is madness in pursuit and in possession achieved. Indulged in, and in pursuit, lust exceeds the bounds of man's moral boundaries. It is an imagined joy in having, and once had, a welling up of grief. Beforehand it is pleasure contemplated, and on reflection afterwards, a fleeting fantasy.

All this the world well knows; yet none knows well To shun the heaven that leads men to this hell.

All of this everyone knows to be true, but not well enough to avoid the deceitfully promised enjoyment that leads men to the hellish woe that follows.

COMMENTARY

Sonnet 129 on lust follows on the heels of Sonnet 128 on envy. Shakespeare clearly states that engaging in lustful conduct despoils the soul. "*Th' expense of spirit in a waste of shame.*" Lust fosters untruth, injury, blame, and a host of "*Savage, extreme, rude,* [and] *cruel*" results.

Like all temptations, there is an expectancy of joyous anticipation almost immediately followed by shame or woe. "*Enjoyed no sooner but despised straight.*" "*A bliss in proof, and proved, a very woe; Before, a joy proposed; behind, a dream.*"

Mankind is almost universally aware of the dangers of lustful conduct, but still many are not wise enough "*To shun the heaven that leads men to this hell.*"

Sonnet 129 is a straightforward comment on the moral and mortal danger of engaging in lustful conduct. The statement that lust is "*Th' expense of spirit*" is similar to Sonnet 1 in which one who pursues egoistic desires is "*Making a famine where abundance lies*" and to "*Thyself thy foe, to thy sweet self too cruel.*" (Sonnet 1.7, 8)

BIBLICAL PASSAGES SUGGESTED BY SONNET 129

"But every man is tempted when he is drawn away of his own lust, and enticed. Then when lust hath conceived, it bringeth forth sin: and sin, when it is finished, bringeth forth death. Do not err, my beloved brethren." **James 1:14-16**

"As righteousness tendeth to life: so he that pursueth evil pursueth it to his own death." **Prov. 11:19**

SONNET 130

My mistress' eyes are nothing like the sun;
Coral is far more red than her lips' red;
If snow be white, why then her breasts are dun;
If hairs be wires, black wires grow on her head.
I have seen roses damasked, red and white,
But no such roses see I in her cheeks,
And in some perfumes is there more delight
Than in the breath that from my mistress reeks.
I love to hear her speak, yet well I know
That music hath a far more pleasing sound,
I grant I never saw a goddess go;
My mistress, when she walks, treads on the ground.
And yet, by heaven, I think my love as rare
As any she belied with false compare.

THEME

Egotistical desires and worldly temptations continually lure man away from the spiritual; but in the end the world proves itself false, a mere shadow. Only the Divine is pure Light and Beauty that has no equal.

GLOSSARY

My mistress' eyes are nothing like the sun; Coral is far more red than her lips' red: If snow be white, why then her breasts are dun; If hairs be wires, black wires grow on her head.

> My mistress' eyes are nothing like the sun; coral is a true natural red compared to her lips; if snow is pure white, why then her breasts are dark and empty; if hair would be wires, black wires grow on her head.

I have seen roses damasked, red and white, But no such roses see I in her cheeks, And in some perfumes is there more delight Than in the breath that from my mistress reeks.

> I have seen damasked roses of red and white, but her cheeks are not of roses. There is more delight in some

> perfumes, than in the breath that from my mistress reeks.

I love to hear her speak, yet well I know That music hath a far more pleasing sound; I grant I never saw a goddess go; My mistress, when she walks, treads on the ground.

> I love to hear her speak, and yet I know that music has a more pleasing sound; and I admit I never saw a goddess walk; my mistress when she walks, treads upon the ground.

And yet, by heaven, I think my love as rare As any she belied with false compare.

> And yet, by heaven, I think my love as rare as any that she in her falseness dares compare herself.

COMMENTARY

Sonnet 130 is a presentation of opposites in which the mistress is the dark ego in contrast to the whiteness of snow. Following Sonnet 129, whose theme is how lust is "*The expense of spirit in a waste of shame*," St. Augustine provides an apropos commentary: "There remains the pleasure of these eyes of my flesh, on which to make my confession in the hearing of the ears of thy temple, those brotherly and devout ears, and so to conclude the temptations of the lust of the flesh, which yet assail me, groaning earnestly, and desiring to be clothed upon with my house from heaven. . . . These seductions of the eyes I resist, lest my feet wherewith I walk upon thy way be ensnared; and I lift up mine invisible eyes to thee. . ." (*Confessions of St. Augustine*, p. 240).

The mistress' eyes are in sharp contrast to eyes that are "*like the sun*". These sun-filled eyes are the "invisible eyes" referred to by St. Augustine, and the eye found in **Matt. 6:22**: "The light of the body is the eye: if therefore thine eye be single, thy whole body shall be full of light."

In Shakespeare's time coral was considered a precious jewel. Often it was compared to or associated with the ruby. The Coverdale Bible in Lamentations 4:7 uses the word "coral" instead of rubies, which appears in the King James version. Making the substitution, it reads:

"Nazarites [distinguished ones] were purer than snow, they were whiter than milk, they were more ruddy in body than coral, their polishing was of sapphire." Also, "Who can find a virtuous woman? For her price is far above rubies." (**Prov. 31:10**) Wisdom also exceeds the price of coral, pearls, and rubies (**Job 28:18**).

The mistress of Sonnet 130 is common, and her common lips of lust are anything but the hallmark of a "virtuous" or wise woman as cited in Proverbs above.

The color white in the Bible is purity, and that which is left after sins are nullified "shall be white as snow." (**Isa. 1:18**) The breast represents nurturing and sustenance. St. Bernard, in his Sermon 9, talks at length on his interpretations of the breasts in the Song of Songs. "O my Bridegroom you have honored me so greatly with the nurturing sweetness of your breasts. . . ." "These two breasts are two proofs of native kindness." These are patience waiting upon the sinner and his "welcoming mercy for the penitent." This is in full contrast to the mistress in Sonnet 130: "*her breasts are dun*" meaning dark, and alluring but leading one down to a "*waste of shame.*" (Sonnet 129.1)

The analogy of hair to "*wires*" has a double meaning. In *Anthony and Cleopatra*, it is the whip made of wire that lashes and scourges. One enmeshed in sins is entwined as if wrapped in wires. This also is in sharp contrast to references in the Oxford English Dictionary in which wire or wires may refer to golden wires. In Peele's *David and Bathsheba* of 1599, he refers to hair like the golden wires of King David's extraordinary harp. This ties into Sonnet 128's like reference: "*With thy sweet fingers, when thou gently sway'st The wiry concord that mine ear confounds.*" (Sonnet 128.3-4) The mistress of the dark ego with lustful eyes is more akin to the wiry-headed Medusa who lures the unwitting to their deaths.

The rose is a symbol of beauty and an expression of love. The "*damasked*" colors of "*red and white*" may also connote harmony, as in the merging of the houses of York and Lancaster, represented by the red and white roses. "*No such roses*" of love and harmony are present for one under the spell of the "*mistress' eyes.*"

The next comparison is to sweet "*perfumes*" in contrast to the breath of the mistress, which "*reeks.*"

"And when he had taken the book, the four beasts and four and twenty elders fell down before the Lamb, having every one of them harps, and golden vials full of odors, which are the prayers of saints." **(Rev. 5:8)**

This passage ties into the hairs as wires, which are gold wires in David's harp, and says that odors are the prayers of saints. When the Lord anoints with the "oil of gladness," "all thy garments smell of myrrh." **(Ps. 45:7-8)** "[*T*]*he breath* [that] *from my mistress reeks*" is in contrast to the breath of life given by God to man **(Gen. 2:7)** and the sweet odors of blessing and prayers.

The speech of the mistress is the language of temptation. The music which "*mine ear confounds*" (Sonnet 128.4) hath a more pleasing sound.

The mistress treads "*on the ground*." This is the ground of earthly temptations and sin. "If the ground of sin were greatly diminished and dried up in you, and your soul rightly reformed to the image of Jesus . . . you would find the light of understanding, and no darkness of unknowing. . ." (Walter Hilton, *The Scale of Perfection*, pp. 124-125).

While the mistress "*treads on the ground*," "the Lord cometh forth out of his place, and will come down, and tread upon the high places of the earth." **(Mic. 1:3)**

Finally, the mistress of temptation will entrap and ensnare, but for the Poet: "*I think my love as rare as any she belied with false compare*." The one of false compare "sinneth from the beginning. For this purpose the Son of God was manifested, that he might destroy the works of the devil." **(1 John 3:8)** The struggle between the soul and the ego mirrors the conflict that was "from the beginning" between God and Satan.

BIBLICAL PASSAGES SUGGESTED BY SONNET 130

"Purge me with hyssop, and I shall be clean; wash me, and I shall be whiter than snow." **Ps. 51:7**

"Come now, and let us reason together, saith the Lord, though your sins be as scarlet, they shall be as white as snow; though they be red like crimson, they shall be as wool." **Isa. 1:18**

"Thus saith the Lord, The heaven is my throne, and the earth is my footstool: where is the house that ye build unto me? And where is the place of my rest?" **Isa. 66:1**

"My skin is black upon me, and my bones are burned with heat." **Job 30:30**

SONNET 131

Thou art as tyrannous, so as thou art,
As those whose beauties proudly make them cruel;
For well thou know'st to my dear doting heart
Thou art the fairest and most precious jewel.
Yet, in good faith, some say that thee behold,
Thy face hath not the power to make love groan;
To say they err I dare not be so bold,
Although I swear it to myself alone.
And to be sure that is not false I swear,
A thousand groans, but thinking on thy face,
One on another's neck, do witness bear
Thy black is fairest in my judgment's place.
In nothing art thou black save in thy deeds,
And thence this slander, as I think, proceeds.

THEME

In the nature of creation, both good and evil are to be found as relative, but permanent, aspects. The dark nature of temptation impairs rational judgment causing one to make choices that eventually result in remorseful groans, as opposed to the groans of longing, characteristic of the devotional heart.

GLOSSARY

Thou art as tyrannous, so as thou art, As those whose beauties proudly make them cruel; For well thou know'st to my dear doting heart Thou art the fairest and most precious jewel.

> You are as tyrannous as the dark art of temptation which is your nature, like prideful women who are superficially beautiful, but cruel. Only too well do you know that my heart has paid a dear price for its extremely foolish nature in believing that you alone are the most beautiful, and only dearest treasure, of my heart.

Yet, in good faith, some say that thee behold, Thy face hath not the power to make love groan; To say they err I dare not be so bold, Although I swear it to myself alone.

> Yet in good faith there are those who behold your face and declare that it does not have the power to elicit groans of longing. I would not be so bold as to declare openly that they are wrong in their opinion, although I swear it privately to myself alone.

And to be sure that is not false I swear, A thousand groans, but thinking on thy face, One on another's neck, do witness bear Thy black is fairest in my judgment's place.

> And to confirm that what I swear is not false, I experience a thousand groans of longing just at the thought of your beautiful face. With passions heaped, one upon the other, they bear witness to the fact that your dark nature is only alluring in my mind's deluded judgment.

In nothing art thou black save in thy deeds, And thence this slander, as I think, proceeds.

> In nothing are you dark except in your deeds bent on tempting mankind toward the ego's selfish desires and away from spiritual pursuits. It is because of this that my slander of this dark side of your nature arises.

COMMENTARY

Sonnet 128 explored the theme of envy. The "*saucy jacks*" are happy with common desires. In Sonnet 129, lust is described as "*Enjoyed no sooner but despised straight.*" Sonnet 130 is a presentation of the stark contrast between the darkness of temptation to worldly allurements, and whiteness that represents the purity and light of the Spirit. St. Augustine states there is "the pleasure of these eyes of my flesh," which are the opposite of Sonnet 130's eyes "*like the sun*" that fill the body not with darkness, but Divine light: "if therefore thine eye be single, thy whole body shall be full of light. But if thine eye be evil, they whole body shall be full of darkness. If therefore the light that is in thee be darkness, how great is that darkness." **(Matt. 6:22-23)**

This brings us to Sonnet 131, which describes the dark nature as "*tyrannous.*" It is the "*art*" of this tyrannous nature to be attractive like proud "*beauties,*" when they are essentially "*savage, extreme, rude* [and] *cruel.*" (Sonnet 129.4) There are some who "*in good faith*" see temptation for what it is and declare that is has no "*power to make love groan.*" Our Poet states that he would not openly dispute this, but he knows from his own life experiences that temptation is real. "*To say they err I dare not be so bold, Although I swear it to myself alone.*"

There are "*a thousand groans*" resulting from sinful pursuits, which remind the Poet of times when his poor judgment deemed black to be "*fairest.*" Each groan is a "*witness*" to that which he can now swear to be true. "*And to be sure that is not false I swear.*" In other words, the mind deluded by temptation, judged black to be fair, usurping wise judgment. "*A thousand groans . . . do witness bear Thy black is fairest in my judgment's place.*"

Creation includes both good and evil as part of the Divine plan. The many temptations comprise the dark "*art*" leading to evil "*deeds.*" These deeds of sin are a "*slander*" against the "*fairest and most precious jewel*" of the Spirit. Ultimately, the soul must reject sin and long only for goodness. Again St. Augustine: "to conclude the temptations of the lust of the flesh, which yet assail me, groaning earnestly, and desiring to be clothed upon with my house from heaven. . ." (See Sonnet 130 discussion).

In reality it is the darkness of temptations that ultimately bear witness to the truth that earthly "*beauties*" are tyrannous and are a slander against "*the most precious jewel*" of the Spirit.

BIBLICAL PASSAGES SUGGESTED BY SONNET 131

"Put on the whole armor of God, that ye may be able to stand against the wiles of the devil. For we wrestle not against flesh and blood, but against principalities, against powers, against the rulers of the darkness of this world, against spiritual wickedness in high places." **Eph. 6:11-12**

"Bread of deceit is sweet to a man; but afterwards his mouth shall be filled with gravel." **Prov. 20:17**

"Thou givest thy mouth to evil, and thy tongue frameth deceit. Thou sittest and speakest against thy brother; thou slanderest thine own mother's son. These things hast thou done, and I kept silence; thou thoughtest that I was altogether such an one as thyself: but I will reprove thee, and set them in order before thine eyes." **Ps. 50:19-21**

"Ye are of your father the devil, and the lusts of your father ye will do. He was a murderer from the beginning, and abode not in the truth, because there is no truth in him. When he speaketh a lie, he speaketh of his own: for he is a liar, and the father of it." **John 8:44**

"Because thou hast kept the word of my patience, I also will keep thee from the hour of temptation, which shall come upon all the world, to try them that dwell upon the earth." **Rev. 3:10**

"For it came to pass, when Solomon was old, that his wives turned away his heart after other gods: and his heart was not perfect with the Lord his God, as was the heart of David his father." **1 Kings 11:4**

"He that speaketh truth sheweth forth righteousness: but a false witness deceit." **Prov. 12:17**

SONNET 132

Thine eyes I love, and they, as pitying me,
Knowing thy heart torments me with disdain,
Have put on black and loving mourners be,
Looking with pretty ruth upon my pain.
And truly not the morning sun of heaven
Better becomes the grey cheeks of the east,
Nor that full star that ushers in the even
Doth half that glory to the sober west
As those two mourning eyes become thy face:
O let it then as well beseem thy heart
To mourn for me, since mourning doth thee grace,
And suit thy pity like in every part.
Then will I swear beauty herself is black,
And all they foul that thy complexion lack.

THEME

Even in sin is the sinner remorseful, being smitten by a guilty conscience. The Divine looks with compassion upon the sinner, bringing a measure of solace. The sinner thus feels that the Lord understands the nature of temptation, and pities His children.

GLOSSARY

Thine eyes I love, and they, as pitying me, Knowing thy heart torments me with disdain, Have put on black and loving mourners be, Looking with pretty ruth upon my pain.

> Your eyes I love; and see how they pity me. Knowing thy forgiving heart torments me scornfully. Thine eyes have put on a black aspect, and like loving mourners, look with a kind understanding upon my pain.

And truly not the morning sun of heaven Better becomes the grey cheeks of the east, Nor that full star that ushers in the even Doth half that glory to the sober west

> The morning sun of heaven does not better become the

> grey clouds of my perceptions, nor does the rich light of the evening star that ushers in the eventide show half the glory to the solemn western sky.

As those two mourning eyes become thy face: O let it then as well beseem thy heart To mourn for me, since mourning doth thee grace, And suit thy pity like in every part.

> As those two mourning eyes become thy face, oh let Thy heart mourn for me, as such does Thee grace and show that Thy pity is all-encompassing.

Then will I swear beauty herself is black, And all they foul that thy complexion lack.

> Then I will swear that contained in the nature of creation is an aspect of darkness or temptation, and all else, that lacks Thy compassionate nature, is that which is truly foul in this world.

COMMENTARY

As has been stated, it is in the nature of creation to have forces of good and evil. The remorseful Poet feels the eyes of God or conscience upon him, making him feel ashamed. "*Thine eyes I love, and they, as pitying me, Knowing thy heart torments me with disdain.*" The sinner feels the Lord's reproving eyes upon Him, but also like "*loving mourners,*" they look with "*pretty ruth*" upon the sinner's pain. The eyes of the Lord seem to "*have put on black*" to the conscience-smitten sinner who feels he is weighed down by the Lord's stern judgment.

Just seeing, or sensing the compassionate gaze of those "*two mourning eyes*" is more comforting that the site of "*morning sun of heaven*" casting its light upon the "*grey cheeks*" or tearfully washed face of the remorseful sinner.

It is pity and compassion that are signs of Divine Grace. This forgiving Grace is present in the midst of the sinner's tormented conscience. Grace must be present because the element of temptation or darkness is part of the Lord's creation, even as the serpent inhabits the Garden of Eden. "*Then will I swear beauty herself is black.*" All that lacks the pity and compassion of those "*two mourning eyes*" are "*foul*" or loathsome.

BIBLICAL PASSAGES SUGGESTED BY SONNET 132

"I clothe the heavens with blackness, and I make sackcloth their covering." **Isa. 50:3**

"I am black, but comely, O ye daughters of Jerusalem, as the tents of Kedar, as the curtains of Solomon." **Song of Sol. 1:5**

"There hath no temptation taken you but such as is common to man: but God is faithful, who will not suffer you to be tempted above that ye are able; but will with the temptation also make a way to escape, that ye may be able to bear it." **1 Cor. 10:13**

"Blessed is the man that endureth temptation: for when he is tried, he shall receive the crown of life, which the Lord hath promised to them that love him." **James 1:12**

"Because thou hast kept the word of my patience, I also will keep thee from the hour of temptation, which shall come upon all the world, to try them that dwell upon the earth." **Rev. 3:10**

"The Lord is nigh unto them that are of a broken heart; and saveth such as be of a contrite spirit." **Ps. 34:18**

"For all those things hath mine hand made, and all those things have been, saith the Lord: but to this man will I look, even to him that is poor and of a contrite spirit, and trembleth at my word." **Isa. 66:2**

"And he said unto me, My grace is sufficient for thee: for my strength is made perfect in weakness. Most gladly therefore will I rather glory in my infirmities, that the power of Christ may rest upon me. Therefore I take pleasure in infirmities, in reproaches, in necessities, in persecutions, in distresses for Christ's sake: for when I am weak, then am I strong." **2 Cor. 12:9-10**

"The eyes of the Lord are in every place, beholding the evil and the good." **Prov. 15:3**

SONNET 133

Beshrew that heart that makes my heart to groan
For that deep wound it gives my friend and me;
Is't not enough to torture me alone,
But slave to slavery my sweet'st friend must be?
Me from myself thy cruel eye hath taken,
And my next self thou harder hast engrossed:
Of him, myself, and thee, I am forsaken;
A torment thrice threefold thus to be crossed.
Prison my heart in thy steel bosom's ward,
But then my friend's heart let my poor heart bail;
Whoe'er keeps me, let my heart be his guard,
Thou canst not then use rigour in my jail.
And yet thou wilt; for I, being pent in thee,
Perforce am thine, and all that is in me.

THEME

Man is not just a physical ego-conscious being, but is essentially a soul, the spark of the Divine. The dark temptations of earthly life enslave man and imprison his soul nature as well. As man and God are one, however, that which imprisons the ego, enslaves the soul and the Light of God is also kept away.

GLOSSARY

Beshrew that heart that makes my heart to groan For that deep wound it gives my friend and me Is't not enough to torture me alone, But slave to slavery my sweet'st friend must be?

> Curse that dark heart that makes my heart groan with longing for temptations as it deeply wounds me and my dear soul. Is it not enough to torture me alone but must my soul also be a slave to my ego desires?

Me from myself thy cruel eye hath taken, And my next self thou harder hast engrossed: Of him, myself, and thee, I am forsaken; A torment thrice threefold thus to be crossed.

> Your evil eye has separated me from my soul, and my dearest soul self you have most cruelly encumbered in grossness. From my soul nature, my own self, and my Lord I am forsaken, a torment thrice by three multiplied and to be overcome.

Prison my heart in thy steel bosom's ward, But then my friend's heart let my poor heart bail; Whoe'er keeps me, let my heart be his guard, Thou canst not then use rigour in my jail.

> Imprison my heart in your heartless steely trap, but then allow my entrapment to secure the release of my soulful heart. Whoever keeps me, allow my heart to be his guardian. Then Thou canst not use severity in my place of confinement.

And yet thou wilt; for I, being pent in thee, Perforce am thine, and all that is in me.

> And yet Thou wilt, for I, being confined all within Thee, it is necessarily true that I, and all that is in me, is Thine.

COMMENTARY

The Poet curses the tyrannous "*heart*" that makes him pursue egoistical desires and temptations. "*Beshrew that heart that makes my heart to groan.*" It has been the nature or "*art*" of temptation to ensnare the Poet's "*dear doting heart.*" (Sonnet 131.3) When one pursues selfish desires of the heart, the soul is also enslaved: "*Poor soul, the centre of my sinful earth.*" (Sonnet 146.1)

Not only is the Poet tormented, but his "*sweet'st friend*" also becomes a "*slave to slavery.*" Yielding to the allurements of the world is likened to slavery, and the soul calls the Spirit, of which the soul is a part, his "*sweet'st friend.*"

The "*cruel eye*" is like the evil eye that brings a curse upon man. One so ensnared loses himself in sin, and his soul nature is also alienated, as is his relationship with the Lord; thus the Poet feels utter despair: "*And my next self thou harder hast engrossed: Of him, myself, and thee, I am forsaken; A torment thrice threefold thus to be crossed.*" "*Thus to be crossed*" may be likened to one crossing the wildness in order to reach the promised land. It is necessary to free the spiritual heart from the worldly desires of "*that heart that makes my heart to groan.*"

As creation includes both good and evil, as already discussed, all is part of God's plan. Man suffers by yielding to temptations, and ends up in the "*steel bosom's ward.*" All is in the bosom of God, but Divine law and judgment requires that a price be exacted by one who wrongfully uses free will to engage in sinful conduct. "*(sovereign mistress over wrack), As thou goest onwards, still will pluck thee back, She keeps thee to this purpose, . . . Her audit, though delayed, answer'd must be.*" (Sonnet 126.5-7, 11)

Shakespeare makes the plea that his torment is punishment enough so why imprison his soulful friend as well. He suffers remorse, and his relationship with the Lord also suffers a "*deep wound.*"

In the end, man and his relationship with the Divine will suffer as sin shuts out the Light of the Spirit. But necessarily, as the Heavenly Father and His children are ever-connected, how man uses his free will determines his torment and the "*rigour*" of his self-imposed prison term. "*And yet thou wilt; for I, being pent in thee, Perforce am thine, and all that is in me.*" There is a sense of "*pent*" here, meaning of not just imprisonment, but being repentant as well. This connects to the compassion the Poet feels in Sonnet 132 by sensing the "*mourning eyes*" that are evidence of the Lord's Grace for the contrite sinner.

BIBLICAL PASSAGES SUGGESTED BY SONNET 133

"For what shall it profit a man, if he shall gain the whole world, and lose his own soul?" **Mark 8:36**

"Know ye not, that so many of us as were baptized into Jesus Christ were baptized into his death? Therefore we are buried with him by baptism into death: that like as Christ was raised up from the dead by the glory of the Father, even so we also should walk in newness of life. For if we have been planted together in the likeness of his death, we shall be also in the likeness of his resurrection: Knowing this, that our old man is crucified with him, that the body of sin might be destroyed, that henceforth we should not serve sin." **Rom. 6:3-6**

"I call heaven and earth to record this day against you, that I have set before you life and death, blessing and cursing: therefore choose life, that both thou and thy seed may live." **Deut. 30:19**

"In all their affliction he was afflicted, and the angel of his presence saved them: in his love and in his pity he redeemed them; and he bare them, and carried them all the days of old." **Isa. 63:9**

"And, behold, I am with thee, and will keep thee in all places whither thou goest, and will bring thee again into this land; for I will not leave thee, until I have done that which I have spoken to thee of." **Gen. 28:15**

"Thus my heart was grieved, and I was pricked in my reins. So foolish was I, and ignorant: I was as a beast before thee. Nevertheless I am continually with thee: thou hast holden me by my right hand." **Ps. 73:21-23**

SONNET 134

So, now I have confessed that he is thine,
And I myself am mortgag'd to thy will,
Myself I'll forfeit, so that other mine
Thou wilt restore, to be my comfort still:
But thou wilt not, nor he will not be free,
For thou art covetous and he is kind;
He learned but surety-like to write for me,
Under that bond that him as fast doth bind.
That statute of thy beauty thou wilt take,
Thou usurer, that put'st forth all to use,
And sue a friend came debtor for my sake;
So him I lose through my unkind abuse.
Him have I lost; thou hast both him and me;
He pays the whole, and yet am I not free.

THEME

The soul pays the price of the ego's whims. Eventually man learns to make better choices and thus free himself from the self-inflicted punishment for sin. But, until complete freedom of choice is exercised, man is not redeemed, not even by Christ as redeemer who "*pays the whole*" for mankind.

GLOSSARY

So, now I have confessed that he is thine, And I myself am mortgag'd to thy will, Myself I'll forfeit, so that other mine Thou wilt restore, to be my comfort still:

> So now I made a confession stating that my ego's nature is in your keeping. My soul has been mortgaged as it is your Divine Law or Will which states that misuse of my free will is at the expense of my Spirit. I would gladly forfeit the ego's desires so my other, better part, my soul, may be made whole in devotion to Thee alone.

But thou wilt not, nor he will not be free, For thou art covetous and he is kind; He learned but surety-like to write for me, Under that bond that him as fast doth bind.

But your Divine Law and Will exacts its due, and my ego-enslaved nature has compromised my God-given free will. Thou art a jealous God, and my soul is pure. My Spirit learned how to overcome temptation, and thus, gradually freed my ego from the ruinous habit of choosing sinful allurements that held us both in check.

That statute of thy beauty thou wilt take, Thou usurer, that put'st forth all to use, And sue a friend came debtor for my sake; So him I lose through my unkind abuse.

You fill the world with beautiful temptations for which you will exact your due like a usurer who lends, then charges exorbitant interest. And further you punish both my Spirit and my Savior, who acted for my redemption. So now, through my misuse of free will, I have lost my faith in the Lord Jesus.

Him have I lost; thou hast both him and me, He pays the whole, and yet am I not free.

My soul, and my Redeemer I have lost. Thou hast Him and me. Even though the Bible declares that Christ has paid for all sins, still am I not free.

COMMENTARY

Sonnet 133 states that "*Me from myself thy cruel eye hath taken.*" In other words, the soul-self is imprisoned as long as the eye of evil chooses sinful temptation. The soul is as a prisoner, a "*slave to slavery*" resulting from the misuse of free will.

In Sonnet 134, the Poet makes a confession of sorts that "*he is thine.*" This can be interpreted as the enslaved ego-nature that has "*mortgaged*" the soul. In Sonnet 146, the soul is in the center of the sinful earth, enslaved by the rebellious powers of the senses. Restoration can be achieved, according to Sonnet 146, through "*buy*[ing] *terms divine*" and letting the ego's store "*pine*" by ceasing to indulge in "*costly*" temptations at the expense of the soul. (Sonnet 146.4, 10, 11)

The world is full of allurements and tempting beauties, which like the loans made by usurers, exact a heavy price. "*That statute of thy beauty thou wilt take, Thou usurer, that put'st forth all to use.*"

There is the sense of the Redeemer or Christ in Sonnet 134 as a "*friend came debtor for my sake.*" "Even as the Son of man came not to be ministered unto, but to minister, and to give his life a ransom for many." **(Matt. 20:28)**

The Lord Himself acts for mankind. "For their redeemer is mighty; he shall plead their cause with thee." **(Prov. 23:11)** There is a further connection with Sonnet 133, line 8, "*A torment thrice threefold thus to be crossed*". The reference to "*crossed*" suggests the crucifixion, with Christ dying for the sins of many. In Sonnet 134, line 14, "*He pays the whole, and yet am I not free,*" even the Lord cannot redeem one who wills not to be free: "*nor he will not be free.*" In Sonnet 133 "*Thrice threefold*" may also be interpreted as meaning that man must first overcome the ego in order to allow the soul's nature to blossom and open the way for final union with the Spirit. In successive stages, man's soul passes from ego identification into a process of purification and finally merges into Spirit through salvation.

The Poet in Sonnet 134 sets up his introduction to Sonnet 135 where the "*Will*" becomes a central, recurrent theme. Use and misuse of one's free will is a theme Shakespeare visits often, both in his plays and in his Sonnets.

BIBLICAL PASSAGES SUGGESTED BY SONNET 134

"For I acknowledge my transgressions: and my sin is ever before me. Against thee, thee only, have I sinned, and done this evil in thy sight: that thou mightest be justified when thou speakest, and be clear when thou judgest. Behold, I was shapen in iniquity; and in sin did my mother conceive me. Behold, thou desirest truth in the inward parts: and in the hidden part thou shalt make me to know wisdom." **Ps. 51:3-6**

"Restore unto me the joy of thy salvation; and uphold me with thy free spirit." **Ps. 51:12**

"For ye know how that afterward, when he would have inherited the blessing, he was rejected: for he found no place of repentance, though he sought it carefully with tears." **Heb. 12:17**

"But God commendeth his love toward us, in that, while we were yet sinners, Christ died for us." **Rom. 5:8**

"That as sin hath reigned unto death, even so might grace reign through righteousness unto eternal life by Jesus Christ our Lord." **Rom. 5:21**

"For I know that in me (that is, in my flesh,) dwelleth no good thing: for to will is present with me; but how to perform that which is good I find not. For the good that I would I do not: but the evil which I would not, that I do." **Rom. 7:18-19**

SONNET 135

Whoever hath her wish, thou hast thy Will,
And Will to boot, and Will in over-plus;
More than enough am I that vex thee still,
To thy sweet will making addition thus.
Wilt thou, whose will is large and spacious,
Not once vouchsafe to hide my will in thine?
Shall will in others seem right gracious,
And in my will no fair acceptance shine?
The sea, all water, yet receives rain still,
And in abundance addeth to his store;
So thou, being rich in Will, add to thy Will
One will of mine, to make thy large Will more.
Let no unkind, no fair beseechers kill;
Think all but one, and me in that one Will.

THEME

All that is in the Universe happens through the Divine Will. Let it be each one's wish that his will be united to the Will of God.

GLOSSARY

Whoever hath her wish, thou hast thy Will, And Will to boot, and Will in over-plus; More than enough am I that vex thee still, To thy sweet will making addition thus.

> No matter what anyone may desire, Thou hast Thy Will and Will beyond human understanding that exceeds all Will; more than enough so that I would trouble Thee and Thy sweet Will to make an addition to Thy Will in this way.

Wilt thou, whose will is large and spacious, Not once vouchsafe to hide my will in thine? Shall will in others seem right gracious, And in my will no fair acceptance shine?

> Wilt Thou, whose overarching, all-encompassing Will is capacious enough for all things, vouchsafe to hide my

little will and desire in Thine? Wilt Thou accept what seems to be right and gracious in others' desires, but in my own petition wilt Thou find no merit?

The sea, all water, yet receives rain still, And in abundance addeth to his store; So thou, being rich in Will, add to thy Will One will of mine, to make thy large Will more.

The large ocean is filled with water and still it receives the rain, and to its abundance it adds even more; So Thou so rich in Divine Will, add to Thy Will one small will of mine to make Thy Will still more in abundance.

Let no unkind, no fair beseechers kill; Think all but one, and me in that one Will.

Let no unkindness, no tempting allurements kill the desire in me to surrender my will to Thine; but let all in Thee be one, including me and my human desires at last united to Thy Will.

COMMENTARY

In Sonnet 134, the Poet "*confessed*" that he is "*mortgag'd to thy will.*" Even so a toll must be paid for "*unkind abuse*" of free will just as one pays a "*usurer*" for having incurred a debt. (Sonnet 134.1, 2, 10, 12) "For I know that in me (that is, in my flesh,) dwelleth no good thing: for to will is present with me; but how to perform that which is good I find not. For the good that I would I do not: but the evil which I would not, that I do." **(Rom. 7:18-19)** We see the Poet express in Sonnet 134 that even though "*a friend came debtor for my sake*" that "*yet am I not free.*" (Sonnet 134.11, 14) He is not free because in him is the will, but not the ability "to perform that which is good." **(Rom. 7:18)**

Sonnet 135 contains the Poet's petition to the Almighty, that to God's perfect Divine Will be added the Poet's wish "*to hide my will in thine.*" In other words, he is asking the Lord to remove the desire in his "flesh" for earthly allurements. Shakespeare asks of the Lord why He seems to grant others' prayers or desires and not his? "*Shall will in others seem right gracious, And in my will no fair acceptance shine?*"

The Will of God connotes not only the Divine plan of Creation, but the Biblically- expressed will of the Lord that all His children obey His laws so that they might return to salvation. The Poet therefore argues that to add his small will for fleshly desires to "*thy large Will*" thus fulfills the Divine plan. "*So thou, being rich in Will, add to thy Will One will of mine, to make thy large Will more.*"

Knowing of the possibility of reversion to fleshly allurements ("*fair beseechers*"), the Poet adds to his petition the request that all diverting temptations be kept away from his thoughts. "*Let no unkind no fair beseechers kill.*" Instead, the Poet asks the Lord to fulfill the Lord's desire ("*Will*") that all his children be united with Him as one. "*Think all but one, and me in that one Will.*"

I would be remiss in not mentioning Nicholas Breton's *The Will of Wit* (1599) in which "Will" is also addressed with a capital "W." A preface is written by one, "W.S.". In Breton's work Wit and Will have a discourse between themselves. Will complains that he has lost his way wondering "through a wilderness of woe, which in the Mapp of that Countrey (I find) is called the Desart of Desire." Will goes on to describe the various vanities in which he was engaged in losing his way.

BIBLICAL PASSAGES SUGGESTED BY SONNET 135

"Hear, O Israel: The Lord our God is one Lord." **Deut. 6:4**

"For he remembered that they were but flesh; a wind that passeth away, and cometh not again." **Ps. 78:39**

"In all their affliction he was afflicted, and the angel of his presence saved them: in his love and in his pity he redeemed them; and he bare them, and carried them all the days of old." **Isa. 63:9**

"Because thou hast kept the word of my patience, I also will keep thee from the hour of temptation, which shall come upon all the world, to try them that dwell upon the earth." **Rev. 3:10**

"Therefore by the deeds of the law there shall no flesh be justified in his sight: for by the law is the knowledge of sin. But now the righteousness of God without the law is manifested, being witnessed by the law and the prophets." **Rom. 3:20-21**

"For thy name's sake, O Lord, pardon mine iniquity; for it is great." **Ps. 25:11**

SONNET 136

If thy soul check thee that I come so near,
Swear to thy blind soul that I was thy Will,
And will, thy soul knows, is admitted there;
Thus far for love my love-suit, sweet, fulfil.
Will, will fulfil the treasure of thy love,
Ay, fill it full with wills, and my will one.
In things of great receipt with ease we prove
Among a number one is reckon'd none:
Then in the number let me pass untold,
Thou in thy stores' account I one must be;
For nothing hold me, so it please thee hold
That nothing me, a something sweet to thee.
Make but my name thy love, and love that still,
And then thou lov'st me, for my name is Will.

THEME

Surrender to the Divine Will by abandoning all earthly desires for the one precious love is to fulfill the Divine Commandment (Will) to love the Lord alone with all thy heart, soul, mind, and strength.

GLOSSARY

If thy soul check thee that I come so near, Swear to thy blind soul that I was thy Will, And will, thy soul knows, is admitted there; Thus far for love my love-suit, sweet, fulfil.

> If your reason resists at my intimate approach, affirm to your blind soul that I was Thy Divine Will, and intuitively your soul will respond knowing, that Spirit and soul are bound together; so it appears that out of love, my heavenly petition will so sweetly be fulfilled.

Will, will fulfil the treasure of thy love, Ay, fill it full with wills, and my will one. In things of great receipt with ease we prove Among a number one is reckon'd none:

> Correct use of soulful willing and reason will fulfill the

> treasure of your heart's love. Yes, fill my heart with heavenly desires alone, gathering all my desires into one united wish for Thee alone. In the largest numbers of things we can say easily that one is considered as if it were none.

Then in the number let me pass untold, Thou in thy stores' account I one must be; For nothing hold me, so it please thee hold That nothing me, a something sweet to thee.

> Then among so many let me pass unnoticed, even though in the numbers I must be counted as one; Forgive all and let me pass, and so may a nothing like me be something precious to Thee.

Make but my name thy love, and love that still, And then thou lov'st me, for my name is Will.

> Make my name alone the altar of Thy love, and ever love in Divine stillness, and then thou dost love me according to My Will.

COMMENTARY

In Sonnet 135, the Poet petitions the Lord "*to hide my will in thine.*" He seeks the Lord's grace that "*no unkind, no fair beseechers*" (Sonnet 135.6, 13) of temptation divert his wish to bring his earthly wishes in conformity with the Divine Will.

In Sonnet 136, we see an uneasy surrender of the Poet's soul or reason to the approach of the Divine, also expressed as the desire of the Poet to conform his will to the Divine. "*If thy soul check thee that I come so near, Swear to thy blind soul that I was thy Will.*" The word "*check*" means both to cause the soul to pause or stop but, as in chess, suggests a successful attack upon the opposition. When the Spirit comes "*near,*" the ego-identified soul may seem reluctant or in "*check*" before yielding, as it has been "*blind,*" or unaccustomed, to the bright light of Divine "*Will.*" Spirit, as it awakens the soul, puts the "*blind soul*" in "*check.*" In the Bible it says: "And in that day shall the deaf hear the words of the book, and the eyes of the blind shall see out of obscurity, and out of darkness." **(Isa. 29:18)** Shakespeare states that one must "*swear*" or affirm steadfastly to the "*blind soul that I was thy Will.*" Here is a change of tense from the present in line one, "*If thy soul check thee that I come so near,*" to the past tense in line two, "*I was thy Will.*" The sense here is that behind the soul there always existed from the beginning, the Divine Will: "*I was thy* Will." The soul, identified with the temporal body and senses, and by misuse of free will, became blind to its Divine source.

Proper use of the soul's innate, divinely-conferred, reason "*will fulfil the treasure of thy love.*" This means that the soul's treasure of joy is fulfilled by the correct use of one's will and discrimination to avoid worldly temptations.

In Sonnet 135, Shakespeare asks that his will be taken into the "*large and spacious*" Will of the Divine. In such a large space of the Divine Will, or Divine Intelligence, the addition of one person's will may seem insignificant or "*none.*" "*In things of great receipt with ease we prove Among a number one is reckon'd none.*"

In spite of feeling personally small or insignificant, in comparison to the Lord's vastness, still the Poet says, "*That nothing me, a something sweet to thee.*" Here we see the devotional intimacy of the Poet's heart, trusting that he has a secure and loving niche in the Lord's love for all of His children.

The last couplet seems like a Shakespeare paraphrase of the Biblical injunction to love the Lord with all one's heart, soul, mind, and strength. For the reader of the Sonnet, the couplet, on a spiritual level of interpretation, is a message to use one's free will, the spiritual Will innate to the soul, to conform one's wishes and desires to the love for God. "*Make but my name thy love.*" "After this manner therefore pray ye: Our Father which art in heaven, Hallowed be thy name." **(Matt. 6:9)** The phrase, "*and love that still*" means to love in the stillness of one's heart. "But thou, when thou prayest, enter into thy closet, and when thou hast shut thy door, pray to thy Father which is in secret; and thy Father which seeth in secret shall reward thee openly." **(Matt. 6:6)** (See also Sonnet 27 and Sonnet 52 commentary.)

BIBLICAL PASSAGES SUGGESTED BY SONNET 136

"We grope for the wall like the blind, and we grope as if we had no eyes: we stumble at noonday as in the night; we are in desolate places as dead men." **Isa. 59:10**

"Jesus said unto him, Thou shalt love the Lord thy God with all thy heart, and with all thy soul, and with all thy mind." **Matt. 22:37**

"Are not two sparrows sold for a farthing? and one of them shall not fall on the ground without your Father. But the very hairs of your head are all numbered. Fear ye not therefore, ye are of more value than many sparrows." **Matt. 10:29-31**

"For whosoever shall do the will of my Father which is in heaven, the same is my brother, and sister, and mother." **Matt. 12:50**

"Wherefore come out from among them, and be ye separate, saith the Lord, and touch not the unclean thing; and I will receive you. And will be a Father unto you, and ye shall be my sons and daughters, saith the Lord Almighty." **2 Cor. 6:17-18**

"For thus saith the high and lofty One that inhabiteth eternity, whose name is Holy; I dwell in the high and holy place, with him also that is of a contrite and humble spirit, to revive the spirit of the humble, and to revive the heart of the contrite ones." **Isa. 57:15**

"After this manner therefore pray ye: Our Father which art in heaven, Hallowed be thy name. Thy kingdom come. Thy will be done in earth, as it is in heaven." **Matt. 6:9-10**

"Not unto us, O Lord, not unto us, but unto thy name give glory, for thy mercy, and for thy truth's sake. . . . But our God is in the heavens: he hath done whatsoever he hath pleased." **Ps. 115:1, 3**

SONNET 137

Thou blind fool, love, what dost thou to mine eyes,
That they behold, and see not what they see?
They know what beauty is, see where it lies,
Yet what the best is take the worst to be.
If eyes, corrupt by over-partial looks,
Be anchor'd in the bay where all men ride,
Why of eyes' falsehood hast thou forged hooks,
Whereto the judgment of my heart is tied?
Why should my heart think that a several plot
Which my heart knows the wide world's common place?
Or mine eyes, seeing this, say this is not,
To put fair truth upon so foul a face?
In things right true my heart and eyes have erred,
And to this false plague are they now transferred.

THEME

By habitually engaging in immoral conduct and sensual pleasures, one's higher Divine reason, and the heart's soulful longings are silenced, and one becomes anchored in the shallow places of life.

GLOSSARY

Thou blind fool, love, what dost thou to mine eyes, That they behold, and see not what they see? They know what beauty is, see where it lies, Yet what the best is take the worst to be.

> Thou blind fool, love, what you have done to deceive my eyes, that they see but do not perceive what is real. They know what beauty is and see where it lies, yet what is truly to be cherished, is tossed away, as if worthless.

If eyes, corrupt by over-partial looks, Be anchor'd in the bay where all men ride, Why of eyes' falsehood hast thou forged hooks, Whereto the judgment of my heart is tied?

> If eyes are corrupted by looking at the darker aspects of life, it is because the vision of most men is anchored in

> the shallows frequented by common minds. Why have you placed before man scenes which are tempting but ensnare his reason and cause the judgment of my heart likewise to be mired in the mud of falsehood.

Why should my heart think that a several plot Which my heart knows the wide world's common place? Or mine eyes, seeing this, say this is not, To put fair truth upon so foul a face?

> Why should my heart be deceived into thinking that something is singular and special when it knows truly that it is but commonplace in the world? My blinded eyes deny what the heart knows inwardly to be true and attribute fair beauty to the ugliness before them.

In things right true my heart and eyes have erred, And to this false plague are they now transferred.

> In the world of things, both my doting heart and blind eyes have erred, And now through ignorance they succumb as though stricken by the plague.

COMMENTARY

As discussed in Sonnets 134, 135, and 136, the proper exercise of man's free will is necessary to allow the higher spiritual nature to "*restore, to be my comfort still.*" (Sonnet 134.1, 4) One cannot abrogate one's free will to the Creator by requesting: "*Wilt thou, whose will is large and spacious, Not once vouchsafe to hide my will in thine?*" (Sonnet 135.5-6) To succeed one must heed Divine counsel: "*Will will fulfil the treasure of thy love, Ay, fill it full with wills, and my will one.*" (Sonnet 136.5-6) It is necessary to exercise one's God-given, free will in a manner that shows repeated effort to conform one's wishes to the Divine Will and plan. One is exhorted to have but one wish, one love: "*Make but my name thy love.*" (Sonnet 136.13)

In Sonnet 137, the Poet complains about the false nature of creation. One sees with longing eyes that are blinded. The reason knows better, but is habituated to succumbing to temptations. "*Thou blind fool, Love, what dost thou to mine eyes, That they behold, and see not what they see? They know what beauty is, see where it lies, Yet what the best is take the worst to be.*" Man's conscience knows intuitively what the Truth is and what are lies. The phrase, "*where it lies*" suggests the falsehood of deceitful "*beauty.*" Such a beauty is a forgery of the real Beauty of the Spirit. Eyes become corrupted by constant exposure to the shallow waters of life. This is "*the bay where all men ride.*" It is interesting to note that one who is "*anchor'd in the bay*" cannot ride anywhere. The "*eyes' falsehood*" correspond to the "*forged hooks*" of temptation. "*Forged*" suggests a grappling hook, but may also mean that these "*hooks*" are a forgery, a false allurement. "*Whereto the judgment of my heart is tied,*" suggests that one who is habituated to seeing and partaking of falsehood and temptation becomes "*tied*" or anchored in the common pools, or "*bay*" of life. A "*bay*" is also subject to change by the tides. This suggests, of course, that man vacillates upon the waves of life, being directed not by sound reason, but by the ebb and flow of the tides of earthly temptations.

The result of abdicating his Divinely-conferred reason and will is that man sits "*anchor'd*" in the "*world's common place.*" He deceives himself into believing that the "*foul*" aspects of life are somehow really "*fair.*" "*To put fair truth upon so foul a face.*"

Finally the realization surfaces that "*In things right true my heart and eyes have erred.*" The Poet realizes that the events of his life are not special, not a "*several plot,*" but are "*the wide world's common place,*" and he is but a common player plagued by falsehoods that blind his sight and bind his heart. "*And to this false plague are they now transferred.*"

Walter Hilton, the fourteenth century Christian mystic has written: "Bad thoughts and impure affections: . . . They either take away the life of the soul by mortal sins, or enfeeble the soul and make it sick. . . . If you want to know what you love, look at what you think about; for where the love is, there is the eye, and where the pleasure is, there is the heart thinking most." (*The Scale of Perfection*, pp. 156-157)

BIBLICAL PASSAGES SUGGESTED BY SONNET 137

"Take heed to yourselves, that your heart be not deceived, and ye turn aside, and serve other gods, and worship them." **Deut. 11:16**

"They have mouths, but they speak not: eyes have they, but they see not." **Ps. 115:5**

"What prayer and supplication soever be made by any man, or by all thy people Israel, which shall know every man the plague of his own heart, and spread forth his hands toward this house." **1 Kings 8:38**

"Because that, when they knew God, they glorified him not as God, neither were thankful; but because vain in their imaginations, and their foolish heart was darkened. Professing themselves to be wise, they became fools, And changed the glory of the uncorruptible God into an image made like to corruptible man, and to birds, and fourfooted beasts, and creeping things." **Rom. 1:21-23**

SONNET 138

When my love swears that she is made of truth,
I do believe her, though I know she lies,
That she might think me some untutor'd youth,
Unlearned in the world's false subtleties.
Thus vainly thinking that she thinks me young,
Although she knows my days are past the best,
Simply I credit her false-speaking tongue:
On both sides thus is simple truth suppressed.
But wherefore says she not she is unjust?
And wherefore say not I that I am old?
O, love's best habit is in seeming trust,
And age in love loves not to have years told.
Therefore I lie with her, and she with me,
And in our faults by lies we flatter'd be.

THEME

Desires of the heart and vanity trump man's reason and foster the continuation of poor judgment and habits.

GLOSSARY

When my love swears that she is made of truth, I do believe her, though I know she lies, That she might think me some untutor'd youth, Unlearned in the world's false subtleties.

> When my love swears that she is truthful, though deep inside myself I know she lies, I go along with her untruths so she might judge me to be a foolish youth, inexperienced in the false subtleties of the world.

Thus vainly thinking that she thinks me young, Although she knows my days are past the best, Simply I credit her false-speaking tongue: On both sides thus is simple truth suppressed.

> So I go on vainly thinking that she judges my actions as those of an unwise youth, although she and I both know that I am not young and unwise. Simply I go on believ-

> ing in lies, and between the two of us, the truth is suppressed.

But wherefore says she not she is unjust? And wherefore say not I that I am old? O, love's best habit is in seeming trust, And age in love loves not to have years told.

> Why doesn't she just admit she is unjust? And why can't I admit that I have the age and wisdom to act more wisely? Love's best known habit is that it seems to trust, and one who is advanced in years does not like to discuss old age.

Therefore I lie with her, and she with me, And in our faults by lies we flatter'd be.

> So I continue in my lie with love, and love does the same with me, and in our mutual deception, we flatter ourselves untruly.

COMMENTARY

The Poet in Sonnet 137 calls his love a "*blind fool.*" (Sonnet 137.1) This is the foolish heart whose worldly desires make the eyes "*see not what they see.*" (Sonnet 137.2) "Take heed, brethren, lest there be in any of you an evil heart of unbelief, in departing from the living God." (**Heb. 3:12**) The eyes in Sonnet 137 are "*corrupt.*" They are in the habit of seeking alluring things thus ensnaring both good judgment and the heart. "*Whereto the judgment of my heart is tied?*" (Sonnet 137.8)

In Sonnet 138, "*love*" refers to desires of a heart that is deceived by "*false*" subtleties and thus "*swears that she is made of truth.*" The Poet pointed out in Sonnet 137 that "*my heart and eyes have erred*" in the false manner in which they have perceived the world. (Sonnet 137.13) This falseness, which has made love a "*blind fool*" and which has cauterized the "*heart's judgment,*" the Poet refers to as a "*false plague.*" (Sonnet 137.14) Like a disease that spreads throughout the country, this falseness in perceiving and judging, and falling victim to life's temptations, has become the "*world's common place*" (Sonnet 137.10), or state of affairs among men. To this plague have "*heart and eyes*" (Sonnet 137.13) succumb and to this "*they are now transferred.*" (Sonnet 137.14)

In such a state of self-deception, we find, in Sonnet 138, "*love*" swearing to the reason that the "*lies*" are truths. This is similar to the false promise made to Eve by the serpent, who said that if she eats the apple, "your eyes shall be opened, and ye shall be as gods, knowing good and evil." (**Gen. 3:5**) What's worse, in spite of inwardly feeling that the mind is being deceived, the Poet says that the heart, in order to justify pursuit of vain worldly desires, goes along with the deceit. "*I do believe her, though I know she lies*."

In Sonnet 133, the Poet writes: "*Beshrew that heart that makes my heart to groan For that deep wound it gives my friend and me.*" In subsequent Sonnets, 134 and 135, we see that the imprisoned heart of Sonnet 133 is due in part because of a will that is too weak to resist temptation. In Sonnet 134 we read: "*Thou wilt restore to be my comfort still: But thou wilt not, nor he will not be free.*" (Sonnet 134.4-5) The individual either refuses, or is unable to exercise the will to "*be free.*" In Sonnet 135, is the plea of one with a weak will to ask the Lord, "*whose will is large and spacious . . . to hide my will in thine.*" The answer to the plea of Sonnet 135 is in Sonnet 136 in which it is declared that one may be free by using the will only to seek and act according to God's law. "*Will will fulfil the treasure of thy love,*" and "*make but my name thy love, and love that still.*"

In Sonnet 137, one's "*eyes, corrupt*" and a heart which "*have erred*" going after temptations of the world, are captured in a "*false plague.*" Again and again, Shakespeare looks at man's eternal and internal struggle; the good and evil in the world at large, and the battle between the ego and soul. When the ego predominates, it is "*The expense of spirit in a waste of shame.*" (Sonnet 129.1) It is a battle which is not easily won because "*Nature (sovereign mistress over wrack), as thou goest onwards still will pluck thee back.*" (Sonnet 126.5)

Shakespeare states in Sonnet 138 that one may pretend, or delude oneself into thinking one does not know what choices are correct like some "*untutored youth, unlearned in the world's false subtleties,*" but the conscience within knows better. Man is gratefully endowed with a conscience which knows that the vainglorious desires of the heart are wrong, and that it is youthful and immature foolishness to go into advancing years yielding repeatedly to the same temptations. "*Thus vainly thinking that she thinks me young Although she knows my days are past their best.*"

Because "*heart and eyes have erred*" and are transferred over to the "*false plague*" (Sonnet 137.13-14) of the "*world's common place*" (Sonnet 137.10), bad habits continually win over well-reasoned judgment and conscience.

Why can't one recognize the "*false subtleties*" in life as "*lies*"? "*Wherefore says she not that she is unjust?*" Why can't I, says the Poet rhetorically, admit that I am old and mature enough to know better how to conduct my life? "*Wherefore say not I that I am old.*"

Having long indulged in satisfying selfish desires tends to create in one the belief that one is acting correctly. "*Love's best habit is in seeming trust*"; and an old fool does not want to admit his foolishness when he ought to have known better. "*And age in love loves not to have years told.*" Apparently Eve felt the same way after eating the apple: "And when the woman saw that the tree was good for food, and that it was pleasant to the eyes, and a tree to be desired to make one wise, she took of the fruit thereof, and did eat, and gave also unto her husband with her; and he did eat." **(Gen. 3:6)** Since Genesis, this internal struggle in man, whether to obey Divine Law, or go after temptations, has continued as Shakespeare points out.

One may choose to pursue the world's "*false subtleties*" that one loves like a "*blind fool*" (Sonnet 137.1) and plod through life deceiving one's true self and flattering the ego. In such an existence, "*thus is simple truth supprest.*" "*Therefore I lie with her, and she with me, And our faults by lies we flatter'd be.*"

SUGGESTED PASSAGES FROM SHAKESPEARE'S PLAYS

> "He that loves to be flattered is worthy of the flatterer." *Timon of Athens*, I.i.226-227
>
> "O that men's ears should be to counsel deaf, but not to flattery!" *Timon of Athens*, I.ii.249-250

BIBLICAL PASSAGE SUGGESTED BY SONNET 138

"None calleth for justice, nor any pleadeth for truth: they trust in vanity, and speak lies; they conceive mischief, and bring forth iniquity." **Isa. 59:4**

SONNET 139

O call not me to justify the wrong
That thy unkindness lays upon my heart;
Wound me not with thine eye, but with thy tongue;
Use power with power, and slay me not by art.
Tell me thou lov'st elsewhere; but in my sight,
Dear heart, forbear to glance thine eye aside;
What need'st thou wound with cunning when thy might
Is more than my o'erpress'd defence can bide?
Let me excuse thee: "Ah, my love well knows
Her pretty looks have been my enemies;
And therefore from my face she turns my foes,
That they elsewhere might dart their injuries."
Yet do not so; but since I am near slain,
Kill me outright with looks, and rid my pain.

THEME

A plea: "Heavenly Beloved, stop using evil temptations to wound me, but deliver me through Thy Divine Power and Grace immediately."

GLOSSARY

O call not me to justify the wrong That thy unkindness lays upon my heart; Wound me not with thine eye, but with thy tongue, Use power with power, and slay me not by art.

> Do not call on me to justify my wrong actions because it is Thy creation full of temptation that has influenced my heart, If I am to be wounded, do not do it by turning away your eye from me but with Thy chastising voice of conscience, use Thy true power over me directly, and do not influence me by the artifice of delusive temptation.

Tell me thou lov'st elsewhere; but in my sight, Dear heart, forbear to glance thine eye aside; What need'st thou wound with cunning when thy might is more than my o'erpress'd defence can bide?

> Plainly tell me Thy love is departed; but do so directly in

> my spiritual sight. Dear love of my heart, please do not close the eye of spiritual sight; why dost Thou cause my soul to be in pain by the wiles of ego temptations when Thy divine power alone could overcome any resistance on my part?

Let me excuse thee: "Ah, my love well knows Her pretty looks have been my enemies; And therefore from my face she turns my foes, That they elsewhere might dart their injuries."

> Let me make an excuse for Thee: "Ah, my Beloved knows that the pretty temptations in creation have been my enemies, and therefore She diverts my attention from evil so these earthy wiles might do harm elsewhere.

Yet do not so; but since I am near slain, Kill me outright with looks, and rid my pain.

> Yet do not do this, but since I am nearly slain, render me lifeless outright with spiritual sight and the breathless state of ecstasy, and rid my pain.

COMMENTARY

The Poet makes his plea to the Lord: "*slay me not by art.*" This art, or divine law in creation, is one in which man's eyes and heart are lured into the "*false plague.*" (Sonnet 137.14) Again and again one is played false by temptations or "*forged hooks.*" (Sonnet 137.7) This is just how things are: "*the wide world's common place.*" (Sonnet 137.10)

Repeated indulgence in earthly vanities, or following the desires of the heart, eventually leads one to question whether such actions are correct. "*When my love swears that she is made of truth, I do believe her, though I know she lies.*" (Sonnet 138.1-2) Yielding to "*the world's false subtleties*" continues as "*love's best habit is in seeming trust.*" Old habits persist and often without resolution. "*Therefore I lie with her, and she with me, And in our faults by lies we flatter'd be.*" (Sonnet 138.4, 11, 13-14)

In Sonnet 139, the Poet says "*O call not me to justify the wrong That thy unkindness lays upon my heart.*" In other words, do not call upon me to justify the order or harmony of things in creation whereby the battles between good and evil, and ego and soul, continue. I have eyes to see good or evil, and You created my eye and put before it temptations in this world. In this way, you "*wound me.*" Instead of temptations, speak to my soul directly, and I will listen. "*Wound me not with thine eye, but with thy tongue.*" Use Your Divine power to turn my heart's desires to you ("*Use power with power*"), and "*slay me not by art,*" meaning by the artifice of worldly allurements.

In several sonnets, Shakespeare refers to the spiritual eye which, when opened, brings one into a state of peace, joy, and grace. "*Mine eye hath play'd the painter and hath stell'd Thy beauty's form in table of my heart; . . . That hath his windows glazed with thine eyes. . . . Mine eyes have drawn thy shape, and thine for me Are windows to my breast, where-through the sun Delights to peep, to gaze therein on thee.*" (Sonnet 24.1, 2, 4, 10-12)

"The greatest scholar on earth cannot with all his wit imagine what this opening of the spiritual eye is, or fully declare it with his tongue, for it cannot be acquired by study or through human toil alone, but principally by the grace of the Holy Spirit." (Walter Hilton, *The Scale of Perfection*, p. 281)

So in Sonnet 139, the Poet makes the plea, "*Dear heart, forbear to glance thine eye aside.*" In other words, do not use the artifice of temptation to "*wound me,*" but with all of your "*power with power,*" which is "*more than my o'erpress'd defence can bide . . . rid my pain.*" Shakespeare is saying that worldly temptations are killing for they have corrupted eyes and heart into "*this false plague.*" (Sonnet 137.14) It would be better, says the Poet, if your "*Dear heart . . . in my sight,*" meaning the sight of the spiritual eye, would "*Kill me outright with looks.*" This is not literally to cause him death, but in one sense to cause the "*death*" in him of desires for worldly pleasures.

Again quoting the Christian mystic Walter Hilton: ". . . when a soul sighing to see the face of Jesus is touched through special grace of the Holy Spirit, it is suddenly changed and turned from the plight that it was in to another way of feeling. It is wonderfully separated from the love and pleasure of all earthy things and drawn first into itself, so much that it has lost the savor of the bodily life and everything that is, save only Jesus." (*The Scale of Perfection*, p. 281) If the Poet's spiritual eye is opened, this would end all suffering, so he pleads: "*Kill me outright with looks, and rid my pain.*"

BIBLICAL PASSAGES SUGGESTED BY SONNET 139

"For I know that thou wilt bring me to death, and to the house appointed for all living." **Job 30:23**

"I protest by your rejoicing which I have in Christ Jesus our Lord, I die daily." **1 Cor. 15:31**

"And if thou deal thus with me, kill me, I pray thee, out of hand, if I have found favor in thy sight; and let me not see my wretchedness." **Num. 11:15**

SONNET 140

Be wise as thou art cruel, do not press
My tongue-tied patience with too much disdain;
Lest sorrow lend me words, and words express
The manner of my pity-wanting pain.
If I might teach thee wit, better it were,
Though not to love, yet, love, to tell me so;
As testy sick men, when their deaths be near,
No news but health from their physicians know.
For, if I should despair, I should grow mad,
And in my madness might speak ill of thee:
Now this ill-wresting world is grown so bad,
Mad slanderers by mad ears believed be.
That I may not be so, nor thou belied,
Bear thine eyes straight, though thy proud heart go wide.

THEME

Often life seems so difficult with its many temptations. We might complain and lament at the many pitfalls, to a God who will always hear our supplications for relief and release in spite of our own shortcomings.

GLOSSARY

Be wise as thou art cruel, do not press my tongue-tied patience with too much disdain; Lest sorrow lend me words, and words express the manner of my pity-wanting pain.

> Be wise as Thou art cruel; do not oppress me so much with disdain that I can no longer hold my tongue, and then out of sorrow, I give voice to my unpitied pain.

If I might teach thee wit, better it were, Though not to love, yet, love, to tell me so; As testy sick men, when their deaths be near, No news but health from their physicians know.

> If it were possible to impart wisdom to Thee, it would be that it is better not to love (the things of this world)

> and yet have heavenly Love teach this to my heart; but stubborn, sick men on their death beds only hear words of good health from their doctors and nothing else.

For, if I should despair, I should grow mad, And in my madness might speak ill of thee: Now this ill-wresting world is grown so bad, Mad slanderers by mad ears believed be.

> If I should lose all hope, I would grow mad, and in such madness I might speak ill of Thee. These days everything people hear is interpreted in the worst possible way. Madmen who are slanderers are believed by deluded listeners.

That I may not be so, nor thou belied, Bear thine eyes straight, though thy proud heart go wide.

> So I may not become mad as they, nor Thou be slandered, hold my vision, these eyes that Thou gavest me, straight ahead, though this proud heart, with which Thou endowed me, strays from its mark.

COMMENTARY

Sonnet 139 is a plea to be released from "*pain*" in a time when the Poet declares: "*I am near slain.*" In Sonnet 140, the Poet pleads that wisdom be equal to the weight of cruelty. "*Be wise as thou art cruel.*" While he has restrained himself from verbally lashing out to this point, he pleads "*do not press my tongue-tied patience with too much disdain.*" In other words, do not oppress me with any more sorrow, "*Lest sorrow lend me words, and words express the manner of my pity-wanting pain.*" He is at breaking point and can bear no more. There is the feeling of being forlorn and unpitied ("*pity-wanting*"), which has added to the depth of pain.

It is going after vainglorious desires of the heart that has caused this sorrow. If the heart could be made more wise ("*If I might teach thee wit*") it might learn "*not to love*" worldly things, but it would be better if the heart could learn from a true spiritual love (as opposed to "*wit*") not to "*love*" or desire the material things in the "*world's common place.*" (Sonnet 137.10)

The heart has been habituated to swearing that "*truth*" is found in the world's "*false subtleties.*" (Sonnet 138.1, 4) So like a "*testy*" dying man, the heart does not listen to the truth but only hears what it wants to hear. "*As testy sick men, when their deaths be near, No news but health from their physicians know.*"

Helen Vendler, in her book *The Art of Shakespeare's Sonnets* (Cambridge: Harvard University Press, 2003), states that this Sonnet describes "chains of verbal and moral consequences that occur" within the sonnet. "These undeflectable chains stand symbolically for the absence of free will" (p. 592). So much of the discussion related to Sonnets 135-140 centers upon the lures of the world and how man's strength of reason and free will have been subverted by temptation. "*In things right true my heart and eyes have erred.*" (Sonnet 137.13) It is as if one does not have the free will to choose, or has lost the freedom through injudicious non-use.

In Sonnet 140, not only does the Poet describe that his sorrow is nearing breaking point, but should he "*despair*" he would "*grow mad,*" in a world filled with madness. "*For, if I should despair, I should grow mad, And in my madness might speak ill of thee: Now this ill-wresting world is grown so bad, Mad slanderers by mad ears believed be.*"

We see a little of the lamentation of Job in these remarks. (See Bible Passages that follow.)

The Lord has given eyes to see good, and a heart to love, but the Poet says "*my heart and eyes have erred, And to this false plague are they now transferred.*" (Sonnet 137.13-14) So the Poet pleads for a spiritual opening of his eyes, even though his heart still loves proudly things of the world. "*Bear thine eyes straight, though thy proud heart go wide.*" In this sense, to "*Bear thine eyes*" means to lift them up, or support these eyes ("*thine eyes*") that the Lord has given him.

BIBLICAL PASSAGES SUGGESTED BY SONNET 140

"I was at ease, but he hath broken me asunder: he hath also taken me by my neck, and shaken me to pieces, and set me up for his mark." **Job 16:12**

"My soul is weary of my life; I will leave my complaint upon myself; I will speak in the bitterness of my soul." **Job 10:1**

"But ye have set at nought all my counsel, and would none of my reproof: I also will laugh at your calamity; I will mock when your fear cometh; When your fear cometh as desolation, and your destruction cometh as a whirlwind; when distress and anguish cometh upon you. Then shall they call upon me, but I will not answer; they shall seek me early, but they shall not find me: For that they hated knowledge, and did not choose the fear of the Lord: They would none of my counsel: they despised all my reproof. Therefore shall they eat of the fruit of their own way, and be filled with their own devices." **Prov. 1:25-31**

"Keep thy heart with all diligence; for out of it are the issues of life. Put away from thee a froward mouth, and perverse lips put far from thee. Let thine eyes look right on, and let thine eyelids look straight before thee." **Prov. 4:23-25**

"We grope for the wall like the blind, and we grope as if we had no eyes: we stumble at noon day as in the night; we are in desolate places as dead men." **Isa. 59:10**

"But if thine eye be evil, thy whole body shall be full of darkness. If therefore the light that is in thee be darkness, how great is that darkness!" **Matt. 6:23**

"Turn away mine eyes from beholding vanity; and quicken thou me in thy way." **Ps. 119:37**

SONNET 141

In faith, I do not love thee with mine eyes,
For they in thee a thousand errors note;
But 'tis my heart that loves what they despise,
Who, in despite of view, is pleas'd to dote.
Nor are mine ears with thy tongue's tune delighted;
Nor tender feeling to base touches prone,
Nor taste nor smell desire to be invited
To any sensual feast with thee alone;
But my five wits nor my five senses can
Dissuade one foolish heart from serving thee,
Who leaves unsway'd the likeness of a man,
Thy proud heart's slave and vassal wretch to be:
Only my plague thus far I count my gain,
That she makes me sin awards me pain.

THEME

Man's intellect and reason are awakened, as is his faith, by spiritual introspection; but the earthly desires of the heart, and man's pride, do not easily yield, and he must keep up the battle between soul and ego until all sensuality and pride are vanquished.

GLOSSARY

In faith, I do not love thee with mine eyes, For they in thee a thousand errors note; But 'tis my heart that loves what they despise, Who, in despite of view, is pleas'd to dote.

> My love is true and constant, and my eyes truly see the faults and temptations in this world, but the desires of my heart, in contemptuous disregard of my eyes' truthful perceptions of love and sin, are content to dote upon temptation.

Nor are mine ears with thy tongue's tune delighted; Nor tender feeling to base touches prone, Nor taste nor smell desire to be invited To any sensual feast with thee alone;

> Neither my ears, which hear truth, are tempted by the tune of physical sounds; nor is the tender loving of my heart attracted by base physical allurements, nor taste, nor smell have any desire to be invited to any sensual feast where unity with Thee alone is sufficient.

But my five wits nor my five senses can Dissuade one foolish heart from serving thee, Who leaves unsway'd the likeness of a man, Thy proud heart's slave and vassal wretch to be:

> But neither my reasoning intellect, nor my fine senses have the power to deter one foolish heart from serving as an example of Thy will. One who acts as a slave and a groveling servitor to his prideful heart and earthly desires is left by Thee to the likeness of an egotistical man.

Only my plague thus far I count my gain, That she makes me sin awards me pain.

> My error-strewn life I count as my gain, and that which leads me to sin rewards me with the instructive judgment of suffering.

COMMENTARY

In contrast to eyes that "*see not what they see*" (Sonnet 137.2), the eyes in Sonnet 141 have changed. These "*in thee a thousand errors note*," but they do not alter the inner "*faith*," which seems now to be awakened. The eyes of Sonnet 141 are also not those of Sonnet 137, which "*have erred, And to this false plague are they now transferred*." (Sonnet 137.13-14) The eyes of Sonnet 141 now "*despise*" the false "*thousand errors*" to which formerly "*the judgment of my heart is tied*." (Sonnet 137.8) In Sonnet 141, the heart is attracted to temptations and "*loves what they* [the eyes] *despise*." There is a contrast to the previous declaration of Sonnet 137.1 in which the eyes were "*blind*"; in Sonnet 141 they are now are able to distinguish between "*faith*" and the "*thousand errors*" that exist. "I have heard of thee by the hearing of the ear: but now mine eye seeth thee. Wherefore I abhor myself, and repent in dust and ashes." **(Job 42:5-6)**

Sonnet 141 goes on to state: "*nor are mine ears with thy tongue's tune delighted; nor tender feeling to base touches prone. Nor taste nor smell desire to be invited To any sensual feast with thee alone:*" Just as stated in Job, above, there is an awakening, a perception that is beyond the physical, material senses. "I have heard of thee by the hearing of the ear: but now mine eye seeth thee." **(Job 42:5)** "Thine eyes shall see the king in his beauty." **(Isa. 33:17)** These are eyes that are "*in faith*" and perceive that which the physical eyes cannot. "Now faith is the substance of things hoped for, the evidence of things not seen." **(Heb. 11:1)** This faith does not come by hearing delightful words of the human tongue: "*nor are mine ears with thy tongue's tune delighted.*" The "*faith*" with which the Poet describes as being invested in line 1 is further described thus: "So then faith cometh by hearing, and hearing by the word of God." **(Rom. 10:17)**

"*Nor tender feeling to base touches prone*" means that sensual experience is eschewed in favor of soft, loving sensations of a spiritual nature. "Thy lips, O my spouse, drop as the honeycomb: honey and milk are under thy tongue; and the smell of thy garments is like the smell of Lebanon." **(Song of Sol. 4:11)** These Biblical verses show that the physical senses have an aspect that transcends earthly, material sensualities. One may have the wit to reason and the heightened senses or sensibilities to perceive a higher truth, but a heart that "*is pleased to dote*" is still mired in base habits, and "*loves what they* [the opened eyes] *despise,*" and "*leaves unswayed the likeness of a man.*"

In Sonnet 141 we have a "*foolish heart*" that has sold the divinity of man, made in the likeness of God, to one who is made in the "*likeness of a man.*" He is still of "*the wide world's common place*" (Sonnet 137.10), the slave of a "*proud heart,*" a wretched servitor that "*loves what they despise.*" He is not one who has dominion "over all the earth" **(Gen. 1:26)** as a master, but he is a "*vassal wretch.*"

In spite of this, the Poet says that "*only my plague thus far I count my gain, That she that makes me sin awards me pain.*" (Sonnet 141.13-14) "*She*" is the "*(sovereign mistress over wrack)*" (Sonnet 126.5) who keeps her "*audit,*" but the Poet with eyes now opened truly sees. "*For they in thee a thousand errors note.*"

The Poet keeps his own audit now and because of his "*plague*" can count his "*gain.*" The "*false plague*" to which the Poet's "*eyes, corrupt by over partial looks*" (Sonnet 137.14, 5) were condemned, seems to have been lifted, or healed by "*faith.*" "Blessed is the man whom thou chasteneth, O Lord, and teachest him out of thy law." **(Ps. 94:12)**

St. Augustine: "But what do I love, when I love thee? Not beauty of bodies, nor the fair harmony of time, nor the brightness of the light, so gladsome to our eyes, nor sweet melodies of varied songs, nor the fragrant smell of flowers, and ointments, and spices, not manna and honey, not limbs acceptable to embracements of flesh. None of these I love, when I love my God; and yet I love a kind of light, and melody and fragrance, and meat, and embracement, when I love my God, the light, melody, fragrance, meat, embracement of my inner man" (*Confessions of St. Augustine*, pp. 211-212; compare to Sonnet 141.4-8). "My will the enemy held, and thence made a chain for me, and found me. For a froward will, was lust made; and lust served, become custom; and custom not resisted, became necessity. . . . But that new will which had begun in me, freely to serve Thee, and wish to enjoy Thee, O God, the assured pleasantness, was not yet able to overcome my former willfulness, strengthened by age. Thus did my two wills, one new, and the other old, one carnal, the other spiritual, struggle within me; and by their discord, undid my soul. Lust served became custom or habit which is not easily lodged" (*Confessions of St. Augustine*, p. 159).

When reading Sonnet 141, it is clear that the eyes are newly awakened, as is "*faith*"; however, "*the heart that loves what they despise . . . is pleas'd to dote.*" St. Augustine explains that his "new will" struggled with his old "carnal" will, which is like the will or the desires of the "*foolish heart*" in Sonnet 141 to obstinately, "*in despite of view,*" to go the way it "*pleas'd.*" The result is that he is left in "*the likeness of a man,*" or as Augustine states it: the struggle of wills "undid my soul."

So the Poet finally considers the "*plague*" as "*gain.*" This can only be so if his afflictions have a refining influence on his life. "*That she makes me sin awards me pain.*"

BIBLICAL PASSAGES SUGGESTED BY SONNET 141

"That the trial of your faith, being much more precious than of gold that perisheth, though it be tried with fire, might be found unto praise and honor and glory at the appearing of Jesus Christ." **1 Pet. 1:7**

"And not only so, but we glory in tribulations also: knowing that tribulation worketh patience; And patience, experience; and experience, hope." **Rom. 5:3-4**

SONNET 142

Love is my sin, and thy dear virtue hate,
Hate of my sin, grounded on sinful loving.
O but with mine compare thou thine own state,
And thou shalt find it merits not reproving,
Or if it do, not from those lips of thine,
That have profaned their scarlet ornaments,
And sealed false bonds of love as oft as mine,
Robbed others' beds' revenues of their rents.
Be it lawful I love thee as thou lov'st those
Whom thine eyes woo as mine importune thee:
Root pity in thy heart, that when it grows
Thy pity may deserve to pitied be.
If thou dost seek to have what thou dost hide,
By self-example mayst thou be denied.

THEME

The Lord is hidden behind the veil of creation in which man is tempted to sin. If the Lord is to receive greater love of His children with of all their heart, mind, soul, and strength, then He must show more pity, compassion, and love and tempt his children less.

GLOSSARY

Love is my sin, and thy dear virtue hate, Hate of my sin, grounded on sinful loving. O but with mine compare thou thine own state, And thou shalt find it merits not reproving,

> Loving the allurements of this world is my sin, and Thy dear unrelenting virtue is to hate or abhor my sin, which is based on loving and desiring earthly things. But compare my state of being, with Thine own Creation (state), and Thou shalt find it does not deserve censure.

Or if it do, not from those lips of thine, That have profaned their scarlet ornaments, And sealed false bonds of love as oft as mine, Robbed others' beds' revenues of their rents.

> Or if it does, it cannot be from false speaking lips whose lusty, scarlet temptations have sealed the fate of many such as I, who have loved worldly sin, and which has stolen the rightful expectations of those whose beds lie empty or are rented in mourning for their loss.

Be it lawful I love thee as thou lov'st those Whom thine eyes woo as mine importune thee: Root pity in thy heart, that when it grows Thy pity may deserve to pitied be.

> As it is the law of the universe, I love Thee as Thou dost love those who are tempted by sin. Plant the seed of compassion more deeply in Thy heart for Thy children. When it grows, the loss that Thou dost feel for not having the love of Thy wayward children may then be pitied.

If thou dost seek to have what thou dost hide, By self-example mayst thou be denied.

> If Thou dost seek the love of thy children but continue to hide behind the veil of this alluring creation, then the example set, you will be denied the complete, loving surrender of Thy children's love.

COMMENTARY

The Poet seems to complain to the Lord that the allurements of the world have made "*love my sin.*" The exacting nature of the Lord is to punish sin: "*thy dear virtue hate.*" The word "*dear*" here means costly to the sinner as well as a dear, godly quality.

The Poet argues that the Lord should find fault for man's sinning nature in the way the world is arranged with temptations, which draw man away from God. "*O but with mine* [sin] *compare thou thine own state.*"

In all fairness, says the Poet, the "*scarlet ornaments,*" or sinful temptations, have "*sealed false bonds of love.*" In other words, man has falsely or wrongly loved the allurements in creation instead of the Creator. This is enough to "*dissuade one foolish heart from serving thee.*" (Sonnet 141.10)

The Poet loves the Lord as much as the Lord loves his erring children. "*Be it lawful I love thee as thou lov'st those Whom thine eyes woo.*" Even as the Poet's eyes long to see God, "*as mine importune thee.*"

The Poet says in effect to the Lord: "Have more pity and compassion and do not hide Thyself so much behind the veil of creation." It is because the Lord is so much unseen, that His children continue to seek after worldly pleasures instead of spiritual ones. "*Root pity in thy heart, that when it grows Thy pity may deserve to pitied be. If thou dost seek to have what thou dost hide,* [the love of God and the love of His children in return] *By self-example mayst thou be denied.*" As long as You, Lord, are out of reach and sight, the love of your children will be denied you.

The dichotomies of Sonnet 142 are apparent and pointed. That "*love*" is associated with "*sin*" and "*hate*" with "*virtue*" is seemingly incongruent. Shakespeare is saying too that the Lord that wants the love of His children is seemingly inconsistent: He has created a world full of sinful "*scarlet ornaments*" that bind man falsely to a love of all worldly things, which is man's "*sin.*" If the first commandment is to love the Lord, thy God with all thy heart, then why, Shakespeare chides metaphorically, "dost Thou place the apple in the Garden of Eden and the serpent to deceive Eve into sin?"

In a manner of speaking, the Poet makes a plea for mankind: Lord, "*Root pity in thy heart.*" If Thou truly "*seek to have what thou dost hide,*" Lord, that "*sin*" is to be hated and that "*Love*" is to be man's virtue, then the nature of temptation and sin in creation must, out of pity, change. If not, "*by self-example mayst thou be denied.*"

BIBLICAL PASSAGES SUGGESTED BY SONNET 142

"Like as a father pitieth his children, so the Lord pitieth them that fear him." **Ps. 103:13**

"In all their affliction he was afflicted, and the angel of his presence saved them: in his love and in his pity he redeemed them; and he bare them, and carried them all the days of old." **Isa. 63:9**

"With my soul have I desired thee in the night; yea, with my spirit within me will I seek thee early: for when thy judgments are in the earth, the inhabitants of the world will learn righteousness." **Isa. 26:9**

"Then Job answered and said, Even to day is my complaint bitter: my stroke is heavier than my groaning. Oh that I knew where I might find him! That I might come even to his seat! I would order my cause before him, and fill my mouth with arguments. I would know the words which he would answer me, and understand what he would say unto me. Will he plead against me with his great power? No; but he would put strength in me. There the righteous might dispute with him; so should I be delivered for ever from my judge. Behold, I go forward, but he is not there; and backward, but I cannot perceive him: On the left hand, where he doth work, but I cannot behold him, he hideth himself on the right hand, that I cannot see him." **Job 23:1-9**

"Give ear to my prayer, O God; and hide not thyself from my supplication. Attend unto me, and hear me: I mourn in my complaint, and made a noise." **Ps. 55:1-2**

"Hath God forgotten to be gracious? hath he in anger shut up his tender mercies?" **Ps. 77:9**

"How long wilt thou forget me, O Lord? for ever? how long wilt thou hide thy face from me?" **Ps. 13:1**

"Awake, why sleepest thou, O Lord? arise, cast us not off for ever. Wherefore hidest thou thy face, and forgettest our affliction and our oppression? For our soul is bowed down to the dust: our belly cleaveth unto the earth. Arise for our help, and redeem us for thy mercies' sake." **Ps. 44:23-26**

"If thou, Lord, shouldest mark iniquities, O Lord, who shall stand?" **Ps. 130:3**

SONNET 143

Lo, as a careful housewife runs to catch
One of her feathered creatures broke away,
Sets down her babe and makes all swift dispatch
In pursuit of the thing she would have stay,
Whilst her neglected child holds her in chase,
Cries to catch her whose busy care is bent
To follow that which flies before her face,
Not prizing her poor infant's discontent:
So runn'st thou after that which flies from thee,
Whilst I, thy babe, chase thee afar behind;
And play the mother's part, kiss me, be kind.
So will I pray that thou mayst have thy Will,
If thou turn back and my loud crying still.

THEME

Man, in pursuit of worldly things, acts at the expense of the soul's happiness. When man turns from temptation, the Lord responds and brings peace to the soul.

GLOSSARY

Lo, as a careful housewife runs to catch One of her feathered creatures broke away, Sets down her babe and makes all swift dispatch In pursuit of the thing she would have stay,

> Just as a dutiful housewife runs to catch one of her feathered creatures that gets away and puts her little babe down to run in swift pursuit after the things she wishes to stay with her.

Whilst her neglected child holds her in chase, Cries to catch her whose busy care is bent To follow that which flies before her face, Not prizing her poor infant's discontent:

> While her neglected child chases tearfully after its mother, whose only care at the moment is to follow that which flies away from her, not at all showing concern for

> her poor unhappy infant:

So runn'st thou after that which flies from thee, Whilst I, thy babe, chase thee afar behind; And play the mother's part, kiss me, be kind.

> So do you run after that which flies away from you, while I, your precious babe, chase you from far behind; but if you do capture your hopes and dreams, turn back and play the part of a mother, kiss me and be kind.

So will I pray that thou mayst have thy Will, If thou turn back and my loud crying still.

> So I will pray that Thou mayst have Thy Will fulfilled, If Thou turnst back to me and dissolve my anguished tears into stillness.

COMMENTARY

It is the "*wide world's commonly place*" (Sonnet 137.10) to chase after "*creatures*" as if they are more important than the "*babe*" or "*child*," which is the tender soul within. Mankind pursues desires of the heart and eyes that "*have erred*" (Sonnet 137.13) and are "*transferred*" to the "*false plague*" of the world's allurements. (Sonnet 137.14)

In such a state of delusion, one sacrifices that which is dear and precious, like a mother's "*babe*" longing for attention. "*Cries to catch her whose busy care is bent To follow that which flies before her face, Not prizing her poor infant's discontent.*"

In the Bible, it is usually sin or evil that flies in the face of goodness ("*flies before her face*"). "And took off their chariot wheels, that they drave them heavily: so that the Egyptians said, Let us flee from the face of Israel; for the Lord fighteth for them against the Egyptians." **(Exod. 14:25)** Also: "And he said, Hagar, Sarah's maid, whence camest thou? And whither wilt thou go? And she said, I flee from the face of my mistress Sarah." **(Gen. 16:8)**

In Sonnet 143, the housewife has more concern for the "*feathered creatures*" she pursues with "*all swift dispatch.*" This is in contrast to the parable of the lost sheep. "What man of you, having an hundred sheep, if he lose one of them, doth not leave the ninety and nine in the wilderness, and go after that which is lost, until he find it?" **(Luke 15:4)**

Once that which was lost is found "there is joy in the presence of the angels of God over one sinner that repenteth." **(Luke 15:10)**

In Sonnet 143, the babe wants the "*housewife*" (symbolically man's wayward desires that have been the cause of "*false bonds of love*" [Sonnet 142.7] or "*false plague*" [Sonnet 137.14]) to return to the Spirit in kisses and kindness. "*But if thou catch thy hope, turn back to me, and play the mother's part, kiss me and be kind.*"

In the Bible, when the prodigal son returns to the Father here is what occurs: "And he arose, and came to his father. But when he was yet a great way off, his father saw him, and had compassion, and ran, and fell on his neck, and kissed him." **(Luke 15:20)**

The Poet says that he will pray that the Divine Will may be fulfilled. "*So will I pray that thou mayst have they Will.*" This is the Will of Sonnet 135 (See discussion to Sonnet 135).

As in the parables of the lost sheep or that of the prodigal son, it is to the Will of God that His children return. Man, in order to "*turn back*" must regain his "*hope*" or faith in the Lord. "*But if thou catch thy hope, turn back to me.*" "Casting down imaginations, and every high thing that exalteth itself against the knowledge of God, and bringing into captivity every thought to the obedience of Christ." **(2 Cor. 10:5)**

Note how the housewife wishes to capture the temptation that "*flies before her face.*" In contrast, one who catches his "*hope*" is like one who, in Second Corinthians above, brings "into captivity every thought to the obedience of Christ." These were wayward thoughts that fled from the spiritual realm. The "obedience of Christ" is the Divine "*Will*" in line 13 of the Sonnet.

Once one returns to the spiritual path, the "*loud crying*" is stilled. "As for such as turn aside unto their crooked ways, the Lord shall lead them forth with the workers of iniquity: but peace shall be upon Israel." **(Ps. 125:5)**

"Turn again our captivity, O Lord, as the streams in the south. They that sow in tears shall reap in joy." **(Ps. 126:4-5)**

Finally, it is only when one's desires conform to the Divine Will that the soul is quieted. In such a state of right action, the Spirit can "*return*" or once again be reflected in the soul. "*If thou turn back and my loud crying still.*"

"When he giveth quietness, who then can make trouble? and when he hideth his face, who then can behold him? whether it be done against a nation, or against a man only." **(Job 34:29)**

In the poem "The Hound of Heaven" by Francis Thompson, man flies from the Lord.

> I fled Him, down the labyrinthine ways
> of my own mind. . . .
> [The voice of the Lord is heard by the one in flight:]
> Lo, all things fly thee, for thou fliest Me! . . .
> Whom wilt thou find to love ignoble thee,
> Save Me, save only Me?
> All which I took from thee I did but take,
> Not for thy harms,
> But just that thou might'st seek it in My arms.
> All which thy child's mistake
> Fancies are lost, I have stored for thee at home:
> Rise, clasp My hand, and come. . . .
> Ah, fondest, blindest,weakest,
> I am He Whom thou seekest!

SONNET 144

Two loves I have of comfort and despair,
Which like two spirits do suggest me still:
The better angel is a man right fair,
The worser spirit a woman, colour'd ill.
To win me soon to hell, my female evil
Tempteth my better angel from my side,
And would corrupt my saint to be a devil,
Wooing his purity with her foul pride.
And whether that my angel be turn'd fiend
Suspect I may, but not directly tell;
But being both from me, both to each friend
I guess one angel in another's hell.
Yet this shall I ne'er know, but live in doubt,
Till my bad angel fire my good one out.

THEME

There is an ever-raging battle in man between the ego and the soul. Man must learn to use free will guided by wisdom to avoid the avalanche of ever-present temptations and ego desires. Man's temperament is seemingly ever in flux until he is irrevocably established on the correct path heavenward.

GLOSSARY

Two loves I have of comfort and despair, Which like two spirits do suggest me still: The better angel is a man right fair, The worser spirit a woman, colour'd ill.

> There is within me a dualistic nature of good and evil, and right and wrong, which still alternate in their capacity to move me one way or another; the stronger side is ruled by wisdom and right activity, and the lesser by my errant desires and emotions gone awry.

To win me soon to hell, my female evil Tempteth my better angel from my side, And would corrupt my saint to be a devil, Wooing his purity with her foul pride.

> Leading down the road to despair, my emotional ego-desires overcome my self-discrimination, and I am swayed from lofty purposes and pursuits and am again tempted into selfish acts, bowing to vanity and worldly allurements.

And whether that my angel be turn'd fiend Suspect I may, but not directly tell; But being both from me, both to each friend I guess one angel in another's hell.

> I do not know to what depths my soul has plunged, ruled alternately by ego likes or dislikes for this and that, ego and soul are lost to me and my soul may be completely identified with my ego, as in some hell, but I am uncertain:

Yet this shall I ne'er know, but live in doubt, Till my bad angel fire my good one out.

> Nor, will I ever know, till my soul finally extinguishes the ego's hellish fires.

COMMENTARY

In Sonnet 144 Shakespeare continues the theme of the battle between the soul and the worldly-oriented ego. "*Two loves I have of comfort and despair, Which like two spirits do suggest me still.*" The "*comfort*" is the soul aspect of man, and "*despair*" ensues from pursuit of desires of the ego. The "*better angel*" is a virtuous "*man*," and the "*worser spirit*" is a "*woman, colour'd ill,*" being that aspect of the nature that is attracted to worldly temptations.

Temptation is the ammunition used by "*my female evil*" to "*corrupt my saint to be a devil*"; "*my female evil Tempteth my better angel from my side.*" It is the sinful character of pride, inherent in the worldly ego, which distracts the "*saint.*" "*Wooing his purity with her foul pride.*" It is a seemingly endless ebb and flow, a push-pull of the "*two spirits* [which] *do suggest me still.*"

Shakespeare states clearly that the "*spirits*" to which he is referring are both part of his own nature. He makes no adverse judgment about them. "*But being both from me, both to each friend.*" Whether what seems alluring or attractive to "*my angel*" will result in the "*angel being turn'd fiend*" remains uncertain. "*Yet this shall I ne'er know, but live in doubt.*" Until the "*better angel*" extinguishes the "*fire*" of temptation, or is otherwise insulated from "*foul pride,*" the battle for supremacy will continue: "*till my bad angel fire my good one out.*"

The reference to the "*worser spirit a woman colour'd ill*" and "*my female evil*" are not aspersions cast against women. In the esoteric sense, the analogy of the sensuous mind to the female, and the wisdom-guided mind of discrimination to the male has been used by Christian saints and mystics, including the fourteenth century mystic, Walter Hilton. He has stated that the lower, or sensory, mind is like a woman who must be controlled or dominated by the higher mind or consciousness, which Hilton says is likened to a man (*The Scale of Perfection*, p. 213). There is also an obvious Biblical allusion to the female Eve whose bite of the apple brings Adam (man) to the fall. We have seen throughout the "dark lady" sonnets this feminine reference in which the woman, whose "*mistress' eyes are raven black*" (Sonnet 127.9), represents in man the self-centered ego that opposes or battles the soul. In the cosmic sense this refers to the battle between Satan and the Divine or evil against good, perpetually existing in creation trying to "*corrupt my saint to be a devil.*"

St. Augustine: "Lamentable joys strive with joyous sorrows: and on which side is the victory, I know not. Woe is me! Lord have pity on me. My evil sorrows strive with my good joys: and on which side is the victory I know not. . . . Is not the life of man upon the earth all trial, without any interval?" (*Confessions of St. Augustine*, pp. 232-233)

SUGGESTED PASSAGES FROM SHAKESPEARE'S PLAYS

> "My brain I'll prove the female to my soul,
> My soul the father; and these two beget
> A generation of still-breeding thoughts,
> And these same thoughts people this little world."
> *Richard II*, V.v.6-10

> "You ever-gentle gods, take my breath from me;
> Let not my worser spirit tempt me again
> To die before you please."
> *King Lear*, IV.6.218-221

BIBLICAL PASSAGES SUGGESTED BY SONNET 144

"Submit yourselves therefore to God, and he will draw nigh to you. Cleanse your hands, ye sinners; and purify your hearts, ye double minded." **James 4:7**

"I find then a law, that, when I would do good, evil is present within me. For I delight in the law of God after the inward man: But I see another law in my members, warring against the law of my mind, and bringing me into captivity to the law of sin which is in my members. O wretched man that I am! Who shall deliver me from the body of this death? I thank God through Jesus Christ our Lord. So then with the mind I myself serve the law of God; but with the flesh the law of sin." **Rom. 7:21-25**

SONNET 145

Those lips that Love's own hand did make,
Breath'd forth the sound that said "I hate"
To me that languished for her sake:
But when she saw my woeful state,
Straight in her heart did mercy come,
Chiding that tongue that ever sweet
Was used in giving gentle doom;
And taught it thus anew to greet:
"I hate," she alter'd with an end,
That follow'd it as gentle day
Doth follow night, who like a fiend
From heaven to hell is flown away.
"I hate" from hate away she threw,
And sav'd my life, saying "Not you."

THEME

The theme of this Sonnet is expressed in Psalms: "The Lord is nigh unto them that are of a broken heart; and saveth such as be of a contrite spirit." **(Ps. 34:18)**

GLOSSARY

Those lips that Love's own hand did make, Breath'd forth the sound that said "I hate" To me that languished for her sake: But when she saw my woeful state,

> The lips made by Love's own hand breathed forth the sound that said "I hate" to me who languished for her sake: But when she saw my sad state.

Straight in her heart did mercy come, Chiding that tongue that ever sweet Was used in giving gentle doom; And taught it thus anew to greet.

> Quickly was her heart filled with compassion, chiding that tongue that caringly was used to give me instructive correction and taught it to greet me differently,

"I hate," she alter'd with an end That follow'd it as gentle day Doth follow night,

who like a fiend From heaven to hell is flown away.

> And putting an end to "I hate," substituting other words which like the gentle day follow the dark night, who like a fiend is cast flying unto hell.

"I hate" from hate away she threw, And sav'd my life, saying "Not you."

> "I hate" from hateful judgment she cast away and saved my life, saying "not you."

COMMENTARY

In Sonnet 142.2 we read that "*hate of my sin*" is the nature of the law of Creation. The Poet calls this "*hate*," "*thy dear virtue.*" (Sonnet 142.1) It is a virtue because sin begets the suffering that prods man to turn from sin to spirituality. "*That she makes me sin awards me pain*" (Sonnet 141.14) (See discussion to Sonnet 141).

The "*sound that said 'I hate'*" is the Poet's own conscience that speaks to him. It is the inner voice that speaks to each and every one of us. "Wherefore ye must needs be subject, not only for wrath, but also for conscience sake." **(Rom. 13:5)** "For our rejoicing is this, the testimony of our conscience, that in simplicity and godly sincerity, not with fleshly wisdom, but by the grace of God, we have had our conversation in the world, and more abundantly to you-ward." **(2 Cor. 1:12)**

The Poet "*languished for her sake*" means for "conscience sake" **(Rom. 13:5)**, for the sake of needing relief from the "*false plague*" (Sonnet 137.14) and "*sealed false bonds of love*" (Sonnet 142.7), for which he feels the "*hate of my sin , grounded on sinful loving.*" (Sonnet 142.2) The weight of sin led to a conscience so heavy with guilt that the Poet could hear the inner voice, i.e., "*the lips of Love*" breathe "*forth the sound that said 'I hate'.*"

We read in Sonnet 142 that the Poet's eyes "*importune thee*"; that is, they seek a comforting response. The Poet feels like the abandoned "*poor infant*" (Sonnet 143.8) who is left behind by the Lord. This is the Lord of the parable of the lost sheep who runs after the wayward ones to bring them home. (See discussion to Sonnet 143)

In Sonnet 142, the Poet's plea to the Lord is to "*Root pity in thy heart.*" (Sonnet 142.11) In Sonnet 145, he says that "*when she saw my woeful state, straight in her heart did mercy come.*" It is as if the mother in Sonnet 143 heeded the child's "*discontent.*" "*And play the mother's part, kiss, be kind.*" (Sonnet 143.11)

The "*fiend*" of grief, and the Poet's "*woeful state*" are lifted and dissolved by the Lord's ("*mother's*") response. "*'I hate' from hate away she threw, and saved my life, saying 'not you'.*" Ever and anon does the Lord heed the sincere cries of His children and give mercy and comfort.

Sonnet 145, it seems, would have been more appropriately placed after Sonnet 143. The return of the mother in Sonnet 143 will "*my* [the poet's] *loud crying still.*" (Sonnet 143.14) In Sonnet 145, we see that in "*her heart did mercy come.*" This caused the "*fiend*" to fly away. As we saw in Sonnet 143, "*that which flies before her face*" is sin in the Bible verses. Throwing away the pronouncement "*I hate*" is the sign of mercy and forgiveness of sin. In stating that she "*sav'd my life,*" the Poet is expressing the feeling that he has been forgiven, and the judgment of damnation has been lifted. "*Not you*" means that he is free of the judgment of "*hell,*" and that he has been "*sav'd.*" "I acknowledged my sin unto thee, and mine iniquity have I not hid. I said, I will confess my transgressions unto the Lord; and thou forgavest the iniquity of my sin. Selah." **(Ps. 32:5)**

BIBLICAL PASSAGES SUGGESTED BY SONNET 145

"If we confess our sins, he is faithful and just to forgive us our sins, and to cleanse us from all unrighteousness." **1 John 1:9**

"O my God, I am ashamed and blush to lift up my face to thee, my God: for our iniquities are increased over our head, and our trespass is grown up unto the heavens." **Ezra 9:6**

"The Lord is merciful and gracious, slow to anger and plenteous in mercy. He will not always chide: neither will he keep his anger for ever. He hath not dealt with us after our sins; nor rewarded us according to our iniquities. For as the heaven is high above the earth, so great is his mercy toward them that fear him. As far as the east is from the west, so far hath he removed our transgressions from us. Like as a father pitieth his children, so the Lord pitieth them that fear him. For he knoweth our frame; he remembered that we are dust." **Ps. 103:8-14**

"Say to them that are of a fearful heart, Be strong, fear not: behold, your God will come with vengeance, even God with a recompense; he will come and save you." **Isa. 35:4**

"I will praise thee: for thou hast heard me, and art become my salvation." **Ps. 118:21**

"For by grace are ye saved through faith; and that not of yourselves: it is the gift of God." **Eph. 2:8**

SONNET 146

Poor soul, the centre of my sinful earth,
My sinful earth, these rebel powers that thee array.
Why dost thou pine within and suffer dearth,
Painting thy outward walls so costly gay?
Why so large cost, having so short a lease,
Dost thou upon thy fading mansion spend?
Shall worms, inheritors of this excess,
Eat up thy charge? Is this thy body's end?
Then, soul, live thou upon thy servant's loss,
And let that pine to aggravate thy store;
Buy terms divine in selling hours of dross;
Within be fed, without be rich no more:
So shalt thou feed on Death, that feeds on men,
And Death once dead, there's no more dying then.

THEME

Our beautiful, limitless souls are seemingly trapped in these temporal bodies with an endless array of tempting desires. By eschewing sensual excesses, and ridding the soul of dross it shall overcome the fetters of life and defeat even "the last enemy," death.

GLOSSARY

Poor soul, the centre of my sinful earth, My sinful earth, these rebel powers that thee array, Why dost thou pine within and suffer dearth, Painting thy outward walls so costly gay?

> My poor soul identified with this pleasure-seeking body is fooled by the worldly-oriented senses that have been given me. Why, my captive soul, are you pining away in this body and suffering from lack, while the ego dresses up this bodily form with expensive outward garb?

Why so large cost, having so short a lease, Dost thou upon they fading mansion spend? Shall worms, inheritors of this excess, Eat up thy charge? Is this thy body's end?

> Why spend so much on an earthly body when life is so short? Will the worms of disillusionment that inherit this body pay the price of a life lived in excess? Is this the sad meaning of it all?

Then, soul, live thou upon they servant's loss, And let that pine to aggravate thy store; Buy terms divine in selling hours of dross; Within be fed, without be rich no more:

> Then, soul, live by decreasing attention to this temporal body and let that lessened attention on sensory desires increase the soul's self realization. Experience divine gifts by ceasing wasteful, materialistic desires. Feed on the Divine Light within and not on outward materialism.

So shalt thou feed on Death, that feeds on men, And Death once dead, there's no more dying.

> So you shall then know the soul's immortality, destroying worldly desires that are mortal to men's souls. And once the soul is freed it is forever established in everlasting life, never to taste again of bodily death.

COMMENTARY

Shakespeare is directly addressing the "*soul*" as if in a battle against his "*sinful earth*" whose "*rebel powers*" conspire to make the soul "*poor.*" The Poet questions the "*soul*" as to why it would "*pine and suffer dearth*" as a result of choosing to paint "*thy outward walls so costly gay?*" The body is only a temporary abode of the soul, "*having so short a lease.*" Shakespeare calls the body the soul's "*fading mansion*" unlike the heavenly mansion referred to in the Bible. "In my Father's house are many mansions." **(John 14:2)**

There is no wisdom in "*painting*" or indulging the bodily residence. The Poet asks: "*Shall worms, inheritors of this excess, Eat up thy charge? Is this thy body's end?*" What is needed is for the soul to "*live . . . upon thy servant's loss.*" The soul, instead of incurring a "*large cost*" indulging strong earthly desires, thus making itself "*poor,*" must let the body's "*rebel powers . . . pine.*" In this way, the soul will "*Buy terms divine in selling hours of dross.*" The soul will be "*fed*" within and the bodily residence will "*without be rich no more.*"

The soul being "*fed*" within, triumphs over "*rebel powers*" of the "*sinful earth.*" It shall find salvation, and conquer "the last enemy," death: "*So shalt thou feed on Death, that feeds on men, And Death once dead, there's no more dying then.*"

BIBLICAL PASSAGES SUGGESTED BY SONNET 146

"For I have no pleasure in the death of him that dieth, saith the Lord God: Wherefore turn yourselves, and live ye." **Ezek. 18:32**

"The last enemy that shall be destroyed is death." **1 Cor. 15:26**

SONNET 147

My love is as a fever, longing still
For that which longer nurseth the disease;
Feeding on that which doth preserve the ill,
Th' uncertain sickly appetite to please.
My reason, the physician to my love,
Angry that his prescriptions are not kept,
Hath left me, and I desperate now approve
Desire is death, which physic did except.
Past cure I am, now reason is past care,
And frantic mad with evermore unrest;
My thoughts and my discourse as madmen's are,
At random from the truth vainly expressed.
For I have sworn thee fair, and thought thee bright,
Who art as black as hell, as dark as night.

THEME

Prolonged and relentless indulgence in vain desires is ruinous to the health of body and soul.

GLOSSARY

My love is as a fever, longing still For that which longer nurseth the disease; Feeding on that which doth preserve the ill, Th' uncertain sickly appetite to please.

> The tempting loves of my heart are like an irrepressible fever with unquenchable desires for that which feeds my disease. The more I indulge my fancies, the deeper becomes my enslavement to unwholesome pleasures and delights.

My reason, the physician to my love, Angry that his prescriptions are not kept, Hath left me, and I desperate now approve Desire is death, which physic did except.

> My innate good sense and reason, like a physician, tried to dissuade my sinful love, but reason, too, has left me

as I carelessly reject a sane manner of living. Desperate for a cure, I now realize that my unrelenting desires, not curbed by reason or wisdom, will be the death of my total being.

Past cure I am, now reason is past care, And frantic-mad with evermore unrest; My thoughts and my discourse as madmen's are, At random from the truth vainly expressed;

All reason gone, past hope of redemption, my scattered thoughts are ever-increasingly filled with frantic disquietude; and I am like a madman whose wanton worship of vanity separates me from truth.

For I have sworn thee fair, and thought thee bright, Who art as black as hell, as dark as night.

In this state I have sworn that my desires are fair and proper and believed sin to be bright when it is all black as hell and dark as night.

COMMENTARY

In Sonnet 142, the Poet says that "*love is my sin.*" This refers to a love for worldly temptations and is one of the "*two loves*" of Sonnet 144, one being of "*comfort*" and the other "*despair.*" (Sonnet 144.1)

In Sonnet 147, the love has become "*a fever*" and a "*disease.*" This occurs when the "*better angel*" of Sonnet 144 is tempted by the "*female evil*" in order to "*corrupt my saint to be a devil.*" (Sonnet 144.9, 3, 7) If the "*better angel . . . be turn'd friend*" then the outcome "*shall I ne'er know, but live in doubt.*" (Sonnet 144.9, 13)

The battle between good and evil persists in which "*my saint*" or soul, is ever in conflict with the worldly-oriented ego, "*my female evil.*" (Sonnet 144.5, 7) In Sonnet 146, the Poet declares it wise to "*Buy terms divine in selling hours of dross: Within be fed, without be rich no more.*" (Sonnet 146.11-12) Unless such advice is followed, one's physical body ("*thy fading mansion*") will lie in the grave to be food for the worms: "*Shall worms, inheritors of this excess, Eat up thy charge?*" (Sonnet 146.6, 7, 8) This allusion to feeding is carried into Sonnet 147. "*My love is a fever, longing still for that which longer nurseth the disease; feeding on that which doth preserve the ill.*" The "*fiend*" of Sonnet 144 would seem to be winning out. This "*fiend*" is "*black as hell, as dark as night.*" Sonnet 147, might arguably be better placed before Sonnet 145 where "*night, who like a fiend from heaven to hell is flown away.*" (Sonnet 145.11-12) It may also be that whatever security and reassurance is gained in Sonnet 145.14, "*And sav'd my life, saying 'not you',*" was lost because the love of worldly desires remained "*as a fever, longing still.*" The "*false plague*" (Sonnet 137.14) and "*disease*" are perhaps "*past cure.*"

"My will the enemy held, and thence made a chain for me, and bound me. For a froward will, was lust made; and lust served, became custom; and custom not resisted, became necessity." (*Confessions of St. Augustine*, p. 159)

In Sonnet 147, the perpetrator continued "*feeding on that which doth preserve the ill.*" The realization comes that these endless pursuits for earthly temptations and vanities mean "*death.*" "*I desperate now approve Desire is death.*" "*Desire is death*" if it is for a "*sickly appetite,*" and not bent toward enrichment of the soul, "*the better angel . . . my saint*" (Sonnet 144.3, 7), which must overcome and "*feed on Death, that feeds on men.*" (Sonnet 146.13)

The unrelenting "*longing*" and desires for earthly temptations prove physically and mentally ruinous. "*My thoughts and my discourse as a madman's are.*" Thinking "*at random*" that "*desire is death*" while "*feeding on that which doth preserve the ill*" leads to confusion and "*frantic mad*" assertions, like: "*For I have sworn thee fair, and thought thee bright, who art as black as hell, as dark as night.*"

BIBLICAL PASSAGES SUGGESTED BY SONNET 147

"For they that are after the flesh do mind the things of the flesh; but they that are after the Spirit the things of the Spirit. For to be carnally minded is death; but to be spiritually minded is life and peace. Because the carnal mind is enmity against God: for it is not subject to the law of God, neither indeed can be. So then they that are in the flesh cannot please God." **Rom. 8:5-8**

"For if ye live after the flesh, ye shall die: but if ye through the Spirit do mortify the deeds of the body, ye shall live. For as many as are led by the Spirit of God, they are the sons of God." **Rom. 8:13-14**

"But she that liveth in pleasure is dead while she liveth." **1 Titus 5:6**

"My heart panted, fearfulness affrighted me: the night of my pleasure hath he turned into fear unto me." **Isa. 21:4**

SONNET 148

O me! what eyes hath Love put in my head,
Which have no correspondence with true sight;
Or, if they have, where is my judgment fled,
That censures falsely what they see aright?
If that be fair whereon my false eyes dote,
What means the world to say it is not so?
If it be not, then love doth well denote
Love's eye is not so true as all men's: no.
How can it? O, how can Love's eye be true,
That is so vex'd with watching and with tears?
No marvel then, though I mistake my view,
The sun itself sees not till heaven clears.
O cunning Love! with tears thou keep'st me blind,
Lest eyes well seeing thy foul faults should find.

THEME

Indulgence in vanities blurs true vision, perceptions, and reason. It is the "sore travail" that God has given man to wrest himself free. (**Eccl. 1:13-14**)

GLOSSARY

O me! what eyes hath Love put in my head, Which have no correspondence with true sight; Or, if they have, where is my judgment fled, That censures falsely what they see aright?

> Oh me! What eyes has love put in my head, which in no way see what is really true; or if they do see correctly, where has all reason gone, that cannot properly judge what my eyes see as truth?

If that be fair whereon my false eyes dote, What means the world to say it is not so? If it be not, then love doth well denote Love's eye is not so true as all men's: no.

> If it is really beauty that my false-seeing eyes are doting upon, how can the world say it is not so? If my eyes are

not false, then love has shown me things correctly, although the eyes of doting love are not so true as what all men know to be false.

How can it? O, how can Love's eye be true, That is so vex'd with watching and with tears? No marvel then, though I mistake my view, The sun itself sees not till heaven clears.

How can it be? How can love-sick eyes truly see the world when they are so vexed and saddened with tears by what they constantly see. No wonder then that my view of things is mistaken; even the light of the sun cannot see until the clouds are cleared away.

O cunning Love! with tears thou keep'st me blind, Lest eyes well seeing thy foul faults should find.

O cunning Love! With tears of longing you keep me blinded; otherwise, I could perceive with true vision the wicked entrapments all around me.

COMMENTARY

In Sonnet 147, the Poet says that "*reason . . . hath left me, and I desperate now approve desire is death.*" (Sonnet 147.7-8) In Sonnet 148, the Poet takes no responsibility for using free will to engage in his desires, but blames "*love*" for the state he is in. "*What eyes hath Love put in my head.*"

There are double meanings that must be clarified to understand where the Poet takes us in Sonnet 148. If Love refers to God, who lovingly created the world, He has indeed given us physical eyes. If one chooses to have the eyes of Sonnet 137.2, that "*see not what they see*" because they are "*blind*" (Sonnet 137.1), then they understandably may be called "*false eyes.*" If "*Love,*" in line 1, is the kind described in Sonnet 147, "*my love is a fever, longing still*" wherein "*Love is my sin*" (Sonnet 142.1), then this means love of wanton desires and worldly pleasures. In either case, whether "*Love*" is God or "*Love*" is desire for the worldly, if wrongfully used, the eyes are transferred to the "*false plague*" of Sonnet 137.14.

Finally, there is the esoteric interpretation of the physical "*eyes*" in line 1, which "*have no correspondence with true sight.*" "*True sight*" is spiritual vision, which does not depend on the physical eyes. "The light of the body is the eye: if therefore thine eye be single, thy whole body shall be full of light." **(Mt. 6:17)** "Behold, he cometh with clouds; and every eye shall see him, and they also which pierced him: and all kindreds of the earth shall wail because of him. Even so, Amen." **(Rev. 1:7)**

Even if the eyes have the physical ability to see, the mind must be capable of discernment. "*Or, if they have, where is my judgment fled, That censures falsely what they see aright?*" In Sonnet 147, we read: "*my reason . . . hath left me*" and "*my thoughts and my discourse as madmen's are.*" (Sonnet 147.5, 11) It would not be possible, if reason has departed, to determine then whether "*false eyes dote*" upon what is "*fair.*"

The Poet goes on to state that the world may disagree on what is "*true*" or "*fair,*" but love itself may reveal truth. "*If it be not, then love doth well denote.*" Perhaps true love may reveal truth, but if "*love's eye*" means the "*false eyes*" that dote in a love-sick way, then "*Love's eye is not so true as all men's: no.*" In other words, the "*false eyes*" that feed an "*uncertain sickly appetite*" (Sonnet 147.4) are not as reliable as the judgment of mankind in general, i.e. those that understand the temptations that cause one to be "*vexed with watching and with tears.*" "The way of peace they know not; and there is no judgment in their goings: they have made them crooked paths: whosoever goeth therein shall not know peace. Therefore is judgment far from us, neither doth justice overtake us: we wait for light, but behold obscurity; for brightness, but we walk in darkness. We grope for the wall like the blind, and we grope as if we had no eyes: we stumble at noon day as in the night; we are in desolate places as dead men." **(Isa. 59:8-10)**

Even the sun's light cannot shine until the clouds dissipate, so no wonder, says the Poet, that he is mistaken in his view of things. "*No marvel then, though I mistake my view. The sun itself sees not till heaven clears.*" "Dost thou know when God disposed them, and caused the light of his cloud to shine? Dost thou know the balancings of the clouds, the wondrous works of him which is perfect in knowledge?" **(Job 36:15-16)**

The "*cunning love*" that is a "*fever, longing still*" for that which causes "*disease*" is vexation, and this causes tears of sorrow. (Sonnet 142.1, 2) "Behold, my servants shall sing for joy of heart, but ye shall cry for sorrow of heart, and shall howl for vexation of spirit." (**Isa. 65:14**) The "*cunning love*" is both the love of worldly temptations, and the "*the worser spirit a woman, colour'd ill,*" or the self-centered ego that tries to "*corrupt my saint to be a devil.*" (Sonnet 144.4, 7) Without unrelenting worldly desires, or an ego "*who like a fiend*" (Sonnet 145.11) "*keep'st me blind,*" the eyes might be "*well-seeing*" enough to perceive the "*foul faults*" of worldly entrapments.

BIBLICAL PASSAGE SUGGESTED BY SONNET 148

"And I gave my heart to seek and search out by wisdom concerning all things that are done under heaven: this sore travail hath God given to the sons of man to be exercised therewith. I have seen all the works that are done under the sun; and, behold, all is vanity and vexation of spirit." Eccl. **1:13-14**

SONNET 149

Canst thou, O cruel, say I love thee not,
When I against myself with thee partake?
Do I not think on thee, when I forgot
Am of myself, all tyrant, for thy sake?
Who hateth thee that I do call my friend?
On whom frown'st thou that I do fawn upon?
Nay, if thou lour'st on me, do I not spend
Revenge upon myself with present moan?
What merit do I in myself respect,
That is so proud thy service to despise,
When all my best doth worship thy defect,
Commanded by the motion of thine eyes?
But, love, hate on, for now I know thy mind,
Those that can see thou lov'st, and I am blind.

THEME

It is pride that causes one to excuse one's faults and to blame the Lord (or others) for not receiving life's joys. Once one accepts responsibility for one's choices, recognition of the Truth follows.

GLOSSARY

Canst thou, O cruel, say I love thee not, When I against myself with thee partake? Do I not think on thee, when I forgot Am of myself, all tyrant, for thy sake?

> Can Thou, cruel One, say I love Thee not when against my own selfish interests I still have hope in Thee? Do I not think of Thee when I forget all of my selfish, tyrannous behavior for Thy sake?

Who hateth thee that I do call my friend? On whom frown'st thou that I do fawn upon? Nay, if thou lour'st on me, do I not spend Revenge upon myself with present moan?

> Who is Thine enemy that I call my friend? On whom do I wait that Thou frownest upon? Is it not so that if Thou dost scowl at me, that I take revenge upon myself with

deep remorse?

What merit do I in myself respect That is so proud thy service to despise, When all my best doth worship thy defect Commanded by the motion of thine eyes?

> What is there in myself that I respect and hold up with pride as a justification to despise worshipful service to Thee, when all the best that I can muster still worships the deceitful temptations that my false seeing eyes are commanded by the "sore travail" of life to experience?

But, love, hate on, for now I know thy mind, Those that can see thou lov'st, and I am blind.

> But, Love, hate the sin in me, for now I understand Thy reasoning which is that those who can see with true spiritual vision, Thou dost love, and I still am blind.

COMMENTARY

There is still a bit of a complaint expressed by the Poet here. The fault he asserts is that "*what eyes hath Love put in my head . . . keep'st me blind.*" (Sonnet 148.1, 13) So isn't it cruel to apparently love others ("*Those that can see thou lov'st*") when Thou hast put these eyes in my head that "*dote*" and "*which have no correspondence with true sight.*" (Sonnet 148.5, 2) In spite of being possessed by these "*false eyes*" (Sonnet 148.5), do I not still think of You, willing to forget these tyrannous worldly allurements, for Your sake? "*Do I not think on thee, when I forgot am of myself, all tyrant, for thy sake.*" Don't I shun the company of those who are your enemy? Upon whom that you disapprove of do I wait upon?

"Examine me, O Lord, and prove me: try my reins and my heart. For thy lovingkindness is before mine eyes: and I have walked in thy truth. I have not sat with vain persons, neither will I go in with dissemblers. I have hated the congregation of evildoers; and will not sit with the wicked." **(Ps. 26:2-5)** If I feel your censure in my conscience, I am sorely aggrieved. "*Nay if thou lour'st on me, do I not spend Revenge upon myself with present moan?*"

"Do not I hate them, O Lord, that hate thee? And am not I grieved with those that rise up against thee?" (**Ps. 139:21**) In the Psalm's passage, King David says he is grieved with those who are against the Lord. In

Sonnet 149, the Poet is grieved ("*present moan*") from the pricks of a guilty conscience. This is the conscience "*born of love*" in Sonnet 151.2. Conscience is a saving grace when "*reason . . . hath left*" (Sonnet 147.5, 7) and "*judgment fled.*" (Sonnet 148.3)

In his "*present moan,*" the speaker shamefacedly admits that he has no merit to justify his proud or prideful behavior in shunning service, in the sense of religious service. Instead of worshipful service, in the religious sense, all he can muster is sacrilegious worship of "*thy defect,*" which are the "*foul faults*" (Sonnet 149.14), or worldly temptations inherent in creation. He blames this poor behavior, however, upon the command or coercion of the wanton eyes that "*Love hath put in my* [his] *head.*" (Sonnet 148.1) They "*worship thy defect*" because they are "*frantic mad with ever more unrest*" (Sonnet 147.10) and are "*vex'd with watching and with tears.*" (Sonnet 148.10) This is the constant "*motion*" of "*thine eyes*" ever "*longing still for that which longer nurseth the disease.*" (Sonnet 147.1-2) In his pride, he still blames those "*false eyes.*" (Sonnet 148.5) "For all that is in the world, the lust of the flesh, and the lust of the eyes, and the pride of life, is not of the Father, but is of the world." **(1 John 2:16)**

Apparently having long lamented and moaned, it dawns upon the Poet that perhaps the fault is not with the "*cruel*" one in line 1, for he now addresses the Lord as "*love.*" "*But, love, hate on, for now I know thy mind. Those that can see thou lov'st, and I am blind.*" To say he knows "*thy mind*" signifies an understanding that the Lord loves those who "*can see,*" meaning those who do not see with "*false eyes*" (Sonnet 148.5), but with spiritual vision. (See discussion to Sonnet 148) These are the ones seemingly favored and loved by the Lord in the scriptures. "The Lord openeth the eyes of the blind: the Lord raiseth them that are bowed down: the Lord loveth the righteous." **(Ps. 146:8)**

SONNET 150

O from what power hast thou this pow'rful might,
With insufficiency my heart to sway,
To make me give the lie to my true sight,
And swear that brightness doth not grace the day?
Whence hast thou this becoming of things ill,
That in the very refuse of thy deeds
There is such strength and warrantise of skill,
That, in my mind, thy worst all best exceeds?
Who taught thee how to make me love thee more,
The more I hear and see just cause of hate?
O though I love what others do abhor,
With others thou shouldst not abhor my state:
If thy unworthiness rais'd love in me,
More worthy I to be belov'd of thee.

THEME

The power by which evil influences deceive man is overcome eventually by the greater redeeming power of the Lord who feels the suffering of his lost children, and through His pity and grace, lifts them up.

GLOSSARY

O from what power hast thou this pow'rful might, With insufficiency my heart to sway, To make me give the lie to my true sight, And swear that brightness doth not grace the day?

> From what source hast Thou this overwhelming might to sway me toward delusive things, but the inability to turn my head toward good? How is it that I am seemingly compelled by an overwhelming force to betray my spiritual sight by believing evil is good, and further compelled even to swear that the sun does not grace the day with its light?

Whence hast thou this becoming of things ill, That in the very refuse of thy deeds There is such strength and warrantise of skill, That, in my mind, thy worst all best exceeds?

> From what place dost Thou derive the power to make evil look tempting, that in the most scurrilous deeds and actions there is such cunning power and skill; to my mind, all the temptations of this world appear more alluring than the sweeter aspects of life Thou hast to offer?

Who taught thee how to make me love thee more, The more I hear and see just cause of hate? O though I love what others do abhor, With others thou shouldst not abhor my state:

> In spite of this power of deception, who taught Thee how to make me love Thee more, as I grew to understand, by seeing with opened eyes, and hearing with willing ears, the true reason to hate sinful conduct? While it is true that I love what others hate, have pity and do not be like others and abhor my sinful state.

If thy unworthiness rais'd love in me, More worthy I to be belov'd of thee.

> If the temptations Thou hast put in this world have caused me to love evil, then even more should'st Thou pity me, Thy beloved child.

COMMENTARY

In Sonnet 144.2, we see the power of the "*two spirits*." One "*tempteth my better angel from my side, and would corrupt my saint to be a devil.*" (Sonnet 144.5-6). What kind of power would it take to turn an angel into a devil; or to make evil look good? This is a question posed by Sonnet 150. "*O from what pow'r hast thou this powerful might, With insufficiency my heart to sway, To make me give the lie to my true sight.*" One answer lies in Sonnet 146, describing "*these rebel powers*" that cause the soul to "*pine within and suffer dearth.*" (Sonnet 146.2-3)

This battle between ego and soul has been a theme often repeated in the Sonnets. The power to make the speaker "*swear that brightness doth not grace the day*" is the same that caused him to "*have sworn thee fair . . . who art black as hell, as dark as night.*" (Sonnet 147.13-14). Because "*judgment fled*" (Sonnet 148.3), this same power is unable to turn the speaker's heart away from evil to good. "*With insufficiency my heart to sway.*" Sonnet 150 examines these forces ("*powerful might*") that deceive the mind and judgment into perceiving evil as good. "*Whence hast thou this becoming of things ill.*" "Bread of deceit is sweet to a man; but afterwards his mouth shall be filled with gravel." **(Prov. 20:17)**

Suddenly in the third quatrain, a new question arises; "*Who taught thee how to make me love thee more, The more I hear and see just cause of hate?*" "The hearing ear, and the seeing eyes, the Lord hath made even both of them." **(Prov. 20:12)** Up to this point, the speaker has been plagued by non-seeing "*false eyes*" (Sonnet 148.7) and has not been able to hear the voice of reason. "*My reason, physician to my love . . . Hath left me.*" (Sonnet 147.5, 7) As Vendler, in her comments on this Sonnet says, we begin to see the development of "the speaker's mounting self-knowledge." We are unaware of the source of this new illumination, but it causes the speaker to ask for pity. "*With others thou shouldst not abhor my state.*" It reflects the sentiment of Sonnet 142.11, "*Root pity in thy heart.*" The "*others*" may refer to "*the world*" mentioned in Sonnet 148.6.

Being in such a state of sin, drawn there by the "*rebel powers*" (Sonnet 146.2) and the "*female evil*" (Sonnet 144.5) inherent both in creation and in man, the speaker says he is worthy to be pitied as a beloved child of God. "*If thy unworthiness rais'd love in me, More worthy I to be belov'd of thee.*" "That thy beloved may be delivered; save with thy right hand, and hear me." **(Ps. 60:5)**

The understanding Lord responds through Grace.

BIBLICAL PASSAGES SUGGESTED BY SONNET 150

"How long will ye vex my soul, and break me in pieces with worlds?" **Job 19:2**

"In all their affliction he was afflicted, and the angel of his presence saved them: in his love and in his pity he redeemed them; and he bare them, and carried them all the days of old." **Isa. 63:9**

"For the creature was made subject to vanity, not willingly, but by reason of him who hath subjected the same in hope. Because the creature itself also shall be delivered from the bondage of corruption into the glorious liberty of the children of God." **Rom. 8:20-21**

"Teaching us that, denying ungodliness and worldly lusts, we should live soberly, righteously, and godly, in his present world." **Titus 2:12**

SONNET 151

Love is too young to know what conscience is;
Yet who knows not conscience is born of love?
Then, gentle cheater, urge not my amiss,
Lest guilty of my faults thy sweet self prove:
For thou betraying me, I do betray
My nobler part to my gross body's treason;
My soul doth tell my body that he may
Triumph in love; flesh stays no farther reason,
But rising at thy name doth point out thee
As his triumphant prize. Proud of this pride,
He is contented thy poor drudge to be,
To stand in thy affairs, fall by thy side.
No want of conscience hold it that I call.
Her "love" for whose dear love I rise and fall.

THEME

Conscience can suggest the correct course of action, but alone it is insufficient to trump man's strong desire and will to act, even if such action is against his best interest.

GLOSSARY

Love is too young to know what conscience is; Yet who knows not conscience is born of love? Then, gentle cheater, urge not my amiss, Lest guilty of my faults thy sweet self prove:

> Young love does not know or appreciate correct moral conduct; yet everyone knows that out of true love, conscience is born in man. So then, do not incite me to go amiss, lest it prove that Thou art guilty of my faults.

For thou betraying me, I do betray My nobler part to my gross body's treason; My soul doth tell my body that he may Triumph in love; flesh stays no farther reason,

> For Thou who imprisoned me with sensual desires, I do betray my nobler self or soul to the gross body's treason,

> and my soul tells my body that in loving the Spirit only may it triumph; but my flesh refuses to hear any reason.

But rising at thy name doth point out thee As his triumphant prize. Proud of this pride, He is contented thy poor drudge to be, To stand in thy affairs, fall by thy side.

> But conjuring the voice of reason is enough to point out that sensual excess is the triumphant prize of the body's treason, swollen with the lust of pride. The body is yet content to be a lowly servant in steadfast service to egotistical excesses, while it waxes and wanes, feeding upon a "*sickly appetite.*" (Sonnet 147.4)

No want of conscience hold it that I call. Her "love" for whose dear love I rise and fall.

> It is not for want of a conscience that I call her "love" who is "*my sin,*" and in whose costly indulgence, I rise and fall.

COMMENTARY

In Sonnet 145.2, the speaker hears the voice of conscience in the words "*I hate.*" (See discussion to Sonnet 145 and **Rom. 13:5**: "Wherefore ye must needs be subject, not only for wrath, but also for conscience sake.") Here in Sonnet 151, the Poet again says that there are those "*too young*" to appreciate the moral imperatives of conscience ("*Love is too young to know what conscience is*"), and that man, out of love for the Creator, is innately endowed with a conscience. "*Yet who knows not conscience is born of love?*"

In Sonnet 151, the Poet again points out that there are "*two spirits*" in man (see discussion to Sonnet 144), which are innate to his being. "*But being both from me, both to each friend.*" (Sonnet 144.11) One of these "*spirits*" is the "*gentle cheater*" who has the power to make sin look attractive ("*this becoming of things ill*" [Sonnet 150.5]). So it is this "*gentle cheater*" who bears the guilt for the sins committed by the speaker. "*Then, gentle cheater, urge not my amiss, Lest guilty of my faults thy sweet self prove.*" Note the use of "*gentle*" and "*sweet*" as opposed to "*black as hell, as dark as night*" (Sonnet 147.14) or "*female evil*" (Sonnet 144.5). This is a recognition that the ego-nature in man is part of creation from Genesis on. It is only evil when man wrongly uses his will, reason, or judgment and chooses to love sensuality over virtue: "*love is my sin*" (Sonnet 142.2). So in Sonnet 147 we read of a situation where the will to resist temptation has failed: "*love is as a fever full of disease*" in a "*frantic mad*" state where "*reason*" "*hath left.*" (Sonnet 147.1, 10, 5, 7) In such a state, the love of temptations becomes the "*gross body's treason.*" The sensual appetite will not be stayed by reason: "*flesh stays no farther reason*".

The "*nobler part,*" the soul of Sonnet 146, will "*pine within*" and "*suffer death*" (Sonnet 146.3) as the sensual longings make a "*triumphant prize*" of the body, filled with the excesses of the flesh, "*an expense of spirit in a waste of shame.*" (Sonnet 129.1) Thus the flesh, or selfish ego is merely the lowly servant of the sensual appetites, which come and go, causing the speaker to "*rise and fall*" with the whims of temptation.

Finally, the speaker does not fault his lack of conscience, or the inability to distinguish between moral imperatives, but again makes the case that his "*nobler part*" has fallen victim to his "*gross body's treason.*" His "*love*" for lust, "*proud of his pride,*" is something that costs him dearly as he rises and falls upon the whims of a "*sickly appetite.*" (Sonnet 147.4) "*No want of conscience hold it that I call. Her 'love' for whose dear love I rise and fall.*"

BIBLICAL PASSAGES SUGGESTED BY SONNET 151

"Which shew the work of the law written in their hearts, their conscience also bearing witness, and their thoughts the mean while accusing or else excusing one another." **Rom. 2:15**

"Howbeit there is not in every man that knowledge: for some with conscience of the idol unto this hour eat it as a thing offered unto an idol; and their conscience being weak is defiled." **1 Cor. 8:7**

"Now the Spirit speaketh expressly, that in the latter times some shall depart from the faith, giving heed to seducing spirits, and doctrines of devils; Speaking lies in hypocrisy; having their conscience seared with a hot iron." **1 Tim. 4:1-2**

SONNET 152

In loving thee thou know'st I am forsworn,
But thou art twice forsworn, to me love swearing;
In act thy bed-vow broke, and new faith torn,
In vowing new hate after new love bearing.
But why of two oaths' breach do I accuse thee,
When I break twenty? I am perjur'd most;
For all my vows are oaths but to misuse thee,
And all my honest faith in thee is lost:
For I have sworn deep oaths of thy deep kindness,
Oaths of thy love, thy truth, thy constancy;
And, to enlighten thee, gave eyes to blindness,
Or made them swear against the thing they see;
For I have sworn thee fair; more perjur'd eye,
To swear against the truth so foul a lie.

THEME

Life is a series of trials and battles between the world-centered ego and the soul. The voices of conscience and guilt testify loudly through triumph and defeat.

GLOSSARY

In loving thee thou know'st I am forsworn, But thou art twice forsworn to me love swearing; In act thy bed-vow broke, and new faith torn, In vowing new hate after new love bearing.

In loving Thee, Thou knowest I am a liar, but Thou art twice the liar after swearing love for me. In action Thy vow to my heart was broken, and a new vow of constancy to me was torn asunder, in vowing new hatred after professing love anew:

But why of two oaths' breach do I accuse thee, When I break twenty? I am perjur'd most; For all my vows are oaths but to misuse thee, And all my honest faith in thee is lost.

But why do I accuse Thee of breaking two oaths, when

> I break twenty? I am the greater liar, for all my vows are oaths uttered in a way that treats Thee unfaithfully and all my true faith in Thee has been squandered.

For I have sworn deep oaths of thy deep kindness, Oaths of thy love, thy truth, thy constancy; And, to enlighten thee, gave eyes to blindness, Or made them swear against the thing they see;

> For I have sworn solemn oaths of Thy profound kindness: oaths of Thy love, Thy truth, Thy constancy. And to make the object of my desire look brighter and more attractive, I made my eyes blind to the truth and made them swear falsely against the truth they see.

For I have sworn thee fair; more perjur'd eye, To swear against the truth so foul a lie.

> For I have sworn you are fair and attractive: What a great liar I am, to swear so foul a lie against all that is true.

COMMENTARY

Sonnet 152 is like a confession of all the lies and untruths the speaker has uttered to himself and others. It speaks of the "*hate*" uttered in Sonnets 142, 145, and 149, and repeats the swearing of "*fair*" and "*bright*" in Sonnet 147. It further repeats the theme of "*false eyes*" and the blindness of Sonnet 148; the self betrayal of Sonnet 149 and Sonnet 151; and the "*lie to* [my] *true sight*" in Sonnet 150.3.

In Sonnet 152, the speaker confesses to lying about "*loving thee.*" He confesses to breaking his oath "*twenty*" times. He admits that he unfaithfully acted to "*misuse thee*" in whom he has squandered his truth, faith, and honesty. "*And all my honest faith in thee is lost.*" He further says, in the deepest, most sincere way, "*I have sworn deep oaths of thy deep kindness, Oaths of thy love, thy truth, thy constancy.*" We are uncertain if these "*oaths*" were uttered to one or more persons or whether it means perhaps that in the Poet's works he feels that he glorified "*foul faults*" (Sonnet 148.14) under the delusion or influence of some "*pow'r*" that would make him "*give the lie to my* [his] *true sight*" (Sonnet 150.1, 3).

The Poet claims to have been lied to in at least two instances ("*twice forsworn*"). The first is "*In act thy bed-vow broke,*" and a second time is either in the betrayal of "*new faith torn*" or perhaps rekindling of "*new hate*" after professing new love ("*after new love bearing*"). In the latter case, this may be born out in examining Sonnet 145.14 wherein the Poet declares that "'*I hate' from hate away she threw, And sav'd my life, saying 'not you'.*" "I acknowledged my sin unto thee, and mine iniquity have I not hid. I said, I will confess my transgressions unto the Lord; and thou forgavest the iniquity of my sin." **(Ps. 32:5)** There is evidence that the Poet felt secure in Sonnet 145 after being "*sav'd*"; but apparently this salvation fell by the way as he rekindled old habits, as we see in the Sonnets immediately following Sonnet 145. (See discussion Sonnets 145–150.)

As for the "*bed-vow broke*," there are many scriptural references to beds that suggest that one's bed is the place where one's desires, of heart or soul, are centered. "By night on my bed I sought him whom my soul loveth: I sought him, but I found him not." **(Song of Sol. 3:1)** "Upon a lofty and high mountain hast thou set thy bed: even thither wentest thou up to offer sacrifice. Behind the doors also and the posts hast thou set up thy remembrance: for thou hast discovered thyself to another than me, and art gone up; thou has enlarged thy bed, and made thee a covenant with them; thou lovedst their bed where thou sawest it." **(Isa. 57:7-8)** "The Lord will strengthen him upon the bed of languishing: thou wilt make all his bed in his sickness." **(Ps. 41:3)**

In throwing away "'*I hate*'," the Poet declares, "*she . . . sav'd my life.*" (Sonnet 145.14) But who is it that set up his bed "upon a lofty and high mountain" and "hast discovered thyself to another" **(Isa. 57:8)**? This is one, who in scriptural terms, has committed spiritual adultery. The speaker claims that there was a "*bed-vow*" contract between Spirit and soul, that there was the promised salvation, free of "'*I hate*'," and he was "*sav'd.*" (Sonnet 145.14) But who thereafter breached "*twenty*" oaths? The speaker himself. His justification is found in Sonnet 151.5: "*For thou betraying me, I do betray My nobler part.*" The speaker claims that the "*gentle cheater*," i.e. worldly temptation and bodily sensuality, lured the Poet into "*faults.*" The body or flesh is the "*triumphant prize; proud of his pride.*" (Sonnet 151.3, 4, 10)

Recall that after "*hate away she threw, and sav'd my life*" (Sonnet 145.14), we read in Sonnet 146.2 that the soul is lured by "*rebel powers*"; and in Sonnet 147.2, "*My love is as a fever, longing still for that which nurseth the disease.*" Certainly in all of this indulgence, and being "*at random from the truth vainly expressed*" (Sonnet 147.12), it is no wonder that again the Poet declares, "*I have sworn thee fair and thought thee bright, who art as back as hell, as dark as night.*" (Sonnet 147.13-14) The breach of "*twenty*" oaths seems to be an understatement in Sonnet 152.

There is some redemption expressed in Sonnet 150.9-10: "*Who taught thee how to make me love thee more, The more I hear and see just cause of hate.*" The battle between the "*two spirits*" (Sonnet 144.2), the soul and body (Sonnet 146), is an ongoing tribulation that causes the Poet to "*rise and fall*" (Sonnet 151.14), depending on whether the "*better angel*" or "*worser spirit*" is winning (Sonnet 144.3, 4).

Sonnet 152 is expressed in both the present and past tenses. It is as if a witness at a trial were giving testimony of past events and present reflections. Sonnet 152 is full of legal terminology and trial concepts. This is suggested by the words "*forsworn*," "*swearing*," "*act*," "*broke*," "*torn*," "*vowing*," "*oaths*," "*accuse*," "*break*," "*breach*," "*perjured*," "*vows*," "*oaths*," "*misuse*," "*honest*," "*sworn*," "*truth*," "*enlighten*," "*against*," "*the thing*," "*eyes*," "*lie*," and "*eye*." In all, including repetitions, there are 31 words in a sonnet of 125 words that are suggestive of the law, evidence, and trials.

Metaphorically, the voice of conscience is putting the speaker on trial, and the witness is testifying about what he has forsworn, and what has been sworn to him. The word "*act*" might mean statute, in which case, "*In act thy bed-vow broke*" suggests commission of an offense that is at the foundation or "*bed*" of the entire agreement or accord between the parties.

We further see that the "*accuse*[d]" has twice broken vows, one at the very base, foundation, or "*bed*" of the matter; and further, while the speaker has in good "*faith*" relied upon the "*vows*," the other has "*torn*" the agreement and is therefore in "*breach*" of "*two oaths*."

Now the speaker, in a confessional mood agrees that he "*perjur'd*" himself and used "*vows . . . to misuse*" the accused. In a relationship of trust, "*misuse*," in the sense of exceeding one's legal authority, is a basis for the filing of a lawsuit.

At this stage of the confession, the declarant sets out the many ways he acted to give credence to "*a lie*." He says: "*For I have sworn deep oaths of thy deep kindness, Oath of thy love, thy truth, thy constancy.*" All of this was done to make "*a lie*" appear as truth. In Sonnet 147, the speaker says that "*I have sworn thee fair and thought thee bright*," while knowing all along that the object of his delight or "*desire*" was "*black as hell.*" (Sonnet 147.13, 8, 14) The speaker's entrenched and constant habit of "*longing still*" (Sonnet 147.1) for that which caused his soul to "*suffer dearth*" (Sonnet 146.3) was rationalized by "*oaths*" and "*vows*" that worldly desires were "*fair*" (Sonnet 147.13) in the face of all men saying "*no*" (Sonnet 148.8), it is not so.

In Sonnet 149.14, the speaker says "*I am blind.*" He sees himself in Sonnet 150 as one who needs to be pitied not judged: "*With others thou should'st not abhor my state.*" (Sonnet 150.12) In Sonnet 151, the speaker acknowledges that he has betrayed his soul, his "*nobler part*" on the altar of fleshly enjoyments (Sonnet 151.6). In Sonnet 152, the speaker confesses that he swore perjured oaths to make the "*foul*" lie look "*fair*" in spite of knowing the falsity of his assertions "*and to enlighten thee gave eyes to blindness, or made them swear against the thing they see.*"

In summation, the speaker casts his vote for guilty by saying "*eye,*" a play on "aye" for "yes." There is final acceptance of responsibility for his acts. He says "*more perjur'd eye,*" a further play on "*eye*" as "I," meaning, "I am the true liar."

It is also possible to interpret "*perjured eye*" as "*false eyes.*" (Sonnet 148.5) See also, "*Love's eye is not so true as all men's, no.*" (Sonnet 148.8)

In either instance, the Poet takes responsibility and is blameworthy because he declares: "*For I have sworn thee fair: more perjur'd eye, To swear against the truth so foul a lie.*" His "*disease*" (Sonnet 147.2), like an inflamed addiction "*past cure*" (Sonnet 147.9), has set his "*thoughts and my discourse as madmen's are.*" (Sonnet 147.11) This discourse has taken the shape of "*sworn deep oaths*" of every kind, all "*to enlighten*" the "*eyes*" to see as truth what is really false. "*And, to enlighten thee, gave eyes to blindness, or made them swear against the thing they see.*" In other words, to continue engaging in a "*sickly appetite*" (Sonnet 147.4), it was necessary to lie to himself or betray his "*nobler part*" (Sonnet 151.6) with the "*gross body's treason*" (Sonnet 151.6) by convincing himself that conduct of the "*flesh*" (Sonnet 151.6, 8) was true and correct. It was a very "*powerful might*" (Sonnet 150.1), this "*Love of sin*" (Sonnet 142.1), which contributed to living a life "*against the truth*" and "*so foul a lie.*"

BIBLICAL PASSAGES SUGGESTED BY SONNET 152

"And they bend their tongues like their bow for lies: but they are not valiant for the truth upon the earth; for they proceed from evil to evil, and they know not me, saith the Lord." **Jer. 9:3**

"The heart is deceitful above all things, and desperately wicked: who can know it?" **Jer. 17:9**

"And again he denied with an oath, I do not know the man." **Matt. 26:72**

"If we confess our sins, he is faithful and just to forgive us our sins, and to cleanse us from all unrighteousness." **1 John 1:9**

"For if after they have escaped the pollutions of the world through the knowledge of the Lord and Savior Jesus Christ, they are again entangled therein, and overcome, the latter end is worse with them than the beginning." **2 Pet. 2:20**

SONNET 153

Cupid laid by his brand and fell asleep.
A maid of Dian's this advantage found,
And his love-kindling fire did quickly steep
In a cold valley-fountain of that ground;
Which borrowed from this holy fire of love,
A dateless lively heat, still to endure,
And grew a seething bath, which yet men prove
Against strange maladies a sovereign cure.
But at my mistress' eye love's brand new fired,
The boy for trial needs would touch my breast;
I, sick withal, the help of bath desired,
And thither hied, a sad distemper'd guest,
But found no cure, the bath for my help lies
Where Cupid got new fire; my mistress' eyes.

THEME

The fire of slavery to sense pleasures cannot be abated by worldly cures, or mythical remedies. Only the curative waters of the Spirit can provide healing to body and soul.

GLOSSARY

Cupid laid by his brand and fell asleep. A maid of Dian's this advantage found, And his love-kindling fire did quickly steep In a cold valley-fountain of that ground;

> Cupid lay down beside his torch and fell asleep: A virgin maid of the goddess Diana took advantage of the situation and took Cupid's love-kindling fire. She immediately placed the torch in a cold valley spring nearby.

Which borrowed from this holy fire of love, A dateless lively heat, still to endure, And grew a seething bath, which yet men prove Against strange maladies a sovereign cure.

> The spring borrowed from this holy fire of love an eternally burning heat, and there the water became a healing

bath that men still come to test as a supreme cure against even the strangest illnesses.

But at my mistress' eye love's brand new fired, The boy for trial needs would touch my breast; I, sick withal, the help of bath desired, And thither hied, a sad distemper'd guest,

But at the sight of my mistress' eye, Cupid's torch of love newly ignited my passion. The boy Cupid, to test its effect on me, would touch my breast; and I, sick from the touch of Cupid's flame, desired a cure from the medicinal bath, and there I hastened, a sad and sick visitor to the place of healing.

But found no cure, the bath for my help lies Where Cupid got new fire; my mistress' eyes.

But found that no cure did lie for me in the waters where Cupid got new fire in the form of my mistress' eyes.

As Sonnets 153 and 154 are of a common theme, they are jointly considered in the Commentary and Biblical verses that follow.

SONNET 154

The little Love-god lying once asleep,
Laid by his side his heart-inflaming brand,
Whilst many nymphs that vowed chaste life to keep
Came tripping by; but in her maiden hand
The fairest votary took up that fire
Which many legions of true hearts had warm'd,
And so the General of hot desire
Was, sleeping, by a virgin hand disarmed.
This brand she quenched in a cool well by,
Which from Love's fire took heat perpetual,
Growing a bath and healthful remedy,
For men diseased; but I, my mistress' thrall,
Came there for cure and this by that I prove,
Love's fire heats water, water cools not love.

THEME

The fire of slavery to sense pleasures cannot be abated by worldly cures, or mythical remedies. Only the curative waters of the Spirit can provide healing to body and soul.

GLOSSARY

The little Love-god lying once asleep, Laid by his side his heart-inflaming brand, Whilst many nymphs that vowed chaste life to keep Came tripping by; but in her maiden hand

> The little god of love, Cupid, once asleep, laid his heart-inflaming torch at his side. It happened that many maidens, sworn to chastity, came tripping by; but in her maiden hand,

The fairest votary took up that fire Which many legions of true hearts had warm'd, And so the General of hot desire Was, sleeping, by a virgin hand disarmed.

> The fairest of the maids, took the fire brand that had warmed legions of true hearts. And so it was that Cupid,

> the commanding General of hot desire, was disarmed as he slept.

This brand she quenched in a cool well by, Which from Love's fire took heat perpetual, Growing a bath and healthful remedy, For men diseased; but I, my mistress' thrall,

> The maiden quenched the torch in a cool well nearby, which from the fire of Love absorbed an eternal heat, and became a healing bath providing a healthful remedy to diseased men. But I, a slave to my enchanting mistress,

Came there for cure and this by that I prove, Love's fire heats water, water cools not love.

> Came there for a cure, and coming to the bath, the following I prove to be true: The fire of Love heats water, water cannot cool love.

COMMENTARY

Both Sonnets are based on a theme expressed by Marianus Scholasticus and in various Renaissance stories of cold springs becoming heated by Cupid's love torch (see Stephen Booth, *Shakespeare's Sonnets* [New Haven: Yale Nota Bene, 2000], p. 533n).

In each poem, the sleeping Cupid is the victim of a theft by a virgin nymph who, in an attempt to cool the little love-god's torch, puts it into "*cool*" water. This maid's action was perhaps because Cupid incited people to "*heart-inflaming*" love, meaning a mere infatuation. Such incitement by "*the General of hot desire*" could prove dangerous to one that "*vowed chaste life to keep.*"

Whatever the motive, we find that the speaker has been made a slave to his "*mistress' thrall.*" He seeks relief in the medicinal bath touted to be "*a sovereign cure*" (Sonnet 153.7) for "*strange maladies*" (Sonnet 153.7) and "*men diseased.*" In both Sonnets, the result was that the bath provided no cure. In Sonnet 153, "*the bath for my help lies where Cupid got new fire; my mistress' eyes.*" The implication is that the bath, as a cure, is a lie in the case of inflamed passion from the "*mistress' eyes.*" In Sonnet 154, the waters could not cure as "*love's fire heats water, water cools not.*"

The fire of wayward passions is not a disease of the physical body, so there is no cure in the realm of worldly remedies. It is the "*disease*" (Sonnet 147.2) of feeding a "*sickly appetite*" (Sonnet 147.4). It is base desire, and "*desire is death*" (Sonnet 147.8). In Sonnets 153 and 154, man's affliction was slavery to the mistress of lustful passions. This is the "*worser spirit a woman, colour'd ill*" (Sonnet 144.4). The cure for this disease of the soul could not be found in earthly waters, but requires a spiritual remedy.

BIBLICAL PASSAGES SUGGESTED BY SONNETS 153 AND 154

"Set me as a seal upon thine heart, as a seal upon thine arm; for love is strong as death; jealousy is cruel as the grave; the coals thereof are coals of fire, which hath a most vehement flame. Many waters cannot quench love, neither can the floods drown it: if a man would give all the substance of his house for love, it would utterly be contemned." **Song of Sol. 8:6-7**

"For all that is in the world, the lust of the flesh, and the lust of the eyes, and the pride of life, is not of the Father, but is of the world." **1 John 2:16**

"And they shall go forth, and look upon the carcasses of the men that have transgressed against me: for their worm shall not die, neither shall their fire be quenched; and they shall be an abhorring unto all flesh." **Isa. 66:24**

"For many people have committed two evils; they have forsaken me the fountain of living waters, and hewed them out cisterns, broken cisterns, that can hold no water." **Jer. 2:13**

"But whosoever drinketh of the water that I shall give him shall never thirst; but the water that I shall give him shall be in him a well of water springing up into everlasting life." **John 4:14**

ACKNOWLEDGMENTS

Writing a book such as this cannot be accomplished without the patience and assistance of many, and without the prior work and research of those who have approached the subject of the Sonnets, as well as of Shakespeare and his use and reliance upon the Bible and other scriptural sources. For fear of leaving someone out, I do not list each person, but thank those whose appreciation and love of Shakespeare has inspired them to write and lecture about the author and his body of work.

On a more personal level, I want to thank my personal secretaries Marcia Wareham, Lara Lay, and Alice Harris, who labored reading handwritten notes and keeping track of the many drafts. Alice worked the longest and hardest with me, and I very much appreciate her typing, proofing, comments, kindness, and patience.

I also want to thank friends and family like June, Terry, Jan, Sr., and especially my wife, LeAnn, for their encouragement and support.

INDEX OF FIRST LINES

Accuse me thus: that I have scanted all 346
Against my love shall be, as I am now, 190
Against that time, if ever that time come, 147
Ah wherefore with infection should he live, 202
Alack what poverty my Muse brings forth, 304
Alas 'tis true I have gone here and there, 325
As a decrepit father takes delight 111
As an unperfect actor on the stage, 69
As fast as thou shalt wane, so fast thou grow'st, 31
A woman's face with Nature's own hand painted 59

Being your slave, what should I do but tend 173
Beshrew that heart that makes my heart to groan 404
Betwixt mine eye and heart a league is took, 141
Be wise as thou art cruel, do not press 431
But be contented when that fell arrest, 221
But do thy worst to steal thyself away, 272
But wherefore do not you a mightier way 47

Canst thou, O cruel, say I love thee not, 466
Cupid laid by his brand and fell asleep. 481

Devouring Time, blunt thou the lion's paws, 56

Farewell, thou art too dear for my possessing, 258
For shame deny that thou bear'st love to any, 28
From fairest creatures we desire increase, 1
From you have I been absent in the spring, 291
Full many a glorious morning have I seen 98

How can I then return in happy plight, 84
How can my Muse want subject to invent, 114
How careful was I when I took my way, 144
How heavy do I journey on the way, 151
How like a winter hath my absence been 288
How oft, when thou, my music, music play'st, 384
How sweet and lovely dost thou make the shame 282

If my dear love were but the child of state, 369
If the dull substance of my flesh were thought, 132

If there be nothing new, but that which is 178
If thou survive my well-contented day, 96
If thy soul check thee that I come so near, 415
I grant thou wert not married to my Muse, 244
I never saw that you did painting need, 246
In faith, I do not love thee with mine eyes, 435
In loving thee thou know'st I am forsworn, 475
In the old age black was not counted fair, 379
Is it for fear to wet a widow's eye 25
Is it thy will thy image should keep open 184

Let me confess that we two must be twain, 108
Let me not to the marriage of true minds 343
Let not my love be call'd idolatry, 310
Let those who are in favor with their stars 75
Like as, to make our appetites more keen, 349
Like as the waves make towards the pebbled shore, 181
Lo, as a careful housewife runs to catch 443
Lo, in the orient when the gracious light 19
Look in thy glass, and tell the face thou viewest, 7
Lord of my love, to whom in vassalage 78
Love is my sin, and thy dear virtue hate, 439
Love is too young to know what conscience is; 472

Mine eye and heart are at a mortal war, 138
Mine eye hath play'd the painter and hath stell'd 72
Music to hear, why hear'st thou music sadly? 22
My glass shall not persuade me I am old, 67
My love is as a fever, longing still 458
My love is strengthen'd, though more weak in seeming; 301
My mistress' eyes are nothing like the sun; 393
My tongue-tied Muse in manners holds her still, 252

No, Time, thou shalt not boast that I do change: 366
No longer mourn for me when I am dead 214
No more be griev'd at that which thou hast done: 105
Not from the stars do I my judgment pluck, 41
Not marble, nor the gilded monuments 168
Not mine own fears, nor the prophetic soul 316

O call not me to justify the wrong 427
O for my sake do you with Fortune chide, 328

O from what power hast thou this pow'rful might, 469
O how I faint when I of you do write, 237
O how much more doth beauty beauteous seem, 164
O how thy worth with manners may I sing, 117
O lest the world should task you to recite, 216
O me! what eyes hath Love put in my head, 462
O never say that I was false of heart, 322
Or I shall live your epitaph to make, 240
Or whether doth my mind being crown'd with you, 337
O that you were yourself, but, love, you are 37
O thou, my lovely boy, who in thy power 375
O truant Muse, what shall be thy amends 298

Poor soul, the centre of my sinful earth, 455

Say that thou didst forsake me for some fault, 264
Shall I compare thee to a summer's day? 53
Since brass, nor stone, nor earth, nor boundless sea, 196
Since I left you, mine eye is in my mind, 334
Sin of self-love possesseth all mine eye, 187
So, now I have confessed that he is thine, 408
So am I as the rich, whose blessed key 157
So are you to my thoughts as food to life, 223
So is it not with me as with that Muse, 64
Some glory in their birth, some in their skill, 270
Some say thy fault is youth, some wantonness, 285
So oft have I invok'd thee for my Muse, 232
So shall I live, supposing thou art true, 275
Sweet love, renew thy force; be it not said 170

'Tis better to be vile than vile esteemed, 360
Take all my loves, my love, yea take them all, 120
Th' expense of spirit in a waste of shame 390
That God forbid that made me first your slave, 176
That thou art blamed shall not be thy defect, 211
That thou hast her, it is not all my grief, 126
That time of year thou mayst in me behold, 218
That you were once unkind befriends me now, 356
The forward violet thus did I chide: 293
The little Love-god lying once asleep, 483
Then hate me when thou wilt, if ever, now; 267
Then let not winter's ragged hand deface 16

The other two, slight air and purging fire, 135
They that have power to hurt, and will do none, 278
Thine eyes I love, and they, as pitying me, 401
Those hours, that with gentle work did frame 13
Those lines that I before have writ do lie, 340
Those lips that Love's own hand did make, 451
Those parts of thee that the world's eye doth view, 208
Those pretty wrongs that liberty commits, 123
Thou art as tyrannous, so as thou art, 397
Thou blind fool, love, what dost thou to mine eyes, 419
Thus can my love excuse the slow offence 154
Thus in his cheek the map of days outworn, 205
Thy bosom is endeared with all hearts, 93
Thy gift, thy tables, are within my brain 363
Thy glass will show thee how thy beauties wear, 229
Tired with all these, for restful death I cry, 199
To me, fair friend, you never can be old, 307
Two loves I have of comfort and despair, 447

Unthrifty loveliness, why dost thou spend 10

Was it the proud full sail of his great verse, 255
Weary with toil, I haste me to my bed, 81
Were't aught to me I bore the canopy, 372
What's in the brain, that ink may character, 319
What is your substance, whereof are you made, 161
What potions have I drunk of Siren tears, 352
When, in disgrace with fortune and men's eyes, 87
When forty winters shall besiege thy brow, 4
When I consider everything that grows 44
When I do count the clock that tells the time, 34
When I have seen by Time's fell hand defaced 193
When in the chronicle of wasted time 313
When most I wink, then do mine eyes best see, 129
When my love swears that she is made of truth, 423
When thou shalt be disposed to set me light, 261
When to the sessions of sweet silent thought 90
Where art thou, Muse, that thou forget'st so long 295
Whilst I alone did call upon thy aid, 235
Whoever hath her wish, thou hast thy Will, 412
Who is it that says most, which can say more 249
Who will believe my verse in time to come, 50

Why didst thou promise such a beauteous day, 101
Why is my verse so barren of new pride, 226

Your love and pity doth the impression fill 331

For a glossary of all key foreign words used in books published by World Wisdom, including metaphysical terms in English, consult: www.DictionaryofSpiritualTerms.org.
This on-line Dictionary of Spiritual Terms provides extensive definitions, examples, and related terms in other languages.

BIOGRAPHICAL NOTE

Ira B. Zinman is a writer, filmmaker, and independent scholar who specializes in the Biblical and spiritual elements in Shakespeare's Sonnets. He has taught and lectured on Shakespeare, and was a presenter on Shakespeare's Sonnets at the Ohio Shakespeare Conference. Zinman has also produced and directed a documentary film, entitled *Shakespeare's Spirituality: A Perspective*, on the lifelong work of Dr. Martin Lings, whose scholarship has contributed greatly to our understanding of Shakespeare and the spiritual elements that infuse his works. Zinman has practiced law since 1970 and lives in the Midwestern part of the United States.